The Complete Dambusters

The 133 men who flew on the Dams Raid

The Complete Dambusters

The 133 men who flew on the Dams Raid

Charles Foster

First published 2018
Reprinted 2018

The History Press
The Mill, Brimscombe Port
Stroud, Gloucestershire GL5 2QG
www.historypress.co.uk

British Library Cataloguing in Publication Data.
A catalogue record for this book is available from the British Library.

ISBN 978 0 7509 8808 7

Design + typesetting by Charles Foster
Further information about this title at www.completedambusters.com

Printed and bound in Turkey by Imak

For M . J . M . F.

1924–1987

Contents

Chapter 1: Introduction   13
    A note on RAF structures and training   18

Chapter 2: Planning the raid   21

Chapter 3: Selecting the aircrew   29

Chapter 4: Finalising the crews
    Crew 1: Wg Cdr G.P. Gibson DSO and Bar, DFC and Bar   43
    Crew 2: Flt Lt J.V. Hopgood DFC and Bar   45
    Crew 3: Flt Lt H.B. Martin DFC   47
    Crew 4: Sqn Ldr H.M. Young DFC and Bar   48
    Crew 5: Flt Lt D.J.H. Maltby DFC   51
    Crew 6: Flt Lt D.J. Shannon DFC   52
    Crew 7: Sqn Ldr H.E. Maudslay DFC   55
    Crew 8: Flt Lt W. Astell DFC   56
    Crew 9: Plt Off L.G. Knight   57
    Crew 10: Flt Lt R.N.G. Barlow DFC   58
    Crew 11: Flt Lt J.L. Munro   60
    Crew 12: Plt Off V.W. Byers   61
    Crew 13: Plt Off G. Rice   62
    Crew 14: Flt Lt J.C. McCarthy DFC   64
    Crew 15: Plt Off W. Ottley DFC   65
    Crew 16: Plt Off L.J. Burpee DFM   67
    Crew 17: Flt Sgt K.W. Brown   68
    Crew 18: Flt Sgt W.C. Townsend DFM   69
    Crew 19: Flt Sgt C.T. Anderson   70

Chapter 5: Training for the raid   72

Chapter 6: Operation Chastise
    Wave One: Attacks on the Möhne and Eder Dams   88
    Wave Two: Attacks on the Sorpe Dam   99
    Wave Three: Mobile reserve   105

Chapter 7: The men who flew on the Dams Raid

CREW 1

AJ-G: First aircraft to attack the Möhne Dam. Returned safely.
Pilot: Wg Cdr G.P. Gibson DSO and Bar, DFC and Bar   111
Flight engineer: Sgt J. Pulford   114
Navigator: Plt Off H.T. Taerum   116
Wireless operator: Flt Lt R.E.G. Hutchison DFC   117
Bomb aimer: Plt Off F.M. Spafford DFM   120
Front gunner: Flt Sgt G.A. Deering   121
Rear gunner: Flt Lt R.D. Trevor-Roper DFM   122

CREW 2

AJ-M: Second aircraft to attack the Möhne Dam. Shot down.
Pilot: Flt Lt J.V. Hopgood DFC and Bar   124
Flight engineer: Sgt C.C. Brennan   126
Navigator: Flg Off K. Earnshaw   127
Wireless operator: Sgt J.W. Minchin   128
Bomb aimer: Flt Sgt J.W. Fraser   129
Front gunner: Plt Off G.H.F.G. Gregory DFM   130
Rear gunner: Plt Off A.F. Burcher DFM   131

CREW 3

AJ-P: Third aircraft to attack the Möhne Dam. Returned safely.
Pilot: Flt Lt H.B. Martin DFC   134
Flight engineer: Plt Off I. Whittaker   137
Navigator: Flt Lt J.F. Leggo DFC   138
Wireless operator: Flg Off L. Chambers   139
Bomb aimer: Flt Lt R.C. Hay DFC   140
Front gunner: Plt Off B.T. Foxlee DFM   142
Rear gunner: Flt Sgt T.D. Simpson   143

CREW 4

AJ-A: Fourth aircraft to attack the Möhne Dam. Shot down.
Pilot: Sqn Ldr H.M. Young DFC and Bar   144
Flight engineer: Sgt D.T. Horsfall   146
Navigator: Flt Sgt C.W. Roberts   147
Wireless operator: Sgt L.W. Nichols   148
Bomb aimer: Flg Off V.S. MacCausland   149
Front gunner: Sgt G.A. Yeo   151
Rear gunner: Sgt W. Ibbotson   152

CREW 5

AJ-J: Fifth aircraft to attack the Möhne Dam. Returned safely.

Pilot: Flt Lt D.J.H. Maltby DFC   153
Flight engineer: Sgt W. Hatton   155
Navigator: Sgt V. Nicholson   156
Wireless operator: Sgt A.J.B. Stone   158
Bomb aimer: Plt Off J. Fort   159
Front gunner: Sgt V. Hill   160
Rear gunner: Sgt H.T. Simmonds   162

CREW 6

AJ-L: First aircraft to attack the Eder Dam. Returned safely.

Pilot: Flt Lt D.J. Shannon DFC   163
Flight engineer: Sgt R.J. Henderson   165
Navigator: Flg Off D.R. Walker DFC   166
Wireless operator: Flg Off B. Goodale DFC   167
Bomb aimer: Flt Sgt L.J. Sumpter   168
Front gunner: Sgt B. Jagger   169
Rear gunner: Flg Off J. Buckley   171

CREW 7

AJ-Z: Second aircraft to attack the Eder Dam. Shot down.

Pilot: Sqn Ldr H.E. Maudslay DFC   172
Flight engineer: Sgt J. Marriott   173
Navigator: Flg Off R.A. Urquhart DFC   174
Wireless operator: Wrt Off A.P. Cottam   175
Bomb aimer: Plt Off M.J.D. Fuller   176
Front gunner: Flg Off W.J. Tytherleigh DFC   176
Rear gunner: Sgt N.R. Burrows   177

CREW 8

AJ-B: Crashed on outward flight.

Pilot: Flt Lt W. Astell DFC   179
Flight engineer: Sgt J. Kinnear   180
Navigator: Plt Off F.A. Wile   181
Wireless operator: Wrt Off A. Garshowitz   182
Bomb aimer: Flg Off D. Hopkinson   183
Front gunner: Flt Sgt F.A. Garbas   184
Rear gunner: Sgt R. Bolitho   185

CREW 9

AJ-N: Third aircraft to attack the Eder Dam. Returned safely.
Pilot: Plt Off L.G. Knight   187
Flight engineer: Sgt R.E. Grayston   190
Navigator: Flg Off H.S. Hobday   191
Wireless operator: Flt Sgt R.G.T. Kellow   192
Bomb aimer: Flg Off E.C. Johnson   193
Front gunner: Sgt F.E. Sutherland   194
Rear gunner: Sgt H.E. O'Brien   196

CREW 10

AJ-E: Crashed on outward flight.
Pilot: Flt Lt R.N.G. Barlow DFC   197
Flight engineer: Plt Off S.L. Whillis   198
Navigator: Flg Off P.S. Burgess   199
Wireless operator: Flg Off C.R. Williams DFC   200
Bomb aimer: Plt Off A. Gillespie DFM   203
Front gunner: Flg Off H.S. Glinz   204
Rear gunner: Sgt J.R.G. Liddell   206

CREW 11

AJ-W: Damaged by flak on outward flight and abandoned mission.
Pilot: Flt Lt J.L. Munro   208
Flight engineer: Sgt F.E. Appleby   210
Navigator: Flg Off F.G. Rumbles   212
Wireless operator: Wrt Off P.E. Pigeon   212
Bomb aimer: Sgt J.H. Clay   213
Front gunner: Sgt W. Howarth   214
Rear gunner: Flt Sgt H.A. Weeks   215

CREW 12

AJ-K: Shot down on outward flight.
Pilot: Plt Off V.W. Byers   217
Flight engineer: Sgt A.J. Taylor   218
Navigator: Flg Off J.H. Warner   219
Wireless operator: Sgt J. Wilkinson   220
Bomb aimer: Plt Off A.N. Whitaker   220
Front gunner: Sgt C.McA. Jarvie   221
Rear gunner: Flt Sgt J. McDowell   221

CREW 13

AJ-H: Damaged on outward flight and abandoned mission.

Pilot: Plt Off G. Rice 223

Flight engineer: Sgt E.C. Smith 225

Navigator: Flg Off R. Macfarlane 226

Wireless operator: Wrt Off C.B. Gowrie 227

Bomb aimer: Wrt Off J.W. Thrasher 227

Front gunner: Sgt T.W. Maynard 228

Rear gunner: Sgt S. Burns 229

CREW 14

AJ-T: First aircraft to attack Sorpe Dam. Returned safely.

Pilot: Flt Lt J.C. McCarthy DFC 231

Flight engineer: Sgt W.G. Radcliffe 234

Navigator: Flt Sgt D.A. MacLean 235

Wireless operator: Flt Sgt L. Eaton 237

Bomb aimer: Sgt G.L. Johnson 238

Front gunner: Sgt R. Batson 240

Rear gunner: Flg Off D. Rodger 242

CREW 15

AJ-W: Shot down on outward flight.

Pilot: Plt Off W. Ottley DFC 244

Flight engineer: Sgt R. Marsden 246

Navigator: Flg Off J.K. Barrett DFC 246

Wireless operator: Sgt J. Guterman DFM 248

Bomb aimer: Sgt T.B. Johnston 250

Front gunner: Sgt H.J. Strange 251

Rear gunner: Sgt F. Tees 251

CREW 16

AJ-S: Shot down on outward flight.

Pilot: Plt Off L.J. Burpee DFM 254

Flight engineer: Sgt G. Pegler 255

Navigator: Sgt T. Jaye 256

Wireless operator: Plt Off L.G. Weller 258

Bomb aimer: Flt Sgt J.L. Arthur 258

Front gunner: Sgt W.C.A. Long 259

Rear gunner: Wrt Off J.G. Brady 260

CREW 17

AJ-F: Second aircraft to attack Sorpe Dam. Returned safely.

Pilot: Flt Sgt K.W. Brown   261

Flight engineer: Sgt H.B. Feneron   262

Navigator: Sgt D.P. Heal   263

Wireless operator: Sgt H.J. Hewstone   265

Bomb aimer: Sgt S. Oancia   266

Front gunner: Sgt D. Allatson   266

Rear gunner: Sgt G.S. McDonald   268

CREW 18

AJ-O: Only aircraft to attack Ennepe Dam. Returned safely.

Pilot: Flt Sgt W.C. Townsend DFM   269

Flight engineer: Sgt D.J.D. Powell   270

Navigator: Plt Off C.L. Howard   272

Wireless operator: Flt Sgt G.A. Chalmers   273

Bomb aimer: Sgt C.E. Franklin DFM   274

Front gunner: Sgt D.E. Webb   275

Rear gunner: Sgt R. Wilkinson   277

CREW 19

AJ-Y: Damaged by flak on outward flight. Abandoned mission.

Pilot: Flt Sgt C.T. Anderson   279

Flight engineer: Sgt R.C. Paterson   281

Navigator: Sgt J.P. Nugent   282

Wireless operator: Sgt W.D. Bickle   283

Bomb aimer: Sgt G.J. Green   284

Front gunner: Sgt E. Ewan   285

Rear gunner: Sgt A.W. Buck   285

Chapter 8: After the Dams Raid   287

Chapter 9: Afterword   309

Bibliography   312

Acknowledgements   314

Index   316

Chapter 1

Introduction

IN APRIL 2013, about a month before the 70th anniversary of the Dams Raid, the RAF's most famous Second World War bombing operation, BBC journalist Greig Watson began work on what seemed to be a straightforward enough project. He had an idea for an online feature story: a complete set of pictures of all the aircrew who had taken part in the raid. When the user selected an image, up would pop the name, their nationality, the aircraft they were in and what position they occupied. It seemed a relatively easy task.

However, he soon found that this was not so. Wartime RAF personnel records are not open to the public and, in any case, did not contain photographs. Men moved frequently from unit to unit, and few had any visual archive. And, worst of all, although many big museum collections have hundreds of aircrew photographs, the vast majority have no names attached.

At that stage, I had been writing a regular blog about the Dambusters for about five years. I had started this in 2008, at the same time that my book[1] about my uncle, David Maltby, had been published. David had been a pilot on the celebrated raid but had died four months later on another operation. The blog had built up a significant readership and in the spring of 2013, with the 70th anniversary of the raid fast approaching, I decided that I would use it to publish online profiles of all of the 133 men who had taken part in the raid, aiming to complete them all by the end of the year. I planned to illustrate as many posts as possible with a photograph of the subject, although I knew as I started that I didn't have access to pictures of them all. Maybe the missing pictures would turn up once I began searching for them.

I gave my project the catchy title 'Dambuster of the Day' and started publishing the profiles in late March 2013. Then, a couple of weeks later, I got an email from Greig, asking for help with his search. By coincidence, I was working that same day on the first profile for which I could not find a photograph: a 23-year-old Yorkshireman called David Horsfall, who had joined the RAF before the war as an apprentice technician at the age of 16. By May 1943, he

---

1   Charles Foster, *Breaking the Dams,* Pen and Sword 2008.

had retrained as a flight engineer and had flown on a grand total of two operations, on each cramped into a fold-up seat next to his pilot. His third, and what turned out to be his last, was an attack on the Möhne Dam.

Greig and I spoke on the phone and went through the possibilities. The idea was to publish all the 133 pictures as an interactive 'picturewall'. He explained what would happen as the user moved their mouse over the individual shots. We discussed whether or not the pictures would appear in random order, which was the BBC's plan. This made no sense to me, I argued: surely the members of each crew should appear together, and in the order in which they had flown on the raid itself.

Greig had already accepted the fact that some of the faces would have to be cropped from group shots and we went through some sources for these. The Canadian, Australian and New Zealand survivors from the raid had posed the next day for pictures for their own national newspapers, so that was a good starting point. There was also a series of official RAF pictures taken of 617 Squadron in the summer of 1943 and archived in the Imperial War Museum. So it seemed likely that everyone who had got back from the raid had been photographed at some stage during the war.

It quickly emerged that the main problem was going to be finding pictures of the others, the fifty-three men who had died. The popular myth that the Dams Raid aircrew were all battle-hardened veterans who had flown on dozens of previous operations was just that, a myth. It is true that most of the pilots did have considerable operational experience (although four of the nineteen had actually completed fewer than ten operations) but their crews were another matter. It was quite common for an experienced pilot to be given a new crew, and this had been the case for several of those who met their fate on the night of 16/17 May 1943.

The research continued apace. A few low-resolution shots on obscure websites were considered, but discounted because they lacked corroborative evidence. But there were some successes: a portrait of a flight engineer sold at auction ten years ago was found on the auction house's site. A community news site in West Yorkshire had a photograph of a rear gunner taken at his wedding. A local journalist recalled a bundle of pictures being kept by a bomb aimer's nephew. We were adding in pictures right up to the day of the anniversary, but when it arrived we were still twelve short.

As soon as the picturewall went live, several more families contacted us so we were able to fill some of the gaps. A few more were uncovered in the following few weeks, including one of flight engineer David Horsfall, taken at RAF Halton training college before the war. But by the middle of July 2013 we were still short of five faces, which was very frustrating. It was then that I looked again at my copy of the memoirs of 617 Squadron's first adjutant, Flt Lt Harry Humphries, who had died in 2008. This referred to a crewboard that he had kept in in his office, with pictures of all the squadron arranged in rows. If an aircraft went missing, the pictures were removed and kept in what he called a 'Roll of Honour' in a 'rough squadron diary'.[2]

In the late 1990s, Humphries had decided to sell some of the material which he had collected during the war, and it had been bought by Grantham library. Amongst his collection were three large pieces of card, each mounted with a few small identity card photographs of Dams Raid aircrew. As part of the process of preparing his memoirs for publication Humphries had typed up the captions himself on a manual typewriter.

I had already used the material which was in Grantham. There were seventeen pictures on the three cards – fourteen of aircrew lost in the raid, and three of men who were taken prisoner. They weren't brilliant quality and had been roughly treated over the years. The individual shots had been cut out with scissors and had obviously already been pasted or stapled onto individual cards at some point in the past, and then removed. They had all the hallmarks of a project which had never been completed. But with only seventeen in the library's collection, was it possible that the 'diary' and the further pictures which Harry had mentioned were still in the possession of the Humphries family?

I got hold of a phone number for Harry's son, Peter Humphries, and called him. He said immediately that he remembered there being a file containing sheets of paper pasted up with identity card pictures. It was in his loft, with the rest of his father's papers. 'Give me the names you are looking for', he said, 'and I will check.' I read out the names: Daniel Allatson, Jack Barrett, Norman Burrows, Jack Marriott, Ronald Marsden. A few hours later, he rang me back: 'I have them all.' He read out the names again to check. The following day he emailed me a scan of two pages of yellowing foolscap. Four of the men were on one sheet, the final one was on another.

I rang Greig to tell him the news. 'I'm looking at the last five pictures. All together on two sheets of paper', I said. 'I hardly believe it. In fact, I actually feel a bit shaky.' After a period of mutual congratulation, I sent the scans on to him and he said he would discuss with his editors as to when the complete picture-wall would go on display.

A few weeks later, the BBC published all the pictures. Their release made the national TV news and was covered in all the papers. The importance of the

---

2   Harry Humphries, *Living with Heroes*, Erskine Press 2003, p115.

LINCOLNSHIRE COUNTY COUNCIL

No. 617 SQUADRON. NIGHT FLYING PROGRAMME 16.5.43.

No.	A/C.	Captain.	F/Engr.	Navigator.	W/Optr.	A/Bomber.	Front Gunner.	Rear Gunner.

The list of 617 Squadron crews typed on the morning of the Dams Raid, Sunday 16 May 1943. It was called a 'Night Flying Programme' to maintain secrecy until the last possible moment.

project was brought home to me when I read what George 'Johnny' Johnson, the last British Dambuster, had told Greig: 'I was looking at faces of colleagues I last saw previously at RAF Scampton at the "All Crews" briefing on the afternoon of 16 May 1943,' he had said. Greig took the opportunity of asking Johnny to sign two printed copies of the complete wall, one for him and one for me. My copy now hangs in my office.

The story of the picturewall was just one of the items which showed the continued public interest in the Dambusters story around the time of the 70th anniversary of the raid. A series of events, newspaper stories and TV broadcasts had marked the date, with two of the three living Dambusters, Johnny Johnson and Les Munro – who had flown from New Zealand at the age of 93 – at the forefront of coverage.

So who were the Dambusters, the 133 men who took part in the raid? It is perhaps not surprising that so little is known about some of them, apart from the list of names which appears in the appendices to several books. Those who died during the war are all listed in the Commonwealth War Graves Commission records, but some of these are inaccurate. So the wrong age or place of residence has been copied again and again, unnoticed and unquestioned.

There were nineteen crews, each made up of seven men. Twenty-one crews had been trained up, but two were not available on the day due to sickness. Since it turned out that there were only nineteen serviceable aircraft this was a happy coincidence. A full crew list of all the men who flew in these nineteen crews was typed up in a 'Night Flying Programme' on the morning of the raid. This includes a late substitute in Flt Sgt Ken Brown's crew, where Sgt Daniel Allatson from one of the crews who had gone sick took the place of Sgt Donald Buntaine, who had also been taken ill, in the front gun turret. Exactly the same names were repeated in the Operations Record Book, written up in the days following the raid.

Of the 133 men:
- 86 were from Britain, 31 were from Canada, thirteen from Australia, two from New Zealand and one from the USA.
- 53 died on the raid, three were captured as PoWs.
- 32 died in action later in the war.
- 48 survived the war.

(The nationality figures include two Canadians and one Australian enlisted in the RAF rather than their indigenous air forces. To add confusion, some of the Canadians were born in the UK but emigrated as a child. The US citizen was Joe McCarthy, who had enlisted in the RCAF.)

Now, for the first time in one book an attempt has been made to do justice to them all, with each man who took part in the raid getting his own entry and photograph in the pages that follow.

In researching this book, I have been lucky in that both the Canadian and Australian national archives have now released the personnel files of the men who died in the war, and I was able to access these. But as of 2018 the RAF's files are still closed, and although some 'casualty packs' from the earliest part of the war have now been released to the National Archives it is not clear when this process will reach the year 1943 nor whether these packs will contain the full details of each man's service.

But at least we now have a face for each of the 133 men who took part in the Dams Raid. The lives of some are reasonably well documented, but for a few we still know little more than their dates of birth and death, some information about their previous RAF service and, perhaps, some sketchy family details. So this book is just the start of an ongoing research project. Any further information received will be used for a possible second edition and to update the companion website, www.completedambusters.com. Giving each man his credit for taking part in such a piece of history is the least that they deserve.

A note on RAF structures and training

When the Second World War started, the Royal Air Force was only a little over twenty years old. It had grown rapidly since its formation eight months before the end of the previous conflict and by the late 1930s it had established its own distinct service traditions, many of which reflected those in the older branches of His Majesty's forces. So its officer ranks were given titles such as Flight Lieutenant, Wing Commander and Air Marshal to match those in the Royal Navy and the army, and an officer cadet college at Cranwell mirrored those for the other services at Dartmouth and Sandhurst.

In the period immediately after the 1938 Munich crisis the RAF grew even more swiftly, when the Cabinet gave approval for formation of twelve new fighter squadrons and the gradual re-equipment of the bomber force with heavy bombers. The decision to go for a heavy bomber force was a lucky consequence of the cautious start in rearmament decisions in 1936-7. Earlier rearmament would have left Britain with a fleet of immediately outdated aircraft whereas the arrival of the heavy bomber in 1941-2 eventually made the Allied air forces a much more potent striking force than their Axis equivalent.[3]

Bomber Command came into existence in 1936, as one of the RAF's four commands following that year's reorganisation of the service (the other three being Fighter, Coastal and Training Commands). It was sub-divided into Groups, which by early 1943 were numbered 1–6 and 8. Nos. 1 to 5 Groups were RAF Groups organised by regions, No. 6 Group was under Royal Canadian Air Force command and No. 8 Group was the new Pathfinder force, established in January 1943. Each Group was made up of a number of squadrons.

No. 5 Group had its headquarters in Grantham, Lincolnshire, and its squadrons were spread at various RAF stations over that county and its neighbours. In March 1943, there were ten fully operational squadrons in the group, based at eight different stations.

The prewar expansion of the air force had been done exclusively by recruiting new personnel into the service's volunteer reserve, and this policy would continue throughout the war. Thus all new recruits started at the rank of Aircraftman and it was only after completing training in their allocated 'trade' that some were commissioned as officers.

Tens of thousands of new recruits joined in the first year of the war and this itself gave rise to a whole raft of new problems, with large bottlenecks building

---

3   Daniel Todman, *Britain's War: Into Battle 1937-1941,* Penguin 2017, p99 and p153.

up as they moved through the various stages of training.[4] Many recruits wanted to become pilots, but not all turned out to be suitable. Some were remustered as other aircrew trades, some were told that they weren't suitable for the RAF at all. Others indicated when they joined up that they wanted to serve in other capacities.

At the outset of the war, the RAF had just two 'trades' available for non-pilot aircrew: observer and a combination wireless operator/airgunner, and there was no automatic promotion to Sergeant for those who achieved these qualifications. Over the next three years, this was changed and then the arrival of the heavy bomber which needed a minimum of seven crew led to the two trades being sub-divided into four: the navigator, air bomber (the official name for what was usually known as a bomb aimer), wireless operator and air gunner,. These changes were ratified by a major conference between the RAF and the air forces of the Dominions and the USA, which was held in Ottawa, Canada, in May and June 1942. As much of the training was conducted abroad, especially in Canada, this was an appropriate venue.

Many of the men who would fly on the Dams Raid had been through training earlier in the war, so had begun their operational careers with a variety of different qualifications. Thus the letter they carried on their single-winged flying badge (such as an O to show that they had qualified as an Observer) might not reflect the position in their aircraft which they later occupied, such as bomb aimer.

The final important position in a 1943 heavy bomber crew of seven to be officially designated was that of its flight engineer. It was recognised that with four engines a second pair of eyes were needed in the cockpit in order to monitor their performance, and at first this position was occupied by a fully qualified second pilot. However, getting a man to this level of skill took the best part of a year. The attrition rate amongst bomber crews meant that a lot of invested time and money was lost if a crew with two pilots was shot down or crashed. And, in reality, the role of a second pilot was often superfluous, with him rarely gaining any actual flying experience. Moreover, both the Avro Lancaster and the Handley Page Halifax had only one set of controls, the Short Stirling being the only heavy bomber with two sets. So in early 1942, it was decided that the second pilot should be replaced by a flight engineer. This new trade had been

---

4   Total RAF personnel figures for the first sixteen months of the war are as follows:
     3 September 1939   173,958
     1 January 1940   214,732
     1 January 1941   490,762
     Source: www.rafweb.org [Accessed February 2018].

in existence in some squadrons since late 1940, with training being done at squadron level, but it became formalised in May 1942.

A new training establishment – No. 4 School of Technical Training – was set up at RAF St Athan in Glamorgan and courses were devised to take place there. Initially entrants to this course were recruited from ground crew who had qualified as either fitters or mechanics, although later in 1942, direct entry to the trade were accepted from new recruits. The training was type-specific, as the skills needed to manage the engine performance of a Lancaster, Halifax or Stirling differed considerably. Flight engineers were also given some rudimentary training in flying skills, so that they could take the controls if their pilot was incapacitated. All the flight engineers who took part in the Dams Raid had previously served as ground crew and qualified in their trade between May and November 1942.

As with the other flying trades, each new flight engineer received an automatic promotion to the rank of Sergeant along with his flying badge when he qualified. In all trades – pilots and non-pilots – some men were also commissioned, although in order to achieve this, they were supposed to show they had 'officer qualities'. Some turned down commissions, not convinced that the small increase in pay and change of status was worth the separation from the colleagues with whom they had gone through training. The Dominion air forces were less hidebound by class distinctions than were the British and it is noticeable that a higher proportion of men received commissions in squadrons and other units which were under their direct command.

During the war, automatic promotion to Sergeant caused a certain amount of resentment amongst some older men, who felt that they might have to wait years to achieve the same rank, but it was felt by the authorities that aircrew did deserve recognition for the fact that they were voluntarily putting their lives at risk.

Chapter 2

Planning the raid

WELL BEFORE THE SECOND WORLD WAR STARTED the British Air Ministry had set up an Air Targets Sub-Committee to look for possible targets in Germany in the event of war. The power stations and coking plants in Germany's heavily industrialised Ruhr Valley were amongst the important strategic objectives which were identified. It was then argued that neutralisation of these could be achieved by the destruction of just two dams, those at the Möhne and Sorpe. If other dams, such as the Eder, were also destroyed, severe damage to the canal system and drinking water could be added to the effect on hydro-electric power and steelmaking.

The planners however recognised that bombs of sufficient explosive power did not yet exist, and even if one could be developed there was no agreement as to how it should be delivered. Several papers were circulated and suggestions included torpedos and low level bombing of the air side of the dam wall. When war came, an attack on the dams remained on the agenda. Significantly, in July 1940 Air Marshal Sir Charles Portal, at that stage the AOC-in-C of RAF Bomber Command, wrote to the Secretary of State for Air arguing 'that the time has arrived when we should make arrangements for the destruction of the Möhne Dam'.[5] Later that year Portal became Chief of the Air Staff – the head of the Royal Air Force – and it was in this position he was later able to give support for the Dams Raid at a number of crucial points.

It was recognised that in order for a successful attack to be mounted three separate developments needed to occur. There needed to be a bomb or other explosive device of sufficient size, an aircraft big enough to carry it and aircrew who could be trained in any special delivery method.

From the very beginning of the war the assistant chief designer of the aircraft manufacturer Vickers-Armstrongs, Barnes Wallis, had taken an interest in methods for attacking German dams. He and his small staff had been evacuated from the main Vickers works at Weybridge and were given offices in the clubhouse of the nearby Burhill Golf Club. During 1940 Wallis started his own

---

5   John Sweetman, *The Dambusters Raid,* Cassell 2002, p26. This chapter owes much to
     Sweetman's first three chapters.

research, combing through contemporary German articles about the construction of the Möhne Dam in 1913. He was convinced that the standard 1,000lb small bombs would never be effective and devised a much larger 22,400lb bomb with a 'R100' or peardrop shape. (In the late 1920s, Wallis had headed the design team which had built the R100 airship.) Amongst the small group of scientists to see Wallis's early research was Benjamin Lockspeiser, the Deputy Director of Scientific Research at the Ministry of Aircraft Production (MAP), who would later solve the problem of how to calculate and maintain the altitude of a low-flying bomber. Lockspeiser disagreed with the idea of a peardrop shape for such a large bomb, arguing that it should have a sharply pointed nose. However, with no aircraft available which could carry such a huge payload, Wallis turned his attention to finding a different method.

By coincidence, a team of engineers from the Building Research Station in Garston, near Watford, who had been working on the effects of explosives on structures since before the war, were transferred to the Road Research Laboratory in Harmondsworth. Led by A.R. Collins, they had also identified the Möhne Dam as a possible target.

Wallis met Collins, along with Dr W.H. Glanville and Dr A.H. Davis, the director and assistant director of the laboratory, and they discussed how much damage would be caused if a large explosion occurred on the upstream side of the Möhne Dam, very close to the wall. On an unknown date in late 1940, Glanville and Wallis held a meeting with Dr Norman Davey of the BRS,[6] and they decided that the most effective way to determine the weight of explosive needed, and the optimum location to detonate it to breach the dam, was to construct a scale model and then blow it up. Davey agreed to build this at Garston, and so work began in November 1940 in a secluded corner of the site. Some 2 million miniature concrete blocks were made, and the construction took about six weeks. The model was completed on 21 January 1941, and the first explosive test took place the following day. In all, ten explosions were carried out and the model – which can still be seen at Garston – was badly damaged.[7]

Later, at Harmondsworth, Collins made further 1/50-scale models of both the Möhne Dam and a similar one in Italy, and in late 1940 and early 1941 wrote a series of reports for MAP on his results.

Wallis took all this information, and in March 1941 wrote a massive 117-page paper. He circulated more than 100 copies (including sending one to an *Evening Standard* journalist). He sent several to his friend Gp Capt Frederick

6   Dr Norman Davey, *Some reflections on the Möhne Dam,* unpublished paper, Building Research Establishment, 1993. See www.bre.co.uk/dambusters [accessed January 2018].
7   www.bre.co.uk/dambusters.

Winterbotham, the RAF officer who was the Chief of Air Intelligence at MI6. He had become a useful ally with a wide range of contacts and Winterbotham used these to make sure that Sir Henry Tizard, MAP's scientific adviser, and other influential people received copies.

The full title of Wallis's paper, 'A Note on a Method of Attacking the Axis Powers', doesn't do justice to the wide range of subjects covered. With five appendices, eight tables, thirty-two diagrams and a quotation from Thomas Hardy, it described the current bombing campaigns as 'puny efforts' and proposed a different strategy, involving much bigger 4,000 and 10,000lb bombs, and a much larger aircraft in order to deliver them.

The note was eventually considered by various Whitehall committees and sub-committees. Unfortunately for Wallis, the final answer to his proposals was 'No'. As Wallis knew, at that point four-engine heavy bombers were only just becoming available, and there was no enthusiasm for diverting resources into developing an even bigger one. It was also felt that the explosive in a larger peardrop-shaped bomb would not all explode at the same time, thereby reducing its impact.

But at least Wallis's ideas had been considered, and he had got an audience interested in his ideas. Although disheartened, Wallis went back to his research and gave the matter further thought. Then came his brainwave. 'Early in 1942,' he later wrote, 'I had the idea of a missile, which if dropped on the water at a considerable distance upstream of the dam would reach the dam in a series of ricochets, and after impact against the crest of the dam would sink in close contact with the upstream face of the masonry.'[8]

Then began Wallis's famous experiments in his garden in Effingham using his children's marbles, firing them from a catapult across the surface of a tub of water, where they bounced. They landed second bounce on a table, where the fall was marked in chalk by one of his children. He also modified the shape of his bomb, believing that if it was a spherical shape and detonated in the centre the explosion would reach all points on the surface at the same time.

At this stage, thinking that the weapon would be most useful for the Fleet Air Arm, he wrote another paper and sent it to another of his circle of friends, Professor P.M.S. Blackett, the scientific adviser to the Admiralty. Blackett could also see its relevance for the RAF, and informed Sir Henry Tizard at MAP. Tizard had been consulted before about Wallis's earlier paper, but this time he saw merit in the idea and travelled to Burhill Golf Club to meet Wallis again. Wallis found him 'kindly and very knowledgeable' and through him secured

---

8   Sweetman, *Dambusters Raid,* p54. This section draws heavily on the following pages of Sweetman's book.

permission to use the large water tanks at the National Physical Laboratories in Teddington for further research.

Work began at Teddington on 9 June 1942 and continued until September. At some point, Wallis decided to introduce back spin to the projectile, probably following discussions with Vickers employee and keen cricketer George Edwards. A succession of research grandees – including Tizard, Air Vice Marshal F.J. Linnell (from MAP) and Rear Admiral E.de F. Renouf (the navy's Director of Special Weapons) – came to see the tests in action, and Linnell gave permission for a Wellington to be used for test drops.

Meanwhile Collins and his colleagues at the Road Research Laboratory had been given permission to scale up their dam experiments on the disused Nant-y-Gro dam in the Elan Valley in Powys. Wallis travelled to the site to watch the first test using an upstream explosion on 1 May, but this was unsuccessful. However, after further examination of the Harmondsworth models, it was decided to place an explosive charge in contact with the base of the dam. On 24 July a mine with 279lb of explosive was placed in at the centre of the dam, 7ft 6in below its crest, and detonated. The result was so spectacular – a huge waterspout and the centre of the dam punched out – that Collins, who was recording events on a ciné camera, temporarily stopped filming. Extrapolation of the results showed that a similar result could be achieved on a larger dam with a 7,500lb bomb. Crucially, a single bomb of this weight could be carried by the new four-engine Avro Lancaster, which had been in service with the RAF since January that year.

The development of four-engine heavy bombers can be argued as being one of the most crucial prewar decisions taken by the UK government, contrasting with Germany's perseverance with the medium two-engine bomber throughout the war. And the delay in starting rearmament, caused by the vacillation of the Baldwin government before 1936, in fact proved to be a benefit since commissioning of new aircraft at this time would have left the RAF beginning the war with a fleet of immediately outdated aircraft.[9]

The first heavy bomber to go into production was the result of a contract awarded to Short Brothers to build the Stirling aircraft. Another government specification led to contracts for the firms of A.V. Roe (commonly known as Avro) and Handley Page. Avro first developed the Manchester bomber, which used two large Rolls Royce Vulture engines, but this proved unsatisfactory and it was superseded by the four-engine Lancaster, using the smaller but more

---

9   Daniel Todman, *Britain's War*, Penguin 2017, p99.

efficient Rolls Royce Merlin engine. Handley Page's Halifax was also designed with four Merlin engines.

Of these three, the Lancaster quickly became the most potent striking force. Production of the Halifax also continued throughout the war, with more than 6,000 manufactured, but the Stirling, of which some 2,000 were built, fell out of favour. The Lancaster had a massive uninterrupted bomb bay (something which would prove important later in the war when the Barnes Wallis-designed Tallboy and Grand Slam bombs became available) and large fuel tanks, and these put targets in both the east of Germany and Italy in range. By the end of 1942 most of the squadrons in Bomber Command's 5 Group had been equipped with Lancasters, and it would be from this group that the aircrew who would make up the Dams Raid strike force would eventually be selected.

Meanwhile Wallis was busy building a prototype spinning device, and its first airborne trial of a spinning device took place on 4 December. A modified Wellington flown by Joseph ('Mutt') Summers, the Vickers-Armstrongs chief test pilot, with Wallis himself as bomb aimer took off from Warmwell airfield and flew towards the test range at Chesil Beach, on the Dorset coast. Flying parallel to the coastline, Wallis dropped the spherical dummy but it shattered on impact with the water. Further trials took place the following week and into the New Year and it wasn't until the fourth trial on 23 January, when a wooden sphere was used for the first time, that a successful series of bounces occurred. Thirteen were recorded, after the dummy rotating at 485rpm had been dropped from a height of 42ft with the Wellington travelling at 283mph.

Several more were dropped successfully over the following days. Then Wallis set about trying to get agreement to develop two separate versions of the weapon: a large version, called Upkeep, for use in a Lancaster against the dams, and a smaller version, Highball, which could be dropped by a Mosquito against shipping. He began the process of hawking film footage from Chesil Beach and Teddington around Whitehall. To go with this, he had written another paper, 'Air Attack on Dams'. As it also included material on maritime targets it was first sent to Rear Admiral Renouf, and then to various Air Ministry contacts. He also sent it to Lord Cherwell, Churchill's scientific advisor at the Cabinet Office. This was accompanied by a covering letter which claimed that Mosquitoes would be ready to test the Highball weapon in six to eight weeks but 'unfortunately have overshadowed the question of the major German dams.' Wallis went on: 'if a high-level decision' were taken to give equal priority to both weapons 'we could develop the large sphere to be dropped from a Lancaster bomber within a period of two months.'

The one senior RAF officer who was not convinced was the man who commanded the aircrew who would be needed to drop the weapon, Air Marshal Sir Arthur Harris, now the AOC-in-C of Bomber Command. His Senior Air Staff Officer, Air Vice Marshal Robert Saundby sent him a lengthy minute on 14 February, outlining the research and testing of Highball and considering the possibility of a 'similar weapon' for the special purpose of destroying dams, in particular the Möhne. A specially modified Lancaster would be needed and the attack would be need to be made when the dam was full or nearly full. One squadron would have to be nominated, depriving Bomber Command of its strength for 'two or three weeks' for training. The tactics are not difficult, Saundby concluded, somewhat optimistically.

Harris was not at all convinced. He handwrote a scathing note on Saundby's minute:

> This is tripe of the wildest description. ... there is not the smallest
> chance of it working. To begin with the bomb would have to be
> perfectly balanced around it's [sic] axis otherwise vibration at 500RPM
> would wreck the aircraft or tear the bomb loose. I don't believe a word
> of it's [sic] supposed ballistics on the surface. ... At all costs stop them
> putting aside Lancs & reducing our bombing effort on this wild goose
> chase. ... The war will be over before it works – & it never will.[10]

Harris had been in charge of Bomber Command for just over a year, and was busy implementing his strategy of area bombing. Ultimately, he was most concerned that a squadron of his most effective bombers was not going to be available for this task. Although the production of Lancasters was now running at full tilt, only about 120 new ones emerged from the factories every month.

However, Harris was now in a minority in the senior ranks of the RAF. A few days later, on 19 February at Vickers House in London, Wallis got to show his films to the two of the Joint Chiefs of Staff, the heads of both the navy and the air force, Admiral Sir Dudley Pound and Air Chief Marshal Sir Charles Portal.

Harris was still not appeased. Nor was he impressed with the films when Wallis went to visit him at Bomber Command HQ in High Wycombe on 22 February. He sent Portal another of his impassioned letters.

> All sorts of enthusiasts and panacea-mongers are now careering round
> MAP suggesting the taking of about 30 Lancasters off the line to rig
> them up for this weapon, when the weapon itself exists so far only

---

10   National Archives, AIR 14/595.

within the imaginations of those who conceived it. … I am prepared
to bet that the Highball is just about the maddest proposition as a
weapon that we have yet come across – and that is saying something.
… Lancasters make the greatest contribution to our bomber offensive,
which we have to carry on so continuously against such great odds.
The heaviest of these odds arises from the continual attempts to ruin
Lancasters for some specialist purpose or to take them away for others
to use.[11]

Portal tried to smoothe Harris's feathers. He accepted that the weapon might
come to nothing, but it was worth conducting a trial in a Lancaster to see if it
could work. 'I can assure you that I will not allow more than three of your pre-
cious Lancasters to be diverted for this purpose until the full scale experiments
have shown that the bomb will do what is claimed for it,' he wrote. 'I shall ask
for the necessary conversion sets to be manufactured but there will be no further interruption of supply of Lancasters to you until it is known that the dif-
ficulties to which you refer have actually been overcome.'[12] Harris reluctantly
accepted the decision.

However, on 23 February there was nearly a fatal setback. Wallis and the
Weybridge works manager Hew Kilner were called to a meeting in London by
Vickers chairman Sir Charles Craven. Craven said that Wallis was making a
nuisance of himself at MAP and by involving Vickers-Armstrongs directly or
indirectly, he was damaging the company's interests and moreover had offend-
ed the Air Staff. Air Vice Marshal Linnell of MAP had apparently told Craven
that Wallis should 'stop this silly nonsense about the destruction of the dams'.
Wallis was shocked and immediately offered his resignation, whereupon Craven reacted vigorously and accused him of 'mutiny'.[13]

However, Linnell seems to have acted unilaterally, and was not aware that
Portal had approved the allocation of three Lancasters. Two days later, the
storm blew over and Wallis was asked to attend a meeting at MAP the following day, which would be chaired by Linnell himself.

The meeting got underway at 1500, in Linnell's office at the Ministry in
Millbank. Wallis and Craven were there from Vickers-Armstrongs, and Avro
was represented by Roy Chadwick, the designer of the Lancaster. Also present
were Air Vice Marshal Ralph Sorley, Air Cdre John Baker and Gp Capt Wilfred
Wynter-Morgan (Air Ministry) and Norbert Rowe from MAP.

---

11   Harris Papers, H82. RAF Museum, cited in Leo McKinstry, *Lancaster: the Second World
     War's greatest bomber,* John Murray 2009, p266.
12   *Ibid.*
13   Sweetman, *Dambusters Raid,* p78.

Linnell had been thoroughly briefed by Portal, and so there were no re-criminations or repetition of doubts about the project. Instead, the meeting proceeded to set in motion what would soon become known as Operation Chastise. Linnell announced that Portal wanted 'every endeavour' to prepare aircraft and weapons for use in the late spring of 1943, and for both Avro and Vickers-Armstrongs to give the work the highest priority. Three Lancasters were to be prepared for trials as soon as possible, with another twenty-seven to be similarly modified. Baker, the Director of Bombing Operations, said that the best possible date for an attack on the dams would be 26 May, so all aircraft and mines should be delivered by 1 May to allow for training and experiments. Wallis pointed out that 'no detailed scheme' for preparing the modified Lan-casters had yet been agreed, so following discussion the line of demarcation between Avro and Vickers-Armstrongs was settled, with the latter handling the attachment arms and driving mechanism and the mine itself. Avro agreed to send draughtsmen to Weybridge immediately to work on this. Wallis revealed that no detailed drawings for Upkeep yet existed, but that he hoped to be able to send them to the works manager in Newcastle 'in ten days to a fortnight'. Wynter-Morgan said that Torpex explosive was available but that it would take three weeks to fill 100 mines and that it wouldn't be possible to design the self-destructive mechanism until the detailed drawings were ready.

Everything was very tight, and Wallis's often-repeated assertion that the whole process could be done in eight weeks would be tested to the limit. That was almost exactly the timescale now proposed. He recalled later that as he left, he felt 'physically sick' because his bluff had been called and that he realised the terrible responsibility of making good all my claims'.

Norbert Rowe, a religious man, offered to send him the prayer to St Joseph which he himself used at times of stress. Wallis was going to need all the help he could get.

Chapter 3

Selecting the aircrew

THE CLOSE OF THE MEETING IN MILLBANK on Friday 26 February 1943 left Barnes Wallis with much work to do on finishing the design of the proposed weapon and Avro agreeing to start production of three modified Lancasters. Thus, two of the three conditions needed for an attack on the dams were in the process of being fulfilled. The third item, the selection and training of suitable aircrew, began just over two weeks later on Monday 15 March 1943 when the AOC-in-C of Bomber Command, Air Chief Marshal Sir Arthur Harris chose the command's 5 Group to undertake the work. He told the group's Air Officer Commanding, Air Vice Marshal the Hon Ralph Cochrane, that he would need to set up a new squadron to undertake the operation, but emphasised that he should not reduce the efforts of his main force.

Three days later, on Thursday 18 March, Wg Cdr Guy Gibson, who had just finished a tour of operations as CO of 106 Squadron, was summoned to a meeting with Cochrane at Group HQ in Grantham. The day before, Harris's Senior Air Staff Officer, Air Vice Marshal Robert Oxland, had written two important memos. The first was to the Director of Bomber Operations, Air Cdre Sydney Bufton, stating that the Commander in Chief [Harris] had decided 'this afternoon' that a new squadron should be formed.

The second memo was sent to Cochrane. It described the new Upkeep weapon: it was, Oxland said, a spherical bomb which if spun and dropped from a height of 100ft at about 200mph would travel 1,200 yards.

> It is proposed to use this weapon in the first instance against a large dam in Germany, which, if breached, will have serious consequences in the neighbouring industrial area… The operation against this dam will not, it is thought, prove particularly dangerous [sic], but it will undoubtedly require skilled crews. Volunteer crews will, therefore, have to be carefully selected from the squadrons in your Group.[14]

---

14 AIR 14/840, quoted in Sweetman, *Dambusters Raid*, p97.

It is worth noting that Oxland called the weapon a spherical bomb, but it was soon changed to a large cylinder, much the shape and size of the heavy roller used on a cricket field. At first, the cylinder was enclosed in a wooden sphere, but this proved impractical so was not used.

This second memo led to a circular being sent by 5 Group to all its squadrons, asking them to provide a pilot and crew for a new squadron, for a special one-off operation. No copies of the circular survive, but it would seem to have specified that the crew should be experienced, even perhaps have completed a full tour. Individual squadron commanders interpreted this circular in different ways, and most were probably reluctant to lose one of their best crews. Some however entered into the spirit and nominated an experienced captain. Others chose to offload someone with fewer operations, but perhaps the right 'press-on' attitude. In some squadrons – notably 97 Squadron – volunteers were called for. In others, people were told they were moving, perhaps in the time-honoured service tradition of being told that they were volunteering.

At that stage there were ten fully operational squadrons in 5 Group. Nos 44, 49, 50, 57, 61, 97, 106, 207 and 467 Squadrons eventually provided aircrew, some indirectly. No 9 Squadron was the only squadron in the group not to send a crew, although a supernumerary air gunner on its strength, Sgt Victor Hill, was posted to 617 Squadron as a late replacement on 7 May 1943.

The method by which the crews were actually selected is incontrovertible, and directly contradicts the account given by Gibson himself in his book *Enemy Coast Ahead*, written in mid 1944. Here he states that he personally chose not only the pilots but also their crews, giving the names to a staff officer he called Cartwright. He adds that the process took him just an hour:

> It took me an hour to pick my pilots. I wrote all the names down on a piece of paper and handed them over to him. I had picked them all myself because from my own personal knowledge I believed them to be the best bomber pilots available. I knew that each one of them had already done his full tour of duty and should really now be having a well-earned rest; and I knew also that there was nothing any of them would want less that this rest when they heard that there was an exciting operation on hand. Cartwright helped a lot with the crews because I didn't know these so well, but we chose carefully and we chose well.[15]

---

15   Gibson, *Enemy Coast Ahead*, pp239–240. There was a Plt Off J.S. Cartwright listed as a staff officer in the personnel section at 5 Group in July 1942 (Source: www.rafweb.org) but it is not clear whether this is the man to whom Gibson is referring.

He goes on to elaborate his story with a description of finding all his men waiting for him in the officers' mess at Scampton, on the day he arrived. This is then
followed by an impromptu party. Paul Brickhill must have relied on Gibson's
book as his source, since he has a similar account in *The Dam Busters*. Even
though he wrote this six years after the war and therefore had the opportunity
to interview many of the aircrew involved, he evidently didn't bother to check
what had actually occurred:

> A staff officer helped [Gibson] pick aircrew from the group lists.
> Gibson knew most of the pilots – he got the staff man to promise him
> Martin and help him pick the navigators, engineers, bomb aimers,
> wireless operators and gunners; when they had finished they had 147
> names – twenty-one complete crews, seven to a crew. Gibson had his
> own crew; they were just finishing their tour too, but they all wanted to
> come with him.[16]

The 1955 film of the same name follows the same scenario, with both giving a
supporting role to Gibson's famous beer-drinking pet dog.

This whole narrative is nonsense, but unfortunately the story that Gibson
'personally selected' every 'Dambuster' persists, even today. The truth is that
the process was much more drawn out, and the crews arrived over a period of
more than two weeks. The only pilots destined for the new squadron who could
have been at Scampton on the day Gibson arrived were those in 57 Squadron,
which was also based there. But at this stage, they were unaware of their imminent transfer so it is unlikely that Gibson spent the first evening knocking
back pints with them.

We know that Gibson certainly asked for some pilots by name, because he
spoke to Mick Martin, Joe McCarthy and David Shannon by telephone. This
was confirmed by all three after the war. He may have also directly contacted a
few others. One of these was probably John Hopgood who, like Shannon, had
served under him at 106 Squadron. Gibson had never met many of the other
pilots including Melvin Young and Henry Maudslay, who would be his new
flight commanders.

So why did Gibson choose to over-elaborate the story when writing his own
account? The answer, as Richard Morris discovered when writing his biography
of Gibson,[17] is that he probably didn't write the account at all. The myth had

---

16   Paul Brickhill, *The Dam Busters,* Evans 1951, p49.
17   Richard Morris, *Guy Gibson,* Penguin 1995, p208.

It took me an hour to pick my squadron. I wrote the names down on a piece of paper and gave them to a man with a red mustache who was sitting behind a huge desk. Then I got in touch with my wife and told her that our leave was postponed because I had one or two things to do before I could get away.

The next night I arrived in the mess at Dersingham with my batman and my dog trotting happily along at my heels. And there I met the boys. I knew them all. I had picked them myself because I honestly believed from my own personal knowledge of them that they were the best bomber crews in the RAF. I knew that each one of them had already done his full tour of duty and should really now be having a well-earned rest; and I knew also that there was nothing that any of them would want less than this rest when they heard that there was an exciting operation on hand. There was Mickey

It took me an hour to pick my squadron. I wrote the names down and gave them to a man with a red moustache sitting behind a huge desk. Then I got in touch with my wife, and told her our leave was postponed.

The next night I arrived in the mess with my batman and my dog trotting happily along at my heels, and there we met the boys. I knew them all. I had picked them myself because I honestly believed from my own personal knowledge that they were the best crews in the RAF.

Due for a rest

I knew that each one of them had already done his full tour of duty and should be having a well-earned rest, and I knew also that there was nothing any of them would want less than this rest when they heard that there was an exciting operation on hand.

Articles published under Guy Gibson's name in (left) *Atlantic Monthly,* December 1943, and (right) the *Sunday Express,* 5 December 1943.

already been created in a pair of press articles published in December 1943, credited to Gibson but both likely to have been written by 'ghostwriters'. The first was in the American magazine *Atlantic Monthly* in December 1943. The second was in the London newspaper, the *Sunday Express,* on 5 December 1943.

For example, he wrote in *Atlantic Monthly*:

> It took me an hour to pick my squadron. I wrote the names down on a piece of paper and gave them to a man with a red mustache who was sitting behind a huge desk. ...
>
> I knew them all. I had picked them myself because I honestly believed from my own personal knowledge that they were the best bomber crews in the RAF. I knew that each one of them had already done his full tour of duty and should now be having a well-earned rest; and I knew also that there was nothing that any of them would want less than this rest when they heard that there was an exciting operation on hand.[18]

A very similar passage appears in the *Sunday Express* article, as can be seen in the illustration above.

The probable reason for the first article's publication in an American

18   Guy Gibson, 'Cracking the German Dams', *Atlantic Monthly,* December 1943, pp45–50. The man with the red mustache/moustache transmogrifies into 'Cartwright' in *Enemy Coast Ahead.* No records on staff officers' facial hair have ever been traced.

magazine is because it coincided with a four-month tour by Gibson of Canada and the USA. As to who actually wrote it, there is the strong possibility that it was the writer Roald Dahl, then serving as the Assistant Air Attaché at the British Embassy in Washington DC, with the rank of Flight Lieutenant. He was one of the wide range of service people and civic leaders who encountered Gibson on his travels. Earlier in the war, Dahl had been a fighter pilot in both North Africa and Greece, but had been forced to give up flying after an accident. He had arrived in Washington in April 1942, and was mainly involved in intelligence work. By the time Gibson met him sixteen months later he had made contacts with the movie scene in Hollywood and had also developed a career as a writer, with several short stories published and film treatments drafted. Feted as a great new talent, he had also become heavily involved in the Washington social scene.

A few months before meeting Gibson, on 31 May 1943, Dahl had sent a proposition to the Air Ministry in London for a film on the effects of bombing. This didn't specifically involve the Dams Raid, but given that this had taken place only two weeks previously it was doubtless in his mind. He had already been introduced to the American film director Howard Hawks, and he must have also contacted him at this time because, at the end of July 1943, Dahl's colleague in the Air Attaché's office, Sqn Ldr G. Allen Morris, wrote to Air Chief Marshal Harris, the AOC Bomber Command, asking for 'every possible releasable detail' about the Dams Raid. Hawks, he said, had asked Dahl to write a script about it.

By early September, Gibson was in New York, and Dahl travelled to the city to meet him. Dahl wrote in a letter to his mother that Gibson had flown from Canada 'to see me about the "Bombing of the Dams" script which I am trying to do for Hollywood in my spare time. I've got all the material now and all the photos I want. I've got everything, in fact, except the time in which to do it.'[19] By 21 September, he had completed the script, calling it 'The Dam', and sent it to London for vetting.

However, it was not well received. Some readers raised security concerns, but others, such as Harris, thought it unrealistic. It isn't known how Howard Hawks reacted but it is clear that he then became involved in other projects, so 'The Dam' was quietly shelved. However, parts of the script also appear almost verbatim in the 'Cracking the German Dams' article in *Atlantic Monthly,* which adds credence to the theory that Dahl was involved in writing the article and getting it published. Whoever the author was, Gibson may have assisted him,

---

19   Robert Owen, 'Roald Dahl and the Dam', in Richard Morris and Robert Owen (eds), *Breaching the German Dams,* RAF Museum 2008, p62.

but several months later he apologised to Barnes Wallis for the article's inaccuracies, excusing it as propaganda written by someone else.[20]

The *Sunday Express* article was published on 5 December 1943, four days after Gibson got back to Britain. It is written in much the same style, and could be the work of the same author. More likely, it was rewritten from the *Atlantic Monthly* piece by an RAF public relations officer in London.

The truth is, Gibson didn't know all of his pilots – or even most of his own crew – before they arrived at 617 Squadron. Some of the remarks about his crew in the two articles are arrogant, to say the least. However, when the text was incorporated wholesale into the draft of *Enemy Coast Ahead,* Gibson never bothered to change it.

Gibson probably arrived at Scampton on Sunday 21 March, before any pilots or other aircrew had been posted to the station. It seems that some of the administrative staff may have been ready to start but Gibson fell out almost immediately with Flt Lt Charles Pain, who had been posted by 5 Group to be the squadron's adjutant. Gibson arranged for him to be removed, and to be replaced by Flg Off Harry Humphries, who he had met when Humphries had been the Committee of Adjustment Officer at RAF Syerston.[21] Humphries duly turned up on 1 April – along with a promotion to Flight Lieutenant.

The aircrew began arriving a few days after Gibson started work. Records vary considerably between squadron and squadron, so not all transfers are listed in their respective squadron Operations Record Books (ORBs) but the earliest mention is on Wednesday 24 March, in the ORB of 467 Squadron. This is for the crew of the inexperienced Canadian pilot, Sgt Vernon Byers.

Byers, and a full crew (Alastair Taylor, James Warner, John Wilkinson, Neville Whitaker, Charles Jarvie, James McDowell) are shown as being posted on Wednesday 24 March, although they do not appear to have arrived at Scampton until 28 March. Byers had done just five operations and some of his crew even fewer. Byers and his crew were in fact the second choice of the 467 Squadron CO. He had nominated a more experienced crew, but they had turned down the transfer after a ballot amongst them was lost by four votes to three. (See p62.)

In any event, Gibson was not at Scampton on 24 March. This was the day he travelled to the Vickers Company's temporary drawing offices at Burhill Golf Club, near Weybridge in Surrey for his first meeting with Barnes Wallis. At the meeting, Wallis was embarrassed when he realised that he did not have the authority to divulge the target to Gibson.

---

20   Morris, *Guy Gibson,* p208.
21   Morris, *Guy Gibson,* p145.

On the same day at RAF Skellingthorpe, Flt Lt Henry Maudslay of 50 Squadron was surprised to be told that he and his crew were to be posted to a new squadron being formed at Scampton. He wrote to his mother that evening telling her that he was to be promoted to Squadron Leader and would be a flight commander.[22] He had completed a first tour in November 1941, and was now thirteen operations into a second tour.

The next day, Thursday 25 March, brought the biggest influx of crews. Henry Maudslay turned up at Scampton with a complete crew from 50 Squadron (Robert Urquhart, Alden Cottam, John Fuller, William Tytherleigh and Rupert Burrows). Although they had all flown with Maudslay on several occasions, they had only combined together on three operations. Also from 50 Squadron came Plt Off Les Knight and his crew (Ray Grayston, Sydney Hobday, Robert Kellow, Edward Johnson, Fred Sutherland and Harry O'Brien). This crew were all coming to the end of their first tour, and were offered the chance to transfer.

Two individuals who would join Gibson's own crew also arrived on this day. One was another transferee from 50 Squadron: air gunner Flt Lt Richard Trevor-Roper, holder of the DFM for his first tour of operations and now halfway through a second. He may have been suggested by Mick Martin who would have known him from 50 Squadron. Although Martin was not officially transferred by this stage, it seems as though he might have already been contacted by Gibson, and had also been sounded out about who might also be persuaded to come aboard, particularly for the CO's crew.

The other man destined to fly with Gibson was the only member of his 106 Squadron crew to join him in 617 Squadron, wireless operator Robert Hutchison. He had finished his tour on 26 February, and on 19 March he was posted to 1654 Conversion Unit at RAF Wigsley to take up a training role. He was there for just six days, according to his logbook where he records his arrival at Scampton on 25 March. Trevor-Roper and Hutchison would later be joined in the Gibson crew by two more 50 Squadron colleagues, Harlo Taerum and Fred Spafford.

Also arriving on the same day were three crews from 97 Squadron, based at Coningsby. Two, the crews of Flt Lt Joe McCarthy (William Radcliffe, Douglas MacLean, Leonard Eaton, George Johnson, Ronald Batson and David Rodger) and Flt Lt Les Munro (Frank Appleby, Grant Rumbles, Percy Pigeon, James Clay, William Howarth and Harvey Weeks), were all experienced men, mostly coming to the end of a first tour. The third was piloted by Flt Lt David Maltby, who had completed a first tour and had just been posted back to his squadron

---

22   Robert Owen, *Henry Maudslay: Dam Buster,* Fighting High 2014, p248.

to begin a second. He had acquired a brand new crew (William Hatton, Vivian Nicholson, Antony Stone, John Fort, Austin Williams [who did not fly on the Dams Raid] and Harold Simmonds) which had no significant operational experience at all.

McCarthy was one of those who Gibson telephoned personally. Gibson had met McCarthy the previous September, when he was just coming to the end of his training. McCarthy, an American citizen, had joined the RCAF in 1941 along with his boyhood friend, Don Curtin. They had been together through training and the voyage to Britain, but were then split up when they went on operations. Curtin had joined Gibson's 106 Squadron but was shot down and killed in February 1943, on a raid to Nuremburg.

McCarthy had finished his tour, but was persuaded to do one more trip. He recounted later:

> [Gibson] asked me if I'd like to join a special squadron for one mission. He also asked if I could bring my own crew along… He couldn't tell me what we were going to do, where we were going to go, or anything… He said 'If you can't bring the whole crew take as many as you can. We'll probably find some for you, but we would prefer your own.'
>
> I explained it to my crew and I got a lot of flak back, quick, 'Why? What are we going to do?' Same thing I asked and I just had to tell them I didn't know but it was going to be just one trip. I don't know whether I, at that moment, had any decision from them that they would accompany me. But in two days, I arrived at the Officers Mess and I was looking around and I found all my crew there with a brief but proud little grin, and they were all ready and waiting to go again. So I had the original crew all the way through.
>
> The next thing we knew we were at Scampton. Gibby didn't fool around.[23]

McCarthy's colleague Les Munro saw the 5 Group circular and volunteered, along with his crew. He confirmed this in 2007:

> I distinctly remember discussing with my crew the question of whether we should volunteer or not, and I seem to think that Joe McCarthy did likewise on the same day. I was not aware of how or when David

---

23   Dave Birrell, *Big Joe McCarthy*, Wing Leader 2012, p87.

> [Maltby] reached his decision. Can't remember how I was advised
> that our transfer to Scampton was official, but it was certainly not
> by Gibson.[24]

Munro was also fairly sure that they all transferred the few miles to Scampton
in a crew bus, and has the distinct memory of a gathering in the ante-room of
the Officers' Mess in the evening. Perhaps this was the evening that Gibson
wrote about in *Enemy Coast Ahead*.

The final crew listed as being posted on 25 March was that of Flt Lt Harold
Wilson and his crew, whose move was recorded in the 44 Squadron ORB on
this day. Wilson had some fourteen operations to his name. In the end, illness
prevented him flying on the raid.

The first of the two crews who came from 49 Squadron is listed in its ORB
as being transferred on 24 March, but in fact did not arrive for several more
days. This was Sgt Cyril Anderson and his crew (Robert Paterson, John Nugent,
Douglas Bickle, Gilbert Green, Eric Ewan and Arthur Buck), who had all only
been on the squadron for a few weeks, and had only completed two operations
together. Anderson, who had done just two further operations as a second pilot, asked to gain some further experience in 49 Squadron before moving. He
and his crew were therefore sent on three operations in the next five days, flying
to Duisburg on 26 March and Berlin on both 27 and 29 March. By contrast, Sgt
Bill Townsend had almost completed a full tour and his transfer along with five
of his crew (Dennis Powell, Lance Howard, Charles Franklin, Douglas Webb
and Raymond Wilkinson) was listed in the squadron's ORB on 25 March. His
wireless operator declined the transfer as he was getting married. Townsend's
was a crew with a level of experience which fitted the criteria laid down by
Group HQ, but the same could not be said of Anderson's.

Another of Gibson's telephone calls had been to his 106 Squadron colleague,
Flt Lt David Shannon. He was widely regarded as one of the best pilots in
Bomber Command, and had completed his first tour of operations on 28 February, as had most of his crew. Under normal circumstances, the crew would
have broken up and all would have been sent on instructional duties for a period of six months. Shannon, however, wanted to carry on flying and somehow
arranged a transfer to a Pathfinder outfit, 83 Squadron at RAF Wyton. It was
there that he got a call from Gibson, asking him to join him. Although several
of Shannon's previous crew (still at Syerston) were also transferred to the new
squadron, none would be in his final crew. Of all the men who had flown with

---

24   Les Munro, email to author, 8 May 2007.

Shannon in 106 Squadron, only navigator Plt Off Danny Walker, who had finished his tour back in November 1942, and had been instructing at 22 OTU at Wellesbourne Mountford since then, was selected for his Dams Raid crew. (See pp52–55 for a full account of how the Shannon crew came together.)

The biggest single group of aircrew transferred into the new squadron came about when the whole of 57 Squadron's C Flight, numbering five crews, was posted across the station to their new neighbours.

The commander of this flight was Sqn Ldr Melvin Young, who had joined 57 Squadron on 13 March with a full crew. He had taken over a new inexperienced crew a few days before at 1660 Conversion Unit at RAF Swinderby, after their pilot went on sick leave. They were David Horsfall, Charles Roberts, Lawrence Nichols, John Beesley (who did not fly on the Dams Raid), Gordon Yeo and Wilfred Ibbotson. They had each flown on a small number of operations in training, the most experienced being Ibbotson with just three. Although Young had completed two operational tours, these had been on medium bombers, and he had only just finished heavy bomber training. The Dams Raid would be his first and last operation flying a Lancaster.

Flt Lt Bill Astell was also in 57 Squadron's C Flight. He had been posted to the squadron on 25 January 1943, where he had acquired the full crew (John Kinnear, Floyd Wile, Albert Garshowitz, Donald Hopkinson, Frank Garbas, and Richard Bolitho) who would fly with him on the Dams Raid. He had completed a full tour as a Wellington pilot and like Young he was also relatively new to Lancasters. However, he and his crew had flown on a handful of operations in the main squadron before their transfer.

The other three crews from 57 Squadron's C Flight were all relatively new to operational flying, and only one of these would eventually fly on the Dams Raid. This was Plt Off Geoff Rice and crew (Edward Smith, Richard Macfarlane, Bruce Gowrie, John Thrasher, Thomas Maynard and Stephen Burns) who had completed nine trips together. Rice and his crew had gone on leave on 24 March and did not find out about the transfer until they returned on 1 April.[25] The other two pilots were Flt Sgt Ray Lovell and Flt Sgt George Lancaster and their crews.

Nineteen ground crew were also transferred from 57 Squadron on this day. These included one of the new squadron's administrative lynchpins, Sgt Jim Heveron. His colleague, Flt Sgt George ('Chiefy') Powell and ten more ground crew made the same administrative journey the following day, Friday 26 March.

Gibson's old colleague from 106 Squadron, Flt Lt John Hopgood was listed

25   Nigel Press, *All My Life: the story of a Lancaster Crew*, Lancfile Publishing 2006, p17.

on Thursday 25 March as being posted from his instructional duties at 1485 Bombing Gunnery Training Flight at RAF Fulbeck. He flew over to Scampton in a Gipsy Moth that day.[26]

The day's final entry in the new squadron's Operations Record Book ends optimistically, recording that the squadron had a number, 617, and was 'ready to fly'.

On Saturday 27 March, a week or so after he had arrived at Scampton, Gibson began to get a better idea of what was expected from the squadron when a set of 'most secret' orders was given to him by Gp Capt Harold Satterly, Senior Air Staff Officer at 5 Group. These told him that the operation would involve low flying and precision bombing and that it would be 'convenient to practise this over water'.

By now, a number of ordinary Lancasters had arrived for training purposes and in the afternoon, the first crew got airborne. Flt Lt Bill Astell was dispatched to photograph nine lakes that Satterly had identified as being suitable for practice.

Another member of the Gibson crew may have arrived at Scampton on this day. This was the Australian bomb aimer, Fred Spafford, who had finished a tour with 50 Squadron and had been posted to 1660 Conversion Unit on 24 March. His future colleague, Canadian navigator Harlo Taerum, had also completed a tour in 50 Squadron but was by then an instructor in 1654 Conversion Unit, along with Martin. The fact that Spafford and Taerum were well known to Martin suggests that he may have had a hand in selecting them. Martin was yet to arrive on 617 Squadron but there is also evidence that he was putting together his old crew in the last week of March 1943.[27]

On Monday 29 March the only crew transferred directly from Gibson's previous command at 106 Squadron arrived at Scampton. It was captained by a Canadian, Flt Sgt Lewis Burpee, and he brought his complete crew (Guy Pegler, Thomas Jaye, Leonard Weller, James Arthur, William Long, Gordon Brady). Although Burpee was not yet commissioned, he was nearing the end of his first tour with twenty-eight operations. Gibson reckoned that he had the right 'press on' attitude and was happy to have him on the team.

The other crew to arrive on that day were much less experienced, but had not been given any option by their CO at 44 Squadron. It was captained by

26   Jenny Elmes, *M-Mother: Dambuster Flight Lieutenant John 'Hoppy' Hopgood*, History
      Press 2015, p213.

27   Tom Simpson, *Lower than Low*, Libra Books 1995, pp77–8. Simpson was also friendly
      with Spafford.

another Canadian Flight Sergeant, Ken Brown, and was made up of Basil Feneron, Dudley Heal, Herbert Hewstone, Stefan Oancia, Donald Buntaine (who
did not fly on the Dams Raid) and Grant McDonald.

Another man destined for Gibson's crew also arrived, the Canadian air gunner George Deering. He was instructing in 22 OTU at Wellesbourne Mountford, after completing a full tour in 103 Squadron.

This was the day on which Gibson was summoned to Group HQ and told
the target by Cochrane. He was shown models of the Möhne and Sorpe dams,
the same models which were dramatically unveiled again to all the crews at the
briefing on the day of the raid.

John Hopgood, who had arrived on the Thursday, must have returned to
his previous posting by road, as his next flight is listed in his logbook as taking
place on Tuesday 30 March, back to Scampton in an Avro Manchester, with a
Flg Off Jones as his second pilot. Hopgood's previous operational crew from
his completed tour in 106 Squadron had largely dispersed, but he was able to
contact Charles Brennan, his old flight engineer. Tony Burcher, who had served
on 106 Squadron but not in his crew, would also join him at Scampton as his
rear gunner. Hopgood then took leave between 31 March and 11 April, in order
to attend an investiture at Buckingham Palace on 9 April, where he received a
bar to his first DFC. (See pp45–7 for a full account of how the Hopgood crew
came together.)

Flt Lt Mick Martin finally arrived on 31 March, having been contacted several days previously. Martin's crew from their completed tour in 50 Squadron
had been dispersed, but he was able to contact four of them (Ivan Whittaker,
Jack Leggo, Toby Foxlee, Thomas Simpson), although they didn't all arrive at
Scampton together. Simpson was probably the last to arrive, on 4 April. They
were joined by another Australian 50 Squadron tour veteran, bomb aimer Bob
Hay, and an RNZAF wireless operator from 75 Squadron, Len Chambers.

The last day in March was exactly a fortnight after Air Vice Marshal Oxland
had sat at his desk in High Wycombe and written his two important memos. In
that time, a lot of progress had been made. There were eighteen crews or part-
crews nominally on the squadron strength, although some had gone on leave.
A number of borrowed Lancasters were also available and training schedules
and routes were in the process of being drawn up.

Plt Off Geoff Rice and crew returned to Scampton from their leave on 1 April.
When they had left they were in 57 Squadron's C Flight, but they found that in
their absence they had been posted across the station to the new 617 Squadron.

The final two men in Gibson's crew arrived over the next three days. Navigator Harlo Taerum had been posted to 1654 Conversion Unit, but was

summoned from there, and arrived at Scampton on 3 April. Flight engineer John Pulford was posted from 97 Squadron at Coningsby on Sunday 4 April.

The last two of the 19 crews who would take part in the Dams Raid arrived at Scampton on Sunday 4 and Wednesday 7 April. The first of these was an experienced crew from 207 Squadron, based at RAF Langar. This was piloted by Plt Off Warner Ottley, and comprised Ronald Marsden, Jack Barrett, Jack Guterman, Thomas Johnston, Harry Strange and Fred Tees. They had all flown with Ottley at some point over the previous few months. Jack Guterman, the wireless operator, had in fact come to the end of his tour on 8 March but as Ottley didn't yet have a regular replacement he must have volunteered to return to the crew.

The following day, Flt Lt Norman Barlow of 61 Squadron and a full crew (Leslie Whillis, Philip Burgess, Charles Williams, Alan Gillespie, Harvey Glinz and Jack Liddell) arrived, having taken the week's leave which was owing to them. Only two of these had been in Barlow's crew before, but they were all well known to each other. Four, including Barlow himself, had finished a full tour. They had been based at RAF Syerston, where Gibson had himself been stationed until a couple of weeks previously.

No new pilots would join 617 Squadron after 7 April, but there were a few further changes to crews which are detailed in the individual sections about each crew in the following chapter.

Experience levels of pilots and crews

The experience levels of both pilots and crews varied enormously, something which was not mentioned by Gibson or others writing at the time. In *Enemy Coast Ahead*, Gibson overexaggerates how well decorated they were: 'Soon it became obvious, even to the casual observer, that this was no ordinary squadron … Many of them had two DFCs, and most of them wore one, some had the DSO.'[28] In fact, only three – Gibson himself, Young and Hopgood – had a Bar to their DFCs, and there were no holders of the DSO, again with the exception of Gibson. Official lists show that at the time of the raid, twenty-nine of the 133 aircrew had received either the DFC or the DFM for their previous operational service, but this is misleading. A number of decorations were not awarded until April or May 1943, and some did not come through until after 17 May. At least three men died on the Dams Raid not knowing that they had been decorated. Their medals were eventually sent to their grieving relatives.

---

28   Gibson, *Enemy Coast Ahead*, p242.

Of the nineteen pilots who took part in the raid, fifteen could justifiably be described as 'experienced' and thirteen had been decorated. By contrast, four – Anderson, Brown, Byers and Rice – had all completed fewer than ten operations, as had all of their crews. Furthermore, two more crews, those of Melvin Young and David Maltby, were made up mainly of newly qualified aircrew. Both these pilots, however, had substantial experience – Young had completed two full tours, Maltby one. In another coincidence, both would also have a late substitute in their crews and thereby gain a seasoned flyer, respectively Vincent MacCausland and Victor Hill.

Background of aircrew

The 133 aircrew who flew on the Dams Raid were a microcosm of the type of men who flew in Bomber Command at that time. Of the British, a few came from the country's top public schools and rather more from other independent schools a little lower down the pecking order. The largest number had been to grammar schools, but some had no education at all beyond elementary level. The so-called Dominions provided nearly a third of the men, bringing a more relaxed attitude to class and background, but they too came from many different family situations, ranging from university graduates to men brought up on farmsteads hundreds of miles from the nearest big city with little in the way of formal education.

Chapter 4

Finalising the crews

Crew 1: Wg Cdr G.P. Gibson DSO and bar, DFC and bar

GUY GIBSON HAD RETURNED FROM THE FINAL TRIP of his tour of operations with 106 Squadron, an attack on Stuttgart, in the early hours of Friday 12 March 1943. It was his twenty-eighth operation with the squadron – the first had been almost a year before, on 22 April 1942.

Although the members of his crew changed regularly, in the latter part of his 106 Squadron career Gibson had built up a core team of four men, all of whom had taken part in at least half of his tour of operations. These were Plt Off F. Ruskell (navigator) with nineteen sorties, Plt Off R.E.G. Hutchison (wireless operator) with eighteen, Flt Lt W.B. Oliver (mid-upper gunner) with fourteen and Flg Off J.F. Wickens (rear gunner) with twenty-three.

However, in the course of his tour, the positions of flight engineer/second pilot and bomb aimer were filled by many different men, with no one flying on more than a handful of operations with their squadron CO. Gibson was in the habit of taking squadron new boys, especially pilots, to fill the seat in the cockpit beside him as their first operation. Some new flight engineers were also selected for this honour. Some undoubtedly found this a daunting experience, others warmed to the task. A new young Canadian pilot, Walter Thompson, fulfilled this role on Gibson's last trip on 12 March:

> 'You must be Thompson,' [Gibson] said, walking across the room and extending a strong hand. Before I could acknowledge he said, 'My name is Gibson, will you have a drink?' 'Thank you, sir, a half of bitter would be fine.' The barman drew a glass as Gibson turned to the adjutant and I heard him say, 'Maybe he'll be another Joe McCarthy.'
>
> I had met McCarthy during my incarceration at Grantham, where he had landed one day. He was from New York. I forgave Gibson for blurring the distinction between Canadians and Americans. He said, 'You're just in time, you'll be flying tonight.' I hoped he hadn't seen me gulp as I asked, 'With my own crew, sir?'

'No, you'll be coming with me, so get yourself settled in and I'll see you at briefing.' I had only a sip of the beer.'[29]

Thompson must have enjoyed the experience and took a shine to his new CO as, a few days later, he volunteered to join the new squadron at Scampton. His request was however turned down.

Wireless operator Robert Hutchison was the only one from Gibson's core 106 Squadron crew transferred to his new crew in the fledgling squadron. It doesn't seem that any of the others were approached. A decision was obviously made to find him a crew with plenty of experience, but Gibson himself didn't do the headhunting. Three of his crew came from 50 Squadron, where Mick Martin had recently finished a tour, which suggests that Martin might have had a hand in selecting them for his boss. Of this trio, rear gunner Richard Trevor-Roper was the first to arrive, on 25 March. He was one of the most experienced air gunners in Bomber Command, having almost completed a second tour of operations in 50 Squadron. His upper class manner and reputation as a hellraiser might well have endeared him to Gibson. Fred Spafford, the Australian bomb aimer, had completed a tour of operations. He was posted to 617 Squadron on 29 March. His friend and colleague Harlo Taerum, the Canadian navigator, arrived two days later, on 1 April. He had also completed a tour in early 1943 and after a spell as an instructor in the squadron's conversion flight, had moved to 1654 Conversion Unit, also as an instructor. While there, he flew with Mick Martin on two operations to Berlin on 16 and 17 January 1943.

Meanwhile Hutchison had arrived at Scampton on 25 March. He was followed by George Deering, an experienced Canadian mid-upper gunner, who was transferred on 29 March from training duties. The crew was completed on 4 April by John Pulford, a flight engineer from 97 Squadron, who had the least experience of them all but had still clocked up thirteen operations.

Gibson's logbook records that he took his full crew out for the first time on 1 April, on a local training flight. Although Pulford is recorded as the flight engineer, this could be an error, and he took someone else. Gibson's next training flight was on 4 April, a trip to a 'Lake near Sheffield', but his entry just says 'Crew'. This may in fact be the first time Pulford flew with his new skipper.

With the exception of Hutchison, the Dams Raid was therefore the first operation in which the crew flew with Gibson as their skipper. In fact it turned out to be the only sortie on which all seven flew together. This is in stark contrast to what Gibson wrote about 'my crew' in *Enemy Coast Ahead,* where you are

---

29   Walter Thompson, *Lancaster to Berlin,* Goodall 1985, pp53–4.

given the impression that they had flown together regularly and were therefore the closest of pals.

In a book which is littered with typing and proofreading errors, there are several in Gibson's account of his Dams Raid crew. George Deering, his Canadian front gunner, is called Jim, Tony and Joe at different points in the text. Rear gunner Richard Trevor-Roper is given the additional forename Algernon. And John Pulford, his flight engineer, is never referred to by his first name at all and described as a Londoner, when he was born and bred in Hull and according to all other accounts had a distinct Yorkshire accent. These points are noted by Gibson's biographer, Richard Morris, who writes wryly: 'In the cockpit of Gibson's Lancaster there was a distinct air of master and servant. In the fuselage as a whole his crew represented Britain's class structure in microcosm and the pattern of Empire beyond.'[30]

Crew 2: Flt Lt J.V. Hopgood DFC and Bar

As we have seen, not all the pilots were personally known or recruited by Gibson. However with John Hopgood there is no doubt that Gibson wanted him by his side. Hopgood had impressed him when he first arrived to take command at 106 Squadron, and they had become friends as well as colleagues.

Hopgood had officially finished his tour of operations with 106 Squadron at the end of October 1942, but as he was still at Syerston he flew on another trip to Berlin on 16 January. This was the same operation on which Richard Dimbleby flew with Gibson, reporting for the BBC. By early March, he was working at 1485 Bombing and Gunnery Flight at RAF Fulbeck as an instructor, and it was there that he was contacted by Gibson.

Hopgood flew to Scampton on 30 March in one of 1485 Flight's Manchesters, with a Flg Off Jones as his second pilot. The next day, he went on a local familiarisation trip with his old squadron colleague David Shannon. He was, however, due at Buckingham Palace to receive a Bar to his DFC on 6 April and had booked leave to cover this event. So he did not fly again until 11 April, when he took an unnamed crew on a low-level cross-country flight.

It is not clear exactly who made up this crew, but it certainly included his regular flight engineer from 106 Squadron, Sgt Charles Brennan. It is likely that the remainder were the five others listed in Hopgood's logbook on another low-level cross-country flight two days later. Four of these do not appear to have been previously known to him. The navigator was Flg Off George Osborne,

---

30   Morris, *Guy Gibson*, p152.

who had come from 97 Squadron. Sgt John Minchin, the wireless operator, had done a full tour of operations in 49 Squadron but came direct from a posting in 26 OTU. The bomb aimer, Sgt William White, had come from 49 Squadron. The mid-upper gunner was Plt Off George Gregory, who had completed a tour in 44 Squadron and been awarded the DFM. He was also working as an instructor, in 16 OTU. The final member of Hopgood's crew, rear gunner Plt Off Tony Burcher, had previously served in 106 Squadron and was therefore known to his new pilot. He was also working as an instructor, in his case in 1654 CU, and had received the DFM after his first tour.

A few days later, on 20 April, Hopgood wrote to his mother telling her about his crew:

> I like my new crew – all very experienced types and damn good chaps as well. My flight engineer is my old one, but the rest are new faces, except my rear-gunner, who was in my last squadron though not in my crew. There are 3 officers besides myself, which is much better than an all sergeant crew which I had before.[31]

However, two changes then swiftly followed. Bomb aimer William White was deemed to be somehow unsatisfactory, and had to be replaced. A replacement was called up from 50 Squadron – Flt Sgt John Fraser, a Canadian, who had just finished his first tour and was due to be posted to an OTU. He first flew with Hopgood on 21 April. Two days later, on 23 April, Fraser wrote to his fiancée, Doris, describing the rest of the crew:

> There is one Australian P/O DFM in the crew called Tony, one Scot P/O DFM called Jack [Gregory], a sergeant wireless op called Minchie, a navigator P/O called Ossie, engineer sergeant called Charlie (a Canadian who came over here seven years ago and settled in Leeds, an attempt to colonize this country) the pilot called 'Hoppy' (F/L DFC and Bar) and me. I feel a bit strange after flying with Pop, but everything should work out OK.[32]

The second and final change to AJ-M's crew happened a few days later, although the exact date is not certain. George Osborne went sick. Hopgood then sent a telegram to his old 106 Squadron navigator, Plt Off William Bates, who was by then an instructor at RAF Harwell. This is dated 25 April and Bates apparently

31   Elmes, *M-Mother*, p221.
32   Owen et al, *Dam Busters: Failed To Return*, p54.

responded immediately. He was told to meet Hopgood and Guy Gibson for tea at Simpson's in the Strand in London, and to bring his kit. Bates set off to London, but his train was delayed and by the time he reached Simpson's the others had gone. With no way of contacting them he returned to Harwell.[33]

Osborne was instead replaced by Plt Off Ken Earnshaw, who had been in the same crew at 50 Squadron as John Fraser. He arrived at Scampton on 29 April, the day Fraser had a day off in order to get married.[34] It is hard not to think that Fraser had some influence in choosing his former comrade, and this is corroborated by Hopgood in a letter he wrote to his mother on 3 May, telling her about the changes:

> I have made two alterations in my crew just recently – a new
> Navigator and a new Bombardier. My old Navigator went sick
> and my old Bombardier proved unsatisfactory. The replacements are
> grand chaps – both Canadians who have been flying together for a
> long time. My aircraft letter is once again an 'M' and I am having my
> old crest painted on.[35]

The complete crew had flown together for the first time two days earlier, 1 May, taking part in a Wings for Victory 'Beat Up' of nearby Horncastle in formation with other 617 Squadron crews, and then going on a low-level training flight.

Crew 3: Flt Lt H.B. Martin DFC

At the time 617 Squadron was formed, Mick Martin was just coming to the end of a spell as an instructor at 1654 Conversion Unit at RAF Wigsley. Several months previously Gibson had met him at an investiture and they had discussed low flying methods, so he was an almost automatic choice for the project.

Martin was keen to recruit some of the aircrew who had previously flown with him and set about contacting them. It says something about the devotion with which they regarded him in that they all gave him an immediate yes. Back in February 1942 he had skippered the first all-Australian crew to fly in Bomber Command when navigator Jack Leggo and air gunners Toby Foxlee and Tom Simpson had set off on a trip to Cologne in a 455 Squadron Hampden. All three needed no persuading to return to his command.

33 William Bates, son of Plt Off W.P. Bates, letter to Jenny Elmes, 20 April 2015.
34 Flg Off K. Earnshaw, RCAF personnel file, National Archives of Canada.
35 Elmes, *M-Mother*, pp225–6. There is, however, no evidence that the crest was actually painted onto his aircraft.

The furthest away was Tom Simpson, who was in an instructional job in an OTU in Kinloss, in north-east Scotland. Angry at being confined to barracks for a uniform violation, he had telephoned Martin who told him not to worry because 'something was cooking'. Simpson was posted to the nearby station at Lossiemouth and then given two days' leave. He travelled down to meet Martin at Wigsley who told him that when he got back to Lossiemouth he would be told he was being posted to Scampton. Martin said: 'I'm getting in touch with Toby and Jack and we will link up again in about a week's time and we'll try and find out what it is all about when we get there.'[36]

Simpson arrived at Scampton on 5 April, the last of Martin's crew to show up, and was greeted at the guard house by Toby Foxlee, who told him that they would be sharing a billet on the station built as married quarters. After he had stowed his kit, Foxlee took him to meet the rest of the crew. Two of them had come from 50 Squadron, Martin's last operational squadron. Ivan Whittaker had been his flight engineer for several months. From Wallsend in Northumberland, he was the only Englishman in the crew. Bomb aimer Bob Hay, from Adelaide, South Australia, had done a full tour in 50 Squadron with another crew, and was widely recognised as one of the best at his trade in Bomber Command. The final member of the crew was a New Zealander, Len Chambers, who had a full tour under his belt as a wireless operator in 75 (NZ) Squadron, and where he had been the squadron Signals Leader. In typical Martin fashion, the whole crew went off to Lincoln that evening to celebrate.

It was the measure of the experience level of the Martin crew that two of its members became the squadron's leaders in their trades: Jack Leggo as the Navigation Leader, and Bob Hay as the Bombing Leader.

Crew 4: Sqn Ldr H.M. Young DFC and Bar

At the beginning of 1943 Sqn Ldr Melvin Young DFC was in the USA. He had a number of postings there, the last being working as a liaison officer at a flying training school in Georgia. But he was keen to get back to operational flying, and eventually arrived back in the UK in early February. Although he was a two-tour veteran, he had yet to fly the new generation of heavy bombers, and was therefore sent for training.[37]

It was common practice for an experienced pilot like Young to be given a new crew to work with, and this is how the crew who would eventually fly AJ-A on the Dams Raid was formed. Young first met his crew in early March 1943

---

36   Simpson, *Lower than Low,* p77.
37   Arthur G. Thorning, *The Dambuster who cracked the Dam,* Pen and Sword, 2008, p113.

at 1660 Conversion Unit, flying with them first on 4 March. At this stage, the crew comprised David Horsfall (flight engineer), Charles Roberts (navigator), Lawrence Nichols (wireless operator), John Beesley (bomb aimer), Gordon Yeo (mid-upper gunner) and Wilfred Ibbotson (rear gunner). Nine days later, on 13 March, Young and this crew were posted to 57 Squadron at Scampton to start a new operational tour.

Most of the crew, however, had been together since at least the previous September, when they were at 10 Operational Training Unit at RAF Abingdon, training on Whitley aircraft. Roberts, Nichols and Beesley were part of a five man crew skippered by a Canadian pilot, Sgt Graham Bower. Wilfred Ibbotson was also in this OTU at the same time, flying mainly in a crew headed by Sgt Ivan Morgan.

In September 1942, the OTU was asked to supply crews for maximum effort operations on Düsseldorf on 10 September, Bremen on 13 September and Essen on 16 September. On the first of these dates, Bower flew with Roberts in his crew and Ibbotson was in a crew captained by Sqn Ldr J. Hurry DFC. On the Bremen raid three days later, Bower, Roberts, Nichols and Beesley all flew together, with the final gunner position occupied by Sgt L. Pickford. Ibbotson flew on the raid on Essen on 16 September, in Sgt Morgan's crew.

At the end of December, Bower and his crew moved on to 1660 Conversion Unit at Swinderby for the final stage of heavy bomber training. It would seem that it was here that Wilfred Ibbotson joined the crew, as did Gordon Yeo and David Horsfall who had come straight to the unit from air gunner training and flight engineer training respectively.

The crew flew on about ten training flights between 31 December 1942 and 13 January 1943[38], but then Bower was taken ill and sent to the RAF Station Hospital at Cranwell[39]. Even though they now had no pilot of their own the crew was detailed for an operation on 16 January 1943, an attack on Berlin, with the experienced instructor Plt Off Vincent Duxbury DFC[40] taking command. Another instructor, Flt Lt V. Blair, flew as the navigator, rather than Charles Roberts. This was the first operation for both David Horsfall and Gordon Yeo. Wilfred Ibbotson's name is recorded as 'M. Hibberton' in the Conversion Unit's Operations Record Book, but this is an

---

38   Sgt John Beesley, logbook. (Courtesy Nichols family.)

39   Wrt Off G.W. Bower, RCAF personnel file, National Archives of Canada.

40   Vincent Duxbury had previously served in 207 Squadron and had been awarded the DFC after completing his first tour. For part of this tour his crew had included Jack Barrett and Jack Guterman, who would later form part of Bill Ottley's crew on the Dams Raid. Duxbury was still an instructor when he was killed in a flying accident in October 1943.

obvious transcription error. The following day two more CU crews were detailed for another operation on Berlin. Horsfall flew as flight engineer on one crew skippered by another instructor, Flg Off Harold Southgate and Beesley was the bomb aimer in another piloted by Plt Off Stanley Harrison. Harrison's flight engineer on this trip was Charles Brennan, who was doing an instructional spell having previously flown in 106 Squadron as John Hopgood's flight engineer. He would rejoin the Hopgood crew for the Dams Raid. Harrison and his crew eventually turned back with a problem in the oxygen supply, an event the captain blamed on the reluctance of other members of the crew (neither Beesley nor Brennan) to undertake such a dangerous operation while on instructional duties.[41]

With Bower still off sick (he did not return to active service until mid-March) the crew does not appear to have flown again after the Berlin operations. However, they were kept on at 1660 CU and then in early March were allocated to Sqn Ldr Melvin Young, freshly arrived at Swinderby. He had been posted to 1654 CU at RAF Wigsley on 1 March, but the following day went on to 1660 CU. According to Beesley's logbook, Young made sixteen training flights in Lancasters with his new crew between 4 and 11 March, some with an instructor pilot but the majority on his own.[42]

On 13 March they moved to 57 Squadron at Scampton, where they would have expected to become a fully operational crew. Young had been made flight commander of the squadron's new C Flight. Forming a new third flight in an operational squadron to be used as as the nucleus of a new squadron would later become a common practice in Bomber Command, but in March 1943 it would seem to have just been regarded as an administrative convenience. Young and his crew had a few more days at Scampton to make better acquaintance with each other, and then, and it seems without much consultation, it was decided that the whole flight would move over to the new 617 Squadron, being formed in the station's adjacent hangars.

Young was then appointed as the flight commander of the new squadron's A Flight. His well-known organisational skills were used to devise training routines for the squadron: bombing practice runs at the Wainfleet range and flying exercises which would criss-cross the country at low level. At first, these were done in ordinary Lancasters sequestered from other squadrons. In late April, the special 'Type 464' Lancasters specially built for the operation began to arrive, and the training switched to them.

Shortly before the new aircraft arrived, a decision was reached to replace

---

41   Stanley Harrison, *A Bomber Command Survivor,* Sage Pages Australia, 1992, pp107–9.
42   Sgt John Beesley, logbook. (Courtesy Nichols family).

Sgt John Beesley, the bomb aimer.[43] He was replaced by Canadian bomb aimer, Vincent MacCausland, who had recently returned to his old unit, 57 Squadron at Scampton, in order to start a new tour. He had done a full tour in the same squadron earlier in the war, and since then had been on instructional duties for over twelve months.

By the time of the raid, Young and his crew had done some sixty hours of flying, including twenty-one hours undertaken at night. The intense period of training seems to have bonded them together as a crew. Young drove his men hard, but he had also become proud of those who served under his command in A Flight. He had told his wife Priscilla of 'the especially good type of boy he had in his flight and of how much he liked his new squadron.'[44] However, it is worth noting that of the three crews who lined up for the Dams Raid as the second section in Wave One, two – Young's and Maltby's – each had five members who had between zero and three operations under their belts.

Crew 5: Flt Lt D.J.H. Maltby DFC

David Maltby had finished a full tour of operations in 97 Squadron in June 1942. He then spent several months commanding a specialist Air Bomber Training Section in 1485 Target Towing and Gunnery Flight before returning to active operations with his original squadron on 17 March 1943.

Less than a month before this, on about 22 February 1943, a new crew had arrived at 207 Squadron to begin operations. The skipper, Flt Lt William Elder, was a Scotsman who had spent the first part of the war as an instructor, and had received the unusual award of the Air Force Cross for his 'exceptionally meritorious service.'[45] The rest of the crew were flight engineer William Hatton, navigator Vivian Nicholson, wireless operator Antony Stone, bomb aimer John Fort and gunners Austin Williams and Harold Simmonds.

Three days later, Elder was sent as second pilot on his first operation, on a trip to Nuremberg with an experienced crew captained by Flg Off M.K. Sexton. Nothing more was heard from the aircraft and it was recorded as 'missing'. Losing their pilot meant that the rest of the crew were left kicking their heels while the authorities decided what to do with them. In the next three weeks, Hatton and possibly Simmonds flew on a couple of operations, but other than

---

43 Beesley was posted to 97 Squadron. He flew on more than twenty operations before his aircraft was shot down in September 1943. He was captured and spent the rest of the war as a PoW.

44 Thorning, *Dambuster who cracked the Dam*, p123.

45 AIR 2/9544, recommendation drafted 27 May 1941.

those, they saw no other action. Then the crew was moved on to 97 Squadron at Coningsby, where they were allocated to Maltby.

Maltby took them on three brief training flights between 20 and 22 March before the whole crew was transferred to the new squadron being formed at Scampton on 25 March. The crew made its first training flight on 31 March, a two-hour low-level cross-country and bombing exercise.

Training proceeded throughout April, but on 2 May a decision was taken to replace Austin Williams as front gunner, for unknown disciplinary reasons. He was posted to the Air Crew Refresher Course at Brighton. With the operation so close, an experienced gunner was needed to step into the breach, and Sgt Victor Hill was hurriedly summoned from 9 Squadron at RAF Bardney. He arrived at Scampton on 7 May. After the Dams Raid, on 20 May, Williams returned to the squadron and was then allocated to Bill Divall's crew, one of the two crews who had completed training for the Dams Raid but did not fly on it because of illness.

Unlike the rest of Maltby's crew, Hill had plenty of operational experience, with twenty-two operations between October 1942 and March 1943. He was thus the only man to transfer from 9 Squadron to 617 Squadron in the period before the Dams Raid.

Crew 6: Flt Lt D.J. Shannon DFC

At the end of February 1943, David Shannon finished his tour of operations in 106 Squadron with a trip to St Nazaire. This was the thirty-sixth sortie in a run which stretched back to June 1942, shortly after his 20th birthday. During his tour, he had generally flown with a core crew made up of Danny Walker, navigator, Wallace Herbert, bomb aimer, Arnold Pemberton, wireless operator, Douglas McCulloch, mid-upper gunner and Bernard Holmes, rear gunner. Over the course of the tour Shannon flew with a number of different flight engineers and/or second pilots, but in the last few months Sgt Cyril Chamberlain became the regular flight engineer.

An enforced change happened in November 1942, when Danny Walker came to the end of his own tour. He was posted to No 22 OTU at Wellesbourne Mountford as an instructor and thereafter a number of different navigators filled the seat in the Shannon crew. These included two very experienced men in Norman Scrivener and Winston Burnside, both of whom also navigated for Guy Gibson in this period.

Shannon's last operation in 106 Squadron on 28 February appears to have coincided with the end of the tours of Herbert, Pemberton, McCulloch and

Holmes. Under normal circumstances, the crew would have broken up and all would have been sent on instructional duties for a period of six months. Shannon, however, wanted to carry on flying and somehow arranged a transfer to 83 Squadron at RAF Wyton, a Pathfinder outfit. It was there that he got a telephone call from Gibson asking him to join him at Scampton where he was forming a new squadron.

In the meantime, Chamberlain, Herbert, Pemberton, McCulloch and Holmes were apparently all still at Syerston, waiting for new postings. Consideration was obviously given to reconstituting Shannon's 106 Squadron crew, since Chamberlain, Pemberton, McCulloch and Holmes were all transferred to the new 617 Squadron at Scampton on or about 25 March 1943. Herbert appears either not to have been asked or to have declined the offer. At the same time, Shannon's old crewmate Danny Walker was specifically sought out to fill the post of navigator, and was brought over to Scampton from 22 OTU.

It is not clear exactly what happened next. Shannon undertook two training flights on 28 and 31 March, but he only recorded the names of the other pilots with whom he flew (Flt Lt William Dierkes[46] on 28 March, Flt Lt John Hopgood on 31 March). His next flight wasn't until 6 April, when he did a five-hour cross-country and bombing trip. This was repeated, over a different route, two days later on 8 April. On both of these flights, a five man crew is recorded. This consisted of Walker and McCulloch, both from his 106 Squadron days, Larry Nichols, a wireless operator borrowed from Melvin Young's crew, and two new names – bomb aimer Len Sumpter and flight engineer Robert Henderson.

After the war, Len Sumpter described how he and Henderson had been recruited to the squadron. At that stage, he had completed 13 operations in 57 Squadron, based at Scampton. Then his pilot was grounded with ear trouble and the crew were told they would be broken up. He and his erstwhile crewmate Henderson knew that a new squadron was being formed in the next two hangars, and heard that Shannon was looking for a bomb aimer and a flight engineer, so they sought him out. 'We looked him over and he looked us over – and that's the way I got on to 617 Squadron.'[47] No date is given for this 'interview', but it must have occurred sometime between 31 March and 4 April, since on the latter date the 57 Squadron ORB records the posting of '2 aircrew

---

46   Dierkes was in 61 Squadron and was midway through his first tour. He was an American citizen who had joined the RCAF. Flg Off Harvey Glinz, who would fly on the Dams Raid in AJ-E with Norman Barlow, had been in Dierkes's crew in 61 Squadron. Quite what Dierkes was doing at Scampton on 28 March is a matter of conjecture.
47   Max Arthur, *Dambusters: A Landmark Oral History*, Virgin 2008, p18.

NCOs' to 617 Squadron. They are not named, but Sumpter and Henderson are the only two men who could fit this description.

Sumpter goes on to say that the crew didn't get their own wireless operator until the end of April. He didn't know – or didn't mention – that there were four members of Shannon's old crew, including wireless operator Arnold Pemberton, kicking their heels on the ground.

On 11 April, Shannon's logbook records the first flight of a new crew member, rear gunner Jack Buckley. He had been transferred from No 10 OTU, where he was working as an instructor. He was an experienced gunner and had been commissioned, having completed a full tour of operations with 75 (NZ) Squadron. Albert Garshowitz (misspelt as Gowshowitz) from Bill Astell's crew was the borrowed wireless operator on this occasion.

Two days later, on 13 April, a complete squadron crew list was compiled, under the title 'Order of Battle'. This is preserved in a file in the National Archives (AIR14/842) and is reproduced on p74 of this book. It shows Shannon's crew as: Henderson, flight engineer; Walker, navigator; Sumpter, bomb aimer; McCulloch, mid-upper gunner and Buckley, rear gunner. The position of wireless operator is left blank. The A Flight Gunnery Leader is listed as Flg Off McCulloch. Four names are listed as 'spares', amongst whom are the other three members of Shannon's 106 Squadron crew: Pemberton, Holmes and Chamberlain.

Another two days later, on 15 April, Douglas McCulloch attended an Aircrew Selection Board. He must therefore have previously applied for remustering. However, he returned to the squadron and flew on more training flights with Shannon on 19 and 21 April. He was eventually posted to No 13 Initial Training Wing on 1 May.

On 17 April, Bernard Holmes and Arnold Pemberton's time at 617 Squadron ended, with them both being recorded as being posted to No 19 OTU at Kinloss. Chamberlain was apparently posted to 1654 Conversion Unit at about the same time. Holmes's son Robert recalls that his father apparently told his wife at the time that he and Pemberton were bored and frustrated through not being kept busy, and asked for a transfer.[48]

Eleven days later, on 24 April, another squadron crew list was published. The Shannon crew shows two changes. The wireless operator position has been filled by Flg Off Goodale DFC and the mid-upper gunner has the handwritten name of Sgt Jagger in a space which had been left blank by the typist. The A Flight Gunnery Leader is now shown as Flg Off Glinz (from Norman Barlow's crew) and there are no longer any names listed as spares.[49] This date coincides

48　Email from Robert Holmes to author, 12 February 2016.
49　National Archives: AIR14/842.

with Goodale's first appearance in Shannon's logbook. It is notable that Brian Jagger's name appears here, but in fact he did not fly with Shannon until 4 May.

Both men came with a great deal of experience. Brian Goodale had completed a full tour and was recruited from No 10 OTU, where Jack Buckley had also been an instructor. Brian Jagger came from 50 Squadron. He had previously flown with John Fraser and Ken Earnshaw, two Canadians in John Hopgood's crew, and all three seem to have joined 617 Squadron at about the same time.

On this date, Tuesday 4 May, David Shannon's Dams Raid crew was finally established, and they would fly together for the next few months. Quite why three members of his crew from 106 Squadron were earlier brought over to Scampton but never used remains a mystery.

Crew 7: Sqn Ldr H.E. Maudslay DFC

Flt Lt Henry Maudslay returned to active duties on 1 January 1943 when he joined 50 Squadron at RAF Skellingthorpe. His first tour, in 44 Squadron, had finished more than a year previously and he had spent some of the intervening period testing the new Avro Lancasters, getting them ready for operational use. He had then been posted to instructional duties and had flown on three operations in the middle of 1942, one in a Lancaster.

In order to get back into the swing of things, he went on a trip on 8 January to Duisburg as second pilot with one of the squadron's flight commanders, Sqn Ldr Peter Birch. This crew contained Birch's regular rear gunner, Richard Trevor-Roper, who would fly on the Dams Raid a few months later. On this operation Birch's skills were tested in evading an enemy night fighter.

Without a crew of his own, Maudslay then took over one previously skippered by another 50 Squadron flight commander, Sqn Ldr Philip Moore, an Australian who had completed a second tour. On 9 January 1943 he wrote to his mother, that he 'met them today and like them'.[50] Two of Moore's crew would go on with Maudslay to 617 Squadron and the Dams Raid: Canadian navigator Flg Off Robert Urquhart and rear gunner Sgt Norman Burrows. The remainder were flight engineer Sgt R. Clarke, wireless operator Sgt K.M.D. Lyons, bomb aimer Sgt W.A. Miller and mid-upper gunner Plt Off C.W. Gray. After several training flights, the crew set out on their first operation together to Essen on 21 January.

Over the next few weeks, the other four men who would fly on the Dams Raid joined the crew, replacing those as they finished their tours. The first was

---

mid-upper gunner Plt Off William ('Johnny') Tytherleigh, with one tour already under his belt, who joined the crew on 2 February. The other three, flight engineer Sgt Jack Marriott, wireless operator Sgt Alden Cottam (a Canadian) and bomb aimer Sgt John Fuller, would all make their first trips with their new skipper on 3 March, on a trip to Hamburg. (Fuller, however, had flown on the crew's previous two operations as a passenger.)

The crew would fly together on three further operations in 50 Squadron, the last being a trip to St Nazaire on 21 March 1943. Three days later, and by then only about halfway through his second tour, Maudslay was surprised to find out that he was to be transferred to a new squadron which was being formed at Scampton. He was told that he should take his regular crew with him. He was pleased about this posting because he knew that his old friend Bill Astell was in 57 Squadron at this station, so they would be sharing a mess. He told his mother: 'My Wing Commander here tells me that they are making me a Squadron Leader and giving me a Flight but please don't take this too seriously yet – I'm not anyway.'[51]

Maudslay and his crew transferred from Skellingthorpe to Scampton by road the following day, Thursday 25 March.

Crew 8: Flt Lt W. Astell DFC

The crew who would eventually fly with Bill Astell on the Dams Raid had a similar experience to the one which flew with David Maltby. It had been built up over several months in the way standard at the time in Bomber Command. In September 1942, navigator Floyd Wile, wireless operator Albert Garshowitz, bomb aimer Donald Hopkinson and gunner Richard Bolitho all arrived at 19 OTU at RAF Kinloss, and crewed up with pilot Sgt Max Stephenson.

They spent a month training on Whitley aircraft before being posted to 1654 Conversion Unit at RAF Wigsley for the final phase of heavy bomber training. By coincidence one of the extra gunners who had arrived at Wigsley was another Canadian and a childhood friend of Albert Garshowitz, Frank Garbas. Garshowitz must have pushed successfully for Garbas to join them, and was pleased to tell his family about their new colleague in a letter dated 20 October 1942: 'The [new] Gunner is from our fair city of Hamilton – I used to play football with him for Eastwood Park. He went to Wentworth Tech – He's a swell fellow. His name is Frank Garbas.'[52] John Kinnear, a newly qualified flight

---

51 Letter dated 24 March 1943: Owen, *Maudslay*, p248.
52 Albert Garshowitz, letter to Garshowitz family, 20 October 1942.

engineer, also joined up with the crew at this time. The flight commander at 1654 Conversion Unit was Henry Maudslay.

After completing training, the crew was posted to 9 Squadron at RAF Waddington on 23 December, and undertook their first training flight the following day, Christmas Eve. A few further training sessions followed, but on 8 January 1943, Max Stephenson flew as second pilot on an operation to Duisburg with another crew, and was shot down. So, without a pilot, the crew was posted to 57 Squadron at RAF Scampton on 22 January, where they were allocated to the new C Flight under the command of Melvin Young. They became the crew of Bill Astell, as part of the squadron's new C Flight. They undertook their first training flight with Astell on 8 February.

Before then, in another letter home dated 28 January 1943, Garshowitz described Astell as a 'veteran at the trade' and 'an experienced and gen pilot'. He went on to describe how Garbas had only just had his first shave and 'tore his whole side of the face – laughs galore'. It's a sobering reminder that he would in fact die before his 21st birthday.

The new Astell crew flew on their first operation in 57 Squadron on 13 February 1943, a trip to Lorient, and had completed seven more before being transferred to 617 Squadron on 25 March.

Crew 9: Plt Off L.G. Knight

After his training as a pilot, Les Knight was posted to 14 OTU in May 1942 and on to 1654 Conversion Unit in August 1942. During this period he formed a full crew, five of whom would fly with him throughout the rest of their operational careers. These were navigator Sydney Hobday, wireless operator Robert Kellow, bomb aimer Edward Johnson and the two gunners Harry O'Brien and Fred Sutherland. The crew's flight engineer was Eric Sunderland, but he would leave shortly after the crew joined 50 Squadron. Kellow was an Australian and O'Brien and Sutherland were both Canadians.

The crew was posted to 50 Squadron at RAF Skellingthorpe on 22 and 23 September 1942, and flew their first operation on a trip to Wismar on 1 October 1942. They had completed seven trips by 22 November, when Eric Sunderland was replaced by Sgt Ray Grayston, a flight engineer who had arrived on the squadron a few weeks previously. The seven men flew that night on an operation to Stuttgart and on eighteen more trips over the next four months.

Knight had reached twenty-six operations by this time, but then the opportunity came for them to transfer into the new squadron being formed at Scampton. They went as a group, as his wireless operator, Bob Kellow, later explained: 'The offer presented to us sounded interesting and with our faith in each member's ability we made up our minds there and then that we would accept the offer and move over as a crew to this new squadron.'[53] The crew's faith was probably because they had together recognised that Knight was an exceptional pilot, even though he couldn't ride a bicycle or drive a car. They arrived at Scampton on 25 March 1943.

Crew 10: Flt Lt R.N.G. Barlow DFC

When the request for an experienced crew for the new squadron reached 61 Squadron, also based at RAF Syerston like Gibson's 106 Squadron, there were a number of pilots and crews who would have fitted the request. It is not clear whether the Australian pilot Norman Barlow himself volunteered or was simply nominated by his CO, but he met all the criteria. He had just finished a full tour of operations and been recommended for a DFC. He was also apparently keen to move on to an immediate second tour, rather than taking the usual between-tours rest in an instructional role.

Barlow set about building a crew to accompany him. Two came from his own crew. His bomb aimer Alan Gillespie had also completed a full tour but he volunteered to carry on with his skipper. Flight engineer Leslie Whillis was near the end of his tour and must have thought that carrying on with Barlow gave him the chance to finish it with a pilot he trusted. The other four all had substantial experience. Charlie Williams and Philip Burgess had been flying with New Zealander Ian Woodward, who had also just finished his first tour. Williams, the wireless operator and another Australian, had also completed his tour. He wanted to go on with a second tour immediately, so he could go home to Queensland to be with his seriously ill father. Burgess, the navigator, had flown on eighteen operations, the majority with Woodward and Williams. The two gunners were the Canadian Harvey Glinz, who had flown on ten operations, and Jack Liddell, still a teenager but with a full tour under his belt.

Together, they were an unusual group. Three were in their 30s. Four were officers, with two more recommended for commissions which would come through before the Dams Raid. This left only the young Jack Liddell still a sergeant. They took the leave that was owing to them (probably without consulting their new CO) and didn't arrive until the first week in April, so their training was delayed. Their first training flight was on Friday 9 April and the crew had the frightening experience of a bird strike, which resulted in a collision

---

53   Sweetman, *Dambusters Raid*, p98.

with the top of a tall tree. The flight engineer's and bomb aimer's canopies were smashed and two engines badly damaged. Barlow didn't mention the incident when he wrote to his mother a few days later, but he did tell her about his crew:

> I am now at a new Squadron that is just forming, hence we will not
> be operating for some weeks, you will be pleased to know, all we do is
> fly, fly and fly, getting plenty of training in. Today I flew for five hours
> with two other crews doing low level formation flying it was really
> good fun … I have practically a new crew now, you can hardly blame
> the boys for wanting a rest after all the trips we have done over there,
> so now I have four officers in my crew and two of the sergeants who
> have been with me all the time are getting their commissions so we
> will have six out of seven officers, I haven't heard of that before. A chap
> doesn't get a commission unless he knows his work, so you can guess
> we have a pretty good crew. I have an Australian in the crew, (Charlie
> Williams) a damn fine chap from the country, he is the W/Op. and we
> share a room together.[54]

A shortage of aircraft meant that crews could not be certain exactly when they would be training, nor of the route they would be instructed to undertake. However, if you were the navigator, like Philip Burgess in the Barlow crew, it was sometimes possible to make minor variations during a session. Burgess explained how he had done this in a letter to his girlfriend, Edna Mitchell, on 15 April:

> We came over Guildford last Sunday [11 April] at 4.30 p.m, just did
> a couple of circuits over the house – we couldn't shoot the place up
> properly as we had a 'Group Captain' [Probably Gp Capt Charles
> Whitworth, Scampton's station CO] on board as a passenger, and we
> weren't supposed to be over Guildford anyway. We were supposed to go
> to Haslemere but I thought it would be better to go to the home town
> as it was so near. We are hoping to get down that way again in the near
> future and do a real shoot up of the place.[55]

---

54   Norman Barlow, letter to Frances Barlow, 13 April 1943, Barlow family.
55   Philip Burgess, letter to Edna Mitchell, 15 April 1943, RAF Museum.

Crew 11: Flt Lt J.L. Munro

After initial training in New Zealand Les Munro was sent to Canada to complete bomber training and qualified as a pilot in February 1942, receiving a commission at the same time. After arriving in England, and the usual delays that followed, he was sent for further training.

The core of the crew who would fly with Munro throughout most of his career began to be assembled at 29 OTU at RAF North Luffenham, when navigator Jock Rumbles and wireless operator Percy Pigeon first teamed up with him. They undertook two operations in September 1942, while still at 29 OTU. The second of these, when they were scheduled to attack Bremen, nearly ended in disaster when their Wellington's engines lost power shortly after take-off and they crash-landed in a nearby field.

Munro moved onto heavy bomber training at the end of September 1942, along with Rumbles and Pigeon, and they were joined by flight engineer Frank Appleby and gunner Bill Howarth. All five joined 97 Squadron at Woodhall Spa in December 1942, to begin operational flying. Their first operation on 8 January 1943 was minelaying, followed on 13 January by an attack on Essen.

Some 17 further operations would follow in the next ten weeks, but in that time the crew flew with no fewer than eight different bomb aimers, including a Sub Lt Bill Lett RN, seconded for a period to the RAF. Then, towards the end of March a new opportunity presented itself. In a 2010 interview, Munro recalled: 'A letter from 5 Group went up on the noticeboard. I quite distinctly remember this, and I called my crew together and said "Look, there's been a call for volunteers to form a new squadron."'[56]

Most of the crew decided that they would go to the new squadron, but they were still without a regular bomb aimer, and the rear gunner chose not to accompany them. So they were joined by bomb aimer Jimmy Clay and rear gunner Harvey Weeks, who had both almost completed their operational tours with another 97 Squadron crew piloted by the Canadian, Marcel Cuelenaere.

Two other 97 Squadron crews, captained by David Maltby and Joe McCarthy, had also been selected for the new squadron. Guy Gibson had telephoned McCarthy, whom he had met while McCarthy was training, and asked him to join the new squadron, but it seems that he did not previously know either Maltby or Munro.

---

56   Interview with James Holland 2010.
      www.griffonmerlin.com/wwi-iinterview/les-munro [Accessed May 2014].

Crew 12: Plt Off V.W. Byers

Vernon Byers joined the RCAF in his native Saskatchewan in May 1941, and qualified as a pilot in March 1942. He then set off for the UK, where he finished his training over the next few months. The final stage was at 1654 Conversion Unit at Wigsley, which he joined on 8 December 1942, and where one of his instructors was Mick Martin. Here he built up a full crew, of whom four would later take part in the Dams Raid. These were flight engineer Alastair Taylor, flight engineer, navigator James Warner, wireless operator John Wilkinson, and gunner James McDowell, the only other Canadian in the crew. Along with bomb aimer Sgt John McKee and air gunner Sgt Robert Haslam they were transferred to 467 Squadron at RAF Bottesford on 5 February 1943 to begin active operational duties.

467 Squadron was notionally an Australian squadron under RAF command. However by no means were all its personnel Australian: they came from all parts of the Commonwealth, as well as Britain. The squadron had been founded in November 1942, but its first operational flying took place on 2 January 1943. One of the squadron's new crews was piloted by Sgt Henry Vine, and it contained Arthur Whitaker as bomb aimer and Charles Jarvie as mid-upper gunner. The Vine crew had undertaken a handful of operations by the time the Byers crew arrived in February at which time, for some reason, these two swapped with McKee and Haslam. This was a bad move for McKee and Haslam as exactly a fortnight after they had arrived at Bottesford they were lost when Vine's aircraft was shot down on an operation targetting Wilhelmshaven. They were probably the victims of a German nightfighter pilot, and crashed into the North Sea ironically not far from the coastal island of Texel where Byers and his crew would be shot down three months later.

Meanwhile, Byers and his crew were preparing for their first operation as a crew. In preparation, Byers himself flew as 'second dickey' on two operations with other crews. On 28 February, he flew with Plt Off Graeme Mant to bomb St Nazaire and on 5 March he accompanied Flt Lt 'Jimmy' Thiele to Essen.

On 9 March, Byers and his crew took off on their first operation. As was customary at the time, this was a mine-laying sortie ('gardening' as it was called) in the Silverthorne area. Two nights later, the crew was sent on its first bombing operation, to Stuttgart. Twenty miles away from the target the rear turret lost power, meaning that James McDowell could only operate the swivelling mechanism by hand. Despite this, Byers pressed on and successfully dropped his bombs from 16,000ft. A few days later, on 22 March, the crew carried out their third and final operation in 467 Squadron, bombing St Nazaire.

At around this time, 467 Squadron's CO, Wing Cdr Cosme Gomm, must have been asked to nominate a crew for the new as yet unnamed squadron to be set up at Scampton for a top secret mission. However it appears that Byers was not the first choice. Gomm first offered the place to Sgt Frank Heavery, whose crew had at the time completed twelve operations. He gave him twenty-four hours to think about it until Heavery had talked it over with his crew. The crew were split evenly – three for, three against, so Heavery had the casting vote and he decided to stay. Gomm had talked to Heavery about keeping his experienced crews to help the new crews who would be arriving soon, and that he could use this as an argument with Cochrane should he object. Cochrane must have accepted this argument, and Vernon Byers was selected instead.[57]

Heavery and his crew survived the war, so it could be argued that he made the right decision. Meanwhile, Byers and his crew, with their record of just three operations, plus Byers's two second dickey trips, would shortly find themselves en route to Scampton, and a place in history. Their transfer is noted in the 467 Squadron Operations Record Book on 24 March 1943.

Crew 13: Plt Off G. Rice

Geoffrey Rice joined the RAF in 1941 and was selected for pilot training, which he undertook in Canada. He qualified as a pilot in February 1942. On his return to the UK he underwent further training.

He was posted to 19 Operational Training Unit at RAF Kinloss in July where he crewed up with navigator Sgt Richard Macfarlane, wireless operator Sgt Bruce Gowrie, bomb aimer Sgt John Thrasher and air gunner Sgt Charles Challenger. With the exception of Challenger, this crew would stay together for the rest of their RAF career. They moved on to 1660 Conversion Unit at RAF Swinderby in October 1942 to complete their heavy bomber training. The crew was then completed with the addition of flight engineer Sgt Edward Smith and a second gunner, Sgt Thomas Maynard.

On 9 December 1942, the crew was posted to 57 Squadron at RAF Scampton to begin their operational career. However, heavy rain and snow for most of the winter months meant that Scampton's grass runways became almost unusable and some of the squadron were transferred to Swinderby. It was from there on New Year's Eve that Rice and his crew set off on their first operation – a mine-laying trip to Gironde, off the French coast. The trip went relatively smoothly: in his diary, Tom Maynard recorded that they laid their 'eggs' from a height of 500ft, and sang 'old [sic] Lang Syne' as the New Year came in.[58]

---

57   Tony Redding, *Flying for Freedom*, Mulberry 2008, p1.
58   Press, *All My Life*, p7.

A few weeks later, on 7 February, rear gunner Charles Challenger moved to another crew and was replaced by Sgt Stephen Burns, who had flown on several operations with other crews after arriving in 57 Squadron in November 1942. At first, it seems that the swap wasn't permanent as Challenger flew with the Rice crew again on a couple more occasions but eventually Burns held onto this position.

On 15 March, after the crew had undertaken nine operations, they learned that they were to be transferred to the squadron's new C Flight, under the command of Sqn Ldr Melvin Young, who had joined the squadron to embark on a first tour on Lancasters after winning a DFC and Bar for two tours on Whitleys and Wellingtons. Maynard, who was getting frustrated at the number of operations which had been cancelled at the last moment, wrote that this was a 'Bad show as we were well satisfied in B Flight.'[59]

By 25 March the flight comprised five crews, captained by Melvin Young, Bill Astell, Geoff Rice, Sgt George Lancaster and Sgt Ray Lovell. It was decided to post the whole flight over to the new squadron being formed at the same base to undertake training for a special mission. Rice and his crew had actually gone on leave the day before, and they did not find out about the transfer until they returned to base on 1 April. Rice protested at the transfer, but to no avail. Maynard recorded that they had 'got back to find we are in a new squadron, 617, very hush-hush'. The next two entries cover what happened next:

> April 2nd. Had our interview with our new CO, Wing Commander Gibson DSO & Bar, DFC & Bar, very young. He told us we (the squadron) were formed for a special mission of which even he had not the faintest idea and we have to spend the next weeks training low level by day and by night. We changed billets to the new squadron.
>
> April 3rd. The weather is not too bad. We did a five and a half hour low level trip today and it was wizard over Wales and south west England. Lost our trailing aerial in the Bristol Channel. Ended by bombing at Wainfleet from 100ft. This is the goods when you are authorised to get down to the deck.[60]

After writing this, Maynard must have decided to take the emphasis on security seriously, since this is the final entry in his diary.

---

59   Press, *All My Life*, p19.
60   Press, *All My Life*, pp19–22.

Crew 14: Flt Lt J.C. McCarthy DFC

In September 1942, Plt Off Joe McCarthy was posted to 97 Squadron's conversion flight for his final training on Lancasters. Flight engineer Sgt Bill Radcliffe, a Canadian, wireless operator Len Eaton and air gunner Ron Batson, both British, all joined the squadron at about the same time and became regular members of Joe McCarthy's crew. These four would stay together for the next twenty-one months, coming off operations at the same time in July 1944.

The conversion course finished, and McCarthy and his crew were initially posted to 106 Squadron at Coningsby. At the last minute, McCarthy was sent instead to 97 Squadron at Woodhall Spa, as one of the replacements for a series of heavy losses it had undergone. 97 Squadron had recently been designated as a Pathfinder squadron, marking targets for the rest of Bomber Command's main force. The other three members of McCarthy's crew at this time were navigator Flt Sgt W. Brayford, bomb aimer Sgt Alan Westwell and rear gunner Sgt Ralph Muskett.

In early December, after several operations, there was a change in his crew. Brayford, the navigator, left and Westwell, the bomb aimer who was also a trained navigator, moved into his job. The replacement bomb aimer was Sgt George 'Johnny' Johnson, who had been on the squadron for a few months but had no regular crew. He had flown on a number of operations as a gunner. His first trip with McCarthy was on a raid on Munich on 22 December 1942.

In January, the crew flew on an operation to Duisburg using Lancaster ED340 for the first time. They would use this aircraft for most of the rest of their tour, and named it 'Uncle Chuck Chuck' after a small toy panda which Bill Radcliffe always carried. They had the name and a picture of the panda painted on its nose, and would have similar pictures painted on most of the aircraft they used regularly during the rest of the war.

Later in January, rear gunner Sgt Muskett left the crew, after suffering bad reactions during corkscrews and other necessary evasive actions. His replacement was Flg Off Dave Rodger, another Canadian. On 12 March, navigator Sgt Westwell finished his tour after a trip to Essen and was replaced by the crew's third Canadian, Flt Sgt Don MacLean. This meant that the crew who would fly with McCarthy on the Dams Raid was now complete.

By 22 March 1943 McCarthy had completed a tour of 33 operations. He was promoted to Flight Lieutenant, and recommended for a DFC. He had been considering transferring to the USAAF, but had not yet made a decision. Then he had a phone call from Guy Gibson to ask him personally to join the new squadron he was setting up for a special secret operation.

McCarthy recalled later that his whole crew volunteered to go with him.

However, when they arrived at Scampton, they hit a problem. Orders had been issued that since training for the special operation was to begin straightaway, all leave was cancelled. McCarthy and his crew had been due to go on a week's leave, and bomb aimer Johnny Johnson had arranged to get married during this time, on Saturday 3 April.

When he told McCarthy about his plans McCarthy reacted quickly, gathering the entire crew together and marching them into Gibson's office. Johnson recalled later:

> Joe laid it on the line. 'The thing is, sir,' he said, very forcibly, 'we've all just finished our tour and we are all entitled to a week's leave. My bomb aimer is due to be married on the third of April and let me tell you he is going to get married on the third of April!'
>
> There was a short pause while the others, no doubt, wished they were anywhere else except standing in the office of Wg Cdr Guy Gibson DSO, DFC and Bar, who had a fearsome reputation as a strict disciplinarian and had been known by the crews of 106 Squadron as 'The Arch-Bastard'.
>
> He looked us up and down and said, 'Very well. You can have four days. Dismissed.'
>
> Thank you Joe! I left for Torquay immediately, before our new CO could change his mind.[61]

In fact, McCarthy and his crew didn't know that several other crews had been told by their previous COs that they could take leave before their new posting, and therefore would not arrive at Scampton for several more days. Gibson himself was probably relieved not to have all his new men arriving at once. He would have known at this stage that he didn't yet have enough aircraft for his new squadron to train on, so a crew going on leave for four days was hardly going to upset the schedule too much.

Crew 15: Plt Off W. Ottley DFC

Warner ('Bill') Ottley qualified as a pilot in August 1941 after training in Canada. After further training in the UK he was sent to his first operational squadron, 50 Squadron, in June 1942, but was then immediately reposted to 83 Squadron, then based at Scampton. Between 29 July and 6 August 1942 he

---

61 George 'Johnny' Johnson, *The Last British Dambuster*, Ebury Press 2013, p133.

flew on four 'second dickey' operations with Flt Sgt L.T. Jackson as pilot. These were to Saarbrucken, Düsseldorf, Gironde (mining) and Duisburg. He was then transferred to 207 Squadron at RAF Langar and flew on several more operations before being transferred to the squadron's conversion flight. There he was teamed up with most of the men who would later make up his Dams Raid crew: Sgt Ronald Marsden, flight engineer; Sgt Thomas Johnston, bomb aimer; Sgt Jack Guterman, wireless operator; Sgt Fred Tees, air gunner; and Plt Off Jack Barrett, navigator. The crew transferred back to the main squadron and undertook their first operation together on a mine-laying trip to Biarritz on 23 November 1942. The mid-upper gunner on this operation was Sgt Walker. On the same day, the final member of Ottley's Dams Raid crew, Harry Strange, flew as mid-upper gunner on a bombing operation to Quakenbruck with Sgt G. Langdon as pilot.

Ottley went on to fly on twenty further operations with this crew between December 1942 and April 1943, although there were the occasional minor changes in personnel. Jack Guterman reached the end of his tour on 8 March 1943 and so in each of the crew's last three operations there was a different wireless operator. The crew's final operation in 207 Squadron was on 4 April 1943, with a trip to bomb Kiel.

Meanwhile, the tour-expired Guterman was still at Langar. He had been told by his flight commander that he was likely to be sent to an OTU as an instructor for his six-month 'rest' period, but he was keen to stay with Ottley and his crew. He and Ottley had become good friends (they were both interested in music and the arts) and had been room mates. So it seems that he had become aware that Ottley was about to be posted to Scampton and that there was still a vacancy for a wireless operator in his crew. In a letter dated just 'Wednesday' he wrote to his sister that he was likely to be posted to 'the station in Lincolnshire' where he had previously done a gunnery course. It would seem that this letter was composed on either 24 or 31 March.

Ottley and his Dams Raid crew were then transferred to 617 Squadron, and were one of the last crews to arrive. As he didn't at this point have a regular wireless operator, the tour-expired Guterman must have volunteered to go along with them. Guterman's letter to his sister, dated Tuesday 6 April, confirms that his transfer took place on the afternoon of Sunday 4 April[62] but Ottley and the remainder of the crew flew on their final operation in 207 Squadron that night, a trip to Kiel. By this point, Ottley had been commissioned and also recommended for a DFC, although the decoration wouldn't be confirmed

---

62   Jack Guterman, letter to Babs Guterman, 6 April 1943, Guterman family.

until June 1945, two years after his death on the Dams Raid. His navigator, Flg Off Jack Barrett also received the DFC at the same time. Their awards were backdated to 16 May 1943.

Crew 16: Plt Off L.J. Burpee DFM

Lewis Burpee qualified as a pilot in September 1941 and embarked for the UK shortly afterwards. While training in 16 OTU he crewed up with two men who would stay with him until the Dams Raid. The first was fellow Canadian, air gunner Gordon Brady, and later with flight engineer, Guy Pegler. The pair were in Burpee's crew when he was posted to 106 Squadron in October 1942.

After three trips as a 'second dickey', the last of which was with David Shannon as pilot. Burpee undertook his first trip as a captain on 7 November 1942 on a mission to bomb Genoa. This was abandoned, but his first successful operation was later that month.

By the time air gunner William Long joined his crew on a trip to Duisburg on 20 December 1942, the crew had completed four operations. In the six operations in the first three weeks of January 1943, Lewis Burpee flew with five different navigators. However, Thomas Jaye established himself as Burpee's regular navigator on a trip to Essen on 21 January and they went on a further sixteen operations before being transferred out on 29 March.

At 0040 in the early morning of 14 February wireless operator Flt Sgt Eddie Leavesley DFM completed a second tour of operations, after a six-hour trip to Lorient. Then, at 1830 the same day, the crew set off again on a ten-hour operation over the Alps to Milan, with a new wireless operator on board, Len Weller. (Eddie Leavesley would survive the war, and earned a rare Bar to his DFM for his second tour.)

The final member of Burpee's Dams Raid crew to join him was another Canadian, bomb aimer James Arthur. He had been posted to 106 Squadron to begin operations in February 1943, but it wasn't until 12 March that he flew on his first operation. Lew Burpee's bomb aimer George Goodings had come to the end of his tour, so the chance of joining an experienced crew with two other Canadians probably looked like a good choice. Their trip took them to Essen, which they bombed successfully from 19,000ft. They reported very heavy flak and 'scores of searchlights'.

Arthur's first operation turned out to be the last that Burpee and his crew would fly in 106 Squadron, and it was therefore the only time that the complete Dams Raid crew would fly together before the raid itself. By 29 March they were at RAF Scampton, training for the secret mission which would be their last.

Crew 17: Flt Sgt K.W. Brown

After finishing his pilot training in his native Canada, Ken Brown was recommended for fighter service. However, when he arrived in England, things
changed. He was reallocated to bomber training and sent to 19 OTU in Kinloss. At the beginning of the crewing-up process, he quickly teamed up with
a couple of other Canadians, bomb aimer Stefan Oancia and gunner Grant
McDonald. Between them they decided on a proactive approach, did some research and then went looking for a particular navigator, Dudley Heal. They
soon found him:

> 'Your name Heal?' asked the pilot, a tall, well-built chap. 'Yes,' I said.
> 'Then you're going to be our navigator,' he said. I looked questioningly
> at him. 'Who says so?' I asked. 'I've just been to the Navigation Office,'
> he said. 'You were top of your course at AFU so we want you to be our
> navigator.' I looked at the other two who were obviously in complete
> agreement with him. I liked the look of all of them and if I considered
> it all my reaction would have been that here was someone who was
> interested in survival, which couldn't be bad. I agreed to join them
> without further ado. His name was Ken Brown. We shook hands;
> he introduced the bomb-aimer, Steve Oancia, and the rear gunner,
> Grant McDonald, and off we went to the NAAFI for a cup of tea. I can
> honestly say that I never regretted that decision. We then acquired a
> wireless operator, Hewie Hewstone and from that time on, our being
> together as a crew was everything.[63]

After finishing this stage of their training, this five-man crew would normally
have been posted to a Conversion Unit for heavy bomber training. However, in
October 1942, the crew were sent to a Coastal Command station, RAF St Eval
in Cornwall, to conduct anti-submarine sweeps in Armstrong Whitley aircraft.
In early 1943, this posting came to an end and they went to 1654 Conversion
Unit for the final stage of heavy bomber training.

One of the instructors at this unit was Mick Martin. The low-flying specialist
was reportedly impressed by Brown's abilities in this challenging activity. The
complete crew also came together at this unit when engineer Basil Feneron and
gunner Don Buntaine joined. On 5 February 1943, the seven were posted to
44 Squadron at Waddington to begin operations.

On 27 March, after five operations, they were briefed for their first trip to

---

63   Dudley Heal, *Dudley's War,* unpublished manuscript, c.1993.

Berlin. Before they left, Brown was pulled aside for a meeting with the squadron CO, Wg Cdr John Nettleton VC:

> He said, 'You are transferred to a new squadron.'
>
> I wasn't too happy about that. I said, 'Sir, I'd rather stay here and finish my tour with Forty-four.'
>
> He explained in his very curt manner. This was impossible. It was a name transfer[64] and he could do nothing about it.
>
> So we went to Berlin and on our return we got packed up and off we went to No. 617. But before we went, the Wing Commander wished me well and said, 'Do you realize Brown, you're going to be the backbone of this new squadron.'
>
> Well, we arrived over at Scampton and we started to look around as to who was there. There were an awful lot of DFCs, not so many DFMs. We realized that perhaps we weren't really all what we were set up to be.
>
> My wireless operator sauntered up to me and said, 'Skip, if we're the backbone of this squadron. We must be damn close to the ass end.' I began to wonder how I'd got there.[65]

Brown and his crew arrived at Scampton on 29 March.

Crew 18: Flt Sgt W.C. Townsend DFM

William Townsend had transferred into the RAF from the army in May 1941. He was selected for pilot training, qualified as a pilot early in 1942 and in June of that year was posted to 49 Squadron. After spending some time in the squadron's conversion flight he was reposted into the main squadron on 7 September 1942 along with a crew which included Lance Howard and Douglas Webb, both of whom would later fly on the Dams Raid. Charles Franklin, who would become his bomb aimer, was already in the squadron and Ray Wilkinson and Dennis Powell both joined it a few weeks later.

Townsend, Howard and Webb went on two 'gardening' operations during September 1942, and their first bombing trip was to Wismar on 1 October. By the new year, Townsend had built a regular crew which included five of the men who would fly with him on the Dams Raid: flight engineer Denis Powell,

---

64   The 'name transfer' raises the possibility that it was suggested by Mick Martin, his instructor at 1654 CU.

65   Source: Speech at Bomber Command Museum of Canada. www.bombercommandmuseum.ca/kenbrown.html [Accessed March 2017].

navigator Lance Howard, bomb aimer Charles Franklin, and air gunners Doug Webb and Ray Wilkinson. Their last trip in 49 Squadron was a trip to St Nazaire on 22 March 1943. By this time, Townsend had completed twenty-six operations and been recommended for a DFM. The crew therefore fitted precisely into the category from which 617 Squadron's crews were supposed to have been selected.

In the 49 Squadron Operations Record Book, the posting of the Townsend crew is shown as 25 March 1943, the day after the listing for the crew of the far less experienced Cyril Anderson.

The sixth man in Townsend's regular crew, wireless operator Jack Grain, declined the opportunity to transfer to 617 Squadron because he was getting married, so when the crew arrived at Scampton on 25 March they did not have anyone to fill this position. However, George Chalmers, a Scot who had already done a full tour in 35 Squadron, had also arrived at the station as a supernumerary. Chalmers told Mick Martin that he would prefer to be allocated to an all-NCO crew if possible. Martin was a bit taken aback by this (perhaps knowing that there were very few of these in the new squadron) but as it had turned out that Townsend didn't have a wireless operator he could be accommodated.[66] Townsend's crew did not remain all-NCO for long – by the time of the Dams Raid, Lance Howard had been commissioned, and Townsend also received one shortly afterwards.

Their first training flight in 617 Squadron was on 4 April.

Crew 19: Flt Sgt C.T. Anderson

Cyril Anderson joined the RAF in 1934 and served as ground crew. When the war started, he volunteered for aircrew and was selected for pilot training in August 1940. He qualified as a pilot in 1942.

In the final stages of training at 1654 Conversion Unit at RAF Wigsley he crewed up with all the six men with whom he would fly on the Dams Raid: Robert Paterson (flight engineer), John Nugent (navigator), Douglas Bickle (wireless operator), Gilbert 'Jimmy' Green (bomb aimer), and Eric Ewan and Arthur Buck (gunners). They were posted together from Wigsley to 49 Squadron at Fiskerton in February 1943. Anderson's first two operations were the usual trips as second pilot, when he flew with Sgt B.A. Gumbley and his crew on trips to Nuremberg and Cologne on 25 and 26 February. (Gumbley, a New Zealander, would join 617 Squadron later in the war. He took part in a number

66   Max Arthur, *Dambusters,* pp15–16.

of raids including the attacks on the Tirpitz but was shot down in March 1944, and died along with his crew.)

The crew's first operation together was an eventful attack on Essen on 12 March 1943. After a successful bomb drop, they lost power in one engine on the way home. Their second trip was to St Nazaire on 22 March.

At this point, it seems that the request from Group HQ to send a crew to the new squadron being formed at Scampton was received by 49 Squadron. The CO nominated the crews of Bill Townsend and Cyril Anderson.

Anderson, with just two operations under his belt, did not demur from the request, but asked to gain some further experience in 49 Squadron before moving. He and his crew were therefore sent on three operations in the next five days, flying to Duisburg on 26 March and Berlin on both 27 and 29 March. They then left for 617 Squadron and probably arrived at Scampton on 31 March.

Chapter 5

Training for the raid

AT THE SAME TIME that the final decision had been taken to proceed with Operation Chastise, the end of February 1943, Avro were given the order to begin building the special Lancasters needed to drop the new Upkeep weapon. These were to be modified versions of the standard Lancaster III models being built at Woodford, near Manchester, and were given the name 'Type 464 Provisioning'. However, they were not scheduled to be ready until some time in April 1943, several weeks after the squadron was formed. So 617 Squadron began its training on ordinary Lancasters, borrowed from other squadrons.

Shortly after aircrew had begun arriving on the station, Gibson held a meeting to discuss the training programme with his two flight commanders, Melvin Young and Henry Maudslay, and the squadron's newly appointed navigation and Bombing Leaders, Jack Leggo and Bob Hay. By then Gibson had travelled to Weybridge in Surrey to meet Wallis for the first time, but had not yet been told the target. He had also been sent instructions from Gp Capt Harold Satterley, the Senior Adminstrative Staff Officer at 5 Group, which detailed the type of training which the squadron should follow. The squadron would be attacking a number of lightly defended targets in moonlight with a final approach at 100ft at a speed of about 240mph. The orders stated that, in preparation for the attack, it would be 'convenient to practise this over water' and crews should be able to release their 'mine' within 40 yards of a specified release point. Various lakes and reservoirs were listed as being suitable for this. Night flying would be simulated by making the pilot and bomb aimer wear special amber-coloured goggles with blue Perspex screens fitted to the windows.[67] Young and Maudslay were sent away to draw up a training programme.

Bill Astell was the first pilot to take to the air. On 27 March, the day Satterly's instructions arrived, he was sent off to photograph nine lakes and reservoirs on the pretext that they might be needed for training crews at conversion units. In the days that followed, other crews began their work. A number of different training routes were devised, taking the crews up to the north of Scotland,

---

67   Sweetman, *Dambusters Raid*, p101.

out over the Irish Sea or to the western tip of Wales. Bombing was carried out over the range at Wainfleet on the northern side of the Wash, dropping smoke bombs as markers.

The problem of how to judge the aircraft height at very low altitude was solved relatively early in the training period. After some experiments with trailing wires, the Deputy Director of Scientific Research at the Ministry of Aircraft Production, Benjamin Lockspeiser, came up with an idea. (Lockspeiser had earlier been involved with the development of the Upkeep mine, and had attended many of the Whitehall meetings.) He suggested using spotlights fixed so that their beams would converge at a specified height, a technique which had been developed in the First World War. Despite some initial scepticism (including some from Air Chief Marshal Harris), it was decided to try this out.

On 4 April Henry Maudslay, three of his crew (Robert Urquhart, Alden Cottam and John Fuller) and a member of ground staff, AC Chaplin, flew in one of the borrowed Lancasters to the Royal Aircraft Establishment at Farnborough and stayed there several days whilst modifications were undertaken. These included the fitting of two Aldis lamps so that the pilot could maintain the correct height for the attack on the dams. One was located in the front camera slot by the bomb aimer's position, the second fitted in the rear of the bomb bay. The beams were adjusted to form a figure of eight (two touching circles) at the required height, and could be seen just forward of the leading edge of the starboard wing. The navigator could clearly see the circles through the Perspex blister on the starboard side, and could advise the pilot to adjust his height. On their return to Scampton on 8 April, Maudslay and Urquhart made test runs across the airfield and then later the same evening at Skegness and in the Wash, which showed they could successfully keep to the required height.[68]

On the same day, 8 April, a summary of the training undertaken so far was sent to Satterly. By then half the crews had undertaken four or five low level exercises, with some getting well in excess of twenty hours flying time. Bill Ottley, however, who had joined late had only been on one, of just under five hours. Harold Wilson, for some reason, had also only completed one.

The following day, on Friday 9 April, the first wholesale change in personnel occurred. Sgt Ray Lovell and his crew were returned to 57 Squadron on the grounds that they 'did not come up to the standard necessary' for the new squadron. In their place came another 57 Squadron crew captained by Sgt Bill Divall, joining 617 Squadron the following day. As they were already based at Scampton the transfer was of course relatively easy.

---

68 Owen, *Maudslay*, pp255–6.

NO. 617 SQUADRON , ORDER OF BATTLE AS AT 13.4.43

PILOT	F/ENG	NAVIGATOR	W/OPER	B/AIMER	MID-UPPER	REAR GUNNER
Leader:-						
W/CDR. GIBSON	Sgt. Pulford	P/O. Taerum	F/Lt. Hutchison	P/O. Spafford	F/Lt. Trevor-Roper	F/Sgt. Deering
'A' FLIGHT						
S/Ldr. YOUNG	Sgt. Horsfall	Sgt. Roberts	Sgt. Nichols	Sgt. Beesley	Sgt. Yeo	Sgt. Ibbotson
F/Lt. ASTELL	Sgt. Kinnear	P/O. Wile	Sgt. Garshowitz	F/O. Hopkinson	Sgt. Garbas	Sgt. Bolitho
F/Lt. MALTBY	Sgt. Hatton	Sgt. Nicholson	Sgt. Stone	P/O. Fort	Sgt. Williams	Sgt. Simmonds
F/Lt. SHANNON	Sgt. Henderson	F/O. Walker		F/Sgt. Sumpter	F/O. McCulloch	P/O. Buckley
F/Lt. BARLOW	Sgt. Willis	P/O. Burgess	F/O. Williams	Sgt. Gillespie	F/O. Glinz	Sgt. Liddell
P/O. RICE	Sgt. Smith	F/O. MacFarlane	Sgt. Gowrie	F/Sgt. Johnston	Sgt. Maynard	Sgt. Burn
P/O. OTTLEY	Sgt. Marsden	F/O. Barrett	Sgt. Guterman	F/Sgt. Thrasher	Sgt. Tees	Sgt. Strange
F/Sgt. LANCASTER	Sgt. Jackson	F/O. Cleveland	F/Sgt. Sparks	F/Sgt. Clifford	Sgt. McCredie	Sgt. Williams
F/Sgt. BROWN	Sgt. Feneron	Sgt. Heal	Sgt. Hewstone	Sgt. Oancia	Sgt. Buntaine	F/Sgt. McDonald
Sgt. BYERS	Sgt. Taylor	P/O. Warner	Sgt. Wilkinson	Sgt. Whitaker	Sgt. Jarvie	Sgt. McDowell
Sgt. DIVALL	Sgt. Blake	P/O. Warwick	Sgt. Simpson	Sgt. McArthur	Sgt. Allatson	Sgt. Murray
Flight Bombing Leader , P/O. FORT.		Flight Gunnery Leader , F/O. McCulloch.		Flight Nav. Officer , F/O. MacFarlane.		
'B' FLIGHT						
S/Ldr. MAUDSLAY	Sgt. Marriott	F/O. Urquhart	Sgt. Cottam	F/Sgt. Fuller	F/O. Tytherleigh	Sgt. Burrows
F/Lt. MUNRO	Sgt. Appleby	F/O. Rumbles	Sgt. Pigeon	Sgt. Clay	Sgt. Howarth	F/Sgt. Weeks
F/Lt. MARTIN	Sgt. Whittaker	F/Lt. Leggo	F/O. Chambers	F/Lt. Hay	F/Sgt. Foxlee	F/Sgt. Simpson
F/Lt. HOPGOOD	Sgt. Brennan	F/O. Osborne	Sgt. Minchin	Sgt. White	P/O. Gregory	P/O. Burcher
F/Lt. McCARTHY	Sgt. Ratcliffe	F/Sgt. MacLean	Sgt. Eaton	Sgt. Johnson	Sgt. Batson	F/O. Rodger
F/Lt. WILSON	Sgt. Johnson	F/O. Rodger	Sgt. Mieyette	P/O. Coles	Sgt. Payne	Sgt. Hornby
P/O. BURPEE	Sgt. Pegler	Sgt. Jaye	Sgt. Weller	Sgt. Arthur	Sgt. Long	F/Sgt. Brady
P/O. KNIGHT	Sgt. Grayston	F/O. Hobday	Sgt. Kellow	P/O. Johnson	Sgt. Sutherland	Sgt. O'Brien
Sgt. TOWNSEND	Sgt. Powell	F/Sgt. Howard	F/Sgt. Chalmers	Sgt. Franklin	Sgt. Webb	Sgt. Wilkinson
Sgt. ANDERSON	Sgt. Paterson	Sgt. Nugent	Sgt. Bickle	Sgt. Green	Sgt. Ewan	Sgt. Buck
Flight Bombing Leader , F/O. Johnson.		Flight Gunnery Leader , F/O. Tytherleigh.		Flight Nav. Officer , Urquhart.		
Signals Leader , F/Lt. Hutchison	SPARES.	P/O. WOOD.	P/O. PEMBERTON.	F/O. HOLMES.	Sgt. CHAMBERLAIN.	
Bombing Leader , F/Lt. Hay						
Gunnery Leader , F/Lt. Trevor-Roper						
F/Engr. Leader , Sgt. Johnson						
Nav. Officer , F/Lt. Leggo						

Typing and spelling as in original. Source: AIR 14/842

Reconstruction of a complete crew list for 617 Squadron, dated 13 April 1943. Of the men on this list, 127 would eventually fly on the Dams Raid.

The training summaries in the archives contain two complete crew lists and each gives an interesting snapshot of the state of the squadron at that time. The first of these is dated 13 April 1943, and contains the names of 127 of the 133 men who would take part in Operation Chastise some five weeks later.

There are twenty-two crews listed above. One, piloted by Flt Sgt George Lancaster, would shortly leave the squadron and not be replaced. Two more, those of Sgt William Divall and Flt Lt Harold Wilson would complete the training but owing to sickness would not take part in the Dams Raid (although Sgt Daniel Allatson from Divall's crew was a late substitute in Ken Brown's aircraft, when his front gunner, Don Buntaine, was also ill). In the remaining nineteen crews, only six men were replaced between 13 April and 16 May.

By the time the next crew list was compiled, eleven days later on 24 April, Lancaster and his crew had left and five out of the other six changes had been made. Flg Off MacCausland had taken over as bomb aimer in the Young crew, Flg Off Goodale and Sgt Jagger as wireless operator and mid-upper gunner in Shannon's, and Flg Off Earnshaw and Flt Sgt Fraser as navigator and bomb aimer in Hopgood's. The only substitution made later than this would be that of Sgt Victor Hill for Sgt Austin Williams as front gunner in the Maltby crew, which took place in the first week in May.

Lancaster and his crew left because they objected to a plan to replace

Flg Off Cleveland, their navigator. In a case of 'one out, all out' they went as a unit to 61 Squadron. The crew's bomb aimer, Flt Sgt Clifford, had been one of the star bomb aimers in the early test flights and was mentioned by Gibson in *Enemy Coast Ahead* as getting free beer for his prowess.[69] George Lancaster himself went on to complete his tour in 61 Squadron and later in the war won the DFM for his efforts.

Meanwhile the training continued. It involved low flying for days at a time, something they all found exhilarating. At one point McCarthy was flying at about 100 feet above the ground when another Lancaster flew below him. McCarthy was livid, as he wasn't prepared for this and could only think of the possible disastrous consequences. Everyone he asked denied responsibility, although later Les Munro confessed it was him.[70]

There were a number of other near misses. In one, Munro and his crew were flying low over the North Sea when they suddenly saw a naval convoy ahead and had to climb steeply to avoid it. As referred to on p59 above, Barlow suffered a bird strike which resulted in a collision with the top of a tall tree. Maudslay also damaged his Lancaster in an incident with another tree.

Jack Guterman, the wireless operator in Bill Ottley's crew, wrote about his training flights in some of his letters home. In one, dated 18 April, he replied to his sister who had told him she had seen a Lancaster flying over their house a few days earlier:

> I cannot think that the aircraft (which sounded like a Lancaster) you
> mentioned having seen in yesterday's letter was ours because the dates
> don't seem to agree but I am certain that when you receive the letter I
> wrote you on that day, (Friday) when we flew over gfd, you will be able
> to check up on it definitely.[71]

Two days later, in a letter to his sister written in flight and dated 20 April 1943, Guterman described another flight in detail. Guterman was a gifted artist, and often wrote vivid descriptions of what he had seen in his letters:

---

69 Gibson, *Enemy Coast Ahead,* p260.
70 Johnson, *Last British Dambuster,* p146.
71 Jack Guterman, letter to Babs Guterman, 18 April 1943, Guterman family. [Spelling and punctuation as in original.] The letter he refers to, written 'on Friday' which would have been 16 April, does not seem to have survived. It is possible that the Guterman family saw another 617 Squadron Lancaster over Guildford, piloted by Flt Lt Norman Barlow. On Sunday 11 April this flew over another Guildford house, the home of Edna Mitchell, who was the girlfriend of Barlow's navigator Flg Off Philip Burgess. See p59.

I should have been in Lincoln this afternoon, but as you will have probably detected from the uncertainty of my writing I am flying instead; I did not have to (really) but another "tour" of Cornwall on such a glorious afternoon is not to be missed and the mountains in N. Wales, which bring to my mind [landscape artists] Richard Wilson and David Cox look quite magnificent on a day such as this. At the moment we are flying low over a bottle green sea; blue cloud shadows thrown from a clear sky scattered with slow moving lozenge clouds, make dark patches in the water and a long strip of dazzling gold denotes the sandy shore of the English coastline. What could be more idyllic. Proust would have made something of it – as subtle Suggestiveness to recreate a particular scene remembered through the time misted years – but always the golden pink mist of extasy. You have a lovely afternoon in Surrey, I can see from here for if I look out of my port side window the sky above the hills which lie North of the Thames and Surrey is almost cloudless – and up here its boiling. The large wheat-fields are still the threadbare carpets of Spring with the young corn turning them a colour halfway between brown and green, and the old red farms amongst orchards dazzling with white blossoms look up at you from the shallow valleys. There is so much to be seen that you become quite discontented about missing so much.[72]

On 22 April the first of the modified Type 464 Lancasters arrived on the base. All the crews took the opportunity to inspect the new arrivals, which must have given them an inkling as to how special the operation was going to be. Both the bomb bay doors and the mid-upper turret had been removed, and beneath the bomb bay hung a pair of calipers with discs at the end of the arms, specially designed to hold some sort of weapon, as yet unseen. This would apparently be rotated as one of the discs was connected to a drive belt.

The absence of a mid-upper turret confirmed what the crews already knew, that one gunner would have to fly in the less-used Lancaster front turret. Each crew made its own choice as to who was to occupy this position.

Meanwhile, although the crews were training in low flying from their base in Lincolnshire, testing of the weapon that they would eventually use had moved to Reculver on the Kent coast, close to RAF Manston where the aircraft could be kept securely. On 12 April, Gibson took Bombing Leader Bob Hay down to Kent to watch the first test runs which occurred the next day. They saw the

---

72   Jack Guterman, letter to Babs Guterman, 20 April 1943, Guterman family. [Spelling and punctuation as in original.]

Wrt Off Albert Garshowitz, map reading in the cockpit of a Lancaster in flight. This photograph was probably taken on a training flight for Operation Chastise, but this is not certain.

first test Upkeep weapon dropped successfully by a Wellington, but then the second, dropped by a Lancaster, broke up. Flying back in a small Magister, Gibson and Hay had a lucky escape when its single engine failed. Gibson managed to crash-land in a field near Birchington which was full of devices designed to stop enemy gliders landing. Further tests of Upkeep followed in the weeks that followed, and Plt Off Henry Watson, 617 Squadron's armaments officer, was sent to stay at Manston to follow the tests.

Watson returned from his three week attachment on 2 May and was called into Gibson's office to report on progress. Gibson was very perturbed by some of what Watson told him, and sat down immediately to write a report of the conversation for Gp Capt Harold Satterly at 5 Group Headquarters. He was so concerned to maintain the utmost secrecy that he wrote the body of the memorandum in his own handwriting, not even trusting the details being given to a typist. He wrote:

(1) Within three days of arriving at Manston, P/O Watson was shown a file which I think you have seen. This contained:
   a. Sectional drawings of certain objectives.
   b. A map of the Ruhr showing these objectives.

c. Various secret details in connection with Upkeep.

(2) That P/O Watson, an armament officer in this squadron, thus knows more about this operation than either of my Flight Commanders and at the time, more than I did myself.

I have had a long talk with this officer and am satisfied that he understands the vital need for security, and the disregard of security will lead to most distressing results. But I consider that there is no need for a squadron armaments officer to be given such information.

P/O Watson, tells me moreover, that he read this file in company with a F/O Rose, who belongs to 618 Squadron, Coastal Command. This officer is engaged in the same type of work as ourselves, but has no connection with any matter concerning Upkeep.

P/O Watson informs me that he was shown this file by W/C Garner of M.A.E.E. In fairness to W/C Garner I should like to point out that he has been doing excellent work whilst he has been in charge of the trials at Manston. However, I do feel that the more people who know, the looser the security will be.[73]

At the bottom of the page there appears in Gibson's handwriting the phrase 'Seen by me', and below is Watson's own signature. Gibson apparently wanted to ensure that Watson knew the importance of keeping the secret by getting him to countersign the memorandum.

Shortly after this, on 6 May, Gibson called a training conference in his office. All the captains were present, along with Watson and the engineering officer, Plt Off Cliff Caple. Of the men in the room, only Gibson and Watson knew the targets, and Gibson still didn't divulge it to the wider meeting. He did, however, indicate that the operation would take place within the next fortnight and that the squadron would now move from individual training flights to flying in formation. The groups of three would fly on a new route which would carry out simulated attacks on both the Eyebrook and Abberton reservoirs, while another six would use the Derwent dam as a target. The remainder would carry out bombing over the Wash. On all these, the aircraft would fly at the maximum all up weight, to simulate the load needed for the operation itself. Young was given the task of calculating this, and told to get his figures checked by a flight engineer.

The meeting also decided one other important matter. VHF radio telephony sets, which would allow direct aircraft-to-aircraft communication, would be

---

73   AIR 14-595. Spelling and punctuation as in original.

One of the few pictures of a Type 464 Lancaster in flight. It was taken by Nina Maltby, wife of pilot David Maltby, and shows her husband overflying her parents' house a few miles from RAF Manston. The date is uncertain but it is likely to have been either 12 or 13 May 1943.

installed in all the new Lancasters. (The Dams Raid would in fact become the first time this was used in Bomber Command.) More round-the-clock work was required for this, and on the evening of 8 May Maudslay and Young took off in two separate aircraft to test them out. Bob Hutchison, as Signals Leader, flew in AJ-X with Maudslay. The system was found to work up to about 50 miles at 500ft, and a little less at 200ft.[74]

At around the same time, in the first week in May, the two Vickers test pilots, Sqn Ldr M.V. 'Shorty' Longbottom, an RAF pilot seconded to Vickers, and the civilian Richard Handasyde began testing dummy Upkeeps at Reculver under the supervision of Barnes Wallis. Screens were erected on the beach to simulate dam towers, and for the first time the aircraft flew in at right angles to the shoreline, so that a series of successful bounces would leave the mine on the beach. By 7 May, Wallis had made various adjustments to the caliper arms which held the mine in position, and he recorded in his diary that 'Shorty did two good drops – direct hits'. Frustratingly, the weather then closed in for three days so it wasn't until Tuesday 11 May that more tests were possible.

By that time, the draft operation order had arrived at Scampton. This had

---

74   Owen, *Maudslay*, p261.

List of Pilots and their call-signs

1. W/CDR.	GIBSON.	)			
2. F/LT.	HOPGOOD.	)	Take off	21.55	
3. F/LT.	MARTIN.	)			
4. S/LDR.	YOUNG)				
5. F/LT.	MALTBY	)		22.05	
6. F/LT.	SHANNON	)			
7. S/LDR.	MAUDSLAY	)			
8. F/LT.	MUNRO	)		22.15	
9. F/LT.	MCCARTHY	)			
10. P/O.	KNIGHT		22.18	o/c	22.21
11. F/LT.	ASTELL		22.21		22.24
12. P/O.	OTTLEY		22.24		22.27
13. F/LT.	BARLOW		22.27		22.30
14. F/LT.	WILSON		22.30		22.33
15. SGT.	DIVALL		22.33		22.36
16. P/O.	RICE	)	22.05		
17. SGT.	BYERS	)	22.10		
18. SGT.	TOWNSEND	)	22.15	} Target C. only	
19. SGT.	ANDERSON	)	22.20		
20. P/O.	BURPEE	)	22.25		

Handwriting on original is Gibson's
Typing and spelling as in original. Source: AIR 14/2036

Reconstruction of undated file note showing Gibson's draft 'batting order' for Operation Chastise.

been handwritten by Gp Capt Harold Satterley at 5 Group HQ in Grantham, pulling together information from a number of sources. Satterley asked Whitworth and Gibson for their comments and amendments, and both men sent back their observations. Gibson also added a provisional order of battle to his copy. Nine pilots, in three groups of three aircraft, were listed in the First Wave, scheduled to attack the Möhne and Eder Dams, and they included both Joe McCarthy and Les Munro.

In this note, which is undated but which was probably written on 11 or 12 May, six aircraft were allocated to the Second Wave, which was going to attack the Sorpe Dam. They would take off singly, at three-minute intervals after the First Wave had departed. There appears to be some mistake in Gibson's handwritten additions to the typing in that he allocated the Third Wave, which was supposed to be a mobile reserve, earlier take-off times than the Second

Wave. He also bracketed them together as attacking Target C, the Sorpe. One can only conclude that this indicates some of the pressure he was under.

At this time, four or five days before the operation, all the senior crews had been allocated to the First Wave, so it was perhaps no surprise that changes were made before the final list was drawn up. If breaching the Sorpe Dam was to be treated as a major priority then allocating some of the best crews available would be necessary.

On 11 May, the day after the draft operation order arrived, the Upkeep mine was tested for the first time by crews who would have to drop it for real. Gibson, Hopgood and Martin flew to RAF Manston, each in the aircraft they would use on the Dams Raid. At Manston, they were loaded with inert mines and then took off for nearby Reculver, where they took turns to fly towards the target screens which had been set up on the beach. Each mine worked perfectly, taking several bounces before running up the beach. Gibson noted in his logbook: 'Low level. Upkeep dropped at 60 feet. Good run of 600 yards.'[75] Hopgood recorded the flight to Manston as 'To and from Manston. Low-level formation with Wing/Co. VHF tests.' He followed this with a 35 minute flight recorded as 'Store dropping. 60' 220 IAS.'[76]

On the following days more crews dropped dummy mines. But it appears that it was recognised that there might not be time for all twenty-one crews still in training to get a chance to do a test drop. So when Maudslay, Shannon, Munro and Knight set off from Scampton on Wednesday 12 May, Norman Barlow and Bill Townsend flew as second pilots in the Shannon and Munro crews respectively.

Maudslay and his crew had been allocated Lancaster AJ-X (ED933) for the raid, but he came in at an altitude so low that when the mine was dropped the splash of water and shingle damaged the tailplane and soaked his rear gunner, Norman Burrows.[77] The aircraft limped back to Scampton, but the repairs couldn't be done in time. Fortunately another specially modified Lancaster, ED937, arrived the following day, and Maudslay was given it instead. It was given the code name AJ-Z.

Munro also flew in too low, and suffered less serious damage to his tailplane from the after-effect of his mine drop. His aircraft was repaired back at Scampton. Shannon's bomb aimer, Len Sumpter, contrived to drop his Upkeep 20 yards short of the designated mark and was called in by Gibson the following day to explain himself. This was the only occasion on which Gibson

75   Sweetman, *Dambusters Raid*, p116.
76   Elmes, *M-Mother*, p232.
77   Owen, *Maudslay*, p263.

and Sumpter spoke before the raid.[78] After that time, records are sketchy as to which crews actually dropped mines. However, it would seem that fewer than half of the squadron had actually done so by the time they set off on Operation Chastise the following Sunday.

Thursday 13 May did however see what would prove to be the one and only test drop of a live weapon. It was decided to carry this out further out to sea to reduce the risk of it being observed from shore. The mine was dropped by Longbottom, rather than one of the 617 Squadron pilots. He headed to a spot some 5 miles off Broadstairs, and dropped the mine from 75ft.

Spinning at 500rpm, it bounced seven times over 'almost 800 yards' without deviation. For this trial the theodolite film camera was positioned ashore on the North Foreland almost broadside to the aircraft's track, and Handasyde flew the other Lancaster at 1,000ft and 1,000 yards away from Longbottom, with two cameramen aboard to operate the normal-speed camera. Handasyde had Gibson on board his aircraft as observer, and Gp Capt Wilfred Wynter-Morgan, the RAF's Deputy Director of Armaments, flew in Longbottom's rear turret to watch the behaviour of the mine after release as it slowed to 55mph behind the aircraft.

The film of this test showed that the water-spout when the mine exploded rose to about 500ft above Handasyde's aircraft, and the estimated depth of detonation was about 33ft. For all concerned the day was eminently successful.[79]

The following day, Friday 14 May, what amounted to a full dress rehearsal took place. Nearly all the crews flew on a four-hour simulated attack on the Uppingham and Colchester reservoirs. One definite absentee was David Maltby and his crew, with their aircraft stuck at Avro's factory in Woodford getting repairs done on their bomb bay fairing. Mick Martin also seems to have been absent. Somewhat surprisingly, a few crews carried an extra passenger – one was Flg Off Malcolm Arthurton, the squadron medical officer, who flew with the Maudslay crew.

Friday also saw the final decision to proceed with the operation. The Vice Chiefs of Staff had met in Whitehall on Thursday morning, and had been unable to agree whether to proceed with deploying the Upkeep weapon in the forthcoming moon period, or to wait another month in order for Highball to be ready. The matter had to be referred upwards to the Chiefs of Staff, who were in Washington with Churchill. The reply took until Friday afternoon to arrive,

---

78   Sweetman, *Dambusters Raid*, p116.
79   Sweetman, *Dambusters Raid*, p94.

but when it did, it was positive: 'Chiefs of Staff agree to immediate use of Up-keep without waiting for Highball.'[80]

If the operation was going to be on Sunday evening this left a little over 48 hours to finalise everything. On the Saturday morning, Gp Capt Satterley took the handwritten draft operation order out of his safe and arranged for it to be typed for distribution.

While Satterly was doing this, his boss Cochrane flew to Scampton to tell Whitworth and Gibson. He arrived in the early afternoon of Saturday and left to return to Grantham at about 1600, taking Gibson with him. Meanwhile Barnes Wallis had arrived at Scampton in a Wellington, piloted by Vickers test pilot Mutt Summers. By 1800, Gibson was back at Scampton and at a meeting in Whitworth's house he and Wallis began the process of briefing the crews by calling in four of the key personnel: Melvin Young and Henry Maudslay, the two flight commanders, John Hopgood, who would act as Gibson's deputy at the Möhne, and Bob Hay, the squadron Bombing Leader.

The meeting went through the operation order in detail. Hopgood noted that the route took the squadron over Hüls, which he knew was heavily de-fended, and suggested it be changed. Gibson recalls this rather dramatically in *Enemy Coast Ahead* with the remark 'that night Hoppy saved our lives.'[81]

One of the main topics for conversation was doubtless the attack on the Sorpe, and this may well have been the first time that Wallis told the strike force about the different method needed for attacking it. This led to the decision to beef up the Second Wave who were to be given that task. Both Joe McCarthy and Les Munro had been listed in the First Wave but were now moved, with their places given to Bill Astell and Les Knight. This was not a reflection of the bombing abilities of either crew but rather a late acknowledgement that the Sorpe should be seen as a higher priority.

With hindsight, the lack of a detailed strategy for attacking the Sorpe Dam can be seen as a major failure by Wallis and the operation's planners. Tests had shown that Upkeep had a good chance of working when delivered at right an-gles to a concrete-walled dam, such as the Möhne and Eder. Over the course of the trials, Wallis had been trying to think of an effective way of delivering the same exploding depth charge against the Sorpe embankment-style dam with its sloping wall, built of earth with a concrete core. He had written to Air Cdre Sydney Bufton, Director of Bombing Operations at the Air Ministry,

---

80   Sweetman, *Dambusters Raid*, p129. Highball (see p25) was the smaller version of Upkeep, still being tested by Mosquitoes in Loch Striven in Scotland. The testing process was running at a slower pace than that for Upkeep.
81   Gibson, *Enemy Coast Ahead*, p276.

with his most recent suggestions just five days before the operation. Wallis had originally suggested in January 1943 that the concrete core of the dam could be 'practically self-destroying if a substantial leak can be established within the water-tight core'[82] but he had now modified that view. After studying more aerial photographs, he had concluded that the sloping face on the air side of the dam appeared to be made of 'pretty heavy material', and he felt that this might not disintegrate even if the central core of the dam were cracked. He therefore suggested that craters be made on the air side before any attack from the water side. Then he included calculations showing that if Upkeep were dropped 41ft from the core, it would roll 113ft down the slope and explode 30ft under water. The explosive charge would then generate a lateral movement of 16–20in.[83] There does not ever appear to have been any plan to bomb the air side first, which would surely have required a completely different weapon, so the 617 Squadron crews would be told to drop their mines on the water side of the centre of the dam so that they rolled down the slope before exploding.

It wasn't until the day of the raid itself that the five crews of the Second Wave were suddenly told that the method of attack they had been using in training would not be used. Nor was consideration given to how crews from the Third Wave would have to change their methods depending on which target they were allocated while in the air. The one crew from the mobile reserve to reach the Sorpe, that of Ken Brown in AJ-F, was also unprepared for this target. His bomb aimer, Stefan Oancia, had been planning to get the correct dropping point for his mine from a set of chinagraph marks which he had made on the window of his blister to align with the towers of both the Möhne and Eder Dams.[84] These were made redundant when AJ-F received a signal while in flight to proceed to the Sorpe Dam.

No detailed plan had been devised for how the sequence of attack would be mounted. The five aircraft would not fly in formation but would take off at one-minute intervals, starting at 2127, and ahead of the First Wave. Because they were to take a longer route, this would mean that they would cross the Dutch coast at the same time as the First Wave, but further north.

Wallis had in fact previously expressed the view that it might take the successful drop of five or six Upkeeps by this method for the central core of the Sorpe to be breached. It is clear now that insufficient consideration of this took place in the frantic period before the raid.

At the time of the meeting in Whitworth's house, there were thought to be

82   Sweetman, *Dambusters Raid*, p68.
83   Sweetman, *Dambusters Raid*, p127.
84   Sweetman, *Dambusters Raid*, p110.

CHARLES FOSTER

The briefing for Operation Chastise was held on the first floor in this building at RAF Scampton, the 'Other Ranks' mess. This photograph was taken in 2007. Apart from the pitched roof, the building would have looked much the same in 1943.

twenty flyable Type 464 Lancasters on the station, plus Maudslay's original air-craft, ED 933 AJ-X, which the ground staff were still working on round the clock to repair in time. With twenty-one crews trained and ready, Ken Brown and the crew of AJ-F were therefore left off the list.

Harry Humphries was in his office early the next morning, even though it was a Sunday. Gibson arrived at about 0900. He told Humphries that at last the squadron was going to war, but he didn't want 'the world' to know about it. He instructed him to make out a battle order but to title it 'Night Flying Pro-gramme', and then gave him the crew details and the code orders.[85]

There were nineteen crews on the list as both Bill Divall and Harold Wilson had reported sickness in their crews. Divall himself appears to have been sick for a few days as he doesn't seem to have flown on any training flights after 6 May. However in the run up to the raid, on 13 and 14 May, his rear gunner, Sgt John Murray, had undertaken two flights in Ken Brown's crew. Again, it is not clear whether Brown's front gunner Don Buntaine was on these training flights. He would also miss the raid with sickness, but Divall's other gunner Daniel Allatson would end up substituting for him. It isn't clear what was the problem with the Wilson crew.

---

85   Humphries, *Living with Heroes*, p6. See p16 of this book for a copy of the Programme.

So Ken Brown and his crew were therefore reinstated into the programme, with Allatson's name listed in his crew. He was allocated to the Third Wave, the mobile reserve. Divall and Wilson's absence also led to the promotion of Rice and Byers to the Second Wave, detailed to attack the Sorpe. The Ottley crew were moved into the mobile reserve. Several copies of the typed Night Flying Programme were produced, and they show all these late changes.

With the battle order typed up, the nineteen pilots and nineteen navigators were called to a briefing at about midday, when they were told their targets by both Gibson and Wallis. Around the same time, the wireless operators were called to a separate briefing by Wg Cdr Wally Dunn on code words and protocols. The briefing was held in the first-floor room of the Junior Ranks Mess at Scampton. At some point in the afternoon, bomb aimers and gunners were brought into the picture, with small groups clustered around the models, noting details which would be relevant.

Early in the afternoon, the ground crew working on AJ-X called time on their efforts. They simply would not be able to get it ready to fly that evening. This left nineteen serviceable aircraft at Scampton; with only nineteen crews now flying this would only be all right if none of them had a problem getting ready for take-off. A reserve aircraft was deemed necessary but all the other Type 464 Lancasters ever manufactured were off-base. Two were still at Manston, the ones used by Longbottom and Handasyde, and one more, ED825, was at the research airfield at RAF Boscombe Down in Wiltshire, where it had been used for performance testing. A ferry pilot, Cdr H.C. Bergel, was dispatched to bring this up to Scampton to become the reserve, which he did. Bergel decided to ignore a slight problem which he noticed with its No 3 engine.[86] When it arrived, ground crew quickly got it operation-ready. It was allocated the code AJ-T.

At 1800 the general briefing began. As well as the 133 aircrew sitting on benches in front of a dais holding Gibson, other senior officers and Wallis, there was a civilian interloper in the room by the name of Herbert Jeffree, an engineer at Vickers who worked for Wallis. He bluffed his way past the RAF policeman standing as security at the door with a pass that had given him authority to attend the tests at RAF Manston and Reculver.

Gibson spoke first, and then introduced Wallis who described the weapon, how it had been developed and the arguments for attacking the German dams. His arguments that the loss of the dams would lead to the curtailment of industrial production for a very long time were well remembered by those who heard him. In a 2007 email to the author, Fred Sutherland recalled the briefing:

---

86   Sweetman, *Dambusters Raid,* p148.

I remember the briefing quite well because we had waited for weeks to find out what we were doing and where we were going. The pilots, navigators, and, I think, the bomb aimers had a pre-briefing in the afternoon. The models of the dams, the pictures and maps were all set up in the room under guard. No person was allowed to enter. I remember seeing the targets for the first time and knowing that this was going to be really touch and go. Gibson ended his speech by saying: 'Well chaps if you don't do it tonight you will be going back tomorrow night to finish it off.' All the speakers concentrated on the importance of the dams and the water to the German war effort.[87]

Cochrane spoke after Wallis, briefly emphasising the 'historic' nature of the operation. He ended his remarks by saying that the raid might do a lot of damage but that they might never read about it in the news. 'It may be a secret until after the war. So don't think that you are going to get your pictures in the papers.' Cochrane may have thought that there might be little publicity, but some people at the Air Ministry had other ideas. The Director of Bombing Operations, Air Cdre Sydney Bufton, had already devised a plan for press communiqués after the raid.

Cochrane was followed by Gibson again, who repeated the details of the three waves that he had already given the pilots and navigators. After the briefing, at about 1930, the crews went off for their meal – the traditional eggs and bacon, with an extra egg for anyone flying that night. The WAAFs who worked in the separate messes for the officers and sergeants could not help noticing the extra rations, and were now in on the secret. Operation Chastise was under way.

---

87   Fred Sutherland, email to author, 13 August 2007.

Chapter 6

Operation Chastise

Wave One
Attacks on the Möhne and Eder Dams

GIBSON BELIEVED IN LEADING FROM THE FRONT, and his AJ-G was at the apex of the first group of three Lancasters from the First Wave, which left the ground at Scampton at 2139. The other two aircraft were AJ-M and AJ-P, piloted by John Hopgood and Mick Martin respectively. Four of the aircraft from the Second Wave, with further to fly, were already airborne by this stage. As Gibson and his crew climbed aboard their Lancaster, they were photographed together as a complete crew for the first and only time. Their rather self-conscious pose, with Gibson paused on the top step, was later recreated in the 1955 film. In his account in *Enemy Coast Ahead*, Gibson made it sound as though it was a surprise: 'An RAF photographer came running up and asked to take a picture – these men certainly choose the queerest times,' he wrote.[88] In fact, a decision to send a photographer had been taken back in London by the Air Ministry's Director of Bombing Operations, Air Cdre Sydney Bufton, with an eye on the possible media coverage if the raid was a success. The photographer, Flg Off W. Bellamy, stayed on duty all night. He took several other pictures before the raid, including a picture of a single Lancaster taking off, shown on p90, which was probably AJ-E, piloted by Norman Barlow. He also photographed Gibson's crew being debriefed after the raid.

The trio had a quiet flight across the North Sea but experienced stronger winds than forecast, so they made landfall on the enemy coast late and some distance off course. They had reached Walcheren island rather than the nearby mouth of the Scheldt river. Fortunately the land-based anti aircraft gunners failed to pick them up and they were able to alter course. Again, they were not threatened as they crossed Holland and reached the Rhine. Once more they found themselves off course, 6 miles too far south. Gibson turned and flew up the Rhine towards the intended turning point, a bend in the river near Rees. It

---

88   Gibson, *Enemy Coast Ahead*, p280.

IWM COLLECTIONS CH18005

The crew of AJ-G pose rather self-consciously as they board their aircraft, just before take-off on the Dams Raid. Left to right, Richard Trevor-Roper (rear gunner). John Pulford (flight engineer), George Deering (front gunner), Fred Spafford (bomb aimer), Bob Hutchison (wireless operator). In doorway, Guy Gibson (pilot). Standing on right, Harlo Taerum (navigator). This was the one and only operation on which all seven men flew together.

was on this short section that they encountered their first flak, being fired on by guns positioned on barges on the river and its banks.

The experience of going off course and meeting unexpected flak was repeated several more times as Gibson's trio flew on towards the target. At 0007, wireless operator Robert Hutchison sent a message to Group HQ warning of a particularly nasty attack near Dülmen, which appears to have been the place where Hopgood's AJ-M was damaged. It was rebroadcast to all aircraft four minutes later. Tom Simpson, flying as rear gunner in Martin's AJ-P, wrote an account in his diary of the trip from the Dutch coast:

> Lost Hoppy! later picked up by some searchlights near Rhine – shot some out somewhere – bit off track over some town – bags of shooting – lost Winco – arrived Möhne Hoppy and Winco turned up.[89]

From Tony Burcher's post-war account it would seem that it was at Dülmen

---

89   Quoted in Sweetman, *Dambusters Raid*, p158.

IWM COLLECTIONS CH18006

A Lancaster takes off on the Dams Raid. Photograph taken by official Air Ministry photographer Flg Off W. Bellamy. As it is a single aircraft, it is probably one from the Second Wave, possibly the first to leave the ground: Norman Barlow and his crew in AJ-E.

There has been some discussion on the veracity of this picture, since there is no sign of the Upkeep weapon underneath the Lancaster as it leaves the ground. However, it is likely that either the photographer or a darkroom operative was instructed to paint out the weapon for security reasons. The painting out has been done rather crudely – if there was no weapon, daylight would be visible through the landing gear struts.

Bellamy's 'dope sheet' (a handwritten list of shots taken that day) lists two pictures: 'One of the "Lancs" taking off for the raid as night falls' and 'A "Lanc" takes off as night falls'. The dope sheet itself is in the Imperial War Museum's photographic archive, and was reproduced in Herman Euler's book *The Dams Raid through the Lens*, After the Battle 2001, p210.

that AJ-M was hit by flak, which damaged its port wing. A shell damaged the cockpit, inflicting a head wound on Hopgood himself. Another must have damaged the front turret below him, badly wounding gunner George Gregory. Burcher recalls Hopgood saying: 'Right, well what do you think? Should we go on? I intend to go on because we have only got a few minutes left. We've come this far. There's no good taking this thing back with us. The aircraft is completely manageable. I can handle it OK. Any objections?' And so on he pressed, as flight engineer Charles Brennan stood beside him, holding a handkerchief on his head to stem the bleeding.

Melvin Young in AJ-A led the second section, made up of David Maltby in AJ-J and David Shannon in AJ-L. Maltby's navigator, Vivian Nicholson, was actually flying his first ever operation that night. The section's progress can be accurately tracked by using the details from his log sheet, one of the six which have survived from the raid.[90] At 2210, over the Wash, the crew tested the spotlights which had been set to keep the aircraft at exactly 60ft during the bombing run. They made landfall accurately over the Scheldt estuary on the Dutch coast at 2312, and the mine was then fused. At Rosendaal, Maltby had to take 'evasive action' to avoid flak. At the canal intersection at Beck, Nicholson wrote 'Leader turns soon'. He probably meant 'too soon', as Young's aircraft went slightly off course. At 2342, about 15 miles from the Rhine, he noted that his Gee system was now 'jammed something chronic'. They turned again at Dülmen, avoided more flak which was 'direct at a/c' at Ludinghausen, and also at Ahlen, and arrived at Target X, the Möhne, at 0026. The outward flight had taken two hours and thirty-two minutes.

The final group of three, led by Henry Maudslay, was completed by Bill Astell in AJ-B and Les Knight in AJ-N. Everything seemed to go well until they crossed the Rhine. At this point, Astell was lagging slightly behind Maudslay and Knight, seeming to hesitate as though not sure of a turning point. Shortly afterwards, near Dorsten, they ran into unexpected light flak, possibly from the same position that had damaged Hopgood's aircraft about twenty minutes earlier. Looking back from the astrodome in AJ-N, wireless operator Bob Kellow 'saw two lines of tracer intersecting in a brilliant criss-cross.'[91] Astell flew on with his gunners firing vigorously but he did not survive the ordeal. Kellow watched from two miles distant as AJ-B became swiftly engulfed in flames, and shortly afterwards he and Hobday reported an explosion on the ground. AJ-B crashed at 0015.

---

90 Sgt V. Nicholson, navigator's log sheet, AJ-J. The log sheets which have survived were those kept by Jack Leggo (AJ-P), Vivian Nicholson (AJ-J), Sydney Hobday (AJ-N), Grant Rumbles (AJ-W), Richard Macfarlane (AJ-H) and Donald MacLean (AJ-T).

91 Sweetman, *Dambusters Raid*, p161.

Astell had hit an electrical pylon near Marbeck, where a line of HT cables lay in the path of the attacking force. There was no flak at the site, so it is possible that the tracer lines Kellow saw where in fact electrical flashes. Gibson and Young's trios, a few minutes ahead, had noticed the pylons and flown over them. The Upkeep mine which Astell's aircraft was carrying exploded about ninety seconds later, shattering windows for a distance around, although a roadside shrine to St Joseph somehow survived without damage.

When the first three arrived at the Möhne, they took a few minutes to assess it in real life. The guns on the two sluice towers were already active, and there were further emplacements on the nearby banks.

The Möhne reservoir is the shape of a giant U on its side, the open end facing east, or right. The dam is on the top left part of the curve of the U. Some earlier accounts say that the aircraft approached from the Körbecke bridge at the eastern end, but that is now thought to be wrong. Helmuth Euler interviewed a number of German witnesses after the war[92] and he and others maintain that the aircraft attacked by flying straight at the dam from a south-easterly direction, hopping over a small spit of land (the Heve promontory) and quickly getting down to the right height for the last stretch of about 1 mile. The witnesses confirm that the attacking Lancasters could be seen flying circuits over the Arnsberg forest to the south of the dam.

In that last mile the pilot would have to get down to exactly 60ft and stay level, the flight engineer would maintain the approach speed at 230mph, and the wireless operator would ensure that the mine was spinning backwards at 500rpm. Meanwhile the navigator would switch on the spotlights and check that the beams were touching. Flying at 230mph, the aircraft would cover the 1 mile stretch in about fifteen seconds.

In order to assess the defences at close range, Gibson decided to do a dummy run over the dam. He chose a different angle of approach so not to give too much away to the defences. As he rejoined the waiting aircraft he announced that he 'liked the look of it'. At that point, the first group of three were joined by Melvin Young, David Maltby and David Shannon.

Gibson then prepared to launch the first attack. As he did so, he reminded Hopgood that he should take charge of the operation should anything happen to AJ-G. Brave man that he was, Hopgood does not seem to have told Gibson the extent of the damage he and his crew had already suffered.

Gibson then set off towards the target. After AJ-G had crested the Heve spit Taerum switched on the spotlights and stood by the blister, calling out

92   Euler, *Dams Raid Through the Lens*, p56.

instructions in order to maintain the height at 60ft. Hutchison checked that the mine was rotating, and Pulford kept his hand on the throttles to control the speed. In the front turret, Deering began firing at the defences while Spafford, in the bomb aimer's position below him, prepared to release the spinning mine. He dropped the mine at 0028 at the correct distance, 400 yards from the dam wall. In the rear turret Trevor-Roper saw it bounce three times and then sink, short of the dam. As AJ-G passed over the dam wall, Hutchison, positioned in the astrodome, fired a red cartridge from his Very signal gun. Some ten seconds later, as Gibson turned the Lancaster back towards the holding position, a tremendous sheet of water surged high over the wall. However, when this subsided the dam was seen to be still intact.

The group had to wait about five minutes for the water to settle, whereupon Gibson ordered Hopgood into the attack. As he prepared to do so, Maudslay and Knight from the third group arrived. Hopgood set off, but the gunners on the dam now knew from which direction the attack would come and were waiting for him. The damage which AJ-M had already suffered made it even more vulnerable, as its front gunner George Gregory was almost certainly severely wounded by this time. Both port and starboard wings were hit during the attack and in the confusion bomb aimer John Fraser was late releasing the mine. It bounced over the dam wall and landed near the power station on the other side. A Very cartridge was fired, lighting up the stricken aircraft, which was seen to be engulfed in flames. Hopgood managed to lift it up to about 500 feet and shouted over the intercom 'For Christ's sake, get out of here!' Somehow, the wounded John Minchin managed to drag himself towards the rear escape hatch, with one leg almost severed. Burcher pushed his colleague out of the hatch first, pulling his parachute ripcord as he did so, and then followed him. Sadly, Minchin did not survive the drop, but Burcher did although he was captured and taken prisoner.

Meanwhile, John Fraser was still in the bomb aimer's position. After the war he wrote:

> We flew on and the pilot gave the order to abandon the aircraft within about 25 seconds after we passed over the dam. I knelt facing forward over the escape hatch and I saw that the trees looked awful damn close. I thought there was only one thing to do and that was to pull the rip cord and let the pilot chute go out first and then let it pull the chute out and me after it, and that's what I did.[93]

---

93 Quotation from www.bombercommandmuseum.ca/fraserhoppy.html [Accessed March 2017].

He landed less than a mile away from where the aircraft crashed. Taken prisoner, he was interrogated and forced to give some details of the mission before being sent to a prisoner of war camp. After the war, Fraser was debriefed as a returning prisoner of war, and at this point told his questioner that George Gregory had survived the earlier attack on the aircraft. Fraser last saw him trying to return to the 'rest area' to retrieve his parachute.[94]

The aircraft exploded and crashed near the village of Ostonnen, some 6km from the dam. Minchin's body was found about a kilometre away. The mine also exploded, severely damaging the power station.

Things were not going well. Gibson had six bombed-up aircraft left, but their crews had just seen how simple a target Hopgood had presented to the dam's gunners, although they did not know that the explosion of Hopgood's mine had actually put the left-hand gun tower out of action. The next few minutes were surely what earned Gibson his Victoria Cross. In the words of John Sweetman, 'Gibson's leadership and Martin's courage ensured that the operation would not disintegrate.' In the hope that the gunners would be distracted, Gibson flew alongside Martin and slightly ahead of him, on his starboard side. However, something went wrong with Martin's mine: it veered off leftwards and exploded near the southern shore of the lake. Its casing may have been damaged when the unfused mine had been dropped accidentally onto the hard standing at Scampton after being loaded that morning, or, perhaps, Martin hadn't got the aircraft exactly level as it was released.

By this time a certain amount of desperation must have been creeping in. Gibson and Martin's mines had not been successful and Hopgood had been shot down. Melvin Young in AJ-A was next and Gibson decided to vary his diversion tactics. This time, he flew across the defences on the far side of the dam wall, while Martin came in on Young's starboard side. Young was accurate in his approach, and his bomb aimer, Vincent MacCausland, dropped the mine accurately. It bounced three times, hit the dam and seemed to explode while it was in contact with it, but, as the tumult subsided, there was no obvious breach.

A few minutes later, it was the turn of AJ-J, piloted by David Maltby. As he launched his attack he was accompanied by two other Lancasters: Gibson on his starboard side, Martin on the port. As he approached the dam wall, Maltby suddenly realised that from this close he could see that a small breach had occurred in the centre and that there was crumbling along the crown. Young's mine had been successful after all! He steered slightly to port but stayed dead level as his bomb aimer John Fort steadied himself to press the release. The

94   Plt Off John Fraser, RCAF personnel file, National Archives of Canada.

mine bounced four times and struck the wall. Maltby said afterwards: 'our load sent up water and mud to a height of a 1,000ft. The spout of water was silhouetted against the moon. It rose with tremendous speed and then gently fell back. You could see the shock wave at the base of the jet.'[95] His navigator, Vivian Nicholson, wrote a briefer account in his log, just three words long: 'Bomb dropped. Wizard.'[96]

But at the time, it was still not apparent that a further breach had occurred. AJ-J sent a standard 'Goner' message back to base. But then, as David Shannon in AJ-L was called in to deliver a sixth mine, Gibson realised that the dam was broken, and his wireless operator Bob Hutchison transmitted the code message for a successful attack. Elation followed, and all seven Lancasters present took turns to fly over the dam to observe the results of their work.

After a few minutes, Gibson called for order, and set about the second phase of his night's work. He told Martin and Maltby to make their way home, and ordered Shannon, Maudslay and Knight, who still had mines on board, to proceed with him to the Eder Dam. Young was also told to accompany the party, to act as deputy leader if anything should befall Gibson.

The Eder lake was difficult to locate and Shannon found himself circling over another patch of water nearby. He was guided to the correct location by a flare fired from AJ-G by Bob Hutchison. The attacking force quickly realised that the dam presented a much more difficult target than the Möhne. The lake is smaller and set in a deep valley, meaning that there is a much shorter approach which starts with a very tricky steep dive from over the Waldeck Castle. This is followed by a sharp turn to port. Given the geography, the Germans had obviously discounted the idea of an aerial attack, since there were no gun batteries in the vicinity.

Shannon was the first to try an attack, and made three or four passes without releasing his mine. It was very difficult to get down to the right height after the dive, and then turn. Gibson told Maudslay to try, and he found it just as hard, so Shannon had another go. Two more dummy runs followed until, at last, he got the angle and speed right and dropped his mine. It bounced twice, hit the dam wall and exploded sending up a huge waterspout. At the later debriefing his effort is reported as 'no result was seen' but Shannon in fact felt that he had made a small breach.

Maudslay had another attempt but then something went wrong. His mine was released too late, hit the parapet and exploded. Although his aircraft was beyond the dam by the time this occurred, it may have been damaged, since

95   Sweetman, *Dambusters Raid*, p166.
96   Sgt V. Nicholson, navigator's log sheet, AJ-J.

his progress home was slower than would be expected. Some reports say that something was seen hanging down below the aircraft, perhaps caused by hitting trees on the run in.

Gibson saw that AJ-Z had fired a red Very light signal after passing over the dam wall and called Maudslay on the radio: 'Henry – Henry. Z-Zebra – Z-Zebra. Are you OK?' Nothing was heard, so he repeated the call. This time Maudslay's voice could be heard, although the signal was faint: 'I think so. Stand by …' This signal – confirmed by members of Shannon's and Knight's crews – was the last voice contact anyone made with AJ-Z.[97]

It was now down to Les Knight in AJ-N, who was carrying the only mine left. Shannon advised him on the direction and speed. After a dummy run, which was dangerous enough for rear gunner Harry O'Brien to record afterwards that he 'never thought they would get over the mountain' on the other side of the dam, Knight switched his radio off so that he could concentrate. With a bright moon on the starboard beam, he brought AJ-N into attack. The mine was released, bounced three times and hit the dam wall. Knight climbed steeply and, as the aircraft reached a safe height, saw an explosion which caused a 'large breach in wall of dam almost 30ft below top of dam, leaving top of dam intact.'[98]

Wireless operator Bob Kellow had his head up in the astrodome, looking backwards. It seemed, he said, 'as if some huge fist had been jabbed at the wall, a large almost round black hole appeared and water gushed as from a large hose'.

The climb after the attack was hair raising. Bomb aimer Edward Johnson said later that it 'required the full attention of the pilot and engineer to lay on emergency power from the engines and a climbing attitude not approved in any flying manuals and a period of nail biting from the rest of us not least me who was getting too close a view of the approaching terra firma from my position in the bomb-aimer's compartment.'

Kellow was understandably preoccupied while Knight and Grayston pulled AJ-N up and over the surrounding hills, and his message confirming the drop – 'Goner 710B' – was sent six minutes after the message 'Dinghy', denoting a breach of the Eder, had been transmitted by Bob Hutchison, in Gibson's AJ-J.

Gibson, Young and Shannon and their crews were elated, and more congratulations ensued when Group HQ at Grantham received the signal. Air Chief Marshal Harris rang Air Chief Marshal Sir Charles Portal, the Chief of the Air Staff, who was in Washington DC with the Prime Minister. Portal sent

97   Owen, *Maudslay*, p281.
98   Sweetman, *The Dambusters Raid*, pp171–2. Also the quotations from the Knight crew in the following paragraphs.

congratulations to all the civilian and service personnel responsible, and said he would inform Churchill without delay.

Group HQ then asked Gibson if he had any aircraft left who might be sent on to attack the Sorpe Dam. Gibson answered that he had none, and ordered the three aircraft with him to set off home. He was not able to reach Henry Maudslay, and assumed the worst for him.

In fact, at this stage Maudslay was still trying to limp home in his damaged AJ-Z, and would stay airborne for a further fifty minutes. At 0157, some twenty minutes after they had dropped their mine, his wireless operator Alden Cottam sent his 'Goner 28B' message back to base, which indicates that they were making progress. At about 0230, they had reached the Rhine. The turning point on the return route was supposed to be at the town of Rees, but he headed 20 miles north of this towards Emmerich, which was defended by several Heimat light flak anti-aircraft batteries, largely manned by non-military personnel. Some of the outbound force had in fact passed over the town a few hours earlier so the batteries were on alert for the opportunity to fire on any returning crews. When AJ-Z was heard approaching Emmerich it came within range of the batteries on the south and east edges. They fired on the aircraft, and although it turned to the right to try and avoid the flak, either an engine or a fuel tank was hit, as there was a burst of flame. The aircraft lost height and at 0236 crashed in a field close to the hamlet of Osterholt, between the German town of Klein Netterden and the Dutch town of 's Heerenberg. The following morning, German officials recovered seven bodies from the wreckage. Two were identified as Alden Cottam and Jack Marriott, but the rest were recorded as unidentified. All seven were buried in the Northern Military Cemetery at Düsseldorf.[99]

The squadron's other flight commander Melvin Young and his crew were very unlucky indeed. Young had piloted AJ-A and its crew from the Eder Dam on the same route as Maudslay as far as the Dutch coast, which he reached just before three in the morning.

Then, out over the sea, he hit disaster when the gun battery at Wijk-aan-Zee fired at the rapidly disappearing Lancaster. At that stage, the aircraft was well past the last gun battery and only a few hundred yards from safety. The battery later reported shooting down an aircraft at 0258, which was almost certainly AJ-A. Two bodies, one being Young and the other an unidentified sergeant, were washed ashore on 29 May and they were buried in the General Cemetery at the nearby small town of Bergen two days later. The sergeant was later identified as David Horsfall, who would have been sitting alongside Young in the

---

99   This account is derived from Owen, *Maudslay*, pp284–7.

cockpit. The bodies of the other five of the crew of AJ-A were washed up over the next thirteen days.

By this time, Maltby and Martin were well on their way home. Maltby followed the designated exit route 1, flying to the east of the Ruhr, then to the Ijsselmmer and out into the North Sea across the neck of the Helder peninsula. Apart from some brief evasive action near Ahlen, his flight back was uneventful and he landed at Scampton at 0311. He was followed along the same route by Martin who kept very low the whole way home. His rear gunner Tom Simpson wrote: 'On the way back we saw nothing, thank goodness, but by then I think we were flying at less than 50ft.'[100]

When he left the Eder, Gibson flew back past the Möhne, noting that for 3 miles below the dam the river had swollen to 'several times its normal size'. After a warning of a possible night fighter in pursuit, he dropped down to the lowest level possible. On their port side, the crew also saw an aircraft shot down near Hamm. This was probably Ottley from the mobile reserve. Gibson followed the third of the prescribed exit routes, crossing the Helder peninsula north of Haarlem, deviating to pass through an known gap in the coastal defences near Egmond. At this point he climbed slightly beforehand in order to go over the coast in a fast dive. Having achieved this successfully, the rest of the flight was uneventful and AJ-G landed at Scampton at 0415, the only damage from the night's work being three small holes in the tail.

Shannon had landed a few minutes before him, at 0406. Like Maltby and Martin an hour before, he had followed the first return route. Over the Helder peninsula, 3 miles before the North Sea coast he took AJ-L up to 800ft and crossed the shore in a fast dive at almost 300mph.

Les Knight's AJ-N was the last from Wave One to land, at 0420. He had also headed for home via the Möhne Dam, where the crew noticed how much the water level had already dropped. The trip back was relatively trouble-free – they avoided some flak bursts near Borken, and Fred Sutherland was able to shoot up a stationary train in a small town. They were very lucky, however, not to have fallen at the final hurdle in an incident which only O'Brien noticed: '… at the Dutch coast the terrain rose under us, Les pulled up, over and down. On the sea side of this rise was a large cement block many feet high. This block passed under our tail not three feet lower. As the rear gunner I was the only one to see it.'[101]

---

100 Sweetman, *Dambusters Raid*, p173.
101 Sweetman, *Dambusters Raid*, p175.

Wave Two
Attacks on the Sorpe Dam

Flt Lt Joe McCarthy and his crew in AJ-Q were scheduled to be the first to take off on Operation Chastise, at 2127. The plan was for the five aircraft not to fly in formation but to take off at one minute intervals. They would thus all be in the air ahead of Wave One, but because they were to take a longer route, this would mean that they would cross the Dutch coast at much the same time, but further north.

The McCarthy crew headed out to their designated aircraft, which they had nicknamed 'Queenie Chuck Chuck'. Unfortunately, while the engines were being run up one on the starboard side developed a coolant leak and it was obvious that it could not be used. Determined not to miss the action, McCarthy ordered everyone out, knowing that there was a spare Lancaster, AJ-T, which had only arrived on the base a few hours previously. A series of mishaps then occurred. As the crew threw all the essential equipment out of the windows, McCarthy's parachute caught on a hook and blossomed all over him on the ground. They reached AJ-T, only to find it didn't have its important compass deviation card on board. McCarthy himself charged off in a truck to the flight office to get the card. Adjutant Harry Humphries was in the office and saw him coming. His approach resembled a 'runaway tank', he recalled later. A search for the card followed, while Humphries did his best to calm the big American down. It was found quite quickly and McCarthy headed back to AJ-T.[102] In its rear turret, Dave Rodger had used the spare few minutes getting ground crew to remove its Perspex panels.

AJ-T eventually took to the air some thirty-three minutes later than their scheduled departure time, and after the nine aircraft in the First Wave had departed. Bill Radcliffe's skills as a flight engineer, allowing the maximum possible speed while maintaining fuel reserves, were severely tested as AJ-T flew as fast as possible to catch up. They had made up sixteen minutes by the time they reached the Dutch coast.

McCarthy's enforced delay meant that AJ-E was in fact the first Dams Raid aircraft in the air, with Norman Barlow and his crew on board. He left the ground at 2128. Because they were under instruction to maintain radio silence, nothing more was heard from them, and the crew were therefore listed in the official record as 'missing'. But we now know that they just crossed the border

---

102 Humphries, *Living with Heroes*, p11.

between the Netherlands and Germany, for it was near Haldern, 5km east of the Rhineside town of Rees, that they crashed ten minutes before midnight. It appears that they hit one of the pylons which stretch across the fields in the locality, although it is possible that the aircraft had first been hit by flak. AJ-E came to rest in a small meadow on the edge of a copse. All on board were killed instantly, and their bodies badly burned.

After the war, a witness, Johanna Effing, gave an account to the writer Helmuth Euler:

> [We] saw the field in front of us blazing fiercely. An aircraft flying from the west had hit the top of a 100,000 volt electricity pylon and crashed into the field. A huge bomb had rolled out 50 metres from where the plane had crashed. Even before it got light we had a whole crowd of inquisitive people there despite the danger from exploding ammunition. It was not long before the Mayor of Haldern, Herr Lehmann, was on the scene and he climbed onto what was taken to be a large petrol canister. He said 'I'll tell the Chief Administrative Officer that he needn't send us any more petrol coupons for the rest of the war. We've got enough fuel in this tank.' When he found out later that he had been standing on dynamite he's supposed to have felt quite sick. All the crew were killed and burnt beyond recognition. There were no flak batteries or searchlights here; the plane was just flying too low. The first guards from the scene of the crash came to the house and showed us the valuables which they had found: things like cases, gold rings, watches and a long cylindrical torch. Its owner had scratched all his missions on it – 32 of them. I still remember the name 'Palermo' and also the names of a lot of other towns.[103]

Barlow's crew, like all the others had been given orders to fuse the mine's self-destruct 'pistol' before crossing the Dutch coast. This should have led to the mine exploding after the crash. However, this did not occur – it may not have been fused, or the mechanism may simply not have worked. For whatever reason, this gave the Germans a big bonus. One of Germany's leading bomb disposal officers, Hauptmann Heinz Schweizer, was called. The mine was defused on site and then taken to Kalkum, near Düsseldorf, for examination. Detailed drawings of the whole construction were quickly made, and the fact that it had

---

103 Euler, *Dams Raid Through the Lens*, p93. There is no explanation of why the word 'Palermo' should be written on a torch. If it refers to the town of this name in Sicily, it was out of the range of British-based bombing operations.

been spun before release was deduced (although it is not certain whether they ever worked out that it had in fact been spun backwards).

Meanwhile, the seven bodies found in the wreckage were buried by the Germans in Dusseldorf North cemetery, but they could only positively identify Leslie Whillis and Alan Gillespie. The other five were marked as 'unknown'.

Munro's AJ-W was the second aircraft to take off at 2129 on 16 May 1943. All went well for the first eighty-five minutes, and on reaching the Dutch coast near Vlieland the mine was fused. But then the aircraft was hit by flak. Munro and front gunner Bill Howarth say that this was fired from a land battery, while bomb aimer Jimmy Clay recorded that it was a flak ship which spotted them. Whichever it was, it did severe damage. The intercom was put out of action, the master unit for the compass was destroyed and the tail turret pipes damaged.[104]

Munro kept on flying for a while but sent flight engineer Frank Appleby down to the nose to check with Clay. He passed him a note: 'Intercom U/S – should we go on?' Clay remembered his reply:

> I wrote: 'We'll be a menace to the rest.' Had it been a high-level operation there would have been time to make up some sort of signals between Bomb Aimer, Flight Engineer and Pilot which may have worked. But on a quick-moving low-level operation like this and with other aircraft in close proximity Les could neither give nor receive flying instructions from the navigator nor bombing instructions from the bomb aimer.[105]

The rear gunner, Harvey Weeks, was completely isolated and wireless operator Percy Pigeon was sent to check up on him. In doing so he saw the hole in the fuselage, with a host of broken wiring. He told Munro it would be impossible to fix this while airborne. So, reluctantly, Munro altered course and turned for home. When he got to Scampton he was unable to radio the control tower to tell them that he would be landing, so he went straight in and touched down at 0036, the first crew to return from Operation Chastise. He didn't know that Geoff Rice was circling his own severely damaged aircraft, AJ-H, above the runway getting his crew into crash positions. Fortunately, Rice saw Munro landing and an embarrassing and dangerous incident was narrowly avoided.

Some time later that morning, during the impromptu party that was going on in the Officers Mess, Gibson came up to Munro:

---

104 Sweetman, *Dambusters Raid,* p180.
105 Sweetman, *Dambusters Raid,* pp180–1.

'Well, what happened, Les?' he asked him. Munro told him he had been hit by flak.

'Oh, you were too high,' Gibson replied.

Munro was about to protest and give his side of the story, but Gibson had already turned and walked away. It rankled with Munro, who felt that he had not been given a fair hearing. Nor did he feel that he could raise the matter again; it was the last time either of them ever mentioned it.[106]

Vernon Byers and his crew took off in AJ-K at 2130, one minute after Les Munro. Everything seems to have gone smoothly but then, as the official record says, nothing more was heard from him. However, crew members in both Munro's aircraft, ahead of Byers, and in Geoff Rice's, a minute behind, appear to have witnessed Byers's last moments. Munro's bomb aimer Jimmy Clay saw an aircraft on his starboard side, heading towards Texel island, rather than Vlieland, the prescribed route. Rice's crew saw an aircraft shot down by flak at 300ft 'off Texel' at 2257. According to a post-war Dutch report, having crossed the island, he then seemed to climb to about 450ft.

Despite the fact that he was off course, and had crossed Texel which had more anti-aircraft defences than its neighbour Vlieland, it seems that Byers was very unlucky. The German guns could not depress low enough in order to hit an approaching aircraft flying at just 100ft but because AJ-K had risen a little in height it must have been a speculative shot from behind which hit the aircraft and sent it down into the Waddenzee, 18 miles west of Harlingen. Two German units stationed on Texel were credited with the kill.[107] This point is disputed by author Andreas Wachtel, who thinks that it was more likely that 3/Marine Flak 246 unit on the western end of Vlieland was responsible.[108]

Byers and his crew were thus the first to be lost on the Dams Raid and, like the Barlow crew, died before midnight on 16 May 1943. Six bodies have never been found, but that of rear gunner James McDowell must have been detached from the wreckage at some time as it was found floating in the Waddenzee, in the Vliestrom channel, south of Terschelling near buoy No 2 on 22 June 1943.

AJ-H, piloted by Geoff Rice, took off from Scampton at 2131 and all went well for the first hour and a half of flying time. They crossed the narrow neck of

106 James Holland, *Dam Busters: The race to smash the German Dams,* Bantam 2012, p358.
107 Sweetman, *Dambusters Raid,* pp181–2.
108 Chris Ward, Andy Lee and Andreas Wachtel, *Dambusters: The Definitive History,* Red Kite 2003, p64.

Vlieland at 2259 flying very low and exactly on track. Past the danger point, Rice gained altitude briefly to check position and then went low again to turn south-eastwards towards the Ijsselmeer. The bright moon shining on the water made height difficult to judge and flight engineer Edward Smith was about to warn Rice that the altimeter was reading zero when there was a huge jolt. Instinctively Rice pulled upwards and felt another 'violent jolt'.

AJ-H had hit the water twice. The first impact had torn the mine free and sprayed water up through the bomb bay. The second had forced the fixed tail wheel up through the fuselage and demolished the Elsan lavatory just in front of the rear turret. A revolting mixture of its contents, disinfectant and sea water had poured into the turret and immersed gunner Stephen Burns up to his waist. His shout of 'Christ, it's wet back here!' was pretty understandable.

Everyone else was shaken up, but by some miracle the aircraft and crew had survived. Rice flew on for a minute or two while the damage was assessed and it was confirmed that the mine had been lost. So he then turned for home. The anti-aircraft batteries on both Vlieland and Texel were waiting for him and sprayed flak across the gap between the two islands but he sped underneath their fire.

There was nearly another tragedy as they reached Scampton. The hydraulic fluid in the undercarriage had been depleted, so it had to be manually lowered with an air bottle. This took twenty minutes during which time Rice was circling the airfield at 1,000ft. Uncertain whether the flaps would then work, another warning message was sent to the control tower, and the crew prepared for an emergency landing. Rice and Smith remained in their seats while the rest sat with their backs to the main spar, facing aft. They were just about to make their approach when suddenly Les Munro's AJ-W, which had lost its radio, flew in below them and landed on the main runway. Rice held off and touched down a few minutes later.

The next day, Gibson quizzed Rice over the cause of the loss of his mine, but took no further action. He seemed to accept from his own experiences in training how difficult it could be to judge an aircraft's height when flying low over water.

As the four aircraft who took off on time in Wave Two crossed the coast, Joe McCarthy in AJ-T was still some twenty minutes behind. The wave was already in severe trouble, a fact unknown to the crew who should have taken off first. Byers had been shot down and Munro and Rice had been forced to abandon the operation. Barlow had got through, but would crash in flames less than an hour later. McCarthy ploughed on, although by the time he was in enemy territory he had lost radio contact with base, the GEE navigation system had failed and a light had come on in the nose compartment, which made them a much easier target for the night fighters which they could see above them. The light problem was easily fixed with a blow from flight engineer Bill Radcliffe's crash axe, and later wireless operator Len Eaton managed to reestablish radio contact.

When they reached the Sorpe, they realised that none of the other crews had made it. Surveying the scene, McCarthy realised how difficult the attack was going to be, even though there were no flak batteries present to defend the dam. The Dams Raid crews had only practised one method for attacking the dams – flying across the water straight at the dam wall. The first they were told about the different method needed for the Sorpe Dam had been at the briefing on the afternoon of the raid. There, they had been instructed to attack the dam by flying along its wall and dropping the mine at its centre. They were told that this would then roll down the dam wall on the water side and explode when it reached the correct depth.

The approach to the dam wall involved flying over the small town of Langscheid, which had a prominent church steeple, and then dropping very low so that the mine could be dropped in the exact centre of the dam. After several attempts, McCarthy realised that he could use the steeple as a marker and eventually, on the tenth approach, he managed to make a near perfect run, getting down to about 30ft. Johnson released the weapon, and shouted 'Bomb gone'. 'Thank God' came the reply from Dave Rodger in the rear turret, pretty fed up with the continuous buffeting he was getting from the steep climb necessary at the end of the run.

A few seconds after the drop the mine exploded. It threw a fountain of water up to a height of about 1,000ft, some of which ended up in Rodger's turret, leading to further complaints from him. When McCarthy wheeled round to inspect the damage, they could see some crumbling along the top of the wall, but it was not sufficient to cause a breach.

Disappointed, McCarthy set course for home, but went via the Möhne, having heard over the radio that it had been breached. They saw a clear rift in the wall and noted that the level was already well down. On the return flight they went badly off course and flew over the heavily defended town of Hamm, a place they had been warned to avoid. Realising that the compass was not reading accurately they managed to navigate by sight across the rest of enemy territory, narrowly avoiding being shot down on several occasions. As they came in to land at Scampton, they realised that one of the undercarriage tyres had been shot through, but McCarthy still landed safely.

Wave Three
Mobile reserve

The duty of the five crews in Wave Three, the mobile reserve, was to arrive in the air over Germany while the earlier two waves did their work. They would then be diverted by 5 Group headquarters in Grantham to attack whatever target it deemed necessary.

The wave was led off by Bill Ottley in AJ-C, and his aircraft was airborne at 0009 on Monday 17 May. It crossed the Dutch coast at about 0130 and proceeded on the same route taken earlier by the First Wave towards Ahlen. At 0231, Group sent the code word 'Gilbert' to AJ-C, and the signal was acknowledged. This meant 'proceed to the Lister Dam.' A minute later a change of plan occurred, and the code word 'Dinghy' was sent, instructing AJ-C: 'Eder destroyed, attack Sorpe'.

The second signal was not acknowledged, indicating that AJ-C had met its fate at about 0231. Ken Brown, flying AJ-F a few minutes behind, reported seeing it hit the ground at 0235. He recalled later: 'Ottley, on my right, was hit and pulled up, his tanks exploded then his bomb – the whole valley was lit up in a bright orange.' Both Bill Townsend, AJ-O's pilot, and Lance Howard, its navigator, also saw AJ-C's final demise.

There was however one survivor from the crash, rear gunner Fred Tees. He heard wireless operator Jack Guterman say over the intercom 'Möhne gone'. Almost immediately Ottley started a sentence: 'We go to…,' when 'a hell of a commotion' occurred to interrupt him. The aircraft was suddenly bathed in searchlight and a tremendous barrage of flak struck it, mainly from the port side. Tees then heard Ottley say, 'I'm sorry boys, we've had it,' but thereafter his memory of events became blank.[109]

AJ-C hit the ground at Heessen, 5 miles north-east of Hamm, which suggests that it was probably hit by flak west of Hamm itself. Tees's turret was blown clear of the rest of the aircraft and he regained consciousness on the ground nearby, very badly burnt. He was soon captured and spent the remainder of the war as a prisoner. Bill Ottley and the rest of the crew died instantly. They were buried by the Germans in Hamm.

Lewis Burpee and his crew in AJ-S left the ground at 0011, but never made it as far as the German border. While still over Holland, and approaching the gap between the heavily defended airfields at Gilze-Rijen and Eindhoven, the

---

109 Sweetman, *Dambusters Raid*, p189.

aircraft strayed off course. It climbed slightly, probably in an effort to determine its exact position, but was then caught in searchlights and hit by flak. It crashed on the edge of Gilze Rijen airfield, 6 miles south-west of Tilburg. Its mine exploded on impact, demolishing a large number of buildings and doing damage estimated at 1.5 million guilders.

The demise of the Burpee crew was seen by both Stefan Oancia, bomb aimer in AJ-F, a minute or so behind, and Douglas Webb, still further back in AJ-O's front turret. AJ-S's last minutes were also seen by a German witness, a Luftwaffe airman based at Gilze Rijen called Herbert Scholl, interviewed after the war by Helmuth Euler. He was of the opinion that AJ-S was in fact not hit by flak at all, but was dazzled by a searchlight beam hitting it horizontally. The pilot tried to fly even lower, and then hit some trees.

The next morning, Scholl went to the crash site and saw that it was a total wreck. Only the rear turret and tail unit were intact, and he saw rear gunner Gordon Brady's body, which didn't appear to have any sign of injury. He noticed that Brady was scantily dressed, wearing thin uniform trousers and lace-up shoes with holes in the soles.[110]

After the crash, only the bodies of Burpee, Brady and Weller were positively identified. The other four were buried in a communal grave. They were interred by the Germans at Zuylen Cemetery, Prinsenhage.

Ken Brown and his crew in AJ-F took off a minute after Burpee at 0012. Some time before the raid, Ken Brown's regular gunner Don Buntaine had reported sick. However, Bill Divall's whole crew had also been taken off the flying schedule as someone else in his crew was ill, so one of his gunners, Sgt Daniel Allatson, was hastily reallocated to the front turret of AJ-F.

Before take-off Brown liked to smoke two cigarettes. He had just put the second out when Lewis Burpee came up to him and took his hand. 'Goodbye Ken,' was all he said. Brown's rear gunner Grant McDonald saw this and said to him: 'Skip, you know those guys aren't coming back, don't you?' 'Yeah, I know,' Brown replied. All McDonald could say then was 'Well, damn it!'[111]

Two hours later, Brown and his crew witnessed Burpee's fate when he strayed too close to Gilze-Rijen airfield, and was shot down.

AJ-F pressed on over Germany, keeping so low that at times they were below treetop level. They shot up a train which travelled across their path and just avoided crashing into a castle. Having received the signal that both the Möhne

---

110 Euler, *Dams Raid Through the Lens*, p106.
111 Transcript of speech by Ken Brown in 1993.
         www.bombercommandmuseum.ca/kenbrown.html [accessed March 2017].

and Eder Dams had been destroyed, they were diverted to attack the Sorpe.

On their arrival, they found that the mist which had hampered the only previous attack, by McCarthy two and a half hours previously, had thickened considerably. Working out a line of attack was difficult, and they made several abortive attacks. One of these nearly ended in disaster when they flew into a valley, but quick thinking by Brown and a stall turn got AJ-F out of trouble. Eventually they hit on a plan of marking a circuit with flares, and they dropped their mine successfully at 0314. They had cleared the hill beyond the dam and turned to port when the explosion occurred. Bomb aimer Steve Oancia noted a large waterspout, and the crew observed crumbling of the crown of the dam. But no breach had occurred.

Flying back over the Möhne, they saw the extensive damage but were then fired on by the one gun emplacement still active. McDonald returned fire with gusto, and was pleased to see that the flak went silent. With dawn approaching, Brown got down as low as possible and in flight engineer Basil Feneron's words 'opened up the taps'. AJ-F came through intensive fire at Hamm and at the last danger point, the Helder peninsula on the Dutch coast. The cockpit was flooded with light from searchlights and flak crashed through the perspex. Feneron crouched as low as possible and could see Brown above him to his left, hunched over the instruments.

Somehow, they had all survived, and they landed at Scampton at 0533 in an aircraft full of holes.

Bill Townsend took off at 0014 in AJ-O. He had some difficulty getting the heavily-laden aircraft into the air, just crawling over the hedge which marked the airfield boundary. As they approached the Dutch coast, they saw flak far ahead on their port side, probably that which shot down Lewis Burpee and his crew. Turning correctly at the tip of Schouwen, they crossed the coast at 0131.

At 0145, they received another warning about flak at Dülmen and almost immediately were caught in a searchlight. According to Lance Howard's account Townsend 'threw that heavily-laden Lancaster around like a Tiger Moth and we flew out of it.' Several more incidents followed and at one point they flew along a firebreak in a forest, below the level of the trees.

With all this activity, it is perhaps not surprising that AJ-O did not receive radio messages from Group HQ about the breaching of the Möhne and Eder. However, a message sent at 0226 was acknowledged. This ordered AJ-O to proceed to the Ennepe Dam. At about the same time, Ottley and Anderson were ordered to attack the Lister and Diemel Dams respectively.

With hindsight, it would seem to be a tactical error by Group HQ not to have concentrated attacks by the mobile reserve on the most important remaining target, the Sorpe Dam. Indeed, a second message was sent to Ottley to change to this target but he had already been shot down.

When AJ-O reached the Ennepe Dam, the crew found the target obscured by mist. Also, when they started spinning their Upkeep mine it made the aircraft judder alarmingly. AJ-O had not dropped a dummy mine in practice, so this tendency had never been noticed before the operation. However, after three attempts, they managed to drop it at 0337. Although it bounced twice, it exploded short of the dam which remained intact. Townsend hung around for a while waiting to see if others would arrive, but then set off for home. On the way they passed over the Möhne and saw for themselves the extent of the devastation already wreaked.

John Sweetman has put forward the theory that Townsend and his crew actually attacked the nearby Bever Dam, which has a similar shape to the Ennepe. It was not on the list of Operation Chastise targets. The Bever has an earth core, similar to the Sorpe, and was therefore not suitable for a head-on attack.[112]

With dawn breaking, AJ-O had an eventful journey back to base. As they approached Texel on the Dutch coast the Germans depressed a heavy flak gun and deliberately bounced shells off the water, a tactic which Lance Howard later described as 'hardly cricket'. Townsend and George Chalmers later both recalled seeing the shells actually bouncing over them. Townsend turned to starboard and flew back towards Germany, before turning to port once more and finding a new track through the danger. On the way back across the North Sea an oil gauge showed that one engine was faulty and it was shut down.

They finally landed at 0615, the last crew to return. They were met on the hardstanding by a group of Bomber Command's most senior officers, including Air Chief Marshal Harris, whom the exhausted Townsend didn't recognise and pushed past. It was, however, as front gunner Doug Webb later recalled, a piece of 'superb flying' which had brought them home.

Cyril Anderson and his crew in AJ-Y were the last to take off on the Dams Raid, leaving the ground at Scampton at 0015. Having crossed the Dutch coast successfully they encountered heavy flak north of the Ruhr, and were forced off-track. By then the rear turret began to malfunction, which meant that it was difficult to deal with searchlights. These caused it to divert off-track again five minutes before it reached Dülmen. At 0228, wireless operator William Bickle received the signal 'Dinghy' which directed the aircraft towards the

112 Sweetman, *Dambusters Raid*, pp221–4.

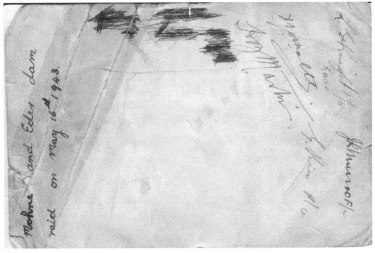

DEAN LEACH

This contemporary print of the photograph of twelve pilots from 617 Squadron, taken on the morning of 17 May 1943, was given to a member of ground crew, Arthur Teal, by Les Knight. It is signed on the back by five of the pilots who appear in it. (Front row, left to right) Cyril Anderson, Geoff Rice, MIck Martin, David Shannon, Les Knight. (Back row, left to right) Bill Townsend, Joe McCarthy, Harold Wilson (did not take part in raid), Guy Gibson, Les Munro, David Maltby, Ken Brown. A circle has been drawn in blue pen around Les Knight's head.

Sorpe Dam. (Some documents claim that it had first been ordered to attack the Diemel Dam, but this is not certain.) By now, a heavy mist was rising in the valleys which made the identification of landmarks almost impossible.

So it was that at 0310, after consulting his crew, Anderson decided that with dawn approaching and a rear turret not working he should turn for home.

Rather than risk following the briefed return routes, he decided to go back the way he had come, crossing the coast at the Schelde estuary. AJ-Y landed at Scampton at 0530, its mine unused.

The next morning, Anderson was photographed along with the rest of the pilots who returned outside the Officers' Mess, but the crew did not remain long on the squadron, and packed their bags that afternoon for a return to 49 Squadron. Gibson was not happy with Anderson's explanation. In particular, he was dismissive of Anderson's account of the valleys being filled with mist. He reasoned that he himself had found his way from the Möhne to the Eder. But this doesn't take into account the fact that Gibson had left the area before 0200, more than an hour before Anderson had turned back, which gave the mist plenty of time to form.

Hindsight suggests that Anderson and his crew were poorly treated. Anderson was an inexperienced pilot, for sure, when he arrived at 617 Squadron – but this was not his fault. But his crew had performed well enough in training and had demonstrated that they had the requisite 'press-on' attitude. They proved that they were a tight-knit bunch when they stayed together on their return to 49 Squadron. They went on a further fifteen operations before being shot down by a night fighter on 23 September 1943, on a trip to Mannheim.

Chapter 7

The men who flew on the Dams Raid

Crew 1: AJ-G
First wave: Attacked Möhne Dam and returned to base.
Lancaster serial number: ED932/G

Wg Cdr G.P. Gibson DSO and Bar, DFC and Bar
Pilot

Guy Penrose Gibson was born on 12 August 1918 in Simla, India, where his father Alexander James (A.J.) Gibson worked for the Imperial Indian Forest Service. He didn't set foot in England until he was 4 years old, when he was brought on a holiday to his grandparents' house in Cornwall. At 6, his mother, Nora, and her three children made a permanent move back and he was sent off to boarding school: first to preparatory schools in Cornwall and Kent and then, aged 14, to St Edward's School in Oxford.

Gibson's time at St Edward's was not particularly distinguished, but it was there that he first became interested in flying. Before he left, he wrote to Captain 'Mutt' Summers at Vickers-Armstrongs (who would later fly the Wellington which dropped the first test 'bouncing bomb' and then collect him at Weybridge station for his first meeting with Barnes Wallis) for advice on how to become a pilot. Summers told him that he should join the RAF. Gibson's first application was refused but he tried again and was accepted onto the No. 6 Flying Training Course at Yatesbury in Wiltshire in November 1936. This was a civilian course, run under the RAF expansion scheme. Pilots who qualified from it were then recruited directly into the RAF and given a short service commission. Gibson became an acting Pilot Officer in early 1937, and then went off on further training until he was sent to his first posting, 83 (Bomber) Squadron at Turnhouse in Scotland, in September 1937.

In March 1938, 83 Squadron was transferred a couple of hundred miles south, to the newly built RAF station at Scampton, Lincolnshire. On the day the war started, 3 September 1939, Gibson piloted one of the first nine RAF aircraft to see action in a raid on German shipping. Apart from one short break, he was to stay at Scampton, flying Hampdens, until he completed his first tour of operations in September 1940.

Although he was supposed to go on a rest period, instructing at a training unit, this only lasted a few weeks as he was drafted over to night fighters due to a chronic shortage of experienced pilots. He joined 29 Squadron in December 1940 and flew some ninety operations in Beaufighters, the last in December 1941, and was credited with several night fighter kills. Having then been sent on instructional duties, he lobbied hard to get back to Bomber Command, where Sir Arthur Harris had just taken over as AOC. Harris knew Gibson and sent him to 5 Group, recommending that he be sent to command one of its new Lancaster squadrons. In the event, he was sent to 106 Squadron based at RAF Coningsby, who were still flying Manchesters but whose Lancasters were expected shortly.

Promoted to Wing Commander, Gibson flew his first operation in a Manchester on 22 April 1942, a 'gardening' trip. By July, he was flying a Lancaster, an aircraft widely regarded as a cut above anything else that had been used before. 106 Squadron moved on to Syerston on 1 October 1942, and Gibson completed his second tour in Bomber Command with an attack on Stuttgart on 11 March 1943.

He was expecting a rest from operations, but instead he was called to a meeting with the Commanding Officer of 5 Group, Air Vice Marshal Ralph Cochrane. 'How would you like the idea of doing one more trip?' Cochrane asked, and Gibson, who hated the idea of being away from the action, readily agreed.

Thus was 617 Squadron born, and the legend began to grow. Based at Scampton again, Gibson, with the support of two excellent flight commanders, Melvin Young and Henry Maudslay, took only two months to mould almost 150 aircrew into a force which would successfully deliver an innovative weapon against a series of targets using astonishing airmanship. On the Dams Raid, he was the first to attack the Möhne Dam, but his mine exploded short of its wall. When the next pilot, John Hopgood, was shot down in the process of dropping his mine, Gibson took it on himself to fly alongside each aircraft to divert the enemy flak as Mick Martin, Melvin Young and David Maltby each made their bombing runs. For this, and his leadership of the raid as a whole, he was awarded the VC.

After the raid, Gibson was taken off operations and was employed what was in effect a full-time publicist for Bomber Command and the RAF. He made public appearances all over the country, and was then sent on a speaking tour

Guy Gibson photographed with five of his Dams Raid crew in July 1943. Left to right: Gibson, Frederick Spafford, Robert Hutchison, George Deering, Harlo Taerum. Missing are flight engineer John Pulford and rear gunner Richard Trevor-Roper.

of Canada and the USA where he met politicians and film stars, but also found time to see ordinary people like the mother of Harlo Taerum, his navigator on the raid. He signed her scrapbook a few days before Taerum was killed, in a costly raid on the Dortmund Ems canal.

By January 1944 he was employed in a desk job in Whitehall, but his real task was to write a draft of his book, *Enemy Coast Ahead.* As discussed above in Chapter 3, pp30–4, much of the text about 617 Squadron was pulled together from material ghostwritten for him, although the earlier sections are probably Gibson's own work. He also found time both to be interviewed for the *Desert Island Discs* radio programme and to be selected as a Conservative candidate for the next General Election.

He changed his mind about going into politics within a few months, but he was still frustrated about being kept off operations. By the late summer he had persuaded the authorities to let him fly on active service again, and he was assigned to an operation on 19 September 1944, to Mönchengladbach and Rheydt. Gibson was to be the controller in a 627 Squadron Mosquito, in charge of other Mosquitoes who were marking the target for the main bomber force.

What happened that night is the subject of much speculation. His aircraft crashed near Steenbergen in Holland, killing both Gibson and his navigator Sqn Ldr James Warwick. There are thought to be three possible causes. The first (and most likely) is that the Mosquito just ran out of fuel because neither Gibson nor Warwick were very familiar with the aircraft and didn't know how to switch to the reserve fuel tank. The second scenario is that they were shot down, either by ground-based anti-aircraft fire or a German night fighter. A third possible account, that they were shot down in a 'friendly fire' episode by a main force bomber, has been put forward by some[113] but there is some doubt about the veracity of the 'confession' of the rear gunner involved.

Gibson was admired by many of his peers and associates, but not by all of them. 'Those who liked or loved him did so intensely,' writes his biographer, Richard Morris. 'More looked upon him with a wary respect. Many thought him unpleasantly rebarbative. A few found him insufferable.'[114] But he was a wartime warrior with a formidable record: few matched his two tours of bomber operations in Hampdens and Lancasters and ninety patrols in a Beaufighter. To quote Morris again: 'He achieved greatness because his combat experience was backed by a practical application of rules of leadership which he had learned: the need to unify his squadrons behind clear aims, to communicate his aims with confidence and to balance discipline with the enlistment of hearts.'[115]

Gibson is buried in the Catholic Cemetery, Steenbergen.

HUMPHRIES FAMILY COLLECTION

Sgt J. Pulford
Flight engineer

John Pulford was born on 24 December 1919 in Sculcoates, near Hull, the second of the four children of George and Ada Pulford. He went to St Paul's School, a local elementary school. He became a motor mechanic and joined the RAF a month before the outbreak of war as ground crew. Like many other ground crew, he volunteered for retraining as a flight engineer in 1942. His brother Thomas was also a flight engineer. By December 1942, Pulford had joined 97 Squadron, based at Coningsby. He flew on 13 operations in Sqn Ldr E.F. Nind's

---

113 James Cutler, 'Who Killed the Dambuster?', *Britain at War,* October 2011.
114 Morris, *Guy Gibson*, p321.
115 Morris, *Guy Gibson*, pxxvii.

crew between December 1942 and March 1943. On 4 April, he was posted to Scampton, and assigned to Gibson's crew. Gibson's logbook actually records Pulford as flying with him on 1 April, but this must be bad record-keeping on the CO's part.

Pulford's father George died on 7 May 1943, and the funeral was fixed for Sunday 16 May in Hull. Pulford was given special permission to attend the funeral, but he was escorted throughout by two RAF policemen in order to ensure he didn't let something slip about the planned operation.[116] It is not clear whether he got back to Scampton in time for the all-crew briefing which took place at 1800 that day.

Despite the fact that they sat side by side throughout their Dams Raid training and on the operation itself, Gibson seems never to have noticed much about Pulford. In *Enemy Coast Ahead* he describes him as a Londoner, obviously unable to identify his Yorkshire accent. But he relied on the Hull man to operate the throttles as they hurtled towards the Möhne Dam at 240mph, calling out the famous words 'Stand by to pull me out of the seat if I get hit.'

All of Gibson's crew were decorated for their actions on the Dams Raid, and John Pulford was awarded the DFM. However, he was sick at the time of the original investiture at Buckingham Palace on 22 June 1943, and collected his medal later in the year. Earlier, he had been home on leave and one night went out for a drink with his brother Thomas. Both men were in civilian clothes and at some point in the evening someone put white feathers in their pockets.[117]

In the run up to Gibson leaving 617 Squadron in the summer, most of his crew – including Pulford – were allocated to the new CO, George Holden. Pulford flew with Holden on his first operation with the squadron on 15 July, a trip to bomb the Italian power stations at Aquata Scrivia and San Polo d'Enza. The detachment flew on to RAF Blida in Algeria. On the return trip nine days later, when bombs were dropped on Livorno, he had swapped to the crew of Ken Brown. The reason why isn't clear. Pulford didn't fly with Holden again, and the new CO then recruited the flight engineer from Bill Townsend's crew, Dennis Powell. Holden, Powell and the remaining four members of the Gibson crew were all killed in the disastrous Dortmund Ems canal operation on 16 September 1943.

By December, Pulford was in another 617 Squadron crew, piloted by Sqn Ldr

---

116 Alan Cooper, *The Men who Breached the Dams,* Airlife 2002, p71.
117 Cooper, *Men Who Breached the Dams,* p113. The practice of handing white feathers to men in civilian clothes had been carried out by some members of the public during the First World War, in order to shame them for not being on military service. It was revived in the Second World War, but not so widely as before.

Bill Suggitt, and completed several more operations. On 12 February 1944, Suggitt's crew bombed the Antheor viaduct in southern France. They had used Ford airfield in Sussex as a staging post and successfully landed there in the early hours of 13 February. Later that day, despite foggy conditions, they took off for the short hop home from Ford to Woodhall Spa and crashed into a hill on the Sussex Downs, near the village of Upwaltham. In 2009, a memorial to this crew and another who died in the area during the war was opened in the local church. John Pulford is buried in Hull Northern Cemetery, in a plot next to his father.

Plt Off H.T. Taerum
Navigator

Harlo Torger Taerum was born in Milo, Alberta on 22 May 1920, the oldest son of the four children of Guttorn and Hilda Taerum. His father was Norwegian, and had emigrated to Canada as a young man. He died in a drowning accident when Harlo was 10.

Despite this tragedy, Harlo was a brilliant student at school. Soon after he left the war started. When he heard how his father's people were being treated in their homeland by the invading Germans, he joined the RCAF. After training in both Canada and Britain, he began operational service with 50 Squadron in January 1942, at first flying on Hampdens, but then moving onto Manchesters and finally Lancasters.

By the end of the year he had completed a full tour of operations and was assigned to the squadron's conversion unit as an instructor. But he continued to fly on operations, including two to Berlin with pilot Mick Martin. It may have been Martin who mentioned both him and bomb aimer Fred Spafford to

BOMBER COMMAND MUSEUM OF CANADA

Guy Gibson at the time of the formation of 617 Squadron, and the pair were quickly slotted into the CO's crew.

Nicknamed Terry, he got on well with Gibson who regarded him as 'one of the most efficient navigators in the squadron' and he received the DFC for his work on the raid. The squadron received huge public attention, and Taerum became one of its stars, making speeches at the Avro factory and Wings for Victory events. 'Can you imagine me giving a speech? We were just about mobbed for autographs afterward,' he wrote to his mother.[118.]When Gibson left the squadron and went to North America on his speaking tour, he met Harlo's mother in Calgary. In front of the press, he praised the work her son had done on the raid. The local press went ecstatic, with headlines reading 'Terry Got Dam Busters to the Job W/C Gibson Tells His Mother Here and 'Modest Dam Buster Hero Gets Enthusiastic Welcome. Gibson's modesty was noted as he: 'spoke little of the escapades which won for him the VC, DSO and Bar, and DFC and Bar. Rather, this young airman, probably the most famous hero yet to emerge from the present war, led the conversation to the splendid job Canadian fliers are doing and to his, "great pal," Flying Officer Harlo "Terry" Taerum DFC, of Calgary.'

A few days later Gibson spent several hours at the Taerum residence. Mrs Taerum showed him a treasured album with letters and photographs about Harlo, and had it autographed. She summed up her experience by saying that it was one of the proudest and happiest times of her life.

Four days later a telegram arrived. Taerum was one of four of Gibson's Dams Raid crew who had flown with the new squadron CO, George Holden, on a disastrous raid on the Dortmund Ems canal on 16 September 1943. Five of the eight 617 Squadron crews were shot down, and thirty-three lives were lost. Taerum is buried in Reichswald Forest Cemetery.

In a tragic postscript for the Taerum family, Harlo's brother Lorne, a gunner just 18 years old, was also killed while serving in the RCAF. His Lancaster was shot down by a fighter on his very first operation in February 1945. The Taerums were one of the three families who lost a son who took part in the Dams Raid and another son serving elsewhere in Bomber Command during the war. (See John Minchin, p128, and David Horsfall, p147.)

Flt Lt R.E.G. Hutchison DFC
Wireless operator

Flt Lt Robert Hutchison was the only person who had regularly been in Guy Gibson's crew in his previous squadron to join the CO at 617 Squadron. Gibson's crew chopped and changed during his time in charge at 106 Squadron, suggesting that a few people found him a hard taskmaster. A more generous interpretation would be that as commanding officer he did not fly as frequently as some of his men, so being part of his crew meant a longer time on active operational duty. In *Enemy Coast Ahead*, Gibson describes Hutchison as 'one of those grand little Englishmen who have the guts of a horse', and says that they

---

118 Taerum family correspondence and newspaper quotes are from
   www.bombercommandmuseum.ca/taerum2.html [Accessed 24 March 2017].

had been on forty operations together. This is a gross exaggeration, since the real number was about eighteen. However, there is no doubt that Hutchison had been one of the small circle of brother officers in 106 Squadron with whom Gibson got on well, and this personal friendship may be what led him to accept the offer of 'one more' operation in a new squadron.

Robert Edward George Hutchison was born in Liverpool on 26 April 1918, the oldest of the four children of Robert and Ada Hutchison. His father worked for the Hall Line, a freight shipping line. Hutchison won a scholarship to the famous Liverpool Institute, whose later old boys would include both Paul McCartney and George Harrison. After leaving school he worked in the principal accountant's department of the Mersey Docks and Harbour Board before joining the RAF soon after the outbreak of war.

The final part of his training as a wireless operator/air gunner was at 25 OTU at RAF Finningley, where he crewed up with Plt Off Horner as his skipper. The crew was posted to 106 Squadron in Coningsby in December 1941, and undertook their first operation to Ostend on 15 December. Hutchison went on to fly on four more operations with Horner and six with Plt Off Worswick. Guy Gibson took over command of the squadron in April, and Hutchison was selected to fly with him as his wireless operator on his fourth operation in his new squadron, a trip to Warnemunde on 8 May 1942.

After five more operations with other pilots, Hutchison became Gibson's regular wireless operator in July and they flew on 18 operations together between that date and February 1943.[119] Hutchison was then recommended for the DFC, where the citation noted the 'numerous operational sorties' he had undertaken. It also specified an attack on Berlin in which Hutchison repaired

defective electrical circuits in the mid-upper turret, despite the intense cold which almost rendered him unconscious during the work.

Having flown on thirty-three operations, Hutchison's tour came to an end on 26 February. On 19 March 1943 he was posted to 1654 Conversion Unit, expecting to be given instructional duties. Within a few days, however, Gibson had been asked to set up the new squadron, and shortly afterwards must have contacted Hutchison, who recorded the transfer in his own logbook as taking place on 25 March.

119 Flt Lt R.E.G. Hutchison, logbook.

Hutchison was a gregarious man – he enjoyed organising concert parties and other activities – and was quick to make friends in all his postings. He was engaged to Beryl Brudenell, who lived in nearby Boston, and was known by the nickname 'Twink'. One of Hutchison's particular friends in 106 Squadron was Canadian navigator Revie (Danny) Walker, who went to stay with the Hutchison family in Liverpool on some of his leave periods. Hutchison must have been pleased when their paths crossed again when Walker rejoined the Shannon crew in 617 Squadron. Another friend had been RAF Syerston's Committee of Adjustment Officer Harry Humphries – another concert party aficianado – and their acquaintanceship continued when Humphries was hastily summoned by Gibson to be the adjutant of the new squadron.

As the senior wireless operator in 617 Squadron, Hutchison was the Signals Leader, responsible for co-ordinating the training of all his colleagues. Individual booths were set up in the crew room so that they could practise their drills. The wireless operators were also given a new responsibility when VHF radios were installed so that voice messages could be passed between aircraft when they were over the target. The Dams Raid would be the first time Bomber Command aircraft had the use of this equipment. In order to test out the radio sets, Hutchison went on a one hour flight with Henry Maudslay as pilot on 8 May.

Hutchison got a bar to the DFC he had received only a few weeks previously for his work on the Dams Raid. As a non-drinker, he might have found the round of parties a little too much, and he didn't go to London on the special train for the investiture.

Hutchison could have gone off operations at any time, as he was well past the number required by then, but he was one of the four members of the Gibson crew who transferred to the new CO, George Holden. He was flying with him on 16 September 1943, the night he was shot down on the Dortmund Ems canal raid.

Revie Walker and Harry Humphries were both devastated when they got the news, and each wrote heartfelt letters to the Hutchison family. Walker said: 'My two year friendship with Bob has convinced me that he was the finest lad I've ever had the pleasure of meeting.' Humphries said that he was 'badly cut up' and anxiously awaiting further news.

Robert Hutchison is buried along with the rest of George Holden's crew in Reichswald Forest Cemetery.

IWM COLLECTIONS TR1127

Plt Off F.M. Spafford DFM
Bomb aimer

Frederick Michael Spafford was always known by the nickname 'Spam' in his RAF days, reflecting the wartime ubiquity of the well-known luncheon meat. He was born as Frederick Michael Burke in Adelaide, South Australia, on 16 June 1918. After his parents died, he was adopted by his maternal grandfather and changed his surname to Spafford.

He joined the RAAF in September 1940 and, after training under the Empire Air Training Scheme, arrived in England in August 1941. After further training, he became a specialist bomb aimer and joined 50 Squadron in May 1942, first flying on Manchesters and then Lancasters.

He flew on most of his operations with pilot Hugh Everitt, one of 50 Squadron's most respected and decorated flyers. Spafford was decorated with a DFM in October 1942 for his skill and 'praiseworthy example'.

He was commissioned in January 1943, and he finished his tour in March. Along with his 50 Squadron colleague, Harlo Taerum, Spafford was then recruited for Gibson's crew. Both may have been recommended by Mick Martin. Spafford obviously hit it off with his new captain, who described him in *Enemy Coast Ahead* as 'a grand guy and many were the parties we had together; in his bombing he held the squadron record.'

On the Dams Raid itself, Gibson attacked first and although his mine was dropped correctly and skipped several times, it sank and exploded some 50yds short of the target. On his safe return, Spafford was awarded the DFC, and was interviewed by the press and on the radio, describing 'the secrecy and hazards of No 617's training for low-level flying, the elaborate briefings, and the attack which was carried out in bright moonlight against enemy fire.'[120]

When Gibson left, Spafford transferred to new CO George Holden's crew, although like Taerum and Hutchison he was technically 'tour expired'. He was killed when Holden was shot down on the raid on the Dortmund Ems canal, on 16 September 1943, and is buried in Reichswald Forest cemetery.

---

120 Australian Dictionary of Biography
     http://adb.anu.edu.au/biography/spafford-frederick-michael-11737
     [Accessed January 2018].

Flt Sgt G.A. Deering

Front gunner

Although of Irish descent, George Andrew Deering was actually born in Kirkintilloch, Scotland, on 23 July 1919. He was the only boy in the family of four children of Samuel and Martha Deering. The family emigrated to Canada when he was a small boy, and his mother died shortly afterwards. His sister, Charlotte, then became the family housekeeper.

Deering went to Essex public school in Toronto, and then trained on a correspondence course in aircraft designing and mechanics while in employment as a shoe worker. He joined the RCAF in July 1940, hoping to become a pilot. However he ended up qualifying as a wireless operator/air gunner and arrived in England in April 1941.

Deering spent about a year in 103 Squadron at RAF Elsham Wolds and completed a full tour of operations. He was then sent to an Operational Training Unit, and was commissioned in February 1943, although this information didn't seem to reach 617 Squadron until after the Dams Raid.

How Deering arrived on 617 Squadron and was then allocated to Gibson's crew is a bit of a mystery. In *Enemy Coast Ahead,* Gibson wrote that he was a novice but this is far from the truth:[121] 'In the front turret was Jim [sic] Deering from Toronto, Canada, and he was on his first [sic] bombing raid. He was pretty green, but one of our crack gunners had suddenly gone ill and there was nobody else for me to take.' Deering was in fact posted into 617 Squadron on 29 March, and had flown on a number of training flights with Gibson in the run up to the Dams Raid.

For his part in the raid, Deering was awarded a DFC, recognition at last that he was an officer by the time of the raid. Along with Taerum, Hutchison and Spafford he transferred to George Holden's crew, and died with all of them when they were shot down on the Dortmund Ems canal operation on 16 September 1943. He is buried in Reichswald Forest War Cemetery.

---

121 Gibson, *Enemy Coast Ahead*, p20.

Flt Lt R.D. Trevor-Roper DFM
Rear gunner

With more than fifty operations, Richard Trevor-Roper was probably the most experienced air gunner to take part in the Dams Raid, and was the squadron's Gunnery Leader. He was also the acknowledged leader of the squadron's hell-raisers, bringing to Scampton a reputation earned in many earlier RAF messes.

Richard Dacre Trevor-Roper[122] was born in Shanklin on the Isle of Wight on 19 May 1915, the son of Charles and Gertrude Trevor-Roper. After leaving Wellington College he spent two years in the Royal Artillery. At the outset of war he joined the RAF, and trained as a wireless operator/gunner.

He was posted to 50 Squadron in October 1940, then flying Hampdens at RAF Lindholme. Most of his operations were flown in the squadron commander Wg Cdr 'Gus' Walker's aircraft and he was recommended for a DFM in October 1941. The citation noted his outstanding service as a wireless operator, and that he had been responsible for the safe return of his crew when severe weather had been encountered. He was also an 'excellent Gunnery Leader' who had dowsed a number of searchlights on two occasions, and was an 'outstanding inspiration to his and all other aircrews'.

Trevor-Roper was commissioned in October 1941 and then spent some time instructing in training units. He went back to 50 Squadron in November 1942, and had flown on another twelve operations, mainly with Sqn Ldr Birch as pilot, before he was brought into 617 Squadron. Gibson obviously recognised Trevor-Roper as a soulmate, describing him in *Enemy Coast Ahead* as one of the 'real squadron characters', although noticing, in a thoughtful moment, that he was quiet on the flight out to the dams, perhaps because his wife was about to have their first baby. He had married Patricia Edwards in 1942 and their son Charles was born on 15 June 1943. (Trevor-Roper was one of four men whose wives were pregnant at the time of the Dams Raid. See also Charles Brennan, p126, David Maltby, p153, and Lewis Burpee, p254.)

After the raid, for which he received the DFC, Trevor-Roper came into his own, leading the pack in the drunken escapades which followed, principally the excursion to London in June for the investiture at Buckingham Palace and the subsequent dinner at the Hungaria restaurant. Card schools were established,

---

122 These are Trevor-Roper's correct forenames. A number of books mistakenly give him an extra forename 'Algernon'. This error would appear to have been originated by Gibson himself in *Enemy Coast Ahead* (p20), where he credits him not only with this single forename but also education at both Eton and Oxford. This might be dismissed as another example of how little Gibson knew about his crew members except for the fact that, as noted below, he furnished the correct facts that Trevor-Roper was married, his wife was living in Skegness and was pregnant.

hipflasks produced and trousers removed, not always voluntarily. The squadron adjutant, Harry Humphries, was a particular target, and various escapades are reported in Humphries's book, *Living with Heroes*. (The same stories appear again, in a more sanitised version, in Paul Brickhill's *The Dam Busters*.)

Eventually 617 Squadron went back on operations, but Trevor-Roper didn't join the core of the Gibson crew which transferred to the new CO, George Holden. In March 1944, after another period in a training unit, he was posted to 97 Squadron based at Bourn, and joined a very experienced crew captained by Flt Lt Rowlands. His luck ran out on Bomber Command's worst night of the whole war, on 30/31 March 1944, when ninety-five bombers were lost from a total of 795 which set out to attack Nuremberg. His aircraft was shot down near Ahorn, by the German nightfighter pilot Major Martin Drewes who claimed five 'kills' that night, and all on board died.

Richard Trevor-Roper is buried in Durnbach War Cemetery.

Crew 2: AJ-M
First wave: Shot down as it attacked Möhne Dam.
Lancaster serial number: ED925/G

Flt Lt J.V. Hopgood DFC and Bar
Pilot

John Vere Hopgood was born in Hurst, Berkshire on 29 August 1921, the son of Harold Hopgood, a solicitor and his second wife Grace. Harold Hopgood's first wife Beatrice had died in 1918, leaving him a widower with two young sons. Harold Hopgood had three more children with Grace, of whom John was the second, and the only boy. He was educated at Marlborough College, and would have gone on to Corpus Christi College, Cambridge, but the war intervened.

He joined the RAF in 1940, and qualified as a pilot in February 1941, and was then commissioned. He spent his first tour of operations flying with 50 Squadron and was then posted to a training unit. In February 1942, he went back onto operations with 106 Squadron, based at Coningsby, which was flying the unreliable two-engined Avro Manchesters. In April, a new Squadron CO, Guy Gibson arrived. He described his first impression of Hopgood in *Enemy Coast Ahead*:[123]

> He was a fair-haired chap about medium height, rather good-looking, except for one prominent tooth. The boys seemed to be always taking him off about this, but he took it very good-naturedly. He was a serious fellow at heart, though, even though he spent most of his time with the boys. As soon as I saw him I thought, 'What an ideal squadron type. I like that chap.'

The squadron was moving over to Lancasters, and Hopgood was one of the first to retrain on this much more powerful aircraft. He was one of the pilots who then had to pass on their new skills to Gibson, something he evidently did with quiet authority, another trait admired by the Squadron CO.

In October 1942, after flying forty-seven operations, he was awarded the DFC, and

---

123 Gibson, *Enemy Coast Ahead*, p175.

commended for his 'magnificent dash and courage when pressing home his attacks whatever the opposition'. This was followed just four months later by a Bar to the DFC for completing a number more successful operations since the first award.

Although Hopgood wasn't one of the flight commanders, Gibson wanted him by his side, and so he was made deputy leader of the attack on the Möhne Dam. As such, he was one of the four who were briefed about the target the night before the raid. At this, Hopgood suggested an important change to the already planned route, pointing out that it went near Hüls, which had heavy defences not marked on the map.

The following day, there were a series of extensive briefings. Then, after their meal and while waiting to board their aircraft, Hopgood was nervous. He sought out David Shannon, his old squadron comrade, and told him that he had a premonition that he wouldn't be returning. Gibson however engaged him with their usual pre-operational banter: 'Hoppy, tonight's the night; tomorrow we will get drunk.'

On the raid itself, Gibson, Hopgood and Mick Martin were the first trio from Wave One to take off. All went relatively smoothly until they reached a heavily defended airfield at Dülmen, where AJ-M was hit by flak and Hopgood and both gunners George Gregory and Tony Burcher were wounded. Hopgood however pressed on and attacked the Möhne Dam ten minutes after Gibson. His already damaged Lancaster was hit again by flak. An engine caught fire, he struggled to keep the aircraft level, and the mine was released too late, bouncing over the dam and into the power station below where it exploded. Somehow, Hopgood was able to gain some height, in an effort to give his crew a chance to bale out. John Fraser, John Minchin and Tony Burcher escaped but Minchin, badly injured, didn't survive the parachute drop. Fraser and Burcher were both captured and taken prisoner. The aircraft crashed in a field near Ostönnen, 6km from the dam. Hopgood, Brennan, Earnshaw and Gregory's bodies were found in the wreckage.

Neither Fraser nor Burcher ever forgot the heroic gesture by Hopgood which saved their lives. Fraser went back to Canada after the war and gave his children names which recognised Hopgood's memory.

Hopgood, Brennan, Earnshaw, Minchin and Gregory are buried together in Rheinberg War Cemetery.

Sgt C.C. Brennan
Flight engineer

Charles Christopher Brennan was born on 22 February 1916 in Calgary, Alberta, Canada and emigrated to the UK in 1928. He was one of the two Canadian-born flight engineers on the Dams Raid. (See also William Radcliffe, p234.)

Brennan joined the RAF in England at the outset of the war, and after training worked as ground crew. When the opportunity came for skilled ground crew to qualify as flight engineers for the heavy bombers, he took the chance, like many other enthusiastic young men who were keen to fly. His course at No 4 School of Technical Training at RAF St Athan finished in June 1942, and he was then posted to 106 Squadron. He joined Hopgood's crew, and flew on his first operation with him on 15 August, on a trip to Düsseldorf. Another fifteen operations followed over the next two months, the last being the attack on the Schneider factory at Le Creusot on 17 October, the final operation of Hopgood's tour.

For some reason, Brennan was not allocated to another crew to finish his tour. Instead, he was posted to 1660 Conversion Unit at Swinderby on 25 November, to train other crews. It would seem that he took the opportunity to fly again with Hopgood when his skipper joined the new squadron. He was posted to Scampton, and undertook his first training flight with Hopgood on 11 April 1943.

One can only wonder as to what conversation passed between Brennan and Hopgood when the young pilot was injured on the fateful journey to the dams. He would have needed all his flight engineering skill to help the pilot keep the aircraft aloft, as one of the engines was damaged and running on reduced revs. Tony Burcher recalls that Brennan was a 'calm chap', so having to hold a handkerchief over Hopgood's head wound at the same time may not have completely fazed him. When they were hit again, as they attacked the Möhne Dam, the pair

must have realised that they would never get off the flight deck themselves, and that all they could do was to give as many of their colleagues as possible the chance to escape. They were both remarkable men. The aircraft crashed in a field near Ostönnen, 6km from the dam. Hopgood, Brennan, Earnshaw and Gregory's bodies were found in the wreckage.

Brennan married Freda Pemberton in Leeds in 1940. He was one of the four men who took part in the Dams Raid when their wives were pregnant. (See also Richard Trevor-Roper, p122,

LINCOLNSHIRE COUNTY COUNCIL

David Maltby, p153 and Lewis Burpee, p254.) His daughter was born in Otley in October 1943.

Charles Brennan is buried in Rheinberg War Cemetery.

Flg Off K. Earnshaw
Navigator

Kenneth Earnshaw was born in Bridlington, Yorkshire, on 23 June 1918, the son of Joseph and Janet Earnshaw. His family emigrated to Canada a year later and took up farming in rural Alberta. He was educated at Camrose High School. He qualified as a teacher at Alberta Normal School in Edmonton, and then taught at Whitebush School in Bashaw, Alberta, before leaving to enlist in the RCAF. He married Mary Heather in November 1941, and they lived in Bashaw.

After training in Canada, at the end of which he was commissioned, he travelled over to England, and was posted to 50 Squadron in November 1942. He was part of a Lancaster crew which flew with pilot Norman Schofield; the crew's bomb aimer, fellow Canadian John Fraser, became a close friend. Together they flew on 30 operations in under six months. Gunner Brian Jagger, who would fly on the Dams Raid with David Shannon in AJ-L, was also in this crew.

By mid April 1943, they were scheduled to go to a training unit for the normal inter-tour rest period. However both Earnshaw and Fraser were recommended when a call came from the new 617 Squadron being set up at Scampton. Pilot John Hopgood needed two new crew members. His first navigator had fallen ill and his bomb aimer had not come up to scratch. Earnshaw and Fraser were recommended and arrived at Scampton at the end of April, some time after training for the Dams Raid had begun.

As navigator, Ken Earnshaw sat immediately behind John Hopgood and Charles Brennan in the cockpit. He must have seen the trouble Hopgood was in, hit by flak before they even reached the Möhne Dam. He had little chance of reaching the escape hatch when Hopgood ordered the crew to bale out, and he died when AJ-M crashed in a field near Ostönnen, 6km from the dam. Hopgood, Brennan, Earnshaw and Gregory's bodies were found in the wreckage.

Kenneth Earnshaw is buried in Rheinberg War Cemetery.

EARNSHAW FAMILY

Sgt J.W. Minchin
Wireless operator

John William Minchin was born on 29 November 1915 in the picturesque Gloucestershire village of Bourton-on-the-Water ('The Venice of the Cotswolds'). He was the third of the six sons of Bertram and Eliza Minchin. His father was a baker. He joined the RAF soon after the onset of war, and after training as a wireless operator/air gunner was posted to 49 Squadron at Scampton in October 1941.

He married Jessie Irving in London on 28 May 1942 but only got three days honeymoon before being recalled to his base to take part in the first Thousand Bomber raid.

In August 1942, he completed a full tour in both Hampdens and Manchesters, and was posted to a training unit. From there he went straight to join John Hopgood's crew in the new 617 Squadron. What happened to Minchin on the Dams Raid is told in an online extract from John Ward's book *Beware A Dog at War*:

> Minchin was badly wounded in the leg when M-Mother was hit by flak en-route to the Möhne Dam. Sgt Minchin sat for almost an hour at his radio set nursing this terrible injury before the target was reached.
>
> M-Mother, the second aircraft to attack, was severely hit by ack-ack on the run-in and set on fire. The bomb was released but hit the parapet wall and exploded. F/Lt Hopgood struggled valiantly to keep his blazing aircraft airborne in order for the crew to bale out.
>
> Tony Burcher evacuated his rear turret and made for the crew door.

> There he was confronted by the pained face of John Minchin, who had dragged himself the length of the fuselage, his leg almost severed.
>
> All Burcher could do to help his comrade was to clip on Minchin's parachute and push him out into the darkness, pulling his D-ring in the process. The Lancaster crashed 3 miles to the north-west of the dam and exploded in flames.[124]

The aircraft crashed in a field near Ostönnen. Hopgood, Brennan, Earnshaw and Gregory's

HUMPHRIES FAMILY COLLECTION

---

124 www.49squadron.co.uk/personnel_index/detail/Minchin_JW
     [Accessed January 2018].

bodies were found in the wreckage. Minchin's body was found about 2km from the crash site.

Tragically, just six weeks after the Dams Raid on 27 June 1943, the family lost another son, Ronald Buckland Minchin, aged 23, who served with 295 Squadron. Both are commemorated on the Bourton-on-the-Water War Memorial.

The Minchins were one of the three families who lost a son who took part in the Dams Raid and another son serving elsewhere in Bomber Command during the war. (See Harlo Taerum, p116, and David Horsfall, p147.)

John Minchin is buried in Rheinberg War Cemetery.

Flt Sgt J.W. Fraser
Bomb aimer

John William Fraser was born in Nanaimo, British Columbia, Canada on 22 September 1922 and joined the RCAF soon after the war started. After qualifying as a bomb aimer he arrived in England in April 1942, and shortly after was posted to 50 Squadron. There he flew a full tour of thirty operations, mostly with Canadian pilot Norman Schofield, whose crew also included two more people who would become Dambusters: another Canadian, the navigator Ken Earnshaw, and gunner Brian Jagger.

By mid April 1943, Fraser and Earnshaw were both scheduled to go to a training unit for the normal inter-tour rest period. However a call came from the new 617 Squadron being set up at Scampton. Pilot John Hopgood needed an experienced navigator and bomb aimer. His first navigator had fallen ill and his bomb aimer had not come up to scratch. Earnshaw and Fraser were recommended, and arrived at Scampton at the end of April, some time after training for the Dams Raid had begun. However, as Fraser had already arranged his wedding for 29 April, he was given special permission to have a day off.

On the Dams Raid itself, Hopgood's aircraft AJ-M was hit by flak well before they reached the Möhne Dam. One engine was damaged, Hopgood himself was wounded, as was George Gregory in the front turret. Fraser released the mine and it bounced over the dam, blowing up the power station on the other side.

But his Lancaster was doomed, and he baled out when Hopgood gave the order. He landed almost a mile away from where the aircraft

FRASER FAMILY

crashed, but was soon captured by the Germans. After interrogation, where he was forced to give some details of the mission, he was sent to a PoW camp.

Released at the end of the war, he saw his wife Doris again in May 1945 for the first time since the day after their wedding. They made their home in Canada. Fraser never forgot the sacrifice made by John Hopgood which saved the lives of two of his crew. The names of all of his children were chosen as a tribute to Hopgood and 617 Squadron. His first son has the given names John Hopgood; his daughter was called Shere, after Hopgood's home village; and his second son was called Guy, after the squadron CO.

Fraser worked in the forestry service, and fulfilled his lifetime ambition to qualify as a pilot. Unfortunately, he was killed in a flying accident, at Saltery Bay in British Columbia on 2 June 1962.

Plt Off G.H.F.G. Gregory
Front gunner

George Henry Ford Goodwin Gregory was born in Govan, Glasgow on 24 June 1917, one of the seven children of Edwin and Agnes Gregory. He worked as a printer before joining the RAF at the outset of the war. He had completed a full tour of operations as a gunner in 44 Squadron by the autumn of 1942, and received the DFM. He then moved on to a training unit and was commissioned. He went back onto operations in March 1943, and was posted to 617 Squadron where he joined John Hopgood's crew.

Gregory was married, but his wife Margaret had remained in Scotland. In the run up to the Dams Raid he was living at RAF Scampton, and sharing quarters with squadron adjutant Harry Humphries. In his memoirs, Humphries recalled the night before the raid:

> Old Greg was a tough proposition, tall, handsome and like most Scots, very independent. If he liked you, all well and good, If he disliked you, well at least you knew… [His] wife had been in Lincoln a few days previously and I really think he needed her in his strung up state. He did not know what he wanted to do. First he wanted to go out in his car and find a drink, then he wanted to play snooker, and then he would talk about bed… I said 'Come on old lad, let's go for a walk around the mess. It's getting damned hot in here.' … Just as we were leaving the anteroom John Hopgood, Gregory's pilot, spotted us and aimed an almost playful kick at his rear gunner's backside, which I am sure would have crippled him if it had landed. When I eventually separated

them, with Greg, needless to say, on top by
sheer brute force, Hopgood or 'Hoppy' as
we knew him, dragged himself painfully
to his feet. 'Just as I said,' he complained
loudly, 'air gunners are all bloody brawn
and no brains.'

They then walked back to their quarters, and
had a cup of tea with their batman in his kitchen:

> Greg was the first to move. 'I think I
> will go to bed,' he said, 'may be working
> tomorrow.' With that he had gone and little did I know that for Greg
> it was probably his last cup of tea in that kitchen. In fact it was his last
> night on earth.[125]

From Tony Burcher's account, we now know that it is likely that Gregory was
severely wounded some twenty minutes before Hopgood's aircraft reached
the Möhne Dam, as he wasn't answering his intercom. In the same flak attack
Hopgood, Minchin and Brennan himself were also wounded. However they
pressed on, the mine was dropped, and moments afterwards Hopgood told
the crew to bale out. According to John Fraser's post-war debriefing after his
release from PoW camp, it would seem that Gregory attempted to get back to
the rest area to retrieve his parachute but never escaped.

George Gregory is buried in Rheinberg War Cemetery.

Plt Off A.F. Burcher
Rear gunner

Anthony Fisher Burcher was born in Vaucluse in Sydney, Australia on 15 March
1922, the fifth of the twelve children of Harvey and Estelle Burcher. He worked
as a wool sorter before volunteering for the RAAF. He arrived in England in
September 1941 and after further training was posted to 106 Squadron. His
first operation was the Thousand Bomber raid on 1 June 1942 when he attacked
Essen in the crew of Wrt Off Peter Merrals. He went on to join Sgt James Cas-
sels's crew where he completed a full tour in November.[126]

---

125 Humphries, *Living with Heroes*, pp1–3.
126 Robert Owen, Steve Darlow, Sean Feast, Arthur Thorning, *Dam Busters: Failed to
Return,* Fighting High 2013, p50.

Burcher was a complicated character and although he was at one point put onto a 'dry' stint by his CO Guy Gibson for scrapping in the mess, Gibson obviously respected his gunnery skills as he was then transferred to the Gunnery Leaders Course at Sutton Bridge in Lincolnshire, with a commission. He also received the DFM for his tour of operations, with the citation particularly noting his part in a skirmish on a trip to Saarbrucken when five enemy fighters were attacked and driven off.

After completing the Gunnery Leaders Course, Burcher was sent to 1654 Conversion Unit at Wigsley as an instructor. One of the pilots there was Mick Martin and according to Burcher's account[127] when Gibson telephoned Martin to ask him to join the new squadron he was told to bring Burcher along as well. As he knew Hopgood from 106 Squadron, he was placed in his crew.

On the Dams Raid itself, Burcher, in the rear turret, could only hear what was going on in the front of the aircraft via the intercom. It would seem that when AJ-M was hit by flak some twenty minutes before the dam was reached, Burcher received superficial wounds to the leg and stomach.

When Hopgood gave the order to bale out after the aircraft was hit again on the final attack, the wounded John Minchin managed to drag himself towards the rear escape hatch, with one leg almost severed. Burcher pushed his colleague out of the hatch first, pulling his parachute ripcord as he did so, and then followed him. Sadly, Minchin did not survive the drop, but Burcher did and he and John Fraser, who had escaped from the front of the aircraft, were captured separately and taken prisoner.

On release from PoW camp in 1945, Burcher married Joan Barnes, a WAAF who had also served in 106 Squadron. They moved to Australia where Burcher continued service with the RAAF, and they had two daughters. At some point in the late 1940s his conduct became unsatisfactory and he suffered a number of health problems. His superiors speculated that some of this behaviour might have been caused by the effects of his wartime experiences. He was transferred to RAAF Overseas Headquarters in London in 1950, and was eventually discharged there in 1952, at the rank of Flight Lieutenant. He was repatriated to Australia at his own expense later that year.

---

127 Burcher, interview with Ken Llewelyn, RAAF, 10 May 1993. This information cannot be confirmed.

He eventually returned to the UK and worked in various businesses. In 1961 he was found guilty of being involved in a criminal fraud case, and was given a prison sentence.[128] He then returned to Australia, and died in Hobart, Tasmania, on 9 August 1995.

128 Details from Flt Lt A.F. Burcher, RAAF personnel file, National Archives of Australia.

Crew 3: AJ-P
First wave: Attacked Möhne Dam and returned to base.
Lancaster serial number: ED909/G

Flt Lt H.B. Martin DFC
Pilot

Harold Brownlow Martin was universally known throughout his long RAF career by his nickname 'Mick'. He was born in the Sydney suburb of Edgecliff, Australia on 27 February 1918, the son of Dr Joseph Martin and his wife Colina. He went to Randwick High School, Sydney Grammar School and Lyndfield College. Before the war, Martin seemed destined for the medical profession like his father. In 1939 he had accepted a place at a medical school in Edinburgh, but shortly after he arrived in Britain his intentions were overtaken by the outbreak of war. He first joined the Australian army, but then in 1940, he transferred to the RAF, and began pilot training. He qualified as a pilot in June 1941, and his first operational posting came in October, when he was sent to 455 (Australia) Squadron, an RAAF outfit flying Hampdens. Two of his regular crew came to include fellow Australians Jack Leggo as navigator and Toby Foxlee as wireless operator/gunner.

On 18 February 1942, another Australian gunner, Tom Simpson, arrived on the squadron and was immediately assimilated into the crew. They flew on a trip to Cologne that night, thereby becoming the first all-Australian crew to fly on operations over Germany. When Simpson reported for duty to the gunnery section the following day, the officer in charge said that he would get him crewed up. Simpson replied:

> 'I am crewed up. I flew last night.' He looked at me in quite blank amazement and said 'Well, who did you fly with? I wasn't told anything about it.'
>
> I said: 'I flew with a Pilot Officer who told me his name was Martin … a Sergeant Foxlee told me that I was in his crew.' The Flight Lieutenant then said 'Well, there's not much hope for you if that's the case because Martin is as mad as a grasshopper; he likes flying his own style.'[129]

The crew went on a further dozen operations together until, in April 1942, 455 Squadron were transferred to Coastal Command. Martin, Leggo, Foxlee and

---

129 Simpson, *Lower than Low*, p40.

This picture of Mick Martin's crew looks like the work of a professional photographer, but cannot be traced in any publication. It must date from the period between September 1943 when Jack Leggo left the crew and February 1944 when Bob Hay was killed. (Left to right) Tom Simpson, unknown welfare officer, Toby Foxlee, Mick Martin, Ivan Whittaker, Bob Hay.

Simpson then moved to 50 Squadron in order to continue their tour in Bomber Command. 50 Squadron was flying Manchesters at the time, but was in the process of moving over to the more powerful Lancasters. Three more Australians (Plt Off Burton, Sgt Paton and Sgt Smith) joined the Martin crew on their first 50 Squadron sortie, the Thousand Bomber raid which attacked Cologne on 30 May 1942. They thereby became the first ever all-Australian crew to fly a Manchester operationally.

By October 1942, Martin had completed his tour, with thirty-six operations, and was awarded the DFC. He had acquired a reputation both as a low flying specialist but also as someone who prepared meticulously for an operation, personally polishing the Perspex on his cockpit canopy, since a smear could easily obscure an approaching fighter. He demanded the same high standards from those who flew with him. According to Max Hastings, he and his crew 'achieved an almost telepathic mutual understanding and instinct for danger.'[130]

It must have been at the investiture ceremony for this DFC that Martin first met Guy Gibson. It is recorded that it was there that they had a conversation

130 Max Hastings, *Bomber Command,* Pan 1999, p165.

about low flying methods. A few months later, Martin was just coming to the end of a spell as an instructor in 1654 Conversion Unit at Wigsley. Gibson recalled the earlier conversation and was quick to recruit him for the new project.

Martin set about bringing back together a crew mainly based on old 50 Squadron comrades, with a New Zealander from 75 Squadron, Len Chambers, as wireless operator. He also seems to have been instrumental in bringing in other men to the new squadron, often other comrades from 50 Squadron.

On the Dams Raid, Martin lined up to attack the Möhne Dam just minutes after disaster had overtaken Hopgood. Gibson joined his attack, flying slightly ahead on his starboard side. This tactic seemed to distract the dam's gunners and Martin was able to drop his mine correctly. However, something must have gone wrong as the mine veered off to the left and exploded some 20 yards short. Later, as both Young and Maltby attacked, Martin joined Gibson in diversionary tactics, putting himself at further risk. Luckily, although one of his fuel tanks was damaged it had already been emptied, and he was able to fly back to Scampton when the Möhne was breached.

After the Dams Raid, Martin was a key figure in many of the celebrations and at the investiture in London, where he received the DSO. The Australian press and broadcasters were very keen to have pictures of their boys shown back at home, and with his distinctive moustache Martin was often recognised.

In September 1943, Martin was acting CO of 617 Squadron in the unhappy circumstances following the catastrophic attack on the Dortmund Ems canal when six pilots and most of their crews were lost in two days. Strangely, this was the only period during the war when he took command of a squadron.

Later, when Leonard Cheshire arrived, Martin participated in attacks on targets in France, Italy and Germany. In February 1944, during an abortive attack on the Antheor Viaduct in the French Riviera, Martin's Lancaster was hit by ground fire, killing the bomb aimer Bob Hay, and causing Martin to force land his crippled aircraft in Sardinia. This was Martin's forty-ninth (and last) heavy bomber operation. However he flew another thirty-four operations in Mosquitos in 515 Squadron.

Martin stayed on in the RAF after the war, and had a distinguished career. He broke the speed record for flying from England to Cape Town in a Mosquito, and then went on to a succession of staff jobs including being an ADC to the Queen, C-in-C RAF Germany and the Air Member for Personnel. He was knighted and rose to the rank of Air Marshal before retiring in 1974. Martin was described by Ralph Cochrane as being the greatest pilot the RAF produced during the war.[131] There would be few who would dispute this view.

Martin married his wife Wendy Lawrence in 1944, and they had two daughters. He died in London on 3 November 1988 after complications following a road accident. He is buried in Gunnersbury Cemetery in London.

Plt Off I. Whittaker
Flight engineer

Ivan Whittaker was born in Newcastle on Tyne on 9 September 1921, the younger of the two sons of William and Jane Whittaker. His father was a seagoing marine engineer. Whittaker attended Wallsend Grammar School and then, in 1938, he joined the RAF as an apprentice at the No 1 School of Technical Training at RAF Halton. He spent the first three years of the war as ground crew. In 1942, he retrained as a flight engineer and was soon posted to 50 Squadron. There he met Mick Martin and flew with him on a number of operations. When he was called into 617 Squadron, Martin gathered together most of his old crew with the newly commissioned Whittaker sitting beside him in the flight engineer's seat.

After the raid, he was promoted again and won his first DFC in September 1943, overdue recognition for a tour completed a year previously. The Martin crew carried on flying throughout the autumn and winter and on 12 February 1944 set off on an operation to attack the Antheor viaduct in Southern France. This was a disaster. Martin's aircraft was hit by a shell which killed bomb aimer Bob Hay, wounded Whittaker and damaged the aircraft severely. Martin's supreme skill as a pilot and Whittaker's careful handling of the engines meant that they were able to make a dangerous landing at a tiny airport in Sardinia.

For his part in this, Whittaker received a Bar to his DFC, and is thought to be the only flight engineer with the double award.

Part of the citation read: 'Whilst over the target the aircraft was repeatedly hit and sustained much damage. Flight Lieutenant Whittaker was

HUMPHRIES FAMILY COLLECTION

---

131 Brickhill, *Dam Busters*, p163.

wounded in both legs but, in spite of this he coolly made a detailed examination of the aircraft and gave his Captain a full report of the damage sustained. He displayed great fortitude and devotion to duty and his efforts were of much assistance to his Captain who flew the damaged bomber to an airfield where a safe landing was effected.'

In March 1944, after forty-four operations, he was finally transferred into a training unit, where he served to the end of the war. He stayed on in the RAF after the war, eventually transferring to the Technical Branch and rising to the rank of Group Captain, finally retiring in 1974.

Whittaker was married with three sons. The family lived in Wendover, near the Halton base where he had first joined the RAF before the war, and he died in its hospital on 22 August 1979.

Flt Lt J.F. Leggo DFC
Navigator

Jack Frederick Leggo was born in Sydney on 21 April 1916, the son of Frederick Henry Leggo and Leah Druce. He was brought up in Newcastle, New South Wales and went to Newcastle High School. He then worked as a bank clerk before joining the RAAF shortly after the outbreak of war.

Like many other Australians, he did part of his training in Canada. After qualifying as a navigator he arrived in England and was posted to 455 (Australia) Squadron, where he crewed up with Mick Martin in the autumn of 1941. Toby Foxlee and Tom Simpson joined Martin and Leggo in the crew over the next few months, and the fact that all four stayed together for almost two years illustrates the bond between them. In April 1942, 455 Squadron

moved to Coastal Command but the four Australians transferred together to 50 Squadron, a heavy bomber squadron, and retrained on Manchesters and Lancasters. They completed a tour there, and then went off separately to various training units. Leggo received a DFC for his work on the completed tour.

When Martin was asked to join the new 617 Squadron, he brought his old team together as the core of the crew of AJ-P. Leggo was made the Squadron Navigation Officer, responsible for all the other navigators.

After the raid, for which he received a Bar to his DFC, he carried on flying with Martin for a while, but then he put in for retraining as a pilot. Martin supported him in this, praising him for his exemplary character, loyalty, conscientiousness, and devotion to duty. 'No higher standard could be asked for,' he added. Leggo qualified as a pilot and moved to 10 Squadron in Coastal Command, where he flew Sunderland flying boats for the rest of the war.

He returned to Australia after the war and went into the sugar industry in Queensland. He married Mary Best in 1947 and they had three children. After a successful business career he received a knighthood in 1982. He died in Brisbane on 14 November 1983.

Flg Off L. Chambers
Wireless operator

Len Chambers was born in Karamea, New Zealand on 18 February 1919. He joined the RNZAF in September 1940. After qualifying as a wireless operator/air gunner, he arrived in England where he was posted to a training unit and then 460 Squadron, an RAAF squadron. He flew on twenty operations there, before being transferred to 75 (NZ) Squadron, where he flew a further thirty-seven operations and became the Squadron Signals Leader.

When Mick Martin joined 617 Squadron he brought most of his old 50 Squadron crew with him, but was short of a wireless operator, so Chambers was brought in. He was awarded a DFC for his part in the raid.

After the raid, he flew on six further sorties before leaving 617 Squadron at the same time as Jack Leggo, in order to qualify as a pilot. However, he did not, apparently, ever fly on any operations in this role.

He returned to New Zealand in November 1944, and left the RNZAF in 1945. After the war, he worked as a carpenter and builder. He died in his native Karamea on 1 March 1985.

CHAMBERS FAMILY

Flt Lt R.C. Hay
Bomb aimer

Aged 30, with a wife and daughter back in Australia, Bob Hay was slightly older than the rest of Mick Martin's crew. Born in Renmark, South Australia on 4 November 1913, Robert Claude Hay was the son of John and Margaret Hay. He attended Renmark High School and graduated from Roseworthy Agricultural College in 1935, where he also excelled in sports. The college swimming pool is now named in his honour.

He joined the RAAF in the summer of 1940, trained in Australia and Canada and arrived in England a year later. His first posting was to 455 (Australia) Squadron, where his time coincided with future colleagues Mick Martin and his crew. Like them, in April 1942 he was posted to 50 Squadron to fly on heavy bombers when 455 Squadron moved to Coastal Command.

He served a full tour of operations, flying mainly as navigator with one of the squadron's best known pilots, Sqn Ldr Hugh Everitt, in a crew which also contained fellow Aussie and future 617 Squadron colleague, Fred 'Spam' Spafford.

By the time 617 Squadron was formed, Hay had been commissioned and been awarded the DFC. As an Australian from 50 Squadron he slotted easily into the crack Martin crew, and his slight age advantage and extensive experience made him the obvious choice for the important role as the squadron's Bombing Leader.

This new job meant that within days of his arrival, he flew to Manston with Gibson to watch a test drop of the new Upkeep weapon at Reculver. The first, dropped by a Wellington, was successful, but the second, dropped by a Lancaster, broke up. Flying back in a small Magister, he and Gibson had a lucky escape when its single engine failed. Gibson managed to crashland in a field full of devices designed to stop enemy gliders landing.

Hay was one of the four who were told the target on the night before the raid, along with Melvin Young, Henry Maudslay and John Hopgood. Although the rest of the squadron didn't know for certain when the operation would take place news that they had been summoned to a meeting in Charles Whitworth's house led to fevered speculation on the base.

Earlier that day, Hay and most of the rest of Martin's crew had been on board AJ-P after it had been loaded with its mine. Intelligence officer Fay Gillon was also inside the aircraft, being given a tour. Suddenly, with a crash, the mine dropped onto the ground and everyone on board and outside beat a hasty retreat in case it exploded. The weapon hadn't been fused, so it did not explode but its delicate mechanism may have been damaged, as when it was finally dropped at the Möhne Dam, it veered to the left and exploded at the side.

Hay received a bar to his DFC for his role on the raid, and played his part in the celebrations that followed. He can be seen in the raucous photo taken at the Hungaria Restaurant, wedged between Tom Simpson and Toby Foxlee, with a glass in his hand.

After the raid, Martin's crew eventually went back on operations, although Leggo and Chambers eventually left to train as pilots. A new CO, Leonard Cheshire, arrived and Hay spent a lot of time working on training his bomb aimers to use a new device, the Stabilised Automatic Bomb Sight (SABS).

Several months passed until February 1944 when, under Cheshire's leadership, a detachment set off to bomb the Antheor Viaduct in southern France, an important rail link to Italy.

Paul Brickhill devotes a whole chapter of *The Dam Busters* to what happened to Martin's crew on this operation, describing in vivid detail his bombing run and the way the aircraft rocked as it was hit by a cannon shell which exploded in the ammunition tray under the front turret.

> Martin was calling the roll round his crew. The tough little Foxlee was all right. Bob Hay did not answer. Whittaker gave him a twisted grin, swearing and hunched, holding his legs. The rest were all right. He called Hay twice more but there was only silence, so he said 'Toby, see if Bob's all right. His intercom must be busted.' Foxlee swung out of his turret and wormed towards the nose. He lifted his head towards Martin. 'He's lying on the floor. Not moving.'[132]

Eventually Martin managed to land his battered Lancaster in Sardinia, on a small airfield run by the Americans. Hay's body was removed from the aircraft and he was buried the next day in a cemetery in Cagliari. He was the only one of Martin's Dams Raid crew who did not survive the war. Martin was himself quite shaken by the episode, and did not fly again on operations with 617 Squadron. A few months later, however, he had recovered his poise and was back in a Mosquito squadron.

After Hay's death, the Principal of Roseworthy Agricultural College wrote:

---

132 Brickhill, *The Dam Busters,* pp154-5.

> We were shocked with the news of the loss of Flt Lt Robert Claude Hay, DFC and Bar and African Star, a much respected and loved member of the College staff and the Gold Medalist in 1935. Before his enlistment in 1940 he was assistant horticulturist at the college. Both as a member of the staff and as a student Bob Hay, with his happy, carefree disposition, more nearly symbolised the life of an agricultural college student than anyone I've known.

Hay had married Honoria (Edna) Thomson in 1938. They had one daughter.

Plt Off B.T. Foxlee DFM
Front gunner

Bertie Towner Foxlee was always known by his nickname 'Toby'. His unusual second name was his mother's maiden name, and was given to him in honour of his uncle, Edgar Towner, who had won the VC in the Australian 2nd Machine Gun Battalion on the Western Front in 1918.

Foxlee was born in Queensland, Australia on 7 March 1920, the son of Herbert and Olive Foxlee. He joined the RAAF in 1940 and trained in Australia and Canada as a wireless operator/air gunner. After further training on arrival in England, he was posted to 455 (Australia) Squadron at Swinderby, where he quickly joined up with Mick Martin and Jack Leggo. Their first operation, in a Hampden, was on 2 January 1942.

After fourteen operations Martin and his crew transferred to 50 Squadron. Foxlee went on to complete a tour of thirty-four operations by 13 September, and was then transferred to a training unit. He received the DFM for his work on the first tour, and was commissioned. In early April 1943, he joined up with

Mick Martin, Jack Leggo and Tammy Simpson again, in the new 617 Squadron, practising for the Dams Raid.

After the raid, he carried on flying with Mick Martin on all his operations. Like his pilot, on 13 February 1944, Foxlee was taken off operations after the Antheor Viaduct trip. He received the DFC in April 1944, and spent the rest of the war instructing in a training unit.

He left the RAAF in 1948, returning to Britain to join the RAF where he worked as an air traffic controller. He married Thelma Madge

IWM COLLECTIONS CH9942

Peacock in 1948 and they had five children. Foxlee finally retired from the RAF in 1957 and, after farming for a while in Kent, took the whole family to live in Australia in 1962. He came back to Britain once more in 1977, and died in Nottingham on 6 March 1985.

Flt Sgt T.D. Simpson
Rear gunner

Thomas Drayton Simpson was born in Hobart, Tasmania on 23 November 1917, the middle of the three children of Thomas Simpson and his wife. His father was a lawyer, and Simpson himself began legal training before enlisting in the RAAF in 1940. On arrival in England, he was first posted to 97 Squadron at Coningsby in October 1941, and flew five operations on Manchesters. In February 1942, he was transferred to 455 (Australia) Squadron who were still flying the older Hampdens, where he quickly teamed up with Mick Martin. It was Martin that gave him the nickname 'Tammy'.

In April 1942, Martin and his crew transferred to 50 Squadron, which meant Simpson was back on heavy bombers. Their first sortie, in a Manchester, was to Cologne on 30 May 1942, the first Thousand Bomber raid, when they became the first ever all-Australian crew to fly a Manchester operationally. By the end of June, they were flying Lancasters. By October Simpson had completed a tour of thirty-seven operations, including his spell at 97 Squadron, and was posted to a training unit. In early April 1943, he joined up with Mick Martin, Jack Leggo and Toby Foxlee again, in the new 617 Squadron, practising for the Dams Raid. He received the DFM for his role on the raid.

After the raid, Simpson carried on flying with Mick Martin on his subsequent 617 Squadron operations, fourteen in all. Like Martin and Foxlee, in February 1944, he was taken off operations after the Antheor Viaduct trip, in which Bob Hay was killed. He had applied for pilot training in the autumn of 1943, but in the end he was posted to an Operational Training Unit for the remainder of the war.

He returned to Tasmania after discharge from the RAAF, and resumed his law studies. He was called to the Bar in 1949, and worked as a lawyer thereafter. He married Esme Reid after the war and they had four children.

Simpson died in Hobart on 2 April 1998.

Crew 4: AJ-A
First wave: Attacked Möhne Dam. Shot down on return journey.
Lancaster serial number: ED887/G

Sqn Ldr H.M. Young DFC and Bar
Pilot
Henry Melvin Young was born in Belgravia, London, on 20 May 1915.[133] His
father was a solicitor, although he was serving in the army at the time of his
birth. His mother was American, from a wealthy Californian family involved
in the real estate business. He had a somewhat disjointed upbringing, spending several years in the USA during his schooldays. He spent two years at Kent
School in Connecticut before leaving at the age of 17 to spend a year at Westminster School in London. He then went up to Trinity College, Oxford to study
law. He had taken up rowing at school and carried on at Oxford, gaining a Blue
for rowing for the university in the 1938 Boat Race. (A rowing contemporary at
Trinity College was Richard Hillary, later to gain wartime fame as a fighter pilot
and the author of *The Last Enemy*.)

Young joined the Oxford University Air Squadron and qualified as a pilot. Another student member was Leonard Cheshire, and Young's instructor
was Charles Whitworth, then an RAF Flight Lieutenant, and later to become
station CO at Scampton at the time of the Dams Raid. Whitworth was fairly
critical of Young's abilities, describing him as 'not a natural pilot' although noting that he had 'improved considerably' and 'was very keen and has plenty of
common sense'.

Young joined the RAFVR in September 1938 and when war came a year later
began formal training to be a service pilot. During this period he wrote to the
headmaster of his old school in Connecticut, in terms which are expressed very
similarly to those of his Oxford contemporary, Richard Hillary:

> Since we had to have a war, I am more than ever glad that I am in the
> air force ... though I haven't yet had to face any of the conflict and
> killing of war, I am not frightened of dying if that is God's will and
> only hope that I may die doing my duty as I should. In the meantime, I
> remain as cheerful, I think, as ever and try to keep others so.[134]

---

133 This account of Young's life is substantially derived from Thorning, *Dambuster who
     Cracked the Dam*.
134 Letter Melvin Young to Rev F.H. Sill, 18 March 1940, quoted in Thorning, *Dambuster
     who Cracked the Dam*, p39.

Young's first operational posting in June 1940 was to 102 Squadron, flying Whitleys. Some of their bombing operations took them as far as Turin in north Italy. It was during this tour that his 'ditchings' took place. The first was on 7 October 1940 when he and his crew spent twenty-two hours in a dinghy in the Atlantic, while on convoy escort duty. The second was on 23 November 1940 in the English Channel south of Plymouth. He finished his tour in February 1941, and was awarded the DFC.

PRESIDENT AND FELLOWS, TRINITY COLLEGE, OXFORD

In September 1941, after a spell at a training unit, Young was promoted to Squadron Leader and started a second tour with 104 Squadron on Wellingtons. A detachment of fifteen aircraft and crews from 104 Squadron was then sent to Malta and then on to Egypt. There he completed another tour, and received a Bar to his DFC.

In July 1942, he was posted to the RAF Delegation in Washington DC. While he was in the USA, he got married to his American girlfriend, Priscilla Rawson. However, he had to leave his new wife behind when he was posted back to England in February 1943. He was sent to 1660 Conversion Unit at RAF Swinderby to begin training on the heavy bomber, the Lancaster, which had come into service in his absence. He began training on 1 March 1943 and it was at this point he was allocated the crew with which he would fly on the Dams Raid. The crew had been without a pilot since their skipper had been sent on sick leave in January. Young first flew a training flight with his new crew on about 4 March, and undertook some fifteen more in the next seven days.

On 13 March they were all posted to 57 Squadron at Scampton, with Young being given command of its new C Flight. Four existing 57 Squadron crews – those captained by Flt Lt Bill Astell, Plt Off Geoff Rice, Sgt George Lancaster and Sgt Ray Lovell – were moved into the new flight.

In the normal course of events, this C Flight would have been built up further, but this was not to be. Within a few days, all five crews in the flight were transferred into a new squadron being established alongside 57 Squadron on the same station.

None of these crews were personally selected by Guy Gibson. But because Young was an experienced pilot with a DFC and Bar and already on the station, it must have been logical for someone at 5 Group HQ to suggest that he and the rest of his flight simply transfer in. Perhaps Young's old flying instructor Charles Whitworth, the station commander at Scampton, had a hand in this.

In the event, only three of the crews – those skippered by Young, Astell and Rice – finally flew on the Dams Raid.

Young's seniority and administrative skills made him the obvious choice to be a flight commander, and it fell to him and his fellow flight commander Henry Maudslay to do a lot of the necessary organising to get more than twenty crews ready for such an important mission. He was popular amongst his fellow officers, with his prowess at beer drinking and eccentric habit of sitting cross-legged on either a desk or the floor much admired. This popularity may have led to his nickname of Dinghy being chosen as the code word to signify a successful attack on the Eder Dam.

On the raid, Young led the second formation in Lancaster AJ-A, the other two being piloted by David Maltby and David Shannon. This trio arrived at the Möhne Dam just a couple of minutes before Gibson began the first attack. By the time Young's turn came, a certain amount of desperation must have been creeping in. Gibson and Martin's mines had not been successful and Hopgood had been shot down.

Young's perfect run resulted in a small breach in the dam wall. This only became obvious ten minutes later when David Maltby, following up with the next mine, saw that the crest of the dam was crumbling. The two explosions combined caused the final collapse. Young was then instructed to go with Gibson to oversee the assault on the Eder Dam, ready to assume command if Gibson was lost. So he witnessed its collapse and then set course for home.

Sadly, he never made it. A gun battery at Castricum-aan-Zee on the Dutch coast reported shooting down an aircraft at 0258, which was almost certainly AJ-A. Two bodies, one Young and the other an unidentified sergeant, were washed ashore on 29 May and they were buried nearby in the General Cemetery at Bergen two days later. The sergeant was later identified as David Horsfall, who would have been sitting alongside Young in the cockpit. The bodies of all seven of the crew of AJ-A were washed up over a period of thirteen days.

Sgt D.T. Horsfall
Flight engineer

David Taylor Horsfall was born in Bramley, Yorkshire on 16 April 1920, the older of the two sons of Robinson and Emma Horsfall. The family moved to Barnsley, and both he and his brother Albert went to Barnsley Grammar School. David joined the RAF in 1936 as a boy entrant at the No 1 School of Technical Training at RAF Halton. He served in ground crew until 1942.

He then took the opportunity to retrain as a flight engineer on heavy

bombers, and met up with his future crew at 1660 Conversion Unit at RAF Swinderby in late 1942. The crew was left pilotless when its skipper Sgt Graham Bower went sick on 14 January 1943. so Horsfall's first operation was to the difficult destination of Berlin on 16 January along with colleagues, Lawrence Nichols, Gordon Yeo and Wilfred Ibbotson, in a Lancaster piloted by Plt Off Vincent Duxbury, an instructor. He flew on a second operation to Berlin the following day, with Flg Off Harold Southgate as pilot, returning on three engines after one failed on the way home.

Melvin Young joined the Conversion Unit later, in early March and took over this new crew there. The full crew were then transferred to 57 Squadron at Scampton on 13 March. On 25 March, they were all reposted to the new 617 Squadron.

The Dams Raid was therefore Horsfall's third operation, and one that they would all have thought had gone well, until they were caught by a burst of flak at the very last moment of real danger.

David Horsfall's body was washed ashore on 29 May, along with his skipper. They were buried together in Bergen General Cemetery.

David Horsfall's brother, Albert, had been killed in 1940 serving as a navigator in 50 Squadron. The Horsfalls were one of the three families who lost a son who took part in the Dams Raid and another son serving elsewhere in Bomber Command during the war. (See Harlo Taerum, p116, and John Minchin, p128.)

Flt Sgt C.W. Roberts
Navigator

Charles Walpole Roberts was born on 19 January 1921 in Northrepps, a village near Cromer in Norfolk. He was the only son of Charles Augustus and Dorcas Roberts. Their marriage broke down when he was very young, and his father moved to Devon. Roberts was brought up by his mother and grandmother, educated at the village school before entering the nearby Paston School, famous as the alma mater of Lord Nelson.

Roberts enrolled in the RAF in 1940, and was selected for training as a pilot. He was sent out to Rhodesia for training at an Elementary Flying Training School. Like many would-be pilots, he ended up qualifying as a navigator.

He then crewed up with Lawrence Nichols and John Beesley in 10 Operational Training Unit at RAF Abingdon in July 1942. The crew was skippered by Graham Bower. On 10 and 13 September, Roberts flew on two operations with Bower, trips to Düsseldorf and Bremen. The crew moved on to 1660 Conversion Unit later that year. Although the crew took part in a raid on Berlin on 16 January 1943, after Bower's departure, Roberts was replaced as navigator by an instructor, Flt Lt V. Blair. Melvin Young joined the Conversion Unit later, in early March, and took over the old Bower crew there.

The full crew were then transferred to 57 Squadron at Scampton on 13 March. On 25 March, they were all reposted to the new 617 Squadron.

Roberts was one of the most inexperienced navigators to fly on the Dams Raid, but he acquitted himself well on the flight to the Möhne Dam, as the trio of Young, Maltby and Shannon maintained formation throughout the trip. Roberts was engaged to Irene Mountney, a WAAF who worked at Scampton packing parachutes.

AJ-A was shot down at the last moment of danger shortly after they had passed over the Dutch coast. On 19 May, Charles Roberts's body was the first of those of the crew of AJ-A to be washed ashore, and he was buried two days later in Bergen General Cemetery.

Sgt L.W. Nichols
Wireless operator

Lawrence William Nichols was born in Northwood, Middlesex on 17 May 1910, and therefore died early in the morning of his 33rd birthday.

Nichols was the oldest of the four children of Edward and Florence Nichols. Edward Nichols was a coal merchant. Lawrence Nichols had married his wife Georgina in 1933, and they had two children. He had worked as a haberdasher in Oxford Street and then as manager of a branch of Currys in North Harrow before volunteering for the RAF in 1940.

After qualifying as a wireless operator/air gunner he then crewed up with Charles Roberts and John Beesley in 10 Operational Training Unit at RAF Abingdon in July 1942, in a crew skippered by Graham Bower. On 13 September, Nichols went on his first operation, flying with Bower on a raid on Bremen.

The crew moved on to 1660 Conversion Unit later that year. On 16 January 1943, after Bower's departure, he went on his second operation, to Berlin with Vincent Duxbury as pilot. Melvin Young joined the Conversion Unit later, in early March and took over this new crew there. The full crew were then transferred to 57 Squadron at Scampton on 13 March. On 25 March, they were all reposted to the new 617 Squadron.

Nichols was a horse racing enthusiast and had plans to set up as a bookmaker after the war, with financial help from his brother Horace, who was running the family coal business. On 5 May 1943, he wrote to his other brother Gerry, who was serving in the army in India, about their plans: 'There is no opposition at all in Northwood and I think it would do very well … after all we are very well known and should get plenty of clients.' He went on to describe to Gerry how he and Horace had cycled over to Windsor to the Easter Monday race meeting. They both backed five winners and also got a successful tip for a race at Pontefract, where they made yet more money.[135]

His colleague, front gunner Gordon Yeo, knew well about his betting skills. He told his parents in a letter sent shortly before the crews took off on the raid that 'Larry (Nichols) our Wireless Operator went to Windsor races last Saturday (1st May) [sic] and won about £12, but he was born lucky.' Maybe he was, but sadly his luck ran out when he died along with the rest of the crew when they were shot down by a gun battery at Castricum-aan-Zee.

Lawrence Nichols's body was washed ashore on 27 May 1943, along with those of Vincent MacCausland and Gordon Yeo. They were all buried in Bergen General Cemetery.

Flg Off V.S. MacCausland
Bomb aimer

Vincent Sanford MacCausland was born in Tyne Valley, Prince Edward Island, Canada on 1 February 1913. He was the oldest of the five children of Burns and Edith MacCausland and worked as a teacher before joining the RCAF in 1940. After training as an observer and then a bomb aimer he completed a first tour in 57 Squadron in late 1941. He received a commission and then spent more than a year in a training unit as an instructor. Keen to get back to a second

135 Lawrence Nichols, letter to Gerry Nichols, 5 May 1943, Ray Hepner collection.

BOMBER COMMAND MUSEUM OF CANADA

tour, which was well overdue, he returned to 57 Squadron in March 1943. His return roughly coincided with the arrival of the inexperienced crew skippered by Melvin Young.

When it was decided that Young's bomb aimer was not suitable for the mission being planned, MacCausland fitted the bill for a replacement. Already at Scampton, with a tour under his belt and further experience training other bomb aimers he could be expected to slot in easily, and he was therefore drafted into Young's crew on 14 April 1943. In a letter home soon afterwards he told his mother what had happened:

You are perhaps wondering what I am doing here. There is really no need to feel over anxious to know that I am back again for my second tour. I really was due back six months after Sept of 41 and had the privilege of joining a well experienced crew and on aircraft that one dreams about. To tell you the honest truth I would not have taken this on had I believed it was a doubtful move. I came up here a couple of days ago (Apr 14th) and we are on revision and conversion for the next month before going over with a few bundles for the squareheads. I know that you will be feeling most anxious during those few months ahead but the time will soon pass and I know that God will be especially with us as were blessed in that first tour. I hope that we shall be writing at least two to three times per week and if you do the same, it will be much happier for us all.[136]

Sadly, the blessings that were bestowed on him in his first tour would not follow him to his second. MacCausland delivered a perfectly placed mine as Young's aircraft flew at the Möhne Dam, and it bounced several times, exploded at the base and caused the initial small breach.

AJ-A was shot down at the last moment of danger shortly after they had passed over the Dutch coast. Vincent MacCausland's body was washed ashore on 27 May 1943, along with those of Lawrence Nichols and Gordon Yeo. They were all buried in Bergen General Cemetery.

---

136 Letter Vincent MacCausland to his mother, 17 April 1943
      www.canadianletters.ca/collections/war/469/collection/20601/doc/221
      [Accessed May 2017].

MacCausland had a girlfriend in Bedford, Rene Warman, and they had a daughter, Angela, born in Bedford in January 1943. Rene Warman made contact with the MacCausland family after he was killed and travelled out to Canada after the war with her daughter to meet them. She would later marry Vincent MacCausland's brother, Howatt. The marriage did not last, and Rene and Angela returned to England.

Sgt G.A. Yeo
Front gunner

Born in Barry Dock, Glamorgan, on 9 July 1922, Gordon Arthur Yeo was the youngest member of Melvin Young's crew. He was the son of Arthur and Ada Yeo and had joined the RAF in 1941, wanting to be a pilot. Having been initially posted to Elementary Flying School in Canada, he eventually qualified as a gunner.

He crewed up with David Horsfall, Charles Roberts, Lawrence Nichols and Wilfred Ibbotson at 1660 Conversion Unit at RAF Swinderby, under skipper Graham Bower. When Bower went sick, most of the crew flew on an operation to Berlin on 16 January 1943, with Plt Off Vincent Duxbury as their pilot. By the time the crew moved to 57 Squadron at Scampton in mid March, Melvin Young had taken over.

Yeo wrote several letters to his parents during his time on 617 Squadron, and they give us some insight into how hard they trained, and what they did in their spare time. Melvin Young drove the crew into Lincoln on a day off from training to watch a parade which was part of the city's 'Wings for Victory' week. This reminded the crew of their skipper's chequered history. 'We had a good laugh at the blokes all dressed up in flying clothes and sitting in the dinghy. [Melvin Young] had a good laugh at them because he had detailed them.' Later, he told his parents about Young's determined efforts to ensure they were trained hard: 'You say you want to know the name of our skipper, well here it is, S/Ldr H.M. Young, he is not so bad lately, I expect that is because we are getting used to him, but he is the cause more or less of us not getting leave.'[137]

HUMPHRIES FAMILY COLLECTION

---

137 Thorning, *Dambuster who Cracked the Dam*, p122.

AJ-A was shot down at the last moment of danger shortly after they had passed over the Dutch coast. Gordon Yeo's body was washed ashore on 27 May 1943, along with those of Lawrence Nichols and Vincent MacCausland. They were all buried in Bergen General Cemetery.

In the months after the raid, Gordon Yeo's mother must have written to Henry Young, Melvin Young's father, as his reply to her dated 13 July 1943 shows. He ends his letter with the sad words: 'With many thanks for your kind sympathy which I feel too for all those who have suffered the same loss.'

Sgt W. Ibbotson
Rear gunner

Wilfred Ibbotson was born in Netherton, near Wakefield, Yorkshire on 18 September 1913, the second son of the four children of Herbert and Anne Ibbotson. His father had been a miner, but Wilfred worked on a farm after leaving school. He married Doris Bray in 1938, and they had two daughters. When war came he was called up and served as an Army motorcycle despatch rider. In 1941 he volunteered for the RAF, and trained as a gunner.

After qualifying, he was posted to 10 Operational Training Unit at RAF Abingdon, and joined a crew piloted by Sgt Ivan Morgan. His future colleagues Charles Roberts, Lawrence Nichols and John Beesley were also in this unit at the same time, but in a different crew, that of pilot Graham Bower. In September 1942, while still training, Ibbotson flew on two operations. In Decem-

ber, he moved on to 1660 Conversion Unit at Swinderby, and it would seem that it was here that he joined Young's future crew, at that stage still skippered by Graham Bower. After Bower's departure on sick leave, Ibbotson flew on one operation to Berlin on 16 January 1943 with Plt Off Vincent Duxbury as the pilot.

The Dams Raid was thus Ibbotson's fourth operation. His body was the last of the crew of AJ-A to be washed ashore, on 30 May.

Ibbotson was buried the following day alongside his comrades in Bergen General Cemetery.

Crew 5: AJ-J

First wave: Attacked Möhne Dam and returned to base.
Lancaster serial number: ED906/G

Flt Lt D.J.H. Maltby DFC

Pilot

David John Hatfeild[138] Maltby was born on 10 May 1920 in Hydneye House, the boys' preparatory school owned by his parents Ettrick and Aileen Maltby, in Baldslow near Hastings, Sussex. He was the second child and the only boy in a family of three. His sisters Audrey and Jean were born in 1917 and 1924 respectively.

He went to prep school at Hydneye and then the nearby St Wilfrid's in Hawkhurst. He went on to Marlborough College, and left there in 1936. In 1938, he decided that he wanted to train as a mining engineer and went to work at Treeton colliery in South Yorkshire, boarding with a local family in the neighbouring village of Aughton.

When the war started he quit his job and tried to sign up for the RAF. Although he went to the recruiting office on 6 September 1939 he wasn't accepted for aircrew training until March 1940 and finally got his call up papers in June. He qualified as a pilot on 18 January 1941 and in June 1941 was posted to RAF Coningsby, which was then the home of two squadrons, Nos 106 and 97. He flew his first six operations in 106 Squadron's Hampdens, but was soon transferred to 97 Squadron then flying Avro Manchester aircraft.

However by January 1942, the new Lancasters were available and 97 Squadron became only the second squadron in the RAF to get them. Maltby took part in a number of famous operations, including two unsuccessful attempts to destroy the German battleship Tirpitz, concealed in a Norwegian fjord.

He finished his first tour of operations in June 1942, and was awarded the DFC. He then spent a few months commanding a specialist Air Bomber Training Section in 1485 Target Towing and Gunnery Flight before returning on 17 March 1943 to active operations with 97 Squadron, still stationed at Coningsby.

IWM COLLECTIONS CH11048

---

138 This is the correct spelling of the name Hatfeild, which was his mother's maiden name.

GRACE BLACKBURN

David Maltby and his crew, photographed in Blida in August 1943. (Standing left to right) Victor Hill, Antony Stone, John Fort, David Maltby, William Hatton, Harold Simmonds. (In front) Vivian Nicholson.

Maltby was given a new crew which had been posted from 207 Squadron after their pilot had been killed on a 'second dickey' trip on 25 February before they could begin operations. This was made up of William Hatton, flight engineer; Vivian Nicholson, navigator; Antony Stone, wireless operator; John Fort, bomb aimer; and Austin Williams and Harold Simmonds, gunners. A few days later, on 25 March, they were all transferred to a new squadron, set up under the command of Guy Gibson, to prepare for a highly secret mission. Les Munro, Joe McCarthy and their crews were also transferred out of 97 Squadron the same day.

Maltby's crew flew on some twenty-three training flights over the next six weeks, with the only hiccough being in early May when front gunner Austin Williams was deemed unsuitable – the reason why is not clear – and was replaced by a new gunner, hurriedly imported from 9 Squadron, Victor Hill.

On the Dams Raid, Maltby and his crew were responsible for dropping the fifth mine at the Möhne, which caused the substantial second breach.

Afterwards Maltby became commander of A Flight and often acted as CO in Gibson's frequent absences on official duties. His signature appears as acting CO on the May entry of all the squadron logbooks. He also took a full and active part in the many festivities that took place, often in conjunction with the squadron's other party animals, such as Richard Trevor-Roper. As both of them had pregnant wives at home, perhaps this gave them a special bond. Maltby's wife Nina gave birth to their son John on 1 July 1943 at their home in Woodhall Spa. (Besides Maltby and Trevor-Roper, two other men with pregnant wives flew on the Dams Raid. See Charles Brennan, p126, and Lewis Burpee, p254.)

Party hard they might, but by September the squadron was back in training for another special mission, an attack on the Dortmund Ems canal, using a special 'thin case' bomb three times the size of a normal 4,000lb 'cookie'. Eight aircraft were assigned – Maltby would lead the second group of four, himself, Dave Shannon, Geoff Rice and Bill Divall. Less than an hour into the flight, word was received at base that the weather conditions at the target had deteriorated. The aircraft were recalled.

Then came disaster. As it turned, Maltby's Lancaster suddenly exploded. Shannon stayed with the wreckage, sending fixes and circling above until air sea rescue launches arrived. It's not clear what caused the explosion. It may have been pilot error. Something may have gone wrong with the bomb. But there is also some evidence that it may have collided with a 139 Squadron Mosquito, returning from a raid on Berlin but out of radio contact.[139]

The only body recovered was that of David Maltby. It was brought ashore, and he was buried the following Saturday in St Andrew's Church, Wickhambreaux, Kent – the same church in which he had been married just sixteen months before.

Sgt W. Hatton
Flight engineer

William Hatton was born in Wakefield, Yorkshire, on 24 March 1920, the oldest boy in a family of four children, two boys and two girls. Their parents were George and Florence Hatton. William Hatton went to Holy Trinity and Thornes House schools in Wakefield.

He joined the RAF at the outbreak of war, and worked in ground crew. In May 1941, he went to RAF Speke in Liverpool where he serviced aircraft in the Merchant Ship Fighter Unit. This was a short-lived scheme in which Hawker

---

139 Foster, *Breaking the Dams*, pp157–64.

Hurricanes were sent to sea on special merchant ships, which were equipped with catapults for launching them. The plan was to enable the Hurricanes to be launched far out at sea to help protect the Atlantic convoys. The only drawback was that they had no way of landing, so the pilot had to bale out of the Hurricane and let the aircraft fall into the sea.

When the opportunity arose for experienced ground crew to become flight engineers on heavy bombers, Hatton applied and was sent to the only flight engineer training facility, No.4 School of Technical Training at RAF St Athan.

After qualifying as a flight engineer in late 1942, Hatton was posted to RAF Swinderby, to join 1660 Conversion Unit on 5 January 1943. There he crewed up with Vivian Nicholson, Antony Stone, John Fort and Harold Simmonds, who had moved into the last phase of training with their pilot Flt Lt William Elder.

On 23 February 1943, the new crew were posted to 207 Squadron to begin operations but unfortunately two days later Elder was killed on a 'second dickey' trip. A month later the pilot-less crew was transferred to 97 Squadron at Coningsby, where they were allocated to David Maltby, returning to operations after his inter-tour break. The whole crew was transferred to 617 Squadron on 25 March 1943.

After the raid, all the aircrew were sent on leave. Such was the excitement that a number of local papers covered the story, with Hatton's arrival back in his home town given the headline 'A Wakefield Hero' in the *Wakefield Express*. The paper sent a photographer to his family house and took the photograph seen above in the street outside.

Four months later, on 14 September 1943, Hatton took off from RAF Coningsby on 617 Squadron's first major operation since the Dams Raid. When their aircraft suffered its final crash it sank with the bodies of all the crew except the pilot, so he has no known grave. William Hatton is commemorated on the Runnymede Memorial.

Sgt V. Nicholson
Navigator

Vivian Nicholson was born on 15 February 1923 in Newcastle on Tyne, the oldest of the eight sons of Arthur and Elizabeth Nicholson, who lived in Sherburn, Co Durham. He worked as an apprentice in the family joinery business but when the war started he volunteered to join the RAF.

He started his training as a navigator in Canada but then moved on to Tuscaloosa, Alabama in the USA for part of his course. Even though the USA was not yet in the war, it was already providing training facilities for the Allies.

On arrival home, he was sent to 10 OTU at RAF St Eval, Cornwall, in September 1942. He arrived there at the same time as bomb aimer John Fort and wireless operator Antony Stone, and it is likely that the trio teamed up there, along with gunner Austin Williams and pilot Flt Lt William Elder.

On 5 January 1943, the fledgling crew were transferred to RAF Swinderby, to join 1660 Conversion Unit, where William Hatton and Harold Simmonds were added. On 23 February 1943, the new crew were posted to 207 Squadron to begin operations but unfortunately two days later Elder was killed on a 'second dickey' trip. A month later the pilot-less crew was transferred to 97 Squadron at Coningsby, where they were allocated to David Maltby. The whole crew was posted together to 617 Squadron on 25 March 1943.

A navigator used a log sheet for each operation in order to record routes taken, changes in bearing, times of fixes etc. All these calculations were, of course, made by hand. Vivian Nicholson was on his first active operation on the Dams Raid, and we are lucky in that his log sheet has been preserved for posterity. Its accuracy has been commended by navigational experts in the years since. There was also space for the navigator to make his own notes during the raid, thus providing one of the few contemporary and he recorded comments such as 'Bomb dropped. Wizard.' immediately after the mine was released.

Nicholson received the DFM for his part in the raid and took an active part in the celebrations at Buckingham Palace and in the Hungaria Restaurant on 22 June 1943. He can be seen in the famous restaurant photograph, sitting behind John Fort and David Maltby, with the arm of Jack Leggo, his Navigation Leader, draped over his shoulders. Doubtless Leggo was proud of the textbook way his young protegé had carried out his first operation.

After their fatal crash into the North Sea on 15 September 1943, Nicholson's mother Elizabeth wrote to David Maltby's father:

> We knew from our son they were a proud and happy crew, and we have at least four different photos of your gallant son, his bomb aimer and our boy together with others taken while in London June 22/23rd.
> It is indeed a terrible and deep wound for us when we look at them so young, happy and beautiful.
> We also knew, as from what my boy told others, that, they knew the

daily risks they had to run, but were prepared to face them as it was for a good cause, which surely makes us feel all the more proud of them, although our loss is at times unbearable.[140]

Vivian Nicholson is commemorated on the Runnymede Memorial.

Sgt A.J.B. Stone
Wireless operator

Antony Joseph Bazeley Stone was born in Winchester, Hampshire, on 5 December 1920, the younger son of a family of two boys who were the children of Joseph and Dorothy Stone. Born in Russia, from where he emigrated in the 1890s, Joseph Stone was a barber and had a shop in the centre of the city. Stone trained as a chef after leaving school, and had worked at several well known London restaurants before volunteering for the RAF in 1940.

He was selected for wireless operator training, and qualified also as an air gunner. He arrived at 10 OTU at St Eval at the same time as navigator Vivian Nicholson and bomb aimer John Fort, and it is likely that the trio teamed up there, along with gunner Austin Williams and pilot Flt Lt William Elder.

On 5 January 1943, the fledgling crew were transferred to RAF Swinderby, to join 1660 Conversion Unit, where William Hatton and Harold Simmonds were added. On 23 February 1943, the new crew were posted to 207 Squadron to begin operations but after Elder was killed on a 'second dickey' trip the crew was transferred to 97 Squadron at Coningsby, and allocated to David Maltby. The whole crew was posted together to 617 Squadron on 25 March 1943.

GARBETT/GOULKDING COLLECTION

When the news of their fatal crash reached his family in Winchester, his mother Dorothy was so shocked she was determined to find out more, and set off by train to Coningsby. Shown into adjutant Harry Humphries' office in a state of shock, she asked him repeatedly: 'Did he suffer? Did he suffer?' She then disarmed him by saying that she was glad that there were brave men like him carrying on the fight. As he noted in his autobiography, sadly, the only battles he fought were against official letters and forms.[141] Antony Stone left a letter for his parents, only

---

140 Foster, *Breaking the Dams*, pp171–4.
141 Humphries, *Living with Heroes*, p61.

to be opened on the event of his death. A fragment of it survives in a typescript version in the possession of the Maltby family:

> I will have ended happily, so have no fears of how I ended as I have the finest crowd of fellows with me, and if Skipper goes I will be glad to go with him. He has so much more to lose and more responsibilities than I and you can rest assured and know that I've taken hundreds with me who lived as you do and never even gloried in the war as I did and I still experience that same thrill every time I fly.[142]

Joseph Stone kept a photograph of his son in his shop until the day he retired, and it is still recalled by the later generations of boys and men who had haircuts there. Antony Stone is commemorated on the Runnymede Memorial.

Plt Off J. Fort
Bomb aimer

John Fort was the oldest member of the crew of AJ-J. He was born in Colne, Lancashire, on 14 January 1912, one of the six sons of George and Martha Fort, and attended Colne Secondary School. He joined the RAF in 1929 as an apprentice at the No 1 School of Technical Training at RAF Halton. On qualification, he won first prize as a fitter. He then went to sea in the aircraft carrier HMS *Glorious*. (Between 1918 and 1937 the RAF operated the aircraft which flew on aircraft carriers, and supplied its own ground staff to service them.)

Back on dry land, he continued in ground crew until the second year of the war, when he volunteered for aircrew training, and was selected as a specialist bomb aimer. At the end of his course he had done well enough to be offered a commission and so it was as a Pilot Officer he arrived at 10 OTU in September 1942, at RAF St Eval at the same time as navigator Vivian Nicholson and wireless operator Antony Stone. It is likely that the trio teamed up there, along with gunner Austin Williams and pilot Flt Lt William Elder.

On 5 January 1943, the fledgling crew were transferred to RAF Swinderby, to join

HUMPHRIES FAMILY COLLECTION

---

142 Foster, *Breaking the Dams*, p174.

1660 Conversion Unit, where William Hatton and Harold Simmonds were added. On 23 February 1943, the new crew were posted to 207 Squadron to begin operations but after Elder was killed on a 'second dickey' trip the crew was transferred to 97 Squadron at Coningsby, and allocated to David Maltby. The whole crew was posted together to 617 Squadron on 25 March 1943.

Fort was one of the most proficient bomb aimers in 617 Squadron, and was the A Flight Bombing Leader. Not all the bomb aimers used the wooden triangular sight devised by Wg Cdr Dann, but Fort did and his was given to David Maltby's father Ettrick shortly after the raid. It is thought to be the only such sight still in existence. It was acquired by a collector in the 1970s and then sold by him in 2015. Fort's accuracy paid dividends on Maltby's run-in to the Möhne Dam, and the crew's mine made the second larger breach which caused its final collapse.

Afterwards there was jubilation, and John Fort joined in the celebrations with much gusto. In the pictures which show the squadron personnel getting on the train to London for the investiture, he can be seen messing about on the locomotive footplate.

After the crash on 15 September 1943, in which he was killed along with all his other comrades, squadron adjutant Harry Humphries, who was a good friend, wrote a short pen portrait which is preserved in the Lincolnshire County Council archives:

> A Lancastrian with an outlook on life difficult to beat. Good humoured, slow of speech, but quick in action. A small fair haired chap, with broad shoulders, well able to carry their responsibilities. He had been in the Service for some years and often said it was a 'piece of cake' compared with the competition & throat cutting of civilian business. A very popular member of the Squadron.[143]

John Fort is commemorated on the Runnymede memorial.

Sgt V. Hill
Front gunner

Early in May 1943, not much more than a week before the Dams Raid was due to take place, a decision was taken to replace David Maltby's front gunner, probably for unknown disciplinary reasons. With the operation so

---

143 Harry Humphries collection, Lincolnshire County Council archives.

close, an experienced gunner was needed to step into the breach, and Victor Hill was hurriedly summoned from 9 Squadron, based at RAF Bardney.

Unlike the rest of David Maltby's crew, Victor Hill had plenty of operational experience. He had flown twenty-two operations on Lancasters between October 1942 and March 1943mand had taken part in some of the war's most famous raids, including the daylight raid on the Schneider works at Le Creusot in France.

Victor Hill had been born in Gloucestershire on 6 December 1921. He was an only child, the son of Harry and Catherine Hill, who both worked at Berkeley Castle. He was brought up on the castle estate and went to the local school. After leaving school, he also worked at the castle, as a gardener.

Hill joined up as ground crew, but volunteered for aircrew and trained as a gunner when the heavy bombers began to arrive and there were many more chances to fly. His first posting was to 9 Squadron in August 1942, round about the time it was posted to Waddington and converted to Lancasters from Wellingtons. He joined a crew piloted by Sgt Charles McDonald, a Canadian, and flew most of his operations with them.

In mid February 1943, most of this crew moved on to 83 Squadron, but Hill was left behind as a spare gunner and flew on his last operation in 9 Squadron on 8 March, with Sgt Doolan as the pilot.

After the Dams Raid, Hill carried on flying with the rest of David Maltby's crew until they all took off from RAF Coningsby on 14 September 1943 on 617 Squadron's first major operation since the Dams Raid.

In common with his pilot, he was also a young father. He had married Evelyn Hourihane in 1941, and at the time of the raid they had a 2-year-old daughter, Valerie. They were living with her parents in South Wales. In a letter dated 10 July 1943, he told his brother-in-law Don that he was looking forward to seeing his wife and daughter again in August:

> I think everyone must know Eve & myself on Cardiff station now as I say cheerio to her there so often. Val made it even harder this time, when I left, she was standing on the door with mam, waving her little hand and saying 'Daddy' that gave me one thought, well this is

certainly worth fighting for. I'm sure you will love her when you see her again Don I don't think Val was walking when you saw her last ... Well Don, roll along August 11th and lets hope we meet this time.[144]

Victor Hill is commemorated on the Runnymede Memorial.

Sgt H.T. Simmonds
Rear gunner

Harold Thomas Simmonds was born on Christmas Day 1921 in Brighton, Sussex, the older of the two children of Thomas and Elizabeth Simmonds. Thomas Simmonds was a gardener. The family lived in the small town of Burgess Hill, and Simmonds went to London Road School and later worked in a government job. Soon after the war started, he volunteered for the RAF. He started his service in ground crew, serving at Kemble in Gloucestershire and Mount Batten near Plymouth. However, he had always wanted to fly, and eventually he was selected for aircrew training, going to the No 2 Air Gunners School in Dalcross, near Inverness.

At the end of his training he was transferred to 1660 Conversion Unit at Swinderby. There he was added to the crew of Vivian Nicholson, Antony Stone

GRACE BLACKBURN

and John Fort, who had moved into the last phase of training with their pilot Flt Lt William Elder. On 23 February 1943, the new crew were posted to 207 Squadron to begin operations but after Elder was killed on a 'second dickey' trip the crew was transferred to 97 Squadron at Coningsby, and allocated to David Maltby. The whole crew was posted together to 617 Squadron on 25 March 1943.

Harold Simmonds is commemorated on the Runnymede Memorial.

---

144 Victor Hill, letter to Don Hourihane, 10 July 1943, Ashton family. [Spelling and punctuation as in original.]

Crew 6: AJ-L

First wave: Attacked Eder Dam and returned to base.
Lancaster serial number: ED929/G

Flt Lt D. J. Shannon DFC

Pilot

David John Shannon was born on 27 May 1922 at Unley Park, South Australia, the only child of Howard and Phoebe Shannon. His father was a farmer and also a member of the state assembly. His grandfather, John Shannon, had also been a member of the assembly, and also later a member of the Australian Senate. Shannon worked briefly in insurance after leaving school but joined the RAAF shortly after his 18th birthday. He had toyed with the idea of joining the navy, but was put off by the longer queue at the recruiting office. He began training as a pilot in March 1941. A year later, he was in England and by July 1942 he had been posted to 106 Squadron at Coningsby.

Shannon arrived with an excellent training record – one instructor thought him the best student he had ever had – but because his squadron CO, Guy Gibson, was on sick leave it took a few weeks for them to become acquainted. Many of the pilots who flew with Gibson were frightened of him but the boyish-looking Shannon was not, and the two flew together on several operations in that first month. Nominally Shannon was the second pilot, but on long flights they would sometimes swap seats.

By August, he was flying with a crew of his own and by February 1943 he had completed a tour of thirty-six operations. On one, to Turin, his load of incendiaries caught fire in the bomb bay and had to be rapidly jettisoned, resulting in the 'largest forest fire ever seen in Italy'. He was awarded the DFC in January 1943 for 'attacks on industrial targets in enemy territory'.

At the end of his tour, he had been posted to 83 Squadron in 8 Group to begin training as a Pathfinder. However Gibson had by then been asked to form a special new squadron and he was quick to track his old comrade down. Shannon agreed to join him, and set about building a crew. (See pp52–5.)

It's at this point in his book *The Dam Busters* that Paul Brickhill brings Shannon into his narrative. He tells us about the 'baby faced' Australian who was growing a moustache to make himself look older but who had a scorching tongue in the air when he felt like it. And he brings to the fore the romantic interludes in the intense training and drinking sessions of the next few weeks caused by Shannon falling for the 'dark, slim' WAAF officer, Ann Fowler. On the evening of 16 May 1943, it is she who notices, with a 'woman's wit', that the aircrew are eating eggs for their evening meal, and therefore deduces that they are going on an operation, rather than yet another training flight.

Indeed they were. A few hours later that evening, at 2147, Shannon took off from Scampton bound for the Möhne Dam, flying alongside Melvin Young and David Maltby. When they arrived, he spent thirty minutes or more circling over the woods beyond the dam waiting his turn to make a bombing run. He was beginning to line up for an attack when it was realised that Maltby's mine had caused the final breach. Elated by the sight, the crews of the three bombers which had yet to drop their mines set off for the nearby Eder Dam, accompanied by Gibson and Young.

Shannon took several attempts until he got the angle and speed right and dropped his mine successfully. He thought he had made a small breach, but it wasn't until Les Knight's later attack that the dam was destroyed.

Shannon sped back to Scampton, landing less than an hour after Maltby and Martin. The party that followed went on through the night and into the afternoon of the next day. According to Brickhill, it was then that Shannon asked Ann Fowler to marry him and she agreed – but only on the condition that he shaved off his moustache.

More parties followed, the biggest being on Shannon's 21st birthday, 27 May. This turned out to be the day the King and Queen visited the station and the decorations were announced. Like all the successful officer pilots, Shannon was awarded the DSO. The King congratulated him on his coming of age, and told

him he should celebrate.

A date was set for Shannon's wedding to Ann Fowler – Saturday 18 September. David Maltby was to be the best man, as the first choice, Gibson, was away in Canada. On the Monday before, Maltby and Shannon set off in a section of four aircraft bound for a raid on the Dortmund Ems

David Shannon and Ann Fowler on their wedding day, 18 September 1943.

CARISSA HOWARD

canal, with the new 12,000lb 'thin case' bomb. At about 0030 the raid was aborted because weather conditions over the target were too poor. Somehow, Maltby crashed into the sea while turning. Shannon didn't see what caused the crash but, hoping that there might be survivors, he circled above the spot for three hours, sending radio fixes until an ASR launch arrived. Maltby's body and some wreckage was all that was found.

The next day the operation was attempted again and even more disasters occurred, with five pilots and four complete crews lost. Shannon, Mick Martin and Geoff Rice were the only three pilots to survive. In appalling weather conditions, Shannon eventually dropped his bomb over the canal, and it exploded on the towpath.

In the autumn, Leonard Cheshire took command of the squadron, and Shannon became one of the flight commanders. He took part in many operations in the next year, using Wallis's giant Tallboy and Grand Slam bombs. Then in August 1944, with sixty-nine operations under his belt, he was removed from active operations and transferred to a long-range transport squadron. By then he had received a Bar to the DSO for 'courage of high order on numerous sorties.'

Shannon left the RAAF after the war and got a job with Shell Oil. He and Ann had one daughter. Although based in England, he travelled widely, but never piloted an aircraft again.

He died in London on 8 April 1993, shortly before the commemoration of the 50th anniversary of the Dams Raid, an event which he had been actively involved in planning. Ann had died three years previously and in 1991 Shannon had remarried, to family friend Eyke Taylor.

David and Ann Shannon are remembered by a pair of plaques in Clifton Hampden churchyard in Oxfordshire.

Sgt R.J. Henderson
Flight engineer

Robert Jack Henderson was born in Tarbrax, Lanarkshire on 17 June 1920, the son of John and Catherine Henderson. He went to West Calder High School and worked briefly as a miner before joining the RAFVR in 1937, where he served in ground crew. He did two stints in 207 Squadron, the second just before going to No 4 School of Technical Training to train as a flight engineer. In October, after he qualified, he was posted to 57 Squadron at Scampton, where he joined the crew of Flt Lt G.W. Curry. Leonard Sumpter also joined this crew at about the same time. Henderson flew on sixteen operations with Curry between November 1942 and March 1943. Hearing about the new squadron, and

HENDERSON FAMILY

anxious to get involved, Henderson and Sumpter approached David Shannon when they found that Curry had been grounded for medical reasons. Shannon recruited both of them for his Dams Raid crew.

After the raid, Shannon's crew carried on flying together for the best part of a year. Henderson notched up a further nineteen operations with Shannon and, when Shannon was taken off active flying, six more with Flt Lt Kearns. He finished his tour in mid 1944, was awarded the DFM and commissioned. He was then transferred to a training unit for the remainder of the war. He married Doreen Bluett in 1943, and they had one child.

Although he had been demobbed, Henderson then rejoined the RAF in 1948, serving at stations all over the UK and in Rhodesia, Malta and Cyprus. He died in the town of Limassol in Cyprus on 18 February 1961 while based at RAF Akrotiri.

Flg Off D.R. Walker DFC
Navigator

Daniel Revie Walker known to some as Danny and others as Revie during the war. He was born in Blairmore, Alberta, Canada on 20 November 1917 and worked for the Alberta forestry service before volunteering for the RCAF in 1940. After training as a navigator, his first active posting was to 106 Squadron as it re-equipped to fly Avro Lancasters, and crewed up with David Shannon.

HUTCHISON FAMILY

He finished a full tour of operations in December 1942, and was awarded the DFC in January 1943. Walker was a gregarious soul, and was particularly friendly with the wireless operator in Guy Gibson's crew, Robert Hutchison.

At the end of March 1943, Walker was serving in 22 OTU. Shannon was contacted by Gibson and told he 'was putting things together' for a new squadron, and would he like to join him. Shannon then assembled an almost completely new crew, with Walker the only man from his time in 106 Squadron to join him.

After the Dams Raid, Shannon and Walker spent some time on leave together near Bradford. So many were the free drinks thrust on them by both friendly members of the public and grateful barmen that Shannon said later that they were in danger of getting alcohol poisoning. Walker received a Bar to his DFC for his work on the raid itself.

In September 1943, when serious operational duties were resumed, Walker became the squadron's Navigation Officer, succeeding Jack Leggo who had been selected for pilot training. Walker flew some seventeen more operations with Shannon before being transferred out of 617 Squadron in April 1944.

Walker went back to Canada and stayed on in the RCAF. He commanded the navigation school in Winnipeg and served with Norad at Tacoma, Washington, before retiring in 1967. He then worked as a manpower commissioner. He died on 17 November 2001 in his native city of Blairmore, Alberta.

Flg Off B. Goodale DFC
Wireless operator

David Shannon's crew was only finalised four weeks before the Dams Raid with the arrival at Scampton on 20 April 1943 of wireless operator Brian Goodale. The crew's members came from quite disparate backgrounds but nevertheless they worked well together and became an important part of the backbone of the squadron. Dedicated fighters in the air, they were also serious revellers on the ground, and thereby added greatly to squadron morale. Goodale, tall and thin with a slight bent and thus known widely by his nickname 'Concave', was described by his colleague Len Sumpter as being 'a bit of a character with a drink in his hand'.

Goodale was born in Addington, Kent on 12 June 1919 and joined the RAF at the outbreak of war. After training as an observer, he became a wireless operator/air gunner and served a full tour of twenty-eight operations in 51 Squadron, starting in September 1940. During this time, he received the DFC and was commissioned. Then, after a period instructing, he was summoned to Scampton to join 617 Squadron when the call came to find an experienced wireless operator for the Shannon crew.

Some of the escapades in which Goodale was involved after the Dams Raid have passed into Squadron folklore. Prominent among them is

GOODALE FAMILY

the trip by train from Lincoln to London for the investiture at Buckingham Pal-ace, where he had to be locked in a lavatory after a drunken trouser-removing incident. (See p296 for a full account.) Many of these incidents were recorded by Paul Brickhill in *The Dam Busters* – items which add to its period charm.

Goodale became the squadron's Signals Leader in September 1943 and car-ried on flying on operations with Shannon for another nine months until he was posted out to another training centre. He was awarded a bar to his DFC. He stayed in the RAF after the war and retired as a Squadron Leader in 1961. He then had a career in business, including five years working for the aircraft manufacturers Short Brothers in Northern Ireland.

Brian Goodale married Vera Beales in 1949, and they had two children. He died on 16 December 1977 in Bury St Edmunds, Suffolk.

Flt Sgt L.J. Sumpter
Bomb aimer

Leonard Joseph Sumpter was born in Kettering, Northamptonshire, on 20 Sep-tember 1911, the son of Joseph and Mary Ann Sumpter. He had already served two stints in the Grenadier Guards before transferring to the RAF in 1941. He had joined the army as a boy soldier in 1928 and left again in 1931. He rejoined his old regiment at the outbreak of war but then in 1941 he persuaded his su-periors to let him transfer to the RAF. After training in England and Canada, he was posted to 57 Squadron at Scampton in September 1942 and flew as the bomb aimer on thirteen operations with Flt Lt G.W. Curry. Curry was then grounded with ear trouble, and his crew were told they had to break up.

However, he and his colleague, flight engineer Bob Henderson, heard a ru-mour that a new squadron was being formed elsewhere at Scampton, and went

looking for David Shannon, who was apparently on the lookout for a bomb aimer and an engi-neer. They both impressed the young pilot, and joined his crew.

After the Dams Raid, for which he received the DFM for his accurate attack on the Eder Dam, Sumpter continued flying in Shannon's crew, as 617 Squadron undertook a series of op-erations. He was commissioned in June 1943.

In 1944 Mosquitoes were introduced into 617 Squadron to mark targets, and Sumpter became Shannon's observer. He received the DFC in

HUMPHRIES FAMILY COLLECTION

Attack on Hitler's mountain lair in Berchtesgarten, 25 April 1945. (Standing left to right)
Flt Lt Leonard Sumpter, Flg Off K. Newley, Flt Lt L.M. Marshall, Flg Off Douglas Webb,
Sgt K. Tollerton. Sumpter and Webb were thereby the only two men to have flown on
617 Squadron's first and last wartime operations..

June 1944. Shannon was finally taken off operations, but Sumpter reverted to
Lancasters for a short time as part of Flt Lt L.M. Marshall's crew. Altogether, by
the end of the war he had flown thirty-five operations. He flew on 617 Squadron's last wartime operation, an attack on Berchtesgarten on 25 April 1945.

He was demobbed from the RAF after the war, but rejoined in 1946 in the
Physical Fitness branch, and served until 1950. He had a son, Leonard, with
his first wife Marjorie MacLean whom he had met in Prince Edward Island in
Canada while training, and a daughter, Jacqueline, with his second wife Hilda
Rose, who was from England.

Leonard Sumpter died in Luton on 30 November 1993.

Sgt B. Jagger
Front gunner

Brian Jagger came from an artistic family from
Yorkshire. His father, David Jagger, was a well-
known portrait painter. His uncle, Charles
Sargeant Jagger, was a sculptor and artist, and
was responsible for many memorials to the dead
of the First World War. His aunt, Edith Jagger,
was also an artist. All three had trained at the
Sheffield Technical School of Art.

Jagger was born on 9 November 1921, in

Painting by David Jagger, 1941. Although the subject is wearing pilot's wings, it is believed that it is actually the artist's son, air gunner Sgt Brian Jagger DFM.

Chelsea, the only child of David Jagger and his wife Catherine, and joined the RAF in 1941. He qualified as an air gunner in the summer of 1942, and was posted to 50 Squadron. Most of his operations were flown in a crew piloted by Sgt Norman Schofield, a Canadian, in a crew which also included two other Canadians who would fly on the Dams Raid in John Hopgood's crew, John Fraser and Ken Earnshaw.

After the Dams Raid, Jagger flew on several other operations with the Shannon crew, and was commissioned in October 1943. He was also awarded the DFM for his time in 50 Squadron, in a citation which also mentioned his role in the Dams Raid:

This NCO has carried out 24 operational sorties with great enthusiasm and efficiency. His sorties have been against targets such as Düsseldorf, Duisburg, Cologne and Hamburg and he has made three trips to targets in Italy. On 16th/17th May, 1943, he flew as front gunner in an aircraft detailed to attack the Möhne Dam and his use of his guns was of great assistance to the success of the operation.

Jagger was transferred to a training unit in the spring of 1944, and was killed in a flying accident at RAF Binbrook on 30 April 1944, in a 49 Squadron Lancaster. The aircraft was taking part in a Fighter Affiliation Exercise, testing a new Automatic Gun Laying Turret. During the flight, which involved strenuous evasion manoeuvres, the dinghy was accidentally inflated and wrapped itself around the tailplane causing the aircraft to crash.[145] (The accidental release of a Lancaster dinghy while in flight was a known fault. A crew had been killed in a similar incident at RAF Syerston in October 1942, and the family of one of the deceased

---

145 Chris Ward, *1 Group Bomber Command,* Pen and Sword, 2014.

was told that the problem would be rectified to prevent it occurring again.)[146]

One of David Jagger's best-known paintings was painted in 1941, and is titled 'Portrait of an officer of the RAF during World War II'. The subject, however, is wearing a greatcoat with sergeant's stripes. The greatcoat is open and on the jacket underneath can be seen a set of pilot's wings. It came up for auction at Christie's in 2008, but was not sold. Although the title says the subject is an officer he is quite clearly wearing sergeant's stripes and bears a strong resemblance to Brian. Confirmation that it is him is provided by David Jagger's recently discovered notes, in which the picture is simply listed as 'Brian'.[147]

Brian Jagger is buried in Cambridge City Cemetery.

Flg Off J. Buckley
Rear gunner

Jack Buckley was one of the most experienced air gunners in 617 Squadron, and one of only eight already commissioned by the time of the Dams Raid. The only son of Hubert and Lucy Buckley, he was born in Bradford on 1 May 1919. He attended Salt's High School in Saltaire, and then worked in the wool trade. He joined the RAF at the outset of war and after training went first to 225 Squadron, and then later to 75 (NZ) Squadron. In the latter, he flew thirty-five operations, mainly with Plt Off Fisher as pilot. He was commissioned in June 1942, and then transferred to a training unit.

Buckley became an important part of the squadron's social activities. Len Sumpter remembered him as owning a racing car, and also usually having a pint in his hand. This reputation looks to have been cemented by the famous 'morning after' picture, taken on the steps of the Officers' Mess on 17 May 1943. Buckley is obviously laughing out loud – perhaps affected by a combination of quite a lot of booze and no sleep.

He was awarded the DFC in July 1943 and flew on several more operations with Shannon. In the summer of 1944, he went back to training and remained there to the end of the war.

After the war, he resumed his career in the wool trade, and died in Bradford on 6 May 1990.

---

146 Letter from Wg Cdr R.M. Coad to the family of Plt Off L.G. Gallaway, RCAF, dated 6 January 1943, in Gallaway's service file. Information from Susan Paxton.
147 Timothy Dickson, *The Art of the Jagger Family* (forthcoming).

Crew 7: AJ-Z
Attacked Eder Dam. Shot down on return flight.
Lancaster serial number: ED937/G

Sqn Ldr H.E. Maudslay DFC
Pilot

Henry Eric Maudslay was born in Leamington Spa on 21 July 1921, the third child of Reginald and Gwendolen Maudslay. His family came from a background in industry: his great-great-grandfather, also Henry Maudslay, was a nineteenth-century inventor, important enough in the history of the British Industrial Revolution to be commemorated on a postage stamp in 2009. Following on the family tradition, his father had founded the Standard Motor Company in the early part of the twentieth century.

Like many boys from his background, Maudslay was sent away to board at a preparatory school at a young age. He went to Beaudesert School in Minchinhampton, Gloucestershire in 1930 and from there to Eton in 1935. His father died shortly before he left Beaudesert. Maudslay excelled at both athletics and rowing at Eton, winning both the mile race and steeplechase several years in succession and rowing in the college's First VIII.

The war started as he entered his final year at school. Maudslay had been determined to join the RAF for a while, and had planned to sit the exam to enter RAF Cranwell as an officer cadet. However, the war put paid to that, and in May 1940 he volunteered directly. He was called up in July 1940, and sent to Canada for his pilot training. He returned to England in February 1941, and was given his first operational posting with 44 Squadron at RAF Waddington, flying Hampdens. There he flew on twenty-nine operations, and won the DFC for a single-handed attack on two enemy cargo vessels.

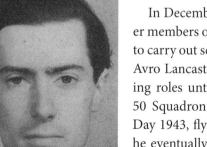

In December 1941 he was attached with other members of 44 Squadron to Boscombe Down to carry out service trials and work with the new Avro Lancaster. He carried on in various training roles until he returned to operations with 50 Squadron at Skellingthorpe on New Year's Day 1943, flying Lancasters. All six of the crew he eventually brought with him to 617 Squadron flew with him at some time in the thirteen operations he undertook over the next three

HUMPHRIES FAMILY COLLECTION

months, although they only appear to have all flown together as a complete crew four times.

Maudslay was promoted to Squadron Leader and became B Flight Commander of the new 617 Squadron. As Guy Gibson was often absent on important meetings, a lot of the organisation of training fell to him and Melvin Young, the other flight commander. Shortly before the Dams Raid Henry Maudslay witnessed his friend Bill Astell's will. The Australian pilot Norman Barlow was the other witness. All three would be lost on the raid.

Maudslay made three attempts on the very difficult Eder Dam. The last was at 0145 when his Upkeep mine was dropped too late and exploded on hitting the parapet of the dam without bouncing. This may have damaged his aircraft. Gibson asked if he was OK, and Maudslay's faint reply was 'I think so, stand by'. Maudslay nursed his damaged aircraft slowly back towards the Dutch border, but his luck ran out near Emmerich at 0243, when he was shot down. AJ-Z crashed in a field in the Osterholt area.

Henry Maudslay and his crew were buried in the military cemetery in Düsseldorf North Cemetery and were reinterred in Reichswald Forest War Cemetery after the war.

Sgt J. Marriott DFM
Flight engineer

Jack Marriott was born on 19 January 1920 in the small village of New Smithy in the Derbyshire Peak District, and went to the local village school at Chinley. He was a factory worker in a local bleach works before the war. At its outbreak, he joined the RAF and worked as ground crew.

As soon as the opportunity arose for experienced mechanics to retrain as heavy bomber flight engineers Marriott volunteered and after training was posted to 50 Squadron at Skellingthorpe on 25 August 1942. There he quickly gained a good reputation and was seen as setting a very high standard. He had amassed twenty three operations in the crew of Flg Off Drew Wyness before joining Henry Maudslay's crew on an operation to Hamburg on 4 March. They flew together on three further operations before they were posted to 617 Squadron on 25 March 1942.

When Marriott left 50 Squadron, his CO

MARRIOTT FAMILY

recommended him for a DFM citing his 'efficiency and enthusiasm for operational flying and his determination in helping to hit the targets' as meriting the award. Sadly, it was only confirmed in July 1943, after his death, but was reported in the local press.

Marriott is buried in Reichswald Forest War Cemetery.

Flg Off R.A. Urquhart
Navigator

Robert Alexander Urquhart was born in Moose Jaw, Saskatchewan, Canada on 2 August 1919, one of the four children of Alexander and Susie Urquhart. His father worked as a clerk. Urquhart himself was educated a local schools and then worked as an apprentice jeweller and a stock manager before the war. He applied to the RCAF in May 1940 and joined up in January 1941. He was initially selected for pilot training and finally qualified as a navigator with a commission in January 1942.

He arrived in England in March 1942, and underwent further training. At one point he flew with Joe McCarthy, later a 617 Squadron colleague. He joined 50 Squadron in August 1942 and undertook fifteen operations with Sqn Ldr Moore as pilot. On 17 December 1942 he joined another crew, piloted by Sqn Ldr Birch, in a raid on Soltau. Richard Trevor-Roper was Birch's regular rear gunner and flew on this operation.

In the New Year, he teamed up with Henry Maudslay almost immediately after Maudslay resumed operational flying in 50 Squadron in January 1943. Maudslay and Uquhart's first operation together was to Essen on 21 January 1943, and they flew another eleven operations together until the whole crew was posted into 617 Squadron on 25 March 1943.

On 4 April Maudslay, Urquhart and three others flew to Farnborough and stayed there several days while two Aldis lamps were fitted to enable the pilot to maintain the correct height for the attack on the dams. The navigator was given the important task of looking through the blister and checking that their beams were touching. On their return to Scampton, Maudslay and Urquhart made test runs across the airfield and then later the same evening at Skegness and in the Wash, demonstrating they could successfully keep to the required height.

By the time of the Dams Raid, Urquhart had amassed twenty-eight operations and had been cited for a DFC for his operational flying in 50 Squadron.
The citation read:

> Since joining this squadron, Flying Officer Urquhart has flown on
> many operations. At all times his navigation has been of the highest
> order and the successes he achieved are due in no small measure to
> his skill. This officer took part in the daylight raids on Le Creusot
> and Milan and at other times on many heavily defended German
> targets. On one occasion during a low level raid on a target in North
> West Germany he was wounded by anti-aircraft fire but continued to
> navigate with accuracy. By his skill and determination Flying Officer
> Urquhart has set a high standard among his fellow navigators.

In fact the recommendation had been made originally on 20 March 1943 by
the Commanding Officer of 50 Squadron, and endorsed by Air Vice Marshal
Cochrane on 4 May 1943. Unfortunately the paperwork got 'lost' in the corri-
dors of officialdom until the closing stages of the war. The Canadian Minister of
National Defence for Air wrote to the Urquhart family on 30 July 1945, apolo-
gising for the delay in the award and enclosing his 'Operational Tour Wings'
and certificate. His DFC was eventually sent by registered mail on 7 November
1949, along with the Canadian War Memorial Cross.

When they got to AJ-Z's crash site, the Germans could not identify the individual remains of Urquhart, Tytherleigh and Fuller, and they were buried
together in a collective grave in Düsseldorf North Cemetery. After the war, the
whole crew was reinterred in Reichswald Forest War Cemetery.

Wrt Off A.P. Cottam
Wireless operator

Alden Preston Cottam was born in Edmonton,
the provincial capital of Alberta on 29 August
1912. His family lived in the small town of Jasper in the Canadian Rocky Mountains, some
225 miles away. The only son of the five children of Edwin and Margaret Cottam, his father
worked as a hostler for the Canadian National
Railway. His parents were both originally from
Nova Scotia in eastern Canada.

HUMPHRIES FAMILY COLLECTION

Cottam went to the local school in Jasper and worked as a clerk and driver before the war. He joined the RCAF in February 1941 and qualified as a wireless operator/air gunner.

After arriving in England he was posted to a training unit, 1654 Conversion Unit. In October 1942, he was sent from there to 50 Squadron at RAF Swinderby. He flew on a number of operations with Sgt A.L. Kitching as pilot, and then joined Henry Maudslay's crew for an operation to Essen on 21 January 1943. He was posted to 617 Squadron in 25 March as part of Maudslay's crew.

Cottam is buried in Reichswald Forest War Cemetery.

Plt Off M.J.D. Fuller
Bomb aimer

Michael John David Fuller, known as John to his family, was born on 28 April 1920 in Reigate, Surrey. After leaving school, he worked for the Post Office as a telephone engineer. He joined the RAF in May 1940, but didn't begin operational training until February 1942. He then qualified as a bomb aimer.

After a short spell in 106 Squadron he was posted to 50 Squadron, and first flew with Henry Maudslay and his new crew on 13 February 1943. He flew on a handful of other operations before the whole crew were posted over to 617 Squadron. By this time, he had been commissioned.

When they got to the AJ-Z crash site, the Germans could not identify the individual remains of Fuller, Tytherleigh and Urquhart, and they were buried together in a collective grave in Düsseldorf North Cemetery. After the war, the whole crew was reinterred in Reichswald Forest War Cemetery.

Flg Off W.J. Tytherleigh
Front gunner

William John Tytherleigh, known in the RAF as 'Johnny', was born in Cambridge on 8 November 1921, the son of Ernest and Julia Lilley (née Bennett). His birth name was William George Lilley. His parents' marriage broke up when he was very young, and his mother moved to London to begin a new life with Albert Tytherleigh. At some point William George Lilley became William John Tytherleigh, and the family moved to Hove in Sussex.

Tytherleigh joined the RAF in 1940, and
qualified as a wireless operator/air gunner the
following spring. He was posted to 50 Squadron in the crew of Sgt Douglas Atkinson (who,
confusingly, was also known by the nickname
of Johnny). This crew completed a full tour in
Hampdens between November 1941 and June
1942. Tytherleigh was commissioned in April
1942. At the end of their tour, he gave his pilot Atkinson an engraved gold propelling pen-
cil, along with a handwritten message 'To help
say thank you Douglas for seeing me through
– Johnny'. This was found by Atkinson's son after the war.

After a spell in a training unit Tytherleigh rejoined 50 Squadron in the autumn of 1942. By then, they were flying Lancasters, and Tytherleigh was stationed in the mid-upper turret. On 2 February 1943, he joined up with Henry
Maudslay, Robert Urquhart and Norman Burrows for the first time, on an operation to Cologne, and he flew a further eight times with this crew, until they
were all transferred to 617 Squadron.

When they got to the AJ-Z crash site, the Germans could not identify the
individual remains of Tytherleigh, Fuller and Urquhart, and they were buried
together in a collective grave in Düsseldorf North Cemetery. After the war, the
whole crew was reinterred in Reichswald Forest War Cemetery.

Like Urquhart, Tytherleigh had been recommended for a DFC at the time of
his transfer from 50 Squadron. He had completed forty-two operations. However, just as happened with his colleague, the recommendation got 'lost' for
over two years, and it was not announced until June 1945.

Sgt N.R. Burrows
Rear gunner

Norman Rupert Burrows was born on 31 August 1914 in the Toxteth area of Liverpool, the
second of the three children of Norman and
Jane Burrows. His father worked as a carter. He
joined the RAF in June 1941, but didn't go to
Air Gunnery School until the following year.
On 28 September 1942, after qualifying as an
air gunner, he joined 50 Squadron based at

Skellingthorpe. Over the following four months he only undertook one operation, before flying for the first time with Henry Maudslay on 27 January 1943
on a raid on Düsseldorf. Following this, he became his regular rear gunner,
taking part in a further nine operations. On one raid, to Cologne on 2 February
1943, when they bombed from 19,000ft conditions were so cold that his guns
froze. The complete crew were transferred to 617 Squadron on 27 March 1943.

Burrows is buried in Reichswald Forest War Cemetery.

Crew 8: AJ-B

Detailed to attack Möhne and Eder Dams. Crashed on outward flight.
Lancaster serial number: ED864/G

Flt Lt W. Astell DFC
Pilot

In his book *Enemy Coast Ahead* Guy Gibson gives a couple of cursory mentions to pilot Bill Astell, describing him rather curiously as a 'grand Englishman
from Derbyshire'.[148] As their paths only crossed for a few weeks in the spring
and early summer of 1943 that may be all that impacted on Gibson, but in fact
Astell had had one of the most eventful careers of any of the Dams Raid pilots.
He had flown on a number of operations and been awarded the DFC, but all his
active service had been in the Middle East and Malta.

Born in Knutsford, Cheshire on 1 April 1920, William Astell, the son of
Godfrey and Margery Astell, was brought up in Derbyshire's Peak District. His
father was managing director of a Manchester textile manufacturer. From his
schooldays in Bradfield College he had been an adventurous spirit, crossing the
Atlantic by cargo boat, climbing in the Dolomites and spending three months
at Leipzig University. With war imminent, he first enlisted in the navy, but then
transferred to the RAFVR in July 1939. By April 1940 he had been selected for
pilot training and was sent to Rhodesia.

After qualifying as a pilot, he had hoped to get back to the UK but found himself sent to another training unit before being posted to a Wellington squadron
in Malta. There he contracted typhoid, so he didn't actually fly on active service
until September 1941, when the squadron had been posted on to Egypt.

On 1 December 1941 he was involved in a horrendous flying accident: another aircraft cut in ahead of him while he was
landing, and he fractured his skull and suffered
severe burns to his back. Back on operations the
next summer, he was shot down over the Western Desert and crash-landed behind enemy
lines. He managed to evade capture and got back
to his base some five days later. For this operation he was awarded the DFC.

He eventually returned to England in September 1942 and was posted to become a flying

---

148 Gibson, *Enemy Coast Ahead*, p285.

instructor. While serving in 1654 Conversion Unit, he became friendly with another instructor called Henry Maudslay, who would later lead his section on the Dams Raid. Astell was then posted to 57 Squadron at RAF Scampton, arriving in January 1943.

His rather unusual career meant that at this point he had no crew, but he was allocated an operationally-ready crew which had formed under pilot Max Stephenson. Stephenson had been killed shortly beforehand in a raid on Duisberg while flying as second pilot with another crew.

The Astell crew's first raid was on Lorient in France on 13 February 1943 and they would fly on a number of other operations until 25 March when the news came that the whole of 57 Squadron's C Flight was to be transferred to a new squadron for a special operation. As they were already at Scampton, this didn't involve too much disruption, but there must have been much speculation as to what the actual target was to be.

Several weeks of intense training was to follow. Astell and his crew were tasked with the new squadron's first flights, taking photographs of all the major lakes in England, Scotland and Wales, and they were also the first to fly the specially modified Lancaster. On 14 May, those captains who had never made a will were instructed to do so, and Astell wrote his. It was witnessed by Norman Barlow and Henry Maudslay. None of them would return from the raid.

Astell's aircraft was damaged by flak and then hit a pylon at Marbeck, and all on board were killed. The next day the bodies of the crew were taken to Borken and buried in the City Cemetery. After the war, they were all reinterred together in the Reichswald Forest War Cemetery.

Sgt J. Kinnear
Flight engineer

John Kinnear was known to his family as Jack, but in the RAF, this was inevitably changed to Jock. He was born on 6 November 1921 in Newport, Fife, a small village on Tayside, the son of William and Helen Kinnear. His father had once been the chauffeur to the Dundee MP and publisher Sir John Leng, and the family had lived on the Leng estate. He was a mechanically-minded young man who had worked as a garage hand before joining the RAF in 1939, at the age of 16.

After more than three years' work on ground crew, Kinnear volunteered for training as a flight engineer and was sent to No. 4 School of Technical Training at RAF St Athan. He qualified from there in the late summer of 1942. He was then posted to a conversion unit, and teamed up with Floyd Wile, Albert

Garshowitz, Richard Bolitho and Don Hopkinson, who had arrived at the unit with pilot Max Stephenson. Frank Garbas was also added to the crew at this time.

When they were ready for operational flying, the whole crew was posted to 9 Squadron. However, before they could fly together Max Stephenson was sent on an operation with another crew as second pilot to gain experience. Unfortunately his aircraft was shot down, and he was killed.

Without a pilot, the crew was then shipped to 57 Squadron, and allocated to Bill Astell and flew their first operation to Lorient on 13 February 1943. After seven more operations, Astell's crew was moved to 57 Squadron's C Flight, under a new Flight Commander Melvin Young. On 25 March the whole flight was transferred to the new 617 Squadron being formed at the same station.

On what turned out to be their last short leave before the Dams Raid, Kinnear and his colleagues, Floyd Wile, Albert Garshowitz and Don Hopkinson all went to stay with the family of rear gunner Richard Bolitho, at Kimberley near Nottingham.

John Kinnear is buried in Reichswald Forest War Cemetery.

Plt Off F.A. Wile
Navigator

Floyd Alvin Wile was born on 17 April 1919 in Scotch Village, Nova Scotia, Canada. His parents Harris and Annabell Wile had seven children, five of whom survived into adulthood. Wile went to local schools in Scotch Village and then worked in the timber trade. He enlisted in the RCAF in May 1941 and was selected for training as a navigator. He qualified as an Air Observer in February 1942. After further training he was posted to Britain, and arrived in May 1942.

He was sent to a further training unit at RAF Kinloss and crewed up with pilot Max Stephenson, wireless operator Albert Garshowitz, bomb aimer Don Hopkinson and gunner Richard Bolitho. The crew was then posted for further training on heavy bombers and Frank Garbas and John Kinnear were added to the crew.

When they were ready for operational flying, the whole crew was posted to 9 Squadron and Wile received a commission. However, before they could fly together Max Stephenson was killed on a 'second dickey' operation.

Without a pilot, the crew was then shipped to 57 Squadron, and allocated to Bill Astell. After eight operations, Astell's crew was moved to 57 Squadron's C Flight, under a new Flight Commander Melvin Young. On 25 March all five crews in the flight were transferred to the new 617 Squadron being formed at the same station.

Floyd Wile is buried in Reichswald Forest War Cemetery.

Wrt Off A. Garshowitz
Wireless operator

Abram Garshowitz, known to his friends as Albert, was born in Hamilton, Ontario, Canada on 11 December 1920, the ninth of twelve children of Samuel and Sarah Garshowitz, who had emigrated from Russia in the first decade of the twentieth century.

At school, he was a keen sportsman, playing many sports but especially American football and rugby. He also played for the Eastwood team in the Hamilton Junior Rugby League, together with another Hamilton boy Frank Garbas, with whom he would ultimately serve in the Royal Canadian Air Force.

Having worked as a salesman before the war, he enlisted in the RCAF in January 1941, indicating on the enrolment form that the reason for leaving his occupation was 'to fight for the country'. He qualified as a wireless operator/

air gunner in April 1942, and on the day of his brother David's Bar Mitzvah his family came to see him in Trenton, and bid him goodbye.

After arrival in England, he underwent further training and was then posted to RAF Wigsley for conversion onto Lancasters. The crew, under pilot Max Stephenson, included his future Dams Raid crewmates Floyd Wile, Donald Hopkinson and Richard Bolitho. By coincidence, Frank Garbas who had also joined the RCAF, was posted to Wigsley at the same time, and Albert seems to have persuaded Max

GARSHOWITZ FAMILY

Stephenson to add him to the crew, along with flight engineer John Kinnear.

When they were ready for operational flying, the whole crew were posted to 9 Squadron. However, before they could fly together Max Stephenson was killed on a 'second dickey' operation.

Without a pilot, the crew was then shipped to 57 Squadron, and allocated to Bill Astell. After eight operations, Astell's crew was moved to 57 Squadron's C Flight, under a new Flight Commander Melvin Young. On 25 March all five crews in the flight were transferred to the new 617 Squadron being formed at the same station.

Known as a gregarious and high-spirited character, Garshowitz was responsible for chalking an inscription on the mine carried by AJ-B on the Dams Raid 'Never has so much been expected of so few', as well as another near the aircraft door saying 'officer entrance only'.

Abram Garshowitz is buried in Reichswald Forest War Cemetery.

Flg Off D. Hopkinson
Bomb aimer

Donald Hopkinson was born on 19 September 1920, in Royton, near Oldham in Lancashire, the second child of Harold and Sarah Hopkinson. His mother died of cancer when he was four months old, and his father remarried. He was educated at Chadderton Grammar School, where he excelled at cricket, and worked as a clerk before volunteering for the RAF in early 1941. After initial training in England he was selected for training as an air observer and sent to Canada. He qualified as a bomb aimer in May 1942, and was commissioned.

Hopkinson was posted to an Operational Training Unit in the summer of 1942, and crewed up with Floyd Wile, Albert Garshowitz and Richard Bolitho, with Max Stephenson as their pilot. In October 1942, all five were sent for heavy bomber training to RAF Wigsley and Frank Garbas and John Kinnear were added to the crew.

When they were ready for operational flying, the whole crew was posted to 9 Squadron. However, before they could fly together Max Stephenson was killed on a 'second dickey' operation.

Without a pilot, the crew was then shipped to 57 Squadron, and allocated to Bill Astell. After eight operations, Astell's crew was moved to

HUMPHRIES FAMILY COLLECTION

57 Squadron's C Flight, under a new Flight Commander Melvin Young. On
25 March all five crews in the flight were transferred to the new 617 Squadron
being formed at the same station.

On his last home leave early in May 1943, Hopkinson mentioned to his family that he had a bad premonition about the forthcoming operation. Unfortunately he was correct. AJ-B was damaged by flak and then hit a pylon at Marbeck, and all on board were killed.

Donald Hopkinson is buried in Reichswald Forest War Cemetery.

Flt Sgt F.A. Garbas
Front gunner

Francis Anthony (Frank) Garbas was born on 13 July 1922 in Hamilton, Ontario, Canada, one of the nine children of Stanley and Mary Garbas, both of
whom had been born in Poland. Many of the families who had moved to Hamilton, attracted by the prospect of work in the steel mills, were also of Polish
descent. He attended the town's Cathedral High School and Technical Institute
where he was good at sports, and went on to play rugby in the local Eastwood
team with Albert Garshowitz. He also played in another team which became
Canadian champions. After leaving school he worked for Otis Elevators, but
joined the RCAF soon after the outbreak of war.

After training in Canada and qualifying as an air gunner he was shipped
over to England in the summer of 1942, and went for further training to the
gunnery school at RAF Stormy Down. He was then posted to a conversion unit
at RAF Wigsley where, by coincidence, his old friend Albert Garshowitz was
also trainng. Garshowitz was in a five-man crew headed by pilot Max Stephenson and must have pushed successfully for Garbas to join them as the extra
gunner when they moved on to heavy bomber
training.

When they were ready for operational flying, the whole crew were posted to 9 Squadron. However, before they could fly together
Max Stephenson was killed on a 'second dickey'
operation.

Without a pilot, the crew was then shipped to
57 Squadron, and allocated to Bill Astell. After
eight operations, Astell's crew was moved to 57
Squadron's C Flight, under a new Flight Commander Melvin Young. On 25 March all five

crews in the flight were transferred to the new 617 Squadron being formed at the same station.

Frank Garbas is buried in Reichswald Forest War Cemetery.

Sgt R. Bolitho
Rear gunner

Richard Bolitho was born on 19 January 1920 in the city of Londonderry, now in Northern Ireland. His father William Bolitho was from Cornwall and worked as a commercial traveller in the seed business. He had stayed on in Ireland after meeting and marrying a local woman, Jane Cuthbertson, the daughter of a land steward. Richard was an only child.

In 1927 the family moved to England, first to Roose in Cumberland, where Richard attended the local school. The family then bought a hotel in Kimberley, Nottinghamshire. Richard moved in with his aunt Emily, who owned a fruit and vegetable shop in the town. He was educated at the local Church Hill School and then won a scholarship to the nearby Heanor Secondary School (later Heanor Grammar School) in 1931. He joined the RAF in 1940, but wasn't selected for aircrew training until early in 1942.

After qualifying as an air gunner, he was posted to an operational training unit, where he crewed up with Max Stephenson, Floyd Wile, Don Hopkinson and Albert Garshowitz. The five were then selected for heavy bomber training and John Kinnear and Frank Garbas were added to the crew.

When they were ready for operational flying, the whole crew were posted to 9 Squadron. However, before they could fly together Max Stephenson was killed on a 'second dickey' operation.

Without a pilot, the crew was then shipped to 57 Squadron, and allocated to Bill Astell. After eight operations, Astell's crew was moved to 57 Squadron's C Flight, under a new Flight Commander Melvin Young. On 25 March all five crews in the flight were transferred to the new 617 Squadron being formed at the same station.

Bolitho spent his last leave before the Dams Raid at his home in Kimberley. He brought two of his Canadian colleagues, Floyd Wile and Albert Garshowitz, and the Scot John Kinnear along as his guests.

In 1946, three years after his death, his parents

returned to Northern Ireland to live in the coastal resort of Portrush, and they lived out their days there. Richard Bolitho is buried in Reichswald Forest War Cemetery.

Crew 9: AJ-N

Attacked Eder Dam and returned to base.
Lancaster serial number: ED912/G

Plt Off L.G. Knight
Pilot

Leslie George Knight was born on 7 March 1921 in Camberwell, a suburb of Melbourne, Australia. He had planned to become an accountant, but the war intervened. He joined the RAAF in 1941, and was sent to England in the autumn of that year.

After training as a pilot, he formed a full crew while training and, with one exception, they would go on to fly with him throughout the rest of their operational life. The crew was posted to 50 Squadron in September 1942. Knight had flown on some twenty-six operations by March 1943, when the crew were offered the chance to transfer into a new squadron being formed at nearby Scampton for a secret mission. They took a joint decision to transfer together.

On the Dams Raid, AJ-N was the ninth and final aircraft of the first wave, tasked with attacking the Möhne and Eder Dams. It was the successful drop of their mine which caused the breach of the Eder Dam.

As a sincere Methodist with a deep faith, Knight was an abstemious character, and although he appears in the 'morning after the raid' photograph taken outside the Scampton Officers Mess he skipped the Hungaria Restaurant party after the London investiture.

The crew went back on training after the raid, but the first action they saw was the raid on the Dortmund Ems canal in September. An extra gunner was allocated to each crew, so Knight's Dams Raid crew was augmented by Sgt L.C. Woollard.

It was a terrible night, with heavy fog blanketing the area. Four of the eight crews taking part had already been shot down when Knight, flying at about 100ft, hit some trees and badly damaged both port engines.

This is one of the stories which Paul Brickhill tells beautifully in *The Dam Busters*. With his tailplane and a starboard engine also damaged Knight managed to pull the Lancaster up to about 1,000ft and called his fellow Aussie Mick

HUTCHISON FAMILY

WM COLLECTIONS CH11049

Les Knight and his crew, photographed at Scampton by an official RAF photographer in July 1943. For some reason, none of the subjects is looking at the camera. (Back row left to right) Sydney Hobday, Edward Johnson, Fred Sutherland, Robert Kellow, Ray Grayston. (Front row) Les Knight, Harry O'Brien.

Martin, who had assumed command after the CO and deputy force head had both come to grief.

> 'Two port engines gone. May I have permission to jettison bomb, sir?' It was the 'sir' that got Martin. Quiet little Knight was following the copybook procedure, asking respectful permission to do the only thing that might get him home.
>   Martin said, 'For God's sake, Les, yes,' and as the bomb was not fused Knight told Johnson to let it go. Relieved of the weight they started to climb very slowly…
>   The controls were getting worse all the time until, though he had full opposite rudder and aileron on, Knight could not stop her turning to port and it was obvious that he could never fly her home. He ordered his crew to bale out and held the plane steady while they did.[149]

The scene inside the aircraft just before the crew began baling out was further described by wireless operator Bob Kellow in his memoirs:

---

149 Brickhill, *Dam Busters*, p121.

[W]e had crossed the Dutch/German border and were about half way to the Dutch coast. We all knew that at this height and with only one motor working properly our chances of getting back to England were slim.

Les had asked our rear gunner, 'Obie' O'Brien, to go to the front gun turret ...

'OK I'm in the turret, Les. What do you want me to do?'

'Good, now reach along below my feet Obie and see if you can find a loose, broken cable,' said Les. 'It belongs to the starboard rudder. When you find it, pull on it for all you're worth.'

In a few minutes Obie announced that he'd found the cable and was pulling it.

The plane began to swing slowly to the right. It was only then that I realized that we'd been steadily swinging to the left for the past few minutes. ...

'I'll have to stop the starboard inner, Les,' said Ray, our flight engineer.

'Try to hold it a bit longer, Ray,' Les replied.

Obie meanwhile warned that his arm was breaking from pulling on the cable and he'd need a break.

'OK Obie, but pull on it again as soon as you can,' said Les.

It was clear Les was putting on a superhuman effort to keep our crippled plane on some sort of course, but I knew we couldn't go on much longer. The plane was down to 1,000 feet and the glide angle was steadily increasing.

'Send out that we're bailing [sic] out, Bob,' Les said to me.

I unhooked my morse key and began tapping out the message.[150]

The crew prepared themselves, and one by one they left the aircraft. Kellow moved forward to the cockpit:

I stood by him as he firmly held the wheel and tried to keep 'Nan' on a steady course, making it easier for each man to jump out. Like a sea captain, he wanted to be sure everyone was safely off before he abandoned ship. His parachute was clipped onto his harness and he looked searchingly at me, probably wondering why I hadn't jumped already.

---

150 Bob Kellow, Paths to Freedom, Kellow Corporation 1992, p21.

Using signs, I asked if he was OK. He nodded his answer and a wry
smile puckered his mouth.

With a last smile, I gave him the thumbs-up sign, checked my
parachute and took my position at the edge of the escape hatch. Then
I bent forward with my head down and tumbled out into the dark
Dutch night.[151]

Knight stayed at the controls and attempted a forced landing in a field. He nearly succeeded, but the aircraft hit a bank running across the field and exploded.
All seven of the rest of the crew landed safely. Five evaded capture, while two
became PoWs. There is no doubt that they all owed their lives to their young
pilot, something that they never forgot.

Knight's crash occurred just outside the village of Den Ham, and he is buried
in the village's general cemetery.

Sgt R.E. Grayston
Flight engineer

Raymond Ernest Grayston was born on 13 October 1918 at Dunsfold, Surrey,
and worked as an automobile engineer before the war.

Like many young men of his generation, Grayston was fascinated by flying
and volunteered for the RAF at the beginning of the war. In a TV documentary
to mark the 60th anniversary of the Dams Raid he described how he loved rid-
ing a motorbike at speed, and that this was one of the things which encouraged
him into the air force. Initially he served as ground crew but then, along with

many others who were mechanically minded,
he was selected to train as a flight engineer on
the new generation of heavy bombers which
needed more personnel.

He was posted to 50 Squadron in October
1942, and teamed up with Les Knight, who had
started a tour of operations about a month earlier with a different flight engineer. He flew on
some eighteen operations with Knight before
they were posted en bloc to 617 Squadron in
March 1943.

After their successful attack on the Eder

---

148 Kellow, *Paths to Freedom*, p22.

Dam, the crew's next operation was the doomed operation against the Dort-mund-Ems canal. After baling out of the aircraft Grayston landed uninjured but was captured almost immediately. He was sent to Stalag Luft III, remaining there until January 1945 when the PoWs were forced to march westwards on what became known as the Long March. He reached Stalag IVA at Lucken-walde where, after three months, he was liberated and flown back to England.

He left the RAF after the war. He then joined the aviation firm Hawker Sid-deley and worked as a quality inspector, retiring in 1984. He died in Woodhall Spa on 15 April 2010.

Flg Off H.S. Hobday
Navigator

Harold Sydney Hobday (known as Sydney by his family and friends) was born in Croydon, Surrey, on 28 January 1912, the only child of Howard and Alice Hobday. After leaving school, he worked in the aviation department of Lloyd's, the insurance business. After joining the RAF in 1940, he underwent part of his training in South Africa before qualifying as a navigator in early 1942, and then being commissioned. In the summer of 1942, he crewed up during training with Les Knight and the others who would form his Dams Raid crew and they joined 50 Squadron in September 1942.

Although some eight years older than his young Australian skipper (still then a sergeant pilot) they obviously bonded well and flew on some twenty-five operations together up until March 1943, when the whole crew volunteered to be transferred to the new squadron at Scampton for the secret mission.

One of the reasons the crew worked so well together may actually have been its disparate nature. There were the two slightly older Englishmen, Hobday and bomb aimer Edward Johnson. The flight engi-neer Ray Grayston was also English but Bob Kellow, the wireless operator, was Australian and both the gunners, Fred Sutherland and Har-ry O'Brien were Canadians. All of them shared the highest regard for their young Melbourne-born pilot.

On their return to Scampton after breaching the Eder Dam, Hobday took part in the celebra-tions with a fair degree of gusto. He was in the group photographed outside the Officers' Mess around breakfast time on the morning after

HUMPHRIES FAMILY COLLECTION

the raid, but fell asleep sometime later and regained consciousness at 1300, slumped in an armchair.

On the night of 16 September 1943, when Knight ordered the crew to bale out after the aircraft was badly damaged over the Dortmund Ems canal, Hobday managed to evade capture.

Within a few hours he had made contact with Dutch resistance supporters. He was taken to a woodland shack near Baarn and reunited with his colleague, Fred Sutherland. The pair were then fed into the escape network, and smuggled the whole way through France to the Pyrenees, then onward through Spain to Gibraltar, and then returned to the UK.

After the war, Hobday returned to Lloyd's and eventually became head of the aviation department. He died in Fakenham, Norfolk, on 24 February 2000.

Flt Sgt R.G.T. Kellow
Wireless operator

Robert George Thomas Kellow was born in Newcastle, New South Wales, Australia on 13 December 1916, the son of George and Violet Kellow. He went to Newcastle High School, the same school as fellow Dambuster Jack Leggo, the navigator in Mick Martin's AJ-P. He worked as a shop assistant after leaving school, but when war came he enlisted in the RAAF.

He was selected to train as a wireless operator/air gunner and was sent to Canada for training. From there, he was posted to the United Kingdom, and arrived in January 1942.

After further training he was crewed up with pilot Les Knight and then posted to 50 Squadron. He completed some twenty-five operations with Knight before the whole crew were offered the chance to transfer to the new secret squadron being set up at Scampton. Shortly before the transfer came about, he was recommended for a DFM and then commissioned. The DFM wouldn't actually be awarded until June 1943.

After the disastrous attack on the Dortmund Ems Canal, Kellow baled out. He made the six-week journey to Spain on his own a day or so ahead of Hobday and Sutherland, and arrived back in England in December 1943. Like all those who had made the perilous return trip he was not allowed to fly over enemy territory again, to protect the networks he had used

HUTCHISON FAMILY

to evade capture, so he returned to Australia in May 1944. He served in the RAAF's 37 Squadron for the remainder of the war, mainly in Australia, but including a deployment to New Guinea.In April 1946 Kellow returned to Newcastle, NSW, after being discharged from the RAAF, with a glowing report from his Commanding Officer who described him as showing 'great possibilities for good leadership', and 'one of the most liked and well known' and 'invaluable' members of the Squadron.

He returned to his job as a shop assistant in Australia, and in 1946 married Doreen Smith, a Canadian who he had met while training there in 1941. By 1952, they had two children and the whole family moved to Winnipeg, Canada, where Kellow worked for the Manitoba Power Commission.

Bob Kellow died in Winnipeg on 12 February 1988, and is buried in the city's Brookside Cemetery.

Flg Off E.C. Johnson
Bomb aimer

There were two bomb aimers called Johnson on the Dams Raid, something that occasionally causes confusion. A third bomb aimer was called Johnston. In the inevitable way of things in the wartime RAF, both Johnsons were also known to their friends and colleagues as 'Johnny'. The older of the two was Edward Cuthbert Johnson, bomb aimer in Les Knight's crew, who was born in Lincoln on 3 May 1912. When his father was killed on the Western Front in 1914, he and his mother moved to Gainsborough, although he was educated at Lincoln Grammar School. On leaving school, he worked for Woolworths and then the catering firm, Lyons, and then in a boarding house business in Blackpool with his wife's family.

He joined the RAF in 1940, qualified as an observer/bomb aimer in early 1942, and was commissioned. After further training he was posted briefly to 106 Squadron, but then sent back to a training unit to be crewed up with Les Knight and his colleagues. They moved to 50 Squadron in September 1942, and Johnson flew on some twenty-two operations with the Knight crew.

Johnson and Hobday were the elder statesmen of the Knight crew, both nine years older than their skipper, and senior to him in rank. But they worked well as a team, each obviously seeing in the younger man the qualities of an outstanding

HUMPHRIES FAMILY COLLECTION

pilot. All three were decorated for their role in the Dams Raid, Knight getting the DSO and Johnson and Hobday the DFC, and were photographed together outside Buckingham Palace on the day of the investiture.

In September, on the fateful Dortmund Ems operation Johnson jumped from the stricken Lancaster when ordered to by Knight. He yelled: 'Cheerio boys. Best of luck. See you in London.' He recalled later: 'The farewells were a little hasty but lacked nothing in sincerity for that.'

Like four of his colleagues, Johnson successfully evaded capture and reached the safety of Spain, with the help of a friendly Dutch farmer and policeman, and various members of the resistance in Holland, Belgium and France. He returned to the UK via Gibraltar. He served out the rest of the war in various ground postings, and left the RAF in 1947. He went back to Blackpool, and joined a company selling fireplaces, where he worked until his retirement.

Edward Johnson died in Blackpool on 1 October 2002.

Sgt F.E. Sutherland
Front gunner

Frederick Edwin Sutherland was born in Peace River, Alberta, Canada on 26 February 1923, the only boy in a family of the three children of Dr Frederick Henry Sutherland and his wife, Clara. His father was a doctor and his mother was a nurse. From a young age, he had wanted to fly and had dreams of becoming a bush pilot, but the war put paid to that. So he joined the RCAF in 1941, as soon as he turned 18. After initial training he volunteered for air gunner duties

He arrived in England in 1942, and crewed up with Les Knight and his future colleagues at a training unit before they were all posted to 50 Squadron in September of that year. He flew on twenty-five operations with Knight before the whole crew volunteered to transfer to the new 617 Squadron in March 1943.

After the Möhne was breached and the crew moved on to the Eder, he realised how difficult the attack was going to be. He recalled the operation in a 2013 TV interview:

We were all afraid of the hill. We had to drop the bomb at the right distance and the right height, and then to make it [Les] had to push the throttles right through the gate, which is not supposed to be done … I didn't

see anything when the bomb went off because I was in the nose, but I heard the rear gunner saying: 'It's gone, it's gone.'[152]

After the raid, Les Knight, Sydney Hobday and Johnny Johnson were decorated. Knight was embarrassed that the whole crew had not been rewarded, Sutherland recalled. 'He felt badly that half the crew got decorated, the other half didn't. He said you know I'm wearing the DSO for all you guys, you all did something for it.'[153]

On the fateful Dortmund Ems raid in September, Knight's crew were in the formation of four aircraft led by the new squadron CO, George Holden. As they flew over the small town of Nordhorn in Holland, Holden was hit by flak, and his aircraft exploded. On board were four of Gibson's Dams Raid crew, including fellow Canadians, Terry Taerum and George Deering. Sutherland in the front turret saw everything:

It was so close I could almost reach out and touch it. Your friends are getting killed and you are scared as hell but you can't let it bother you because if you did, you could never do your job. All you can do is think, 'Thank God it wasn't us.'[154]

Hours later, Sutherland was himself on Dutch soil, having parachuted to safety after being ordered by Knight to bale out. After being hidden by a friendly Dutch farmer, he was put in touch with the underground network, and met up with Sydney Hobday. The two were smuggled all the way through Belgium and France to Spain.

Not long after getting back to the UK he was sent home to Canada. Greeted in Edmonton by his girlfriend, Margaret Baker, he immediately proposed to her. Terry Taerum's mother found out that he had been posted back to Canada, and asked to meet him. She wanted to know whether her son had any chance of escaping the blaze when his aircraft was hit. 'Telling her about it was the hardest thing I ever had to do,' he said in 2013.

Following the war, Sutherland stayed on in the RCAF for twelve more years, and was commissioned. He then studied forestry, and got a job with the forestry service. In 1964 he became forestry superintendent in Rocky Mountain House in his home province of Alberta, and he still lives in the area.

---

152 Interview with Fred Sutherland, CBC, May 2013.
153 John Sweetman, David Coward, Gary Johnstone, *The Dambusters,* Time Warner 2003, p163.
154 *Edmonton Journal,* 9 November 2013.

HUMPHRIES FAMILY COLLECTION

Sgt H.E. O'Brien
Rear gunner

Henry Earl O'Brien, known as Harry, was born in Regina, Saskatchewan, Canada on 15 August 1922. He volunteered for the RCAF soon after he turned 18, and was selected for gunnery training. On arriving in the UK and further training, he crewed up with Les Knight and the rest of his colleagues, and they were all posted to 50 Squadron at the same time. He flew on twenty-three operations with Knight between September 1942 and March 1943.

Like his colleagues, O'Brien hugely admired his pilot. Knight was 'the coolest and quickest thinking person I have ever met. And, in my opinion, the most knowledgeable person on the squadron with respect to his job.'

Four months later, on their final flight together on the attack on the Dortmund Ems canal, O'Brien was one of the two crew members who were captured after baling out over Holland. He spent the rest of the war as a PoW, and returned to Canada after his release.

Harry O'Brien died on 12 September 1985 in Edmonton, Alberta.

Crew 10: AJ-E
Detailed to attack Sorpe Dam. Crashed on outward flight.
Lancaster serial number: ED927/G

Flt Lt R.N.G. Barlow DFC
Pilot

Robert Norman George Barlow was born on 22 April 1911 in Carlton, a suburb of the Australian city of Melbourne. He was always known by his middle
name, Norman. The Barlows were a colourful family: Norman's father Alexander George Barlow, known as Alec, built up a thriving motor business, Barlow
Motors, in the 1920s. He had sponsored the adventurer Francis Birtles and his
older son, Alexander Arthur Barlow (also called Alec), when they undertook
a record-breaking drive from Darwin to Melbourne in 1926. The pair covered
the 5438km distance in eight days and thirteen hours. The car they drove, a
Bean nicknamed 'Sundowner', is now in the National Museum of Australia.

The Barlow family houses, business premises and stables were all designed
by the fashionable architect Arthur Purnell, with whom Alec Barlow Sr went
into business. But many of his ventures were very close to the line and having
defrauded a wealthy merchant of a large sum of money and forged Norman's
name on a loan document, Alec Sr committed suicide in 1937.

Norman Barlow had been working in the family business, but by the time he
joined the RAAF he was running a garage. On his application form his occupation was given as 'service station proprietor'. He had also qualified as a civilian
pilot, so he had a head start in being chosen to carry on that role in the service.

Barlow married his second wife, Audrey, in 1940, shortly before joining
up. He had an infant daughter named Adrianne born in 1938 from his first
marriage, but she was living with his widowed
mother. He left Australia for the last time in the
autumn of 1941, sent to Canada for final training. He received his pilot's flying badge in January 1942, and was also commissioned. By March
he was in the UK, and posted to 16 Operational
Training Unit for bomber training.

In September 1942, Barlow was posted to 61
Squadron, based at RAF Syerston, where he began a successful first tour of operations. His regular crew included flight engineer Leslie Whillis
and bomb aimer Alan Gillespie, both of whom

LINCOLNSHIRE COUNTY COUNCIL

had been in his crew since they had met at 16 Operational Training Unit. Both would also later accompany him to 617 Squadron.

At the end of his tour, Barlow was recommended for the DFC. The citation read:

> Throughout his many operational sorties, this officer has displayed the highest courage and devotion to duty. He has participated in many attacks on Essen, Berlin, Hamburg and Cologne, and on two occasions he has flown his aircraft safely back to base on three engines. During periods of the most extensive operations Flt Lt Barlow has set a magnificent example of courage and determination.

The award was confirmed in the *London Gazette* two days before the Dams Raid. In his last letter home, wireless operator Charlie Williams told his family that '[Barlow] is very thrilled today as he has just been awarded the D.F.C. [H]e is a very good pilot and I have every confidence that he will bring me through my second tour.' In the same letter, Williams confirmed that both his and Barlow's names had featured in a radio broadcast heard by his family at home. This refers to a recording made earlier during their time at 61 Squadron.

Barlow died when AJ-E collided with a pylon near Haldern, and crashed into a small field on the edge of a copse. All seven of the crew were buried in Düsseldorf North Cemetery and they were reinterred after the war in Reichswald Forest War Cemetery.

It took several months for definite news of their fate to reach the British authorities and then to be transmitted onto their counterparts in Australia and Canada. At this stage, Alec Barlow Jr was a Group Captain commanding an RAAF training school, and was quick to use his connections to see if he could find further information. After the war, he had a long career with Qantas, and died in 1972.

Plt Off S.L. Whillis
Flight engineer

Samuel Leslie Whillis, known as Leslie to his family, was born in Newcastle on Tyne on 18 October 1912, the second son of Charles and Edith Whillis. He worked as a commercial traveller before joining the RAF shortly after the outbreak of war, and served as ground crew until 1942. He then, took the opportunity to train as a flight engineer. Having qualified, he was then posted to 1654 Conversion Unit, where it would seem that he first came across both Norman

Barlow and Alan Gillespie. In September 1942, the three moved to 61 Squadron and flew their first operation over the Alps to Turin in Italy on 20 November 1942.

In January 1943, Whillis missed a few operations – perhaps because of illness – so by the time Barlow was at the end of his tour, he had only completed twenty-two operations. When he was offered the chance to move to a new squadron with Barlow, he must have thought that it was a good opportunity to complete his tour with a pilot with whom he had worked well.

Two days before the raid, both Whillis and Gillespie received commissions, backdated to April 1943. At this stage of the war, commissioned flight engineers were rare, so Whillis had obviously impressed his superiors.

Leslie Whillis married Gladys Cooper in Newcastle in 1941. He is buried in Reichswald Forest War Cemetery.

Flg Off P.S. Burgess
Navigator

Philip Sidney Burgess was born in Portsmouth on 19 September 1922, the son of Willis and Marie Burgess. Both his parents died when he was very young, so at the age of 4 he and his brother Carroll were adopted, but by different families. Philip was adopted by his aunt, Gertrude Lewis, in Folkestone, Kent. When she died in 1938, he was then adopted by the Rowland family in the same town. Carroll was adopted by the Brookes family. Philip Burgess was educated at the Harvey Grammar School in Folkestone.

He volunteered for the RAF soon after his 18th birthday, and undertook part of his training in Canada. He was commissioned in May 1942, and after further training was promoted to Flying Officer shortly before being posted to 61 Squadron in January 1943, a few months after he turned 20. Although he arrived with a crew in which he was the bomb aimer, he wanted to be a navigator. He then joined the crew captained by the New Zealander Ian Woodward, in which the wireless operator was Charlie Williams, starting life as its bomb aimer but then becoming its navigator. By the end of March when Woodward and Williams had completed their tours, Burgess had clocked up approximately seventeen operations. Both Burgess and Williams agreed to join the crew being put together by Norman Barlow which would transfer to 617 Squadron for the planned secret mission.

Philip Burgess is buried in Reichswald Forest War Cemetery. Yet to turn 21, he was the youngest officer to take part in the Dams Raid. His brother, Carroll Burgess, served in the Royal Engineers and survived the war.

Flg Off C.R. Williams DFC
Wireless operator

Charles Rowland Williams was born on 19 March 1909 in Townsville, Queensland. He was the middle child of the three surviving children of sheep station manager Horace Williams and his wife Hedwige or Helene (she used both names). His mother seems to have decided to travel to Townsville in order to have the baby. At the time of his birth the family lived in Winton, but then lived at a series of other sheep stations before moving to Telemon, a station near Hughenden, when he was 10 years old. This was a small settlement in inland Queensland, some 250 miles west of Townsville. Australian country districts did not have elementary schools in those days so Williams was tutored at home until he went to Townsville Grammar School as a boarder at the age of 12.

Leaving school at 16, he went home to work on the station his father managed. He also became a skilled mechanic and took up building wireless sets and photography as hobbies. The great crash of the early 1930s led to his father losing his job so, as part of a syndicate, the family bought their own station which they had to work hard to build up.

Like many young men of his generation, Williams had long wanted to fly and took some flying lessons at the aero club in Townsville. When war came, he was already 30 years old. Both he and his brother could have avoided military service on the grounds that their elderly father was ill, and could not run the property on his own but they both joined the army reserve. They agreed between themselves that Doug as the elder should remain in the army so that he could stay in Australia to take responsibility for the family, but younger brother Charlie should volunteer for the air force.

In February 1941, some seventeen months later, Williams began his training. He was posted to Sydney, and then on to a training school in rural New South Wales. By then almost 32, he was mustered as a wireless operator/air gunner. After training, he was commissioned and then posted to England.

He arrived in Bournemouth in November 1941, a few weeks before Pearl Harbor. This traumatic event had another, often overlooked, consequence besides bringing the USA into the war. The Australian government quickly realised how exposed their country was to possible invasion by the Japanese and many aircrew under training were kept back in case they were needed at home.

Caught in a training bottleneck, Williams remained at Bournemouth until being assigned to No 1 Signals School at Cranwell in the middle of February, and then to 14 OTU at Cottesmore in the first week of April. However, his operational experience began very suddenly, when the unit was required to send several Hampdens on the first Thousand Bomber Raid, on Cologne on 30 May 1942. He was also sent on the later raids on Essen and Bremen.

By September, he was ready for operations and had arrived at 61 Squadron at Syerston, as wireless operator in a Lancaster crew skippered by Flg Off Brian Frow, an experienced pilot, who went on to survive the war and rise to the rank of Air Commodore. Their first operation was a raid on Munich and they flew on seven more before Frow finished his tour.

In December, Frow was replaced by a New Zealander, Flt Sgt Ian Woodward, another pilot who also survived the war. Philip Burgess would also join this crew in early 1943. By March 1943, Woodward had completed his tour, but Williams had to do one more as he had missed a couple of operations back in January through illness. He flew on a trip to Berlin, and his CO signed off his logbook as tour complete. He wanted to return to Australia, as his father was seriously ill, which would probably mean he would need to do a second tour. If he went on the normal six-month inter-tour break that would only delay things.

Also, he had broken off his engagement to his Australian fiancée (they hadn't been in touch for several months) as he had become involved with another woman in Nottingham, Gwen ('Bobbie') Parfitt. He wanted to marry her as soon as possible, and then bring her back with him to Australia.

He wrote to his family about his decision:

> Yesterday I made a decision which may or may not be wise, I am joining a crew with an Australian as pilot, he, like myself has nearly finished his first tour and when we have finished we are going to

another squadron and will carry on with our second tour without any rest, the second tour now consists of 20 trips and we believe when we have finished our operations we will have a much better chance of being sent home, and with the summer coming we should finish in three or four months, and I think it is better to do that than have to come back on operations after having been off for six months.

The Australian pilot and the new squadron he mentions in this letter were of course Norman Barlow and 617 Squadron. And so it was that his fate was sealed, for a few weeks later they were leading the second wave of the Dams Raid over Haldern in Germany when they hit the fateful electricity pylon.

Like several other Dams Raid participants Williams had been recommended for a decoration, in his case the DFC, but it was not awarded until after his death. It was eventually presented to his mother. The news that he had broken off his first engagement had not reached Australia by the time of the Dams Raid, so his first fiancée, Millie McGuiness, was contacted by the Australian authorities when his death was confirmed. Eventually his new fiancée, Bobbie Parfitt, was able to set the record straight.

In his final letter to his family, Williams wrote:

> How I wish I could tell you everything I would like to, there is so much I could tell you but until the war is over I cannot tell anyone but I hope in the near future I will be able to tell you some of the amazing things I have seen and experienced.

Because of the delays in the postal service this was the last of the several letters which kept on arriving at home well after his death.

He also wrote and posted a final letter to Bobbie. Timed at 7.30pm, it may be the last written by any of the men who died on the Dams Raid. It reads in full:

> Scampton
> Sunday 16th May 7:30 PM
> My Darling Bobbie.
> Well darling I am very sorry I was unable to get in tonight, I was very disappointed about it also at not being able to contact you at Joans, but I could not ring you after four o'clock as I was too busy, I am almost sure I will be in Monday or Tuesday night, but will phone you and try and let you know.
>   When I do see you I hope to be able to explain why I have not

been able to get in, and I am quite sure that you will then know that it has been absolutely impossible for me to get in during the past two weeks except for the one night I did come in and could not find you.

There is quite a big chance that I may get leave sooner than I expect, and if I do I may not be able to give you more than a few days notice, but will try and let you know as soon as possible, and when I do get that leave I hope you are able to get leave also, so that we can be married.

I will have a lot to tell you when I do see you darling and I can only hope it will be very soon, because I have missed you an awful lot, and it seems ages since I saw you last.

This letter will have to be very short dear as I have very little time, and have work to do, and am only able to let you know that I have not forgotten you.

Cheerio for now darling and believe me when I say I love you very dearly and always will.

All my love dear and kisses

Charles.

Charlie Williams is buried in Reichswald Forest War Cemetery.[155]

Plt Off A. Gillespie DFM
Bomb aimer

Alan Gillespie was born on 16 November 1922 in Hesket, Westmorland. He was the second of the four children of Robert and Margaret Gillespie. His father was a railway porter. The family then moved to Long Marton, near Appleby. Alan Gillespie went to the village school in Long Marton and then Appleby Grammar School. After leaving school he worked as a clerk in a solicitor's practice before volunteering for the RAF in 1940. He was eventually selected

HUMPHRIES FAMILY COLLECTION

---

155 Williams's letters to his family, to Bobbie Parfitt and his other papers are now in the Queensland State Library in Brisbane, with a set of copies of the Parfitt letters also held in the Imperial War Museum. His family papers were used in the biography *An Airman Far Away*, written by historian Eric Fry, who had married Williams's sister Sheila after the war. (Kangaroo Press 1993.)

for aircrew and sent to Canada for training in September 1941.

After returning to the UK, he underwent further training and met up with Norman Barlow and Leslie Whillis at 16 OTU in July 1942. All three were eventually posted to 61 Squadron in September 1942, and did their first operation together over the Alps to Turin on 20 November.

By March 1943, Barlow and Gillespie had both completed their tours. Like his captain, Gillespie's tour ended with a recommendation for a medal, in his case the DFM. The citation read:

> This Air Bomber has carried out 30 successful sorties on all the main targets in Germany and Italy, including six attacks on Essen and five on Berlin. He has frequently obtained excellent photographs, one of his best being the aiming point on Krupps. He has shown himself cool and collected under heavy fire in the target area and has set an excellent example to others in his crew and the rest of the squadron. Strongly recommended for the award of the Distinguished Flying Medal.

When Barlow set about putting together a crew who would accompany him on to 617 Squadron Gillespie and Whillis, who had both been with him since their training days, volunteered to go with him. Both were commissioned two days before the Dams Raid. Whether they had time to move from the Sergeants' to the Officers' Mess is not recorded.

Alan Gillespie is buried in Reichswald Forest War Cemetery. The DFM he had won a few weeks before was presented to his family posthumously. The official notice appeared in the same July 1945 issue of the *London Gazette* as the one for Charlie Williams.

Flg Off H.S. Glinz
Front gunner

Harvey Sterling Glinz was born in Winnipeg, the capital city of the province of Manitoba, Canada on 2 March 1922. His father Ernest was a letter carrier, or postman. Glinz was educated at Lord Roberts and Kelvin Schools, and had worked as a clerk in the Hudson's Bay company until the war intervened.

Having volunteered for the RCAF Glinz was interviewed on 11 September 1941, and deemed to be best fitted for work as an air gunner/wireless operator. It was noted that he was 'A neat clean – athletic young man – sincere – and should be worthwhile addition to aircrew.' He signed up a few weeks later and was sent off for training. Glinz excelled at his air gunnery training, passing out first in his class in February 1942. He then applied for a commission, which was granted after he had left Canada. He arrived in England at the end of March.

After various delays and yet more training, he was finally posted on operations to 61 Squadron in October 1942, as part of a crew captained by Plt Off William Dierkes, an American who had joined the RCAF before the USA entered the war, and who would later transfer to the USAAF. His first operation, however, was a raid on Turin on 28 November 1942, in a crew captained by Flg Off A.E. Foster. This would appear to have been as a replacement for Foster's usual gunner. A week later he flew with Flt Sgt McFarlane, on an operation to Mannheim.

Glinz flew on eight operations with Dierkes between December and February, but then went on sick leave. The medical report shows that he had suffered from catarrh and ear infections caused by the unaccustomed British weather, and that also he was suffering from 'mild anxiety'. This was reported to have been caused by two crashes on landings on both his second and fourth operations. He was also diagnosed as being in a mild 'anxiety state', after being observed sitting on his own in the mess and seldom conversing with people. An RAF Medical Board first recommended that Glinz should see a specialist 'neuropsychiatrist', but then at the end of March reported that:

> He had been thinking things over and wishes to resume operational flying. He has an opportunity of being crewed up with an experienced pilot in whom he has every confidence. This crew is being posted to another unit to form a new squadron. He appreciates that his symptoms are nervous in origin but thinks that he can make the grade and complete his tour … The Board considers this Officer to be a fundamentally good type and should be given a further opportunity to prove himself at operational flying.[156]

So Glinz went to 617 Squadron, along with Barlow and the rest of his ex-61 Squadron crew. There are no further medical reports in his file.

Glinz became 617 Squadron's A Flight Gunnery Leader, a role which would

---

156 Flg Off H.S. Glinz, RCAF personnel file, National Archives of Canada.

have meant he helped organise training for other gunners. He must have been awarded this role because of his rank, rather than experience, as there were other gunners in A Flight with a full completed tour under their belts.

Harvey Glinz is buried in Reichswald Forest War Cemetery. In a sad post-script to the short lives of two of the crew of AJ-E, it emerged in October 1945 that Harvey Glinz and Philip Burgess's service greatcoats had been inadvertently swapped when their possessions were sent back to their families. Glinz's personnel file contains a letter sent to his family, asking them to inspect the coat they had received and see whether its buttons were those of the RAF or the RCAF. It having been ascertained that they were in fact RAF buttons, the two coats were then exchanged. Whether Glinz and Burgess were roommates at Scampton is not known, but the fact their coats were muddled up suggests they might have been.

Sgt J.R.G. Liddell

Rear gunner

Jack Robert George Liddell was the youngest man to take part in the Dams Raid. He was born on 22 June 1924 in Weston-super-Mare, Somerset, the son of Robert and Winifred Liddell. His father died when Jack was a young boy and his mother remarried, so he had one sister and two further half-sisters. He was educated at Weston's Walliscote Road School, and then took up work in the butchery trade. Meanwhile his stepfather was killed at Dunkirk. His sister Sheila Fenwick recalls him dressing in a suit one day in May 1941 and telling her that he was going to Bristol for the day. When he returned, he said that he had volunteered for the RAF. She was not surprised as, like so many other young men of his age, he was 'flying mad'. He must have lied about his age, since he was still only 16.

Liddell was selected for air gunner training, which he completed in May 1942. In September, he was posted to 61 Squadron as the rear gunner in a crew captained by Flt Sgt John Cockshott. This crew completed a full tour of thirty operations together, and as a gesture of thanks to their pilot, they bought him a silver tankard. They weren't able to get it engraved, but they gave him specific instructions to do this at the end of the war along with the wording that should be used. Cockshott rose to the rank of Squadron

LIDDELL FAMILY

Leader and in July 1944 he moved to 617 Squadron to start his second tour. He was the pilot who dropped the second ever Grand Slam bomb, and was involved in the attacks on the Tirpitz and other big targets. He died in 2010, and his family said that the tankard remained one of his most prized possessions.

After completing his tour with Cockshott, Liddell was posted to a training flight as an instructor, but within a week he was called back to fly in the crew being put together by Norman Barlow, which would transfer to 617 Squadron. He was a much more experienced gunner than his crewmate, Harvey Glinz, but it was the officer Glinz who was chosen to be the A Flight Gunnery Leader.

Jack Liddell had still not reached his 19th birthday when he climbed into the rear turret of AJ-E in the early evening of 16 May 1943. He is buried in Reichswald Forest War Cemetery.

Crew 11: AJ-W
Detailed to attack Sorpe Dam. Damaged by flak and returned to base.
Lancaster serial number: ED921/G

Flt Lt J.L. Munro
Pilot

John Leslie Munro was born in Gisborne on the North Island of New Zealand on 5 April 1919, the oldest of three children. His family had a sheep station a few miles outside town. It emerged in about 1999 that his mother had another child, a daughter born in 1913, in an earlier relationship but had given her up for adoption.

Munro was educated in local schools, but left at 14 to work in farming. When the war came he waited until 1940, when he was 21, to volunteer for the RNZAF. He wanted to be a pilot. but he was told that his educational qualifications were 'insufficient for pilot training' and that he would have to be a gunner. Not to be put off, he spent the next twelve months studying at home, doing a maths course before reapplying. This time he was successful and he was enlisted into the RNZAF in July 1941.

After initial training in New Zealand Munro was sent to Canada to complete bomber training and qualified as a pilot in February 1942, receiving a commission at the same time. He undertook further training after arriving in England, and the crew with whom he would fly for most of the rest of his career began to be assembled.

He began his operational career while still at 29 OTU, flying on two sorties. After further heavy bomber training he joined 97 Squadron at Woodhall Spa in December 1942. His crew's first operation on 8 January 1943 was minelaying, followed on 13 January by an attack on Essen. The crew had completed some further seventeen operations by the time they volunteered to join 617 Squadron towards the end of March 1943.

Even though his role in the Dams Raid had come to a premature end, Munro still participated in the events that followed. He was presented to both the King and Queen during the royal visit on 27 May. Gp Capt Leonard Slee, the officer who was accompanying the Queen, didn't seem to know his name, so the forthright Munro stepped in, not aware he was breaking

Les Munro photographed with his crew, probably in the summer of 1943. (Standing left to right) Les Munro, Jimmy Clay, Bill Howarth, Harvey Weeks. (Crouching, left to right) Grant Rumbles, Frank Appleby, Percy Pigeon.

some sort of protocol. 'My name's Munro,' he told her. Then, a few weeks later he was at the famous Hungaria Restaurant party in London given by Avro. He had in fact been decorated with a DFC shortly before the 617 Squadron investiture, awarded for twenty-one operations in 97 Squadron.

617 Squadron went back on operations in July 1943, and Munro's was one of the crews which took part in a raid on Italian power stations from where they flew on to Blida in North Africa. They flew a little too low and a flak hit resulted in a burst tyre and a flesh wound to bomb aimer Jimmy Clay's nose.

His next operation was an abortive attack on the Antheor Viaduct in September. Another short gap followed, but then between November 1943 and July 1944 he undertook almost thirty more operations. He became Flight Commander of the Squadron's B Flight and was temporarily CO of the whole squadron for some of February 1944 while Leonard Cheshire was on leave. In April 1944 he was awarded the DSO.

A month after D-Day, Munro was taken off operations, along with Cheshire, David Shannon and Joe McCarthy. Air Vice Marshal Ralph Cochrane, the CO of 5 Group, decided that all four were by then on 'borrowed time' and should cease immediately.

Munro spent the rest of the war in a training flight, and was finally demobilised in February 1946. He returned to New Zealand, and the business of running a sheep farm. He was active in politics for a while and became Mayor of Waitomo District, where there is now a street named after him.

In 2013 he flew to the UK for the last time, and took a full part in the 70th anniversary commemoration of the Dams Raid. He was accompanied by one of his sons and an official from the New Zealand High Commission. When this official was asked whether he was there as Les's 'minder' he was quick to say that Les didn't need any minding whatsoever.

Shortly before his death Munro made the very generous offer to sell his medals and memorabilia (which include a signed menu from the post-raid dinner at the Hungaria Restaurant) to raise funds for the Bomber Command Memorial in London. He felt strongly that the sacrifice of the 55,000 aircrew who died in the war should continue to be honoured. However, the collection was saved for the Museum of Transport and Technology in Auckland, by being purchased by the British peer and collector Lord Ashcroft.

Les Munro died on 4 August 2015 in Tauranga, New Zealand.

Sgt F.E. Appleby
Flight engineer

Frank Ernest Appleby was born on 3 November 1921 in Eastbourne, Sussex, one of the eight children of Thomas and Ethel Appleby. His father was a fitter in the gas works. Appleby volunteered for the RAF at the age of 18, in August 1939 a few weeks before the outbreak of war. He was assigned to ground crew as a maintenance engineer, but then trained as a flight engineer.

Appleby crewed up with Les Munro, Grant Rumbles, Bill Howarth and Percy Pigeon while at 1654 Conversion Unit in October 1942. He had completed some eighteen operations with Munro in 97 Squadron when they were all transferred to 617 Squadron in March 1943.

The Munro crew's participation on the Dams Raid came to a premature end after they were hit by flak crossing the Dutch coast. They were next back in action two months later on the squadron's next operation, where they flew on to a base in the newly liberated Algeria after attacking Italian power stations. Appleby went on to serve as Munro's flight engineer right through to the end of the crew's tour in July 1944.

In April 1944, Appleby was recommended for the DFM. The citation read:

MUNRO FAMILY

> Flight Sergeant Appleby has completed 39 operational sorties as a
> Flight Engineer against heavily defended targets in Germany, Italy
> and France. He began operating in January 1943, and chose on the
> expiration of his first tour to carry on without a rest period. He has
> always enjoyed the complete confidence of his captain by his capable
> handling of the engines. When the aircraft has been heavily engaged
> by enemy defences, he has always displayed exceptional calmness
> and presence of mind. Since volunteering in March 1943 to join a
> special duties squadron, his utter contempt for personal safety and
> unflinching courage have proved an inspiration to all his crew. He is
> therefore strongly recommended for the award of the Distinguished
> Flying Medal.

Although he was a firm believer in a bomber crew's strict hierarchy (the pilot was 'the leader, the boss, the director of what went on in the aircraft'), the ever-cautious Munro eventually had enough confidence in the man who sat next to him for so long.

> [Munro] learnt that many pilots handed over the controls to their
> flight engineer on their way home. 'This practice became more
> common as the risk of Jerry night fighter attack diminished. I must
> admit that it was a long time before I was prepared to hand over the
> controls to Frank and when I did he handled them quite well. When
> I was confident of his ability to stick to the course and height I would
> take over from the gunners in their turrets and get a feel for their
> contribution to the team effort.'[157]

Munro and all his crew were finally taken off operations in July 1944, each of them having completed more than fifty sorties. Appleby went on to serve in various administrative and training functions in the RAF until the end of the war, when he returned to civilian life.

Frank Appleby died in Eastbourne on 15 September 1996.

---

157 John Sweetman, *Bomber Crew*, Abacus 2005, pp111-2.

MUNRO FAMILY

Flg Off F.G. Rumbles
Navigator

Francis Grant Rumbles was born on 14 September 1920 in Kirtlebridge, Dumfriesshire. His father was the headmaster of Breconbeds School in the village, and the young Grant was educated there. He joined the RAF in October 1940, and inevitably acquired the nickname 'Jock'. He was originally selected for pilot training, but ended up qualifying as a navigator. Part of his training was spent in Port Elizabeth in South Africa, and he was commissioned in April 1942.

Rumbles crewed up with Les Munro at 29 Operational Training Unit in July 1942, along with Bill Howarth, and the crew undertook two operations in September 1942 while still under training. They went on to heavy bomber training and arrived at 97 Squadron at Woodhall Spa in December 1942. At this time, Rumbles and Munro were the only two officers in the crew, so they were given a room in the comparative luxury of the Petwood Hotel, in its wartime role as the station's Officers Mess.

Munro and his crew completed another twenty or so operations in the first three months of 1943, and then volunteered for transfer to the new 617 Squadron at RAF Scampton.

In June 1943, soon after the Dams Raid, Rumbles was awarded the DFC for his twenty-three operations completed while in 97 Squadron. He went on to complete thirty-three more, and was awarded a Bar to the DFC in June 1944.

When the Munro crew were all taken off operations in July 1944, Rumbles was posted to RAF Waddington and later onto a specialist navigation course. Towards the end of the war he became Squadron Navigation Officer for 189 Squadron and then Station Navigation Officer at RAF Bardney.

Rumbles stayed on in the RAF for a short while after the war, serving in Singapore and Japan, before retiring in 1947 as a Squadron Leader. He then moved to South Africa. He died in Port Elizabeth, South Africa, on 26 February 1988.

Wrt Off P.E. Pigeon
Wireless operator

Percy Edgar Pigeon was born on 3 June 1917 in Williams Lake, a small town in the centre of British Columbia, Canada. His family had a small ranch in the area. He attended Williams Lake School, and then worked in a local store.

After initial training and qualification as a wireless operator/air gunner in Canada, he embarked for England. In late 1942 he crewed up at a training unit with the New Zealander Les Munro, Grant Rumbles from Scotland and Englishman Bill Howarth, a quartet who would fly together without interruption for the next two years. They went on two operations in a Wellington in September before moving onto heavy bomber training. They transferred to the front line in December, joining 97 Squadron at Woodhall Spa.

Pigeon went on to fly some twenty further operations with Munro between January and March 1943, and then volunteered to accompany Munro and most of the rest of the crew to the new squadron being formed at Scampton.

In September 1943, Pigeon was recommended for a commission, which duly came through three months later. From November through to July 1944, the crew undertook some thirty more operations and Pigeon was awarded a well-deserved DFC. When they were taken off ops, he went to a training unit before returning to Canada in December 1944.

Percy Pigeon stayed on in the RCAF after the war, serving in its Maritime Air Command and finally retiring in 1962 as a Flight Lieutenant. In 1955, as one of the five Dams Raid veterans still serving in the RCAF, he was flown to London to attend the premiere of the film, *The Dam Busters*.

He died on 23 March 1967 in Williams Lake, BC.

Sgt J.H. Clay
Bomb aimer

James Henry Clay was born on 2 February 1911 in North Shields, Tyne and Wear. His parents, Robert and Mary Clay, had twelve children of whom James was the fifth. Robert Clay worked as a stonemason. Clay went to Queen Victoria School in North Shields.

After joining the RAF and qualifying as an air bomber, Jimmy Clay crewed up with Canadian pilot Marcel Cuelenaere while training, as did his future Dams Raid colleague Harvey Weeks. This crew joined 97 Squadron at Woodhall Spa in October 1942.

Before the Cuelenaere crew saw action, Clay was allocated to the crew of another Canadian pilot, George Lancey, for the famous daylight raid on the

MUNRO FAMILY

Schneider works at Le Creusot on 17 October 1942. This, however, resulted in an early return with engine trouble. The Cuelenaere crew then began a run of almost thirty operations together which ended in March 1943, when their pilot reached the end of his tour. This coincided with the call for volunteers for the new 617 Squadron, which Les Munro and most of his crew decided to accept. However, as they were short of a bomb aimer and rear gunner, Clay and Weeks volunteered to go with them.

On his first operation after the Dams Raid in August 1943, Clay received a flesh wound to the nose during an attack on an Italian power station. He went on to fly with Munro some seventeen more times until May 1944. He was commissioned in November 1943, and received the DFC in July 1944. The citation said that he had completed forty-six operations without a break. He served in various training units until the end of the war and left the RAF in December 1945.

Jimmy Clay returned to Tyneside after the war. He married Patricia Butcher in 1944 and they had two children. He worked as an accountant, and died in Gosforth on 6 August 1995.

Sgt W. Howarth
Front gunner

William (Bill) Howarth was born in Oldham, Lancashire on 29 August 1921. His father was also named William Howarth, and he was a warehouse fore-

HOWARTH FAMILY

man in the cotton industry. His mother was Lily Howarth (nee Martin), and she worked as a cotton operative. Howarth went to Higginshaw School, Oldham, and on leaving school worked as a grocer's manager.

He joined the RAF in 1941, and was eventually selected for gunnery training, which he completed in August 1942. He crewed up with Les Munro, Jock Rumbles and Percy Pigeon at the end of September 1942, during heavy bomber training. Frank Appleby also joined the crew at the same time. These five would serve together uninterrupted for another 20 months. Like his colleagues, he had completed some 20 operations with Munro by the time they volunteered for transfer to the new 617 Squadron. Howarth went on to complete more than 50 operations with Munro by the time the crew were taken off operational duties in July 1944.

He was recommended for the DFM in April 1944. The citation read:

> Flight Sergeant Howarth has completed 41 operational sorties as
> Air Gunner and many of these have been against the most heavily
> defended targets in Germany and Italy. He has operated continuously
> since January 1943, and his last 20 sorties have been carried out against
> objectives in occupied Europe whilst operating with a special duties
> squadron. During these operations, his exceptional coolness and
> marked ability as an Air Gunner has materially assisted his Captain in
> pressing home the attacks against opposition. Flight Sergeant Howarth's
> marked enthusiasm for operations and his outstanding devotion to
> duty merit the highest praise. He is therefore strongly recommended
> for the award of the Distinguished Flying Medal.

Howarth was commissioned in June 1944. He spent the remainder of the war in various training roles, rising to the rank of Flight Lieutenant, and acting as Gunnery Leader in several different establishments. He left the RAF in June 1946 and returned to his former job in the grocery trade for a short time, before joining Prudential Assurance in 1947 where he worked until retirement.

He married Doris Hall, a munitions worker, on 3 July 1943, and they had three sons, one of whom died in infancy. During both his working life and his retirement he was active in fundraising for the Leonard Cheshire Homes.

Bill Howarth died in Oldham on 12 January 1990.

Flt Sgt H.A. Weeks
Rear gunner
Harvey Alexander Weeks was born on 10 December 1919 in Chilliwack, British Columbia, Canada. Chilliwack is a large town some 60 miles from Vancouver.

After joining the RCAF and qualifying as an air gunner, he crewed up with Canadian pilot Marcel Cuelenaere during training, along with his future Dams Raid colleague Jimmy Clay. This crew joined 97 Squadron at Woodhall Spa in October 1942. The Cuelenaere crew had completed almost thirty operations together in March 1943 when their pilot reached the end of his tour. This coincided with the call for volunteers for the new 617 Squadron, which Les Munro

and most of his crew had decided to accept. The rear gunner and bomb aimer declined the invitation, so Weeks and Clay volunteered to take his place, even though Munro told them both that operations with the new squadron would be 'probably special, probably dangerous'.

Weeks settled in with his new crew, although he suffered from being jammed into his turret when it was damaged by a plume of water when Les Munro flew too low on a trial drop on 12 May 1943. On the raid itself he was isolated from the rest of the crew when the intercom was severed by flak over Vlieland, and it was only when Percy Pigeon clambered through to the rear of the aircraft that everyone knew he was all right.

The Munro crew's next operation was some two months later, an attack on an Italian power station. Over the next eleven months, Weeks went on to complete more operations than anyone else in the crew – a total of sixty, made up of thirty-three under Munro's captaincy and twenty-seven in his previous crew in 97 Squadron.

He was commissioned in November 1943, and received the DFC in June 1944. After being taken off operations, Weeks went to 1690 Bomber Defence Training Flight where Munro had been posted as CO. He returned to Canada after the war.

Harvey Weeks died in Chilliwack, BC on 22 March 1992.

Crew 12: AJ-K

Detailed to attack Sorpe Dam. Shot down on outward flight.
Lancaster serial number: ED934/G

Plt Off V.W. Byers

Pilot

Vernon William Byers was born in Star City, Saskatchewan on 24 September 1919.[158] He was one of the four children of Frank and Ruby Byers. When he left school, he worked on a farm, in construction and then as a miner in the town of Flin Flon, Manitoba.

In March 1941 he enrolled with the Canadian Army, where he was assessed as 'a healthy appearing young man desirous of transferring for active service with the RCAF'. He managed this transfer on 8 May 1941, enlisting with the RCAF in Winnipeg. He was determined to become a pilot, and received his wings in March 1942, with his final report concluding that he was a 'dependable average pilot in all phases of work.'

He arrived in the UK in May 1942 and finished his training over the next few months, the final phase being at 1654 Conversion Unit at Wigsley, which he joined on 8 December 1942. Having finished training, he and his crew were transferred to 467 Squadron at RAF Bottesford on 5 February 1943 to begin active operational duties.

Byers flew as 'second dickey' on two operations with other crews, and then completed just three further operations before being posted to the new squadron at Scampton. Byers may not have had much experience as a pilot, but he obviously had a 'press-on' attitude and this along with the skills he exhibited during training must have impressed Guy Gibson. On 17 April he was recommended for a commission, with Gibson noting that he was: 'A good type of NCO who is fully capable of holding down a commission. He keeps his crew in

---

158 Some books and website sources have wrong information about Byers. Some of these errors can be traced back to the Commonwealth War Graves Commission whose record states that he was 32 years old. This could well be a simple typing error since he was in fact 23. In some books he is also said to have already completed a full tour of operations before being transferred to 617 Squadron. Byers' RCAF personnel file was first inspected for the book Owen, Darlow, Feast & Thorning, *Dambusters: Failed to Return,* 2013 and has since been obtained from the National Archives of Canada for this book. It verifies both his date of birth and service record. His operations have also been checked in the 467 Squadron Operations Record Book which lists only the three mentioned below, all undertaken in March 1943. These were the only operations Byers undertook as a pilot before transferring to 617 Squadron.

order, is punctual, and understands discipline. Recommended.'[159]

The commission came through a few days before the Dams Raid. And so the new Pilot Officer Byers lined up AJ-K to take off a minute after Les Munro. Everything seemed to go well until he and his crew were shot down near Texel island in the Waddenzee at about 2257 on 16 May, the first crew to be lost on the Dams Raid. Only one body was ever found, that of rear gunner James McDowell on 22 June 1943.

After the war, this fact allowed a final memorandum to be added to Vernon Byers's RCAF file. 'As the body of F/S McDowell was washed ashore off the Coast of Holland it is assumed that the aircraft was shot down over the sea. Classified. Lost at Sea. Case Closed.'

Vernon Byers and his five other comrades are all commemorated on the Runnymede Memorial.

Sgt A.J. Taylor
Flight engineer

Alastair James Taylor was born in Alves, Morayshire on 19 December 1922. He was the older of the two sons of Stephen and Sarah Taylor, and his brother Charles also served as a flight engineer in the RAF. His home village was just a few miles from two locations – Kinloss and Lossiemouth – which would become very familiar to the personnel of Bomber Command in the war years. He went to Elgin Academy.

He joined the RAF as an apprentice at RAF Halton in January 1939, and served in ground crew until selected for flight engineer training at No 4 School of Technical Training at RAF St Athan in the summer of 1942. After qualification, he was posted to 1654 Conversion Unit in December 1942, where he crewed up with Vernon Byers and his colleagues.

Taylor must have persuaded his pilot to fly low over his family home when they flew to Morayshire on a training run in early May. He wrote to his mother shortly after: 'I hope we didn't scare you too much last Monday. I saw you and Aunt Julia just in front of the house but I could not pick dad out anywhere, so thought he would probably be at a pig sale.'[160]

159 Byers RCAF personnel file, National Archives of Canada
160 aircrewremembered.com/byers-vernon.html [Accessed January 2018].

'Beating up' family houses was quite common in wartime, and this is just one of the instances where even though the crews were undergoing training for a top-secret mission, they would often find time to deviate from a planned course to fly over a crew member's house.

The wave from the cockpit was probably the last time that Taylor and his mother saw each other. A few days later AJ-K set off on its fateful flight on the Dams Raid, and was shot down even before it reached the Dutch coast.

Alastair Taylor is commemorated on the Runnymede Memorial. His brother, Sgt Charles Taylor, survived the war.

Flg Off J.H. Warner
Navigator

James Herbert Warner was born on 19 May 1914 in the small Lincolnshire town of Horncastle, in the heart of the area which would become the home of many Second World War airfields. He was the older of the two sons of Harry and Janetta Warner.

He joined the RAF in 1940 and although initially selected for pilot training was eventually transferred to the observer scheme, from which he qualified in September 1942. He received a commission on completing his training.

By December 1942, he was undergoing the final phase of heavy bomber training at 1654 Conversion Unit, and was crewed up with Vernon Byers and the rest of his crew. They all moved together to 467 Squadron on 5 February 1943.

As a Flying Officer, James Warner was the senior member of the Byers crew by rank. Byers himself was recommended for a commission on 17 April, and bomb aimer Neville Whitaker also received one posthumously.

James Warner is commemorated on the Runnymede Memorial.

WILKINSON FAMILY

Sgt J. Wilkinson
Wireless operator

John Wilkinson was born on 2 May 1922 in the village of Antrobus, near Northwich in Cheshire. His father Thomas was a farmer, and he had an older brother and sister. His mother Ethel died of TB when he was only 1 year old. He went to Antrobus School, and left at 14 to work on the family farm. He joined the RAF as soon as he turned 18. His older brother signed up for the army but was refused because, as a farmer, he was in a reserved occupation.

Wilkinson qualified as a wireless operator/air gunner in the summer of 1942. He was posted to 29 OTU in September, where he appears to have met up with pilot Vernon Byers and others in his crew. Together, they went to finish their training in 1654 Conversion Unit in December 1942 and were posted to 467 Squadron in February 1943.

Towards the end of the training period in 617 Squadron the crew was given some leave, and Wilkinson travelled home to the family farm in Antrobus in time to celebrate his 21st birthday on 2 May. The two Canadians in his crew, pilot Vernon Byers and rear gunner James McDowell, who presumably had no close family in the UK whom they could visit, went with him.

John Wilkinson is commemorated on the Runnymede Memorial.

WHITAKER FAMILY

Plt Off A.N. Whitaker
Bomb aimer

Arthur Neville Whitaker, known to his family as Neville, was born in Blackburn, Lancashire on 8 September 1909, the son of James and Edith Whitaker. He went to Blackburn Grammar School and after leaving school studied accountancy. After qualifying as a chartered accountant, he went to work for a firm of musical instrument dealers in Blackpool.

When the war started, shortly before his 30th birthday, he enlisted in the army, joining the local Blackpool Regiment but then in May 1941 he switched to the RAF. After training at Air Observers School he qualified as a bomb aimer. He was posted to 467 Squadron about the time of its formation in early November 1942 in the crew of Sgt Herbert Vine. Charles Jarvie was also allocated to this crew.

After five operations, Whitaker and mid-upper gunner Charles Jarvie swapped into Vernon Byers's crew. On 28 March the crew was posted to 617 Squadron.

At the briefing for bomb aimers and navigators on the afternoon of Sunday 16 May 1943, Whitaker wrote down some of the key route co-ordinates on the back of an envelope, perhaps before transferring them to an official log for the flight. The envelope was found in his personal effects when they were sent to the family after his death.

Neville Whitaker was commissioned on 13 April, before the Dams Raid, but it was not officially notified until 8 June 1943. He is commemorated on the Runnymede Memorial.

Sgt C.McA. Jarvie
Front gunner

Charles McAllister Jarvie was born in Glasgow on 9 May 1922, one of the two children of Charles and Nellie Jarvie. He joined the RAF in July 1940 soon after his 18th birthday. After a long period awaiting training, he was finally selected for aircrew and underwent gunnery training in September 1942.

He was posted to the new 467 Squadron at RAF Bottesford about the time of its formation in early November 1942 and was crewed up with pilot Sgt Herbert Vine, along with bomb aimer Neville Whitaker. After five operations, Jarvie and bomb aimer Neville Whittaker swapped into the Byers crew and on 28 March they were posted to 617 Squadron.

Charles Jarvie is commemorated on the Runnymede Memorial.

Flt Sgt J. McDowell
Rear gunner

James McDowell was the third Scottish-born member of the crew of AJ-K. He was born in Glasgow on 13 August 1910, the son of John and Agnes McDowell. His father was killed in the First World War, so in 1924 his mother, grandmother and the five McDowell children emigrated to Canada, and took up residence

in Port Arthur, Ontario. McDowell worked first for the Coca-Cola company in Port Arthur and was also involved in a local pipe band. He married Dorothea Edna Craig in 1932, and they had two daughters, Darleen and Marilyn. They then moved to the mining district north of Port Arthur where he found work as a gold miner, ending up at the MacLeod Cockshutt mine in Geraldton between 1935 and 1941.

McDowell joined the RCAF in 1941. After training as an air gunner, he was sent to England and underwent further training before being crewing up with fellow Canadian Vernon Byers, and being posted to 467 Squadron in February 1943.

The crew's first operation together was 'gardening' in the Silverthorne area on 9 March, and they would undertake just two further operations before transferring to 617 Squadron on 28 March.

When the crew was given some leave in early May 1943, McDowell and Byers, the two Canadians, travelled to Antrobus in Cheshire, to spend it with the family of their crewmate John Wilkinson. They were all there for Wilkinson's 21st birthday on 2 May.

After their aircraft was shot down and crashed into the Waddenzee, James McDowell's body was eventually released from its rear turret by the elements and found floating in the Vliestrom channel south of Terschelling near buoy No. 2 on 22 June 1943. He was buried the next day in Harlingen General Cemetery, and remains there today. His comrades are all commemorated on the Runnymede Memorial.

Crew 13: AJ-H

Detailed to attack Sorpe Dam. Lost mine flying too close to sea and returned to base.
Lancaster serial number: ED936/G

Plt Off G. Rice

Pilot

Geoffrey Rice was born on 4 January 1917 in Hinckley, Leicestershire, the son of Frederick and Anne Rice. He went to Hinckley Grammar School and was then apprenticed in the hosiery trade. Rice joined the RAF in 1941 and was selected for pilot training, which he undertook in Canada. He qualified as a pilot in February 1942 and was commissioned.

He was posted to 19 Operational Training Unit at RAF Kinloss in July where he crewed up with three of the men who would make up his Dams Raid crew, Richard Macfarlane, Bruce Gowrie, and John Thrasher. They moved on to 1660 Conversion Unit at RAF Swinderby in October 1942 to complete heavy bomber training. Here, Edward Smith and Thomas Maynard joined the crew.

On 9 December 1942, the crew was posted to 57 Squadron at RAF Scampton to begin their operational career. This started on New Year's Eve, 31 December 1942. On 15 March, after the crew had undertaken nine operations, they were transferred to the squadron's new C Flight, under the command of Sqn Ldr Melvin Young.

By 25 March the flight comprised five crews, captained by Melvin Young, Bill Astell, Geoff Rice, George Lancaster and Ray Lovell. It was decided to post the whole flight over to the new squadron being formed at the same base to undertake training for a special mission. Rice and his crew had actually gone on leave the day before, and they did not find out about the transfer until they returned to base on 1 April. Rice and his crew protested at the transfer, but to no avail.

Tasked with attacking the Sorpe Dam, AJ-H took off from Scampton at 2131 but had to turn back about ninety minutes later. Flying too low after crossing the Dutch coast, they hit the water of the Ijsselmeer, and the impact tore the mine free and damaged the aircraft. Everyone was shaken up, but by some miracle the aircraft and crew had survived. The next day, Gibson

RICE FAMILY

Geoff Rice and his crew, photographed while in 57 Squadron. (Left to right) Charles
Challenger (replaced by Stephen Burns before the Dams Raid), Edward Smith, Richard
Macfarlane, Geoff Rice, John Thrasher, Bruce Gowrie, Thomas Maynard.

quizzed Rice over the cause of the loss of his mine, but took no further action.
Rice flew on the operations to Italy in July and August, and was then selected for the very dangerous attack on the Dortmund Ems canal with the new
12,000lb 'thin case' bomb in September 1943. Of the eight pilots who flew on
that raid, only Geoff Rice, Mick Martin and David Shannon survived. In appalling weather conditions, Rice spent seventy minutes searching for the target
but was eventually ordered home by Martin, who had taken over temporary
command of the operation. He jettisoned his giant bomb over the Waddensee.

On 11 November he took part in an attack on the Antheor viaduct, and
later that month was awarded the DFC. The citation singled out his work at the
Dortmund Ems canal, praising his 'great determination and courage.'

On 20 December, eight 617 Squadron crews, led by the new CO Leonard
Cheshire, were sent on an operation to attack an armaments factory in Liège
in Belgium. Geoff Rice and his Dams Raid crew were amongst them. The target marking wasn't visible so Cheshire ordered the crews to return with their
bombs. However, Rice and his crew were unlucky and were shot down by night
fighter pilot Hauptmann Kurt Fladrich 14,000ft above Merbes-Le Chateau. The
last thing Rice remembered was giving the order to bale out. Unfortunately,
there wasn't time and the aircraft exploded.

Rice appears to have been thrown clear, protected by the pilot's armoured seat. Somehow he had deployed his parachute. However, all his colleagues died as the aircraft crashed. Their bodies were found near the crash site, but Rice regained consciousness in a wood, his parachute snagged in a tree, and with a broken wrist. The first people he met were three farm labourers, who took him to the Resistance. His wrist was set in plaster by a friendly doctor, and he spent the next five months on the run. Unfortunately, he was then betrayed to the secret police and became a PoW, ending up at the notorious Stalag Luft III, scene of the Great Escape. As the Russian army approached, the prisoners were forcibly moved, but were eventually liberated by the Americans.

Rice was repatriated after the war, and left the RAF in 1947. He went on to work for Shell Mex and BP and was very active in setting up the 617 Squadron Association. He died in Taunton, Somerset on 24 November 1981.

Sgt E.C. Smith
Flight engineer

Edward Clarence Smith was born in Cambridge on 26 August 1919, the middle of the three children of Clarence and Annie Smith. He joined the RAF in 1937 as ground crew, trained at the No 3 School of Technical Training at RAF Manston and served in various squadrons until 1942.

It was then that the new category of Flight Engineers was introduced, and Smith volunteered for this position. After training he crewed up with Geoff Rice and his team at 1660 Conversion Unit in October 1942. They joined 57 Squadron in December.

The crew had flown on nine operations before being posted over to the new squadron being formed at the same base to undertake training for a special mission. On the Dams Raid, Smith played an important role in bringing the aircraft home safely to Scampton when hydraulic power for the undercarriage had been lost after AJ-H had hit the sea.

Smith flew with Rice and the rest of his crew on the operations they completed in the period from July to December 1943. When they were shot down over Belgium on 20 December 1943 Rice survived. Smith and the rest of the crew were killed and they were buried in Gosselies Communal Cemetery, near Hainaut, Belgium.

Edward Smith had married Evelyn Tyrell in Cambridge in 1942.

HUMPHRIES FAMILY COLLECTION

Flg Off R. Macfarlane
Navigator

Richard Macfarlane was born in Glasgow on 12 December 1921, the older of the two sons of Daniel and Jessie Macfarlane. He attended Hyndland School and the High School of Glasgow. In 1939 he enrolled at the University of Glasgow to study law, but his studies were interrupted when he joined the RAF in 1941. He was sent to Miami in the USA to train as a navigator, and was commissioned on completing the course.

Macfarlane was posted to 19 Operational Training Unit at RAF Kinloss in July where he crewed up with Rice and two more from his Dams Raid crew, Bruce Gowrie and John Thrasher. They moved on to 1660 Conversion Unit at RAF Swinderby in October 1942 to complete heavy bomber training.

On 9 December 1942, the crew was posted to 57 Squadron at RAF Scampton to begin their operational career. The crew had flown on nine operations before being posted over to the new squadron being formed at the same base to undertake training for a special mission. As the most senior navigator in A Flight, Macfarlane became the Flight Navigation Officer.

Shortly before the raid, Macfarlane travelled home to Glasgow on leave to see his family. In a 2013 newspaper interview, his brother recalled that they were obviously engaged in an important project:

> We gathered he was going back to do something special. But he couldn't tell us what it was. On the morning after the overnight raid we were listening to the wireless and heard the dramatic news. So we were pretty certain that was where Richard had been.

They were given leave immediately and he was back at our home in Broomhill, Glasgow, sitting round the dinner-table and confirming he had been on the Dambuster raid that previous night.[161]

Macfarlane flew with Rice and the rest of his crew on the operations they completed in the period July to December 1943. He is buried in Gosselies Communal Cemetery, Belgium.

HUMPHRIES FAMILY COLLECTION

---

161 *The Herald*, 16 May 2013.

Wrt Off C.B. Gowrie
Wireless operator

Chester Bruce Gowrie, always known as Bruce, was born on 14 April 1918 in the small Canadian village of Tramping Lake, which lies roughly halfway between Edmonton and Saskatoon, in the province of Saskatchewan. His parents were Malcolm and Phyllis Gowrie. He attended the local Tramping Lake School, leaving in 1936. He then worked as a post office clerk for four years, while also gaining experience of farming.

He had thought about applying to join the RCAF before the war, so when the war came it was an obvious path to take. He was accepted as a recruit in February 1941, and was selected for wireless operator training. His pre-war hobby of building radio sets made him a natural choice to be selected for wireless work.

After qualifying, Gowrie spent the Christmas of 1941 on leave and embarked for England in January 1942. He was posted to 19 Operational Training Unit at RAF Kinloss in July where he crewed up with Rice and two more from his Dams Raid crew, Richard Macfarlane and John Thrasher. They moved on to 1660 Conversion Unit at RAF Swinderby in October 1942 to complete heavy bomber training.

On 9 December 1942, the crew was posted to 57 Squadron at RAF Scampton to begin their operational career. The crew had flown on nine operations before being posted over to the new squadron being formed at the same base to undertake training for a special mission.

Gowrie flew with Rice and the rest of his crew on the handful of successful operations between the Dams Raid and December 1943, and he was promoted to a Warrant Officer First Class the same month.

He is buried in Gosselies Communal Cemetery, Belgium.

Wrt Off J.W. Thrasher
Bomb aimer

John William Thrasher was born on 30 July 1920 in Amherstburg, a small Canadian town in the far south west of Ontario, very close to the border with the USA. His parents, Charles and Irene Thrasher had fifteen children altogether, although two died in infancy. His father worked as a clerk in a liquor store. He was educated at St Anthony's Primary School and St Rose's High School, and

HUTCHISON FAMILY

matriculated in 1938. He worked as a printer's apprentice for two years, then moved to be a laboratory worker in a soda ash plant.

He enlisted in the RCAF in May 1941, and was selected for Air Observer training, which he completed on 25 September 1941. His CO described him as: 'Straightforward and assertive. Cautious but fairly aggressive. Quick. Cheerful. Good appearance, and personality. Very good material.' But by December he had only passed out twentieth out of twenty-two, with an average overall mark. In further training it was noted that he was weak on navigation, but had achieved 98 per cent in bombing.

After arriving in the UK, Thrasher was posted to 19 Operational Training Unit at RAF Kinloss in July 1942. It was there that he crewed up with Rice and two more men who would eventually form the AJ-H Dams Raid crew, navigator Richard Macfarlane and Canadian wireless operator Bruce Gowrie. They moved on to 1660 Conversion Unit at RAF Swinderby in October 1942 to complete heavy bomber training.

On 9 December 1942, the crew was posted to 57 Squadron at RAF Scampton to begin their operational career. The crew had flown on nine operations before being posted over to the new squadron being formed at the same base to undertake training for a special mission.

Thrasher flew with Rice and the rest of his crew on the operations they completed in the period July to December 1943. He is buried in Gosselies Communal Cemetery, Belgium.

His brother, Plt Off Charles Thrasher, also joined the RCAF and served as a navigator in the Canadian 424 Squadron, based in Yorkshire and flying Halifaxes. He was awarded the DFC in 1944, with the citation noting his 'fortitude, courage and devotion to duty.' He survived the war.

Sgt T.W. Maynard
Front gunner

Thomas William Maynard was born in Wandsworth, London on 6 September 1923, the son of Sydney and Janet Maynard. His father was a police constable. He was known to some of his family as Bill, but to others as Tom.

He joined the RAF in December 1941, and was selected for training as a wireless operator/air gunner. He crewed up with Geoff Rice and his team at

1660 Conversion Unit in October 1942 and they joined 57 Squadron in December.

Maynard kept a diary for the period between starting operations on 31 December 1942 and his arrival on 617 Squadron in early April 1943. This covers the crew's nine operations in some detail. One of these was an 'early return' and would not have counted towards the tour total. On another ten occasions the operation was cancelled, often at very short notice such on this occasion in January:

> Jan 29th. We were briefed for Lorient tonight. Were in the kite and ready to take off when it was scrubbed. Never felt so cheesed off in my young life as we had a decent kite and it looked like an inviting target. I would like to know who actually scrubs these trips as I reckon he is a bloody fool.[162]

Maynard was promoted to Flight Sergeant and flew with Rice and the rest of his crew on the operations they completed in the period July to December 1943. He is buried in Gosselies Communal Cemetery, Belgium.

Sgt S. Burns
Rear gunner

Stephen Burns was born in Dudley, Worcestershire on 27 December 1920, the oldest of the four children of John and Sarah (Sally) Burns. John Burns was a labourer in a steel works. He had served in the Gordon Highlanders during the First World War, and they moved back to his home town of Manchester for a while during Stephen's childhood. As a reservist, his father was called up at the outset of the Second World War, and served in the Royal Engineers.

Stephen Burns was working in an armaments factory in Dudley when the war started. Although he was in a reserved occupation and therefore not eligible for call up, he volunteered for the RAF in 1941, and after a period working as ground crew trained as an air gunner.

After qualifying, he was posted to 57 Squadron in November 1942. He flew in both the mid-upper and rear gunner's turrets on a number of operations

---

162 Press, *All My Life*, p14.

HUMPHRIES FAMILY COLLECTION

with at least four different pilots between December 1942 and 7 February 1943, when he was first allocated to Geoff Rice's crew, when they flew on a trip to Lorient. On this operation he replaced Charles Challenger, who had previously filled this position. Challenger returned to the Rice crew on a couple more occasions but in early March Burns became its regular rear gunner. He was transferred along with the rest of the Rice crew to 617 Squadron at the end of March.

On the Dams Raid, Burns suffered the ignominy of being soaked by a combination of sea water and Elsan contents when AJ-H flew too low and hit the sea, and its Upkeep mine was torn away. The damage was caused by the tail wheel being forced up into the fuselage. Geoff Rice later recalled his understandable reaction, shouting over the intercom: 'Christ, it's wet back here!' Worse nearly followed since, as the aircraft climbed, all the water flooded into the rear turret, threatening to drown its occupant. Burns had to smash the Perspex window so that it could drain out.

Burns was promoted to Flight Sergeant and flew with Rice and the rest of his crew on the operations they completed in the period July to December 1943. He is buried in Gosselies Communal Cemetery, Belgium.

A few weeks earlier, Burns had been best man at the wedding of Sgt Bill Howarth, Les Munro's gunner. Howarth flew on the same operation on 20 December and apparently witnessed the shooting down of Rice's aircraft. He visited the family afterwards and told them what he had seen. After the war, Burns's brother John visited the grave, and was given a pair of gloves belonging to Stephen Burns, which had apparently been retrieved from the wreckage by local villagers. They had taken articles from all the bodies so that if relatives came visiting they could be given some small memento of their loved one.

Crew 14: AJ-T
Attacked Sorpe Dam and returned to base.
Lancaster serial number: ED825/G

Flt Lt J.C. Mccarthy DFC
Pilot

Joseph Charles McCarthy was born on 31 August 1919 in the small town of St James on Long Island, New York, USA, the older of the two sons of Cornelius and Eve McCarthy. His father worked as a clerk. Shortly after Joe was born, the family moved to the Bronx in New York City, where Cornelius worked as a bookkeeper in a shipyard. Later he became a firefighter.

McCarthy's mother died when he was eleven and his grandmother took over the running of the household. Although they lived in the Bronx, they had a summer home on Long Island and it was there he became a champion swimmer and baseball player, and worked as a lifeguard at various beaches including Coney Island. In his late teens, he and his friend Don Curtin became interested in flying and took lessons at Roosevelt Field on Long Island, then the busiest airfield in the USA.

When the war started, McCarthy made several attempts to join the US Air Corps but was rebuffed because he didn't have a college degree. By May 1941, he was getting frustrated and so he and Curtin decided to take an overnight bus up to Ottawa in Canada. Having located the RCAF recruiting office, they were first told to come back in six weeks.

> Don and I responded that we didn't have the money to return again
> so if the airforce wanted us they had better decide that day. With that
> the officer in charge looked the two young, strong, healthy Americans
> over, realised that they were ideal prospects, and said 'Okay.' Enlistment
> papers were filled out, medical examinations were passed, and Joe and
> Don were enlisted in the Royal Canadian Air Force Special Reserve.[163]

The pair became two of the almost 9,000 American citizens who eventually joined the Royal Canadian Air Force. By the end of 1941, they were both qualified pilots and set sail for the UK.

More training was to follow. On 31 July 1942, both Curtin and McCarthy were at 14 Operational Training Unit, training on Hampdens, when they were

---

163 Dave Birrell, *Big Joe McCarthy*, Wingleader 2013, p19. This account owes much to this title.

both called on to participate in one of the large raids which followed the series of Thousand Bomber Raids. 630 aircraft were mobilised from many different squadrons and OTUs for a raid on Düsseldorf.

McCarthy's operational debut passed off without incident, but Curtin had a more eventful trip, evading two separate fighter attacks and then hit by anti-aircraft fire. He landed in a field in Devon and dragged his wounded crew from the aircraft. For this action, he received an immediate DFC, a very rare occurrence of such an award being made for a first operation.

In September 1942, McCarthy and Curtin were both posted to 97 Squadron's conversion flight for their training on Lancasters. When they qualified the pair were split up, with Curtin and his crew going to 106 Squadron and McCarthy and his crew joining the main 97 Squadron.

McCarthy made the usual 'second dickey' trip on an operation to Krefeld on 2 October 1942, flying as co-pilot with Flg Off C.D. Keir. Three days later, the crew undertook their first full operation together, in an attack on Aachen. On 25 February 1943, McCarthy was just six trips short of a full tour when he set off on a trip to Nuremberg. Don Curtin, flying in 106 Squadron, was also on this raid but unfortunately he was shot down near Furth. When word reached 97 Squadron, someone in authority decided not to tell McCarthy until he had completed his tour.

Towards the end of March, McCarthy was phoned personally by Guy Gibson to ask him to join the new squadron he was setting up for a special secret operation. After discussion with his crew, they decided to accept the invitation, and moved to Scampton. They then negotiated four days' leave, during which 'Johnny' Johnson found time to get married.

On the Dams Raid, the crew were forced to switch to the spare aircraft, AJ-T, which delayed their take off by some thirty-three minutes. Eventually they reached the Sorpe Dam, the only aircraft from the Second Wave to reach the target. It was a very difficult attack and required some ten approaches before the mine was dropped. However, despite it being dropped accurately, it did not appear to do more damage than causing a slight crumbling of the top of the structure.

McCarthy and some of his crew participated enthusiastically in the party which followed their debrief. One of the highlights of the weeks that followed

The McCarthy crew, photographed in July 1943. (Left to right) George Johnson, Donald MacLean, Ronald Batson, Joe McCarthy, William Radcliffe, Leonard Eaton. Rear gunner David Rodger was away on a training course when this picture was taken.

IWM COLLECTIONS TR1128

was the royal visit on 27 May, with McCarthy photographed as he talked to the King with his 'Canada USA' shoulder flash clearly visible. He met the Queen again at Buckingham Palace on 21 June when he received his DSO. He is supposed to 'have turned pink and stammered out answers' as she questioned him about his home life in New York.[164]

McCarthy stayed on in 617 Squadron without a break for another thirteen months after the investiture, flying on thirty-four more operations altogether. His Dams Raid crew stayed with him all this time, with the exception of Johnson, who left in April 1944 shortly before his first child was born. McCarthy had insisted to Johnson that he should move on, knowing that he had done a full second tour, and telling him his duties were to his burgeoning family.

After the war, McCarthy went back to Canada and in 1946 married Alice, the American girlfriend he had met while training in 1941. They went on to have two children. In order to stay in the RCAF he took Canadian nationality, but when he finally retired from the service in 1968, he moved back to the USA. He lived in Virginia and worked in real estate.

Over his career he flew nearly seventy different types of aircraft. McCarthy died in Virginia Beach, VA, on 6 September 1998.

---

164 Brickhill, *The Dam Busters*, p.111.

BOMBEER COMMAND MUSEUM OF CANADA

Sgt W.G. Radcliffe
Flight engineer

William Gordon Radcliffe was one of the two Canadian-born flight engineers on the Dams Raid. (Also see Charles Brennan, p126.) He was born in New Westminster, BC, Canada on 24 September 1919, and educated at New Westminster Central School and I.J. Fopp Technical High School. In March 1939, suspecting that war was on its way, Radcliffe travelled to England with his friend Howard Godfrey, and volunteered to join the RAF in ground crew.

As with many ground crew, he saw the 1942 introduction of the new flight engineer trade as the chance to fly. After training at the No 4 School of Technical Training at St Athan he qualified as a flight engineer in July 1942. He was posted to 97 Squadron and flew on his first operation on 10 September 1942. A few days later, he had teamed up with Joe McCarthy and together with Ron Batson and Len Eaton became the nucleus of a crew which would stay together for almost two years.

Radcliffe was also the owner of the crew's mascot, a small stuffed panda bear which he would tuck into his boot on every flight. Its features were also copied onto the nose art on several of the crew's regular aircraft.

Their first operation as a crew was on 5 October on a trip to Aachen. Most crews were given what was thought to be a relatively easy assignment on their first operation. The McCarthy crew's first outing most certainly was not. In a letter home, Radcliffe wrote:

> You usually get a nice easy trip for the first time and we were told this one was going to be fairly easy. But it didn't turn out that way. …
> When we got up to 10,000 feet we ran into an electrical storm. It sure was pretty at first seeing sparks and flashes all over the windscreen and flashes all over the wings and fuselage and the tips of the props were glowing. But then it started to ice up and then the trouble started. … We weren't much troubled by Jerry and we made the target O.K. and just managed to bomb through a gap in the clouds but couldn't see the results.
> Coming back it got worse and we ran into a lot more ice. We must have dropped over 14,000 feet in less than nothing and the rapid

change in temperature or the ice cracked the perspex windows on each side of the cabin and blew a two foot hole out of each side. Believe me then I was scared. ...

Mac is a wizard at handling the machine. If it hadn't of [sic] been for him ... I think if I had to go through these storm on every trip I'd be grey before I'm 24.[165]

Fortunately not every operation was as eventful as this, and Radcliffe went on to complete his full tour with McCarthy by March 1943. The whole crew was then transferred to the new 617 Squadron.

On the raid itself, because of the late change of aircraft, the McCarthy crew were more than half an hour late leaving the ground. Radcliffe's skills as a flight engineer were put to the test as they pulled out all the stops to make up time and they were only nine minutes late reaching the Sorpe Dam.

Radcliffe went on to fly with McCarthy throughout the rest of their second tour. He was commissioned in November 1943, and awarded the DFC in June 1944. After coming off operations, he served in training units for the remainder of the war, returning to Canada in February 1945.

After the war he became a Customs and Excise Officer, and was also attached to the recruiting branch of the RCAF Reserve. Radcliffe married Joyce Palfreyman, an English WAAF, and they had three children. He died on 5 July 1952 when his car failed to go round a bend in the road and went into the Fraser River, where he drowned. It is thought that he had a blackout.

Following his death, Joyce returned to the UK with the children to be nearer her own family.

Flt Sgt D.A. MacLean
Navigator

Donald Arthur MacLean was born in Toronto, Canada on 2 April 1916, one of the four children of James and Edith MacLean. His father worked as a foreman at Goodyear Tires in the city. He went to Bloor Collegiate school and the University of Toronto, and then qualified as a teacher. He was a good ice hockey player, and this helped him get teaching positions in the small towns of Head Lake and Powassan in Ontario.

MacLean volunteered for the RCAF shortly after the war started. After qualifying as a navigator, he set out for England where he undertook further

---

165 Birrell, *Big Joe McCarthy*, p55.

BOMBER COMMAND MUSEUM OF CANADA

training and was posted to 44 Squadron for a short spell. He arrived at 97 Squadron at the end of 1942. His first operation was with Flt Lt K.G. Tew, when they took part in 'gardening' on 31 December 1942. MacLean then flew on a further seventeen operations over the next three months, all except one with Tew as his pilot.

When Alan Westwell finished his tour MacLean became the McCarthy crew's navigator. He may have seen this as a temporary move, since McCarthy and the others were all near the end of their first tour, but when the chance came for a move to a new squadron he went along with it. The easy rapport between McCarthy and his crew would surely have swayed his decision, along with the fact that it already held two other Canadians. Whatever the reason, with MacLean's arrival, McCarthy's crew was complete and wouldn't change again for another thirteen months.

MacLean's navigation log for the Dams Raid provides an account of AJ-T's journey, along with some fascinating details. At 0020, before the aircraft reached the target, MacLean wrote: 'W.Op fixing TR9 under my table'. He recorded the time of arrival at Target Z as 0030 and at 0046 wrote 'Bombs Gone'. If there were nine or ten runs in all, as Johnny Johnson recalls, then this would mean that they took not much more than ninety seconds each time to get back to the starting point.

MacLean's log doesn't seem to record the fact that AJ-T went off course on the way home, ending up over the heavily defended town of Hamm. Fortunately McCarthy managed to find a way through and the aircraft returned unscathed. The error might have been due to the earlier change in compass deviation cards.

MacLean and Johnson were both awarded DFMs for their work on the Dams Raid. It emerged a few days later that MacLean had in fact been commissioned shortly before the raid, but didn't receive notification until afterwards. This meant that logically, he should have received the officers' medal, the DFC, instead. Adjutant Harry Humphries offered to try and get the draft award changed, but MacLean declined, saying, 'Hell, no!'[166]

MacLean carried on flying with Joe McCarthy throughout the rest of their tour, ending with 57 operations under his belt. He married his wife Josie, who

166 Sweetman, *Dambusters Raid*, p245.

had worked as a wireless operator at Scampton, in Lincoln Cathedral in 1944. She went out to Canada and lived with her parents-in-law until MacLean himself was able to return there later that year.

Don MacLean stayed in the RCAF after the war, and eventually retired in 1967 as a Wing Commander. He was stationed in many locations across Canada and the USA but also had a four year stint from 1957 to 1961 on the Canadian Joint Staff in London. The family, which by then included four children, lived in Croydon at that time. After leaving the RCAF, he worked as Director of the Ontario Health Insurance Program (OHIP) in Toronto. He finally retired in 1981 and died in Toronto on 16 July 1992.

Flt Sgt L. Eaton
Wireless operator

Leonard Eaton, aged 37, was the oldest man to take part in the Dams Raid. He was born in Manchester on 16 March 1906, one of the seven children of Thomas and Edith Eaton. He followed his father's trade as a bookbinder after leaving school. He enlisted in the RAF in 1940 and was eventually sent for training as a wireless operator/air gunner. He was posted to a conversion unit in the late summer of 1942. There he became one of the first people to crew up with Joe McCarthy, flying for the first time with McCarthy, Bill Radcliffe and Ron Batson on 13 September 1942.

The crew joined 97 Squadron, and Eaton flew on seventeen operations during their tour, missing two periods of about a month, presumably through illness. The crew then transferred to 617 Squadron.

When they eventually took off on the Dams Raid, Eaton had a problem with the radio equipment, and lost communication with Group HQ. Aware that this should mean that he abort the trip, McCarthy told him he didn't hear what he said, and ploughed on. Eaton must have got the set working again, as later on they were able to communicate their progress, and he was able to hear the code word for the breach of the Möhne Dam transmitted as AJ-T lined up to attack the Sorpe.

Following the raid he completed a further thirty-four trips with McCarthy, until the whole crew were taken off operations in July 1944. He was promoted to Warrant Officer in June 1944, and awarded the DFM.

IWM COLLECTIONS TR1128

In August 1944, Eaton was posted to a training unit and commissioned. He left the RAF in 1945 and took up employment as an agent for a clothing firm. He carried on this work until his retirement. He died in Manchester on 22 March 1974.

Sgt G.L. Johnson
Bomb aimer

George Leonard Johnson was born on 25 November 1921 in Hameringham, Lincolnshire, the sixth and last child of Charles and Ellen Johnson. He was known as Leonard to his family, but when he joined the RAF he was nick-named 'Johnny', and this is the name by which he is mostly known now. His father was a farm foreman, living in a tied cottage, and the family grew up in very poor conditions. Ellen Johnson died when Johnny was three, and his family life was very disrupted. Eventually his older sister Lena moved back home and he went to a local primary school in Winthorpe.

At the age of 11 he was sent as a boarder to the Lord Wandsworth Agricultural College in Long Sutton, Hampshire. At the time, this was run by a charity catering for the children of agricultural families who had lost one or both parents. He did reasonably well at school and passed the School Certificate as well as playing cricket and football, and winning several athletics events. When he left school in December 1939, he started work as a park keeper in Basingstoke.

Johnson volunteered to join the RAF in June 1940, applying to become a navigator. He was, however, selected for pilot training and eventually joined up in November 1940. He was posted to various training establishments but there was some compensation for all the moving around – at one in Torquay, he met Gwyn Morgan, the woman who would later become his wife.

In June 1941, Johnson was eventually sent for pilot training in Florida. More than one-third of those selected for pilot training were eventually 'washed out', which was what happened to him. As he always doubted he had the necessary skills he was not surprised, and he opted for air gunner training instead, arriving back in the UK in January 1942.

In July 1942, Johnson was posted to 97 Squadron at Woodhall Spa. He was designated as a spare gunner, without a regular crew, and so he flew with various skippers if one of their own gunners went sick. His first operation was on 27 August 1942, flying with Sqn Ldr Elmer Coton on a trip to Gdynia in Poland. However, an engine failure en route led to an early return, so the first time he saw action was the following day, on an operation to Nuremberg.

Johnson flew on a few more operations but then the opportunity came

up to train as a specialist bomb aimer, which
he finished in late November 1942. Within a
month, a vacancy for a bomb aimer came up
in Joe McCarthy's crew. At first Johnson wasn't
keen on flying with an American captain, but a
conversation with McCarthy changed his mind,
and he was introduced to his future crewmates.
What united them, he wrote later, was the fact
that they all had inbuilt confidence in McCarthy, whom they regarded as the best pilot on
the squadron.

Johnson's first trip with McCarthy was an op-
eration to attack Munich on 21 December 1942. It was packed with incident.
In appalling weather, they were attacked by fighters and on the return trip lost
complete power in one engine and suffered problems in another. They were
forced to land at Bottesford.

Johnson went on eighteen more operations with McCarthy, which brought
him to the end of a full tour with 97 Squadron. Knowing that he would then be
entitled to some leave followed by six months working in a non-combat training role, he and Gwyn arranged their wedding for 3 April 1943. The ceremony
was nearly called off when the whole crew were transferred to 617 Squadron
for a new secret mission and all leave was cancelled. His new CO, Guy Gibson,
however relented, and gave them four days off.

In all the training for the Dams Raid Johnson practised dropping the mine
as their aircraft flew straight towards the target at low level. However, on the
afternoon of Sunday 17 May, when the five crews detailed to attack the Sorpe
Dam received their briefing they were told that they had to fly along the dam
wall and drop their mine at its centre. It would roll down the wall and explode
when it reached the correct depth.

Following the delay in setting off and the switch of aircraft to AJ-T, they
realised when they got to the Sorpe Dam that they were the only crew which
had got that far. It took a while to get the approach correct but eventually, on
the tenth try, McCarthy managed to make a near-perfect run, getting down to
about 30ft, and Johnson released the weapon.

Although AJ-T had failed to breach the dam, McCarthy, Johnson and navigator Don MacLean were all decorated for their part in the raid. Johnson received the DFM and travelled up to Buckingham Palace for the investiture.
As a non-drinker, he didn't participate in the festivities that followed. He was
commissioned in November 1943 and went on to fly with McCarthy on all his

subsequent eighteen operations with 617 Squadron, up until April 1944. At that point, knowing that Gwyn Johnson was shortly to have their first child, McCarthy insisted that he stand down.

Reluctantly, Johnson agreed and was sent back to Scampton as a bombing instructor and served out the rest of the war in various training jobs. After the war, he was told that if he qualified as a navigator, he would get a permanent commission. He accepted this offer, and stayed in the RAF until 1962, retiring with the rank of Squadron Leader.

Johnson then retrained again, this time as a teacher. He worked first of all in primary schools and then later in adult education, including a period teaching psychiatric patients at Rampton Hospital.

When he retired, he and Gwyn moved to Torquay, where Gwyn had been brought up. They became active in local Conservative Party politics; Johnson was elected as a councillor, and became chair of the constituency party.

Gwyn Johnson died in August 2005 and for a while Johnson withdrew from public life. But then he started accepting invitations from the media for interviews and documentary appearances, and now he is one of the most familiar of the dwindling number of Bomber Command veterans.

As 'the last British Dambuster', Johnson now occupies an important place in what sometimes seems an insatiable public interest in the Dams Raid. But, as his son Morgan points out in the last chapter of Johnson's autobiography:

> [H]e is the first to recognise that all this attention is not purely about him personally, but is directed at what he represents. The Dambusters became a wartime legend that captured the public imagination and, as the last British survivor of that night, he represents all of them and what they achieved. There are many, many other stories of individual and collective achievements during World War II. Stories of extraordinary courage, of battles won in impossible situations, of acts of heroism against overwhelming odds. But the Dambusters remain high on the list of public affection. And that is what he will be remembered for, by the public at large.[167]

---

167 Johnson, *The Last British Dambuster*, p298.

Sgt R. Batson
Front gunner

Ronald Batson was born on 5 December 1920 in Ferryhill, Co Durham, one of the four children of Joseph and Elizabeth Batson. His father worked as a carpenter. Batson was a grocer's assistant before enlisting in the RAF in March 1941. After qualifying as an air gunner, he was posted to 97 Squadron in early September 1942. He quickly teamed up with Joe McCarthy whose logbook confirms that Batson and Bill Radcliffe first flew with him on the same day, 11 September 1942, in a Manchester on a training flight. Their first operation was on 5 October. Batson was the only one of McCarthy's crew to fly on every single operation in 97 Squadron with his skipper. By late March 1943, they had amassed thirty-one trips.

On the Dams Raid, Batson was in the front turret of AJ-T. On the way back from the Sorpe, he spotted a goods train and asked McCarthy's permission to attack it. The crew hadn't realised, however, that this wasn't an ordinary goods train but an armoured flak train, whose gunners responded with vigour. It was probably a shell from this which punctured a front tyre and caused a problem a few hours later when landing at Scampton.

Batson went on to fly with McCarthy throughout the rest of his tour, and was recommended for a DFM in February 1944. The award was approved in June, with the citation reading:

> Flight Sergeant Batson has completed 37 operational sorties as Mid-upper gunner and has been operating continuously since October 1942. He has flown against many of the most heavily defended targets in Germany including Berlin, the Ruhr, Hamburg and Cologne and took part in the low-level attack on the Sorpe Dam. His enthusiasm and fighting spirit have invariably been of the highest order and he has proved his ability to face the heaviest opposition with complete calm and resolution. It is considered that the exemplary manner in which this NCO has executed his duties with the result that his captain has been able to place complete confidence in him merits the award of the Distinguished Flying Medal.

By the time the McCarthy crew came off operations in July 1944, Batson had reached the rank of Warrant Officer and had completed more than sixty sorties. He was posted to a training unit for the remainder of the war.

Ronald Batson had one brother, Douglas, who also volunteered for the RAF. He was killed in a freak accident on 23 August 1944, when a USAAF B24 Liberator bomber crashed into a cafe in Freckleton, Lancashire. He is buried in Duncombe Cemetery, Ferryhill, Co Durham. How ironic that one brother flew on more than sixty operations over occupied territory and survived, while the other died while eating in a Lancashire snack bar.

After the war Ronald Batson returned to Durham for a while, and worked for the Banda duplicating machine business. He later moved to Fleetwood in Lancashire. He was married twice, and moved back to Leeholme, Co Durham, with his second wife Muriel in the 1990s. He died there on 25 November 2006.

Flg Off D. Rodger
Rear gunner

David Rodger was born on 23 February 1918 in Sault Ste Marie, Ontario, Canada. He went to the local technical school and then worked for the Algoma Steel company. He joined the RCAF in October 1941, and trained as an air gunner before leaving for the UK. By then he had also been commissioned. In September 1942, he joined 97 Squadron at RAF Woodhall Spa and took part in one operation on a trip to Bremen in an aircraft piloted by squadron CO Wg Cdr G.D. Jones. He then suffered a broken kneecap in an accident, and had a spell in hospital.

In January 1943, rear gunner Sgt Ralph Muskett was forced to stand down from Joe McCarthy's crew after prolonged bouts of air sickness, and Dave Rodger was selected in his place. He thus became the third member of the RCAF

in this crew. He went on to take part in fifteen operations with McCarthy in 97 Squadron before they were all transferred to 617 Squadron in March.

Before the Dams Raid, all the rear gunners had set up the turrets of their scheduled aircraft in the way that suited them. Most chose to have the Perspex windshields removed, believing that they had better visibility without them and each would also have made further adjustments to their seats and gun positions. When the McCarthy crew had suddenly to switch from the allo-

BOMBER COMMAND MUSEUM OF CANADA

cated AJ-Q to the spare AJ-T, none of these refinements had been made. Fortunately, Rodger was given a few minutes extra while McCarthy himself went off in hunt of the missing compass deviation cards, so he was able to remove the Perspex with the help of ground staff.

When they reached the Sorpe Dam, Rodger's droll wit was tested to its full by the repeated attempts by McCarthy and Johnson to get into the correct position to drop the Upkeep mine. As Johnson recalled later:

> On our tenth run in, both Joe and I were satisfied that we were right on track. I pushed the button and called 'Bomb gone!' And from the rear turret was heard, 'Thank Christ for that!' As we pulled away, Dave Rodger now had the ringside seat. He said 'God Almighty,' as the explosion threw a fountain of water up to about 1,000 feet. 'Jesus, that spray has come right into the rear turret. Not only have I been knocked about all over the place by you buggers, now you're trying to drown me!'[168]

Rodger continued to fly with McCarthy throughout the rest of the crew's tour. He became 617 Squadron's Gunnery Leader on 11 September 1943, was promoted to Flight Lieutenant and received the DFC in 1944. The citation noted 'his calm resolution in the face of the heaviest opposition, which has been an inspiration to his crew'.

When he was stood down from operational flying, Rodger was offered the chance to return to Canada and work as an instructor for the rest of the war. He decided to take the opportunity, and on his return he married his Canadian girlfriend Nell Barbet. Whilst in the UK he had secretly been taking dancing lessons in order to impress her.

After the war, he returned to work at Algoma Steel in his home town of Sault Ste Marie, and stayed there until retirement. He and Nell went on to have nine children. Dave Rodger died on 1 September 2004 in Sault Ste Marie.

---

168 Johnson, *The Last British Dambuster,* pp171–2.

Crew 15: AJ-C

Detailed to attack Sorpe Dam. Shot down on outward flight.
Lancaster serial number: ED910/G

Plt Off W. Ottley DFC

Pilot

Warner Ottley[169] was born in Battersea, London on 4 March 1922, the oldest of the three sons of Warner Herbert Taylor Ottley and his wife Hilda, née
Edwards. Although given his father's first name, he was always known by the
nickname of Bill. His father was a civil servant, working in the War Office, and
had been awarded the French *Legion d'honneur* for his work with that country
during the First World War.

Ottley was educated at Hurstpierpoint College, and was still at school when
the war broke out. He joined the RAF in 1941, and was selected for pilot training. He went to Canada for training, qualified as a pilot in August 1941 and
returned to the UK three months later.

After further training he was sent to his first operational squadron, 50 Squadron, in June 1942, but then immediately reposted to 83 Squadron, then based at
Scampton. Between 29 July and 6 August 1942 he flew on four 'second dickey'
operations with Flt Sgt L.T. Jackson as pilot.

Ottley was then transferred to 207 Squadron and flew on several more operations before being transferred to the squadron's conversion flight. There he
was teamed up with the bulk of the men who would make up his Dams Raid
crew: Ronald Marsden, flight engineer; Thomas Johnston, bomb aimer; Jack
Guterman, wireless operator; Fred Tees, air gunner; and Jack Barrett, navigator. The crew transferred back to the main squadron and undertook their first
operation together on a 'gardening' trip to Biarritz on 23 November 1942.

Ottley made close friendships with most of his crew, particularly Guterman
and Barrett, with whom he shared an interest in music and art. Guterman provides a vivid description of his skipper in a letter written in late 1942:

> I now occupy the bed next to Ottley (the fellow in between left today
> and we are glad as he was deadly dull) so now I am entertained all
> night by his long and endless store of anecdotes (some of which are

---

169 Ottley had the single forename Warner. His father was Warner Herbert Taylor Ottley,
b.1889, his grandfather was Warner Ottley, b. 1853, and his great-grandfather was
Herbert Taylor Ottley, b.1822. This repetition of forenames across the generations has
often led to confusion. Ottley himself was known by his family by the nickname 'Bill'.

remarkably funny but could hardly be accepted with any degree of morality in the drawing room) so it is impossible to relapse into status melancholis.

I have just read the former paragraph out to Ottley himself whose sole remark was 'Oh Christ' – but he's really quite respectable. We were listening to the news just now and his remark on an announcement concerning the calling up of women (of a certain age) was: 'Oh Yes! My mother gets great sport out of this calling up business. It's the only way of finding out her best friends real ages: "You know Bill, Mrs X once told me she was 35 but she registered today so she must really be 41!"' That's the sort of thing I have to put up with.[170]

Ottley went on to fly on twenty further operations with this crew between December 1942 and April 1943, although there were the occasional minor changes in personnel. Guterman reached the end of his tour on 8 March 1943 and so the last three operations for the crew each had a different person as wireless operator. The crew's final operation in 207 Squadron was on 4 April 1943, with a trip to bomb Kiel.

Ottley and his crew were then transferred to 617 Squadron, one of the last crews to arrive. Ottley had been commissioned and then recommended for a DFC by this point, although the decoration wouldn't be confirmed until after the Dams Raid and was backdated to 16 May 1943.

The Ottley crew undertook their first training flight in the new squadron on 8 April 1943. About five weeks later, they were designated to be the first crew in Operation Chastise's Wave Three, the mobile reserve. Their duty was to be in the air over Germany after the earlier two waves had done their work, and then be diverted by 5 Group headquarters to attack whatever target it deemed necessary.

When they were shot down near Hamm, Ottley and five of the crew died instantly. Rear gunner Fred Tees was thrown clear of the wreckage and captured. Those who died were originally buried by the Germans in Hamm, but were reinterred after the war in Reichswald Forest War Cemetery.

As further proof of Ottley's interest in arts

HUMPHRIES FAMILY COLLECTION

---

170 Jack Guterman, letter to Babs Guterman, dated 'Friday' (probably early October 1942), Guterman family.

and culture, in March 1945 the *Hurst Johnian* school magazine reported that his record collection had been donated to the school's Gramophone Society.

Bill Ottley's father, Warner Ottley, worked in the War Office throughout the Second World War, and received the award of a CB in the New Year's Honours List in 1945. He died in 1980.

Sgt R. Marsden
Flight engineer

HUMPHRIES FAMILY COLLECTION

Ronald Marsden was born on 8 May 1920 in Scarborough, North Yorkshire, one of the five children of William and Emily Marsden. The family lived in Stockton, where he went to school. He joined the RAF in 1935 as a young apprentice at the No 1 School of Technical Training in Halton.

He then served in ground crew in a number of establishments. When the new trade of flight engineers was established, Marsden was quick to apply and qualified at the No 4 School of Technical Training in St Athan.

He qualified as a flight engineer in September 1942, and was posted to a conversion unit to join a crew. It would seem that he met up with Bill Ottley and his colleagues there. Marsden went on to fly with Ottley on all the 20 operations he completed in 207 Squadron, so he is unlikely to have hesitated when offered a posting to the new 617 Squadron. His crewmate Jack Guterman, who was always interested in his colleagues' intellectual life, described Marsden as being 'philosophical' and owning a book on anthropology.[171]

Ronald Marsden is buried in Reichswald Forest War Cemetery.

Flg Off J.K. Barrett DFC
Navigator

Jack Kenneth Barrett was born in Hackney, London, on 9 September 1920, the only child of David and Ethel Barrett. He joined the RAF in 1940, and was sent to South Africa for training as a navigator. On qualification, he was awarded a commission. On arriving back in the UK, he was sent for further training and then posted to 207 Squadron in February 1942, at the same time

---

171 Jack Guterman, letter to Babs Guterman, 20 April 1943, Guterman family.

as wireless operator Jack Guterman, with whom he shared an interest in the arts and cinema. In June 1942 they both joined the crew of pilot Flt Sgt Anthony Walters, which flew on its first 'gardening' operation to the Deodars area on 3 June 1942. The pair flew on some nineteen operations together until September, when Walters was transferred out. Barrett and Guterman were then posted to a conversion unit.

In November, they returned to 207 Squadron, now in a new crew skippered by Bill Ottley. Flight engineer Ron Marsden, bomb aimer Tommy Johnston and gunners Fred Tees and Harry Strange were also all posted to 207 Squadron at about the same time. This was the same crew who would fly on the Dams Raid six months later. The crew went on to fly on some twenty more operations between December 1942 and March 1943, although Barrett was absent for about a month, perhaps through illness. By the end of March 1943, he had reached the end of his tour and could have opted for a training position for a period. He was also recommended for a DFC, the citation for which read:

> Flying Officer Barrett has invariably displayed a high standard of navigation during operational flights. His good work has contributed to the success of the operations in which he has participated. On one occasion, when returning from a raid on Saarbrucken, one engine failed when leaving the target area and a second failed when over the French coast. Although the situation appeared desperate for a time, Flying Officer Barrett continued to give cool and effective navigational directions which greatly assisted the captain in landing the bomber safely. Throughout his operational career, this officer has displayed exceptional skill, courage and devotion to duty.

Unfortunately the award did not come through before the Dams Raid. Jack Barrett is buried in Reichswald Forest War Cemetery.

GUTERMAN FAMILY

Sgt J. Guterman DFM
Wireless operator

Jack Guterman was born in Ramsgate, Kent, on 1 August 1920, the older of the two children of Jack and Jane Guterman. His family then moved to Guildford. His father, an accountant, served on the Western Front in the First World War, and came from a Jewish family who had fled Poland in the 1890s, while his mother was of Irish descent. Guterman went to Sandfield Primary School and on to Guildford Royal Grammar School in 1931. He left school in 1937 and studied at art school in Andover, where his tutor was the artist Dick Hosking. He then went to work in his father's accountancy practice.

When the war came, he volunteered for the RAF and was selected for training as an air observer. He went on to qualify as a wireless operator/air gunner, and finished his training in the autumn of 1941.

Guterman had great potential as an artist, and hung his own oil paintings and drawings on the walls of the various rooms he lived in during his RAF career. He took his paints and drawing materials from base to base and carried on producing quality work. He also loved literature and music, and collected records and books. He wrote regularly to his family, sending them a remarkable series of letters with details of concerts he had heard on the radio, accounts of how his artistic work was progressing, witty pen portraits of his RAF colleagues and vivid descriptions of the countryside over which he had flown.

He was posted to 207 Squadron in February 1942, and started operational flying in June 1942. Along with navigator Plt Off Jack Barrett he joined the crew of Flt Sgt Anthony Walters, and they flew on some nineteen operations together before going first to a conversion unit and then back to 207 Squadron to a new crew skippered by Bill Ottley.

He became good friends with Ottley, and they shared a room together in their quarters at RAF Bottesford. They spent much of their spare time talking about the arts and listening to music. Guterman's last operation in 207 Squadron was on 8 March 1943, on a trip to Nuremburg. With this he finished his tour and could have opted to go to a training unit for at least six months. He was also recommended for a DFM, in which the citation mentioned:

> In both capacities [as air gunner and wireless operator], he has consistently shown the greatest enthusiasm, determination and

efficiency. In the capacity of air gunner, Sergeant Guterman displays a fine fighting spirit, welcoming every opportunity to use his guns against the enemy. On one occasions when returning from Kassel, he successfully attacked light gun and searchlight positions from a low level. His courage, reliability and perseverance have made this airman a most valuable member of aircrew.

Unfortunately the award did not come through before the Dams Raid, and the medal was sent to his family after the war.

Although he could have gone on an instructional role in an OTU, Guterman wasn't enthusiastic at the prospect: 'Ugh! Ugh!', he wrote to his sister on 18 February, and followed this up on 4 March with the news that he was to be posted to a 'wretched training station in the Lincoln vicinity'. He managed somehow to postpone this transfer, so he was still at Langar when Ottley and his crew were nominated for a transfer to 617 Squadron. As they did not have a regular wireless operator, Guterman must have volunteered to join up with his old comrades, and was posted along with them.

Naturally, he took his painting and drawing materials. He told his family that he had been allocated a room in one of Scampton's 'married quarters' which he shared with a 'Scots lad'. In a later letter, he referred to him as 'Johnnie', so this was probably his crewmate Thomas Johnston. One day, when workmen arrived to paint the outside of the quarters they noticed through the window the display on the walls and enquired what they were. Johnston told them that they were 'works of art': 'fleeting fancies materialised in a fleeting form', a description which left the workmen somewhat baffled.

During the training in the run up to the Dams Raid Guterman somehow found quite a lot of time in which he could paint. He began work on a painting which he called 'Gethsemane'. In a letter to his sister which is

Jack Guterman's 'Gethsemane' painting.

GUTERMAN FAMILY

dated 'early May' he told her how excited he was by the work he had done so far on the project:

> My 'Gethsemane' is progressing and flavours of Fra Angelico, the Italian Primitive especially in the 'flora' parts. I get so thrilled about it that I cannot get it out of my mind and rush back to do odd things to it throughout the day. I believe it will turn out to be my chef-d'oevre.

The finished painting was among the large collection of works which were sent back to the family. He didn't however mention it in his last letter home, sent to his sister and dated 16 May. Instead he described a trip to Lincoln the day before, in which he had bought three records and studied some art books in the reference library. All in all, he concluded, he was discovering 'some most quaint corners which each help to raise my opinion of the town'. The letter concluded: 'I'm boring myself so I don't know about you! Fond Love Zak.'

Jack Guterman is buried in Reichswald Forest War Cemetery.

JOHNSTON FAMILY

Sgt T.B. Johnston
Bomb aimer

Thomas Barr Johnston was born on 19 July 1921 in Bellshill, Lanarkshire, the youngest of the three children of Peter and Elizabeth Johnston. His father was a music teacher at Bellshill Academy, and the young Tommy went to school there. After leaving school he went to work in the laboratory of the local steelworks.

Like many young men of his generation, Johnston wanted to fly, and he volunteered for the RAF when the war broke out. He was sent to Canada to train, returning in 1942. He was posted to 207 Squadron[172] in July 1942, and flew on his first operation on 21 July as bomb aimer with Flt Sgt V. Duxbury, on a trip to Duisburg. He took part in three more operations with different pilots in September, and was then posted to a Conversion Unit.

---

172 The 207 Squadron Operations Record Book frequently gives Johnston the initials K.R. in an obvious confusion with Sgt K.R. Johnson, a flight engineer, who was present in the squadron at the same time. The confusion seems to end when K.R. Johnson was killed on operations on 25 February 1943.

It would seem that he then met up with Bill Ottley and his crew and flew on about fourteen more operations in 207 Squadron. By the middle of March 1943 Johnston was established as Ottley's regular bomb aimer and is unlikely to have hesitated when offered a posting to the new 617 Squadron. There was recipe for further confusion in the new squadron, when it emerged that there were already two bomb aimers with the surname Johnson. Sadly, this soon ceased to be a problem for the young Scot as the crew did not complete their first operation, the Dams Raid.

Thomas Johnston is buried in Reichswald Forest War Cemetery.

Sgt H.J. Strange
Front gunner

Harry John Strange was born in Birkenhead on 25 April 1923, the oldest of the six children of Harry and Margaret Strange. He joined the RAF in 1941, soon after his 18th birthday, and was sent for air gunner training in 1942.

He arrived at 1660 Conversion Unit in late 1942, and would seem to have met most of his future crewmates there. Although he joined 207 Squadron from 1660 CU on the same day, 11 November 1942, as most of the rest of the Ottley crew, he flew his first two operations with Sgt G. Langdon as pilot. His first operation with Ottley as his skipper was on 21 December on a trip to Munich. This was the day when the crew who would eventually fly on the Dams Raid with Bill Ottley all flew together operationally for the first time.

Strange flew another operation with Langdon in January 1943, but on 2 February he made a permanent move to Ottley. He went on to fly on another twelve trips with Ottley's crew, their last being their final operation in 207 Squadron, an attack on Kiel on 4 April 1943. He seems to have flown on most of the trips as the mid-upper gunner, but occasionally he swapped with Fred Tees, and flew in the rear turret. On the Dams Raid, Strange flew as AJ-C's front gunner, thereby sealing his fate.

Harry Strange is buried in Reichswald Forest War Cemetery.

Sgt F. Tees
Rear gunner

Frederick Tees was born in Chichester, Sussex on 16 June 1922, one of the five children of Henry and Elizabeth Tees. His father was a barber and had a shop in the town. Tees went to the Central C of E School and the Lancastrian School in Chichester.

He joined the RAF in 1941 and was finally selected for air gunner training in 1942. His final training was at 1660 Conversion Unit, where he joined up with Bill Ottley and the crew who would eventually fly on the Dams Raid. They were posted together to 207 Squadron in November 1942, and took part on their first raid on 23 November. Tees and flight engineer Ron Marsden were the only two who flew on all seventeen operations which Ottley undertook in 207 Squadron between then and April 1943.

Ottley, Tees and the rest of the crew were transferred to 617 Squadron shortly after their last operation in 207 Squadron, on 4 April 1943. They undertook their first training flight in the new squadron on 8 April 1943.

Although they normally flew in the rear and mid-upper turret respectively, Fred Tees and Harry Strange had occasionally swapped positions while serving in 207 Squadron. As the specially adapted Dams Raid Lancasters had no mid-upper turret, it is possible that both tried out the front turret of AJ-C during training. This may explain why some of the documents for the operation, including the Night Flying Programme typed up on the morning of Sunday 16 May, listed Tees in the front turret and Strange in the rear.

When the aircraft took off from Scampton at 0009 on Monday 17 May, however, Tees was definitely in the rear turret, a decision which would later save his life. Ottley flew AJ-C so low that at one point Tees saw a church steeple above him, Tees fired at some searchlights and gun emplacements as they crossed Holland and Germany.

As they neared Hamm, a 'tremendous commotion' occurred and he realised that the aircraft had been hit on the port side. His turret was immobilised and flames began to streak past it. He heard Ottley say 'I'm sorry boys, we've had it', and he recalled thinking 'there's no future at baling out at nought feet with three engines on fire'.[173] Several minutes later, he regained consciousness on

---

173 Sweetman, *Dambusters Raid*, p189.

the ground. His turret had somehow been blown clear of the wreckage, perhaps as a result of a second explosion as the Upkeep mine blew up. He was badly burned and was quickly captured by the Germans. He spent the rest of the war as a PoW.

The fact that Tees had survived did not become known for some months, and so his family were told that he was missing in action. Almost a year after the Dams Raid, on Thursday 11 May 1944, his mother, Mrs Elizabeth Tees, was killed in an accident when a USAAF B24 Liberator crashed on the laundry in Chichester where she was working. It had been damaged by flak on a bombing operation over France. After the pilot set a course for it to crash into the English Channel, the crew baled out. Unfortunately, the aircraft veered off this course and crashed on land, killing three civilians. Some sources say that Mrs Tees defied instructions and ran back into the burning building to collect her handbag. Tees apparently only found out about his mother's death on release from his PoW camp in 1945.

Tees became a hairdresser after the war, the same trade as his father, with a business in Letchworth, Hertfordshire. He took part in a number of 617 Squadron reunions before his death by suicide on 15 March 1982. He was cremated in Luton, but his last wish was for his ashes to be scattered on the graves of his fallen comrades in Reichswald Forest War Cemetery.

Crew 16: AJ-S

Mobile reserve. Shot down on outward flight before receiving final orders.

Lancaster serial number: ED865/G

Plt Off L.J. Burpee DFM

Pilot

Lewis Johnstone Burpee was born on 5 March 1918 in Ottawa, one of the three children of Lewis Arthur and Lilian Agnes Burpee. His father was the manager of Charles Ogilvy, a large department store in the city. He went to Elgin Street Public School and Lisgar Collegiate School in Ottawa, and then on to Queen's University in Kingston, Ontario, where he got a degree in English, history and politics. When war came, he joined the RCAF, enlisting in December 1940.

Burpee qualified as a pilot in September 1941. While training he crewed up first with fellow Canadian air gunner Gordon Brady, and then with flight engineer Guy Pegler. The three were posted to 106 Squadron in October 1942.

While training, Burpee had an accident in a Wellington on 27 August. His starboard engine seized up and he made a poor forced landing at Church Lawford, but avoiding numerous construction obstacles. He was criticised for his choice of emergency airfield, but exonerated over the accident itself.

After three trips as a 'second dickey' Burpee did his first trip as a captain on 7 November 1942 on a mission to bomb Genoa. This was abandoned, but his first successful operation was later that month. He went on to complete some twenty-seven further operations and was recommended for the DFM. He was commended for consistently displaying 'the greatest determination in the execution of whatever tasks were allotted' to him. It noted that he had taken part in

attacks on Berlin, Nuremburg, Stuttgart, Genoa and Turin as well as the highly successful raids on Lorient, St Nazaire, two Essen attacks and the daylight attack against Milan in October 1942. The citation concluded: 'Flight Sergeant Burpee has shown coolness and courage throughout his operational tour and has performed his duties conscientiously and efficiently.'

AJ-S strayed off course shortly before reaching the German border and was shot down near Gilze Rijen airfield, six miles south west of Tilburg. After the crash, only the bodies of

Lewis Burpee and three of the crew who would fly with him on the Dams Raid, photographed after a raid on Berlin in January 1943. (Left to right) Gordon Brady, William Long, Guy Pegler, Lewis Burpee, Edward Leavesley and George Goodings. The latter two had finished their tours in 106 Squadron before Burpee and the rest were transferred.

Burpee, Brady and Weller were positively identified. The other four were buried in a communal grave. They were first interred by the Germans at Zuylen Cemetery, Prinsenhage, but after the war all seven bodies were reburied in Bergen-op-Zoom War Cemetery.

Lewis Burpee was one of the four aircrew who flew on the raid knowing that their wives were pregnant. Richard Trevor-Roper (p122) and David Maltby (p155) would live to see their children being born. Burpee and Charles Brennan (p126) would not. After her husband died, Mrs Lillian Burpee travelled across the Atlantic in order to meet her in-laws for the first time, and have her baby in Canada. Their son, also called Lewis Johnstone Burpee, was born on Christmas Eve 1943.

Sgt G. Pegler
Flight engineer
Guy Pegler was born on 27 September 1921 in Ringwood, Hampshire, the older of the two sons of Claud and Charlotte Pegler. The family would later move to Letchworth in Hertfordshire, where he went to Letchworth Grammar School. Pegler joined the RAF in 1938 as an apprentice at No 1 School of Technical

Training, RAF Halton, and was known by the nickname 'Johnny' during his time in the RAF. He served in ground crew in the early part of the war, mainly servicing aircraft in Fighter Command, before taking the opportunity in 1942 to train as a flight engineer in Bomber Command.

After qualifying, he was posted to 106 Squadron's Conversion Flight where he joined up with Lewis Burpee and gunner Gordon Brady for the final stages of Lancaster training. The trio were posted to 106 Squadron in October 1942.

On 24 October 1942, the day Burpee flew on his final operation as second pilot (in David Shannon's crew), Pegler had the dubious privilege of making his operational debut, accompanying the Squadron CO, Wg Cdr Guy Gibson on a trip to Milan. At that stage in his career, Gibson had a different flight engineer or second pilot on almost every single operations. Whether they volunteered or were chosen by him is not recorded. Pegler survived the experience, and was able to rejoin Burpee and his crew for their first trip together as a crew, on a 'gardening' operation to the Silverthorn area on 16 November 1942. Thereafter, Pegler flew with Burpee on all his twenty-seven operations in 106 Squadron and went with him to 617 Squadron.

Guy Pegler is buried in Bergen-op-Zoom War Cemetery.

Sgt T. Jaye
Navigator

Thomas Jaye was one of the two sons of James and Helena Jaye of Crook, Co. Durham. His father worked as a miner at Roddymoor Collery. He was born on 3 October 1922 and went to Wolsingham Grammar School. After leaving school he worked as an electrical engineer.

He joined the RAF in 1941 and was sent for training as a navigator to the flying school run by Pan-American in Miami, Florida. His final stint of training, after arriving back in the UK, was at 1654 Conversion Unit at RAF Wigsley in November and December 1942, where one of the instructors was Henry Maudslay. He was posted to 106 Squadron on 28 December 1942.

In his six operations in the first three weeks of January 1943, Lewis Burpee had flown with five different navigators. On the afternoon of 21 January Jaye flew with him for the first time on a night flying test and they went on their first operation together that evening, a trip to Essen. Jaye was immediately established as Burpee's regular navigator and they went on a further sixteen operations before joining 617 Squadron.

The Burpee crew were about to leave 106 Squadron when Jaye bumped into an old friend from his home village. Sgt Fred Smooker was about to begin a tour of operations as a bomb aimer in 106 Squadron, and had just arrived at Syerston:

> Having settled in our barracks we all decided to go to the Sergeants' mess for a meal and on our way we noticed numerous black, brooding, Lancasters standing silently at their dispersals, at different parts of the airfield. When we reached the Sergeants' mess, coming down the steps from the main entrance, was a navigator, a young man of about twenty one. I didn't recognise him until he said to me:
> 'Hello, Fred, have you just arrived?'
> I looked again. 'Why,' I said, 'Tom Jaye. We're just going to have a meal.'
> 'Well, that's a pity,' he said, 'I'm just leaving,' and with that I hurried on to catch up with my crew. Tom Jaye was on his way to Scampton to join 617 Squadron.
> Meeting Tom caused me to reminisce about Roddymoor, the village where we both came from, not far from Crook. His father Jimmy Jaye and my father Billy Smooker were coal miners at Roddymoor Colliery, where I would have been had I not volunteered for RAF aircrew. Tom Jaye had gone to grammar school and joined the RAF before me. I remember his mother telling me that he was based in Nottinghamshire while I was on leave, during training.[174]

On their final leave before the Dams Raid, in early May, Jaye spent some time staying with his cousin Derek and family in Durham before continuing to see his mother in Crook.

Thomas Jaye is buried in Bergen-op-Zoom War Cemetery.

---

174 Clive Smith, *Lancaster Bale Out*, Tucann 2013, p62.

Plt Off L.G. Weller
Wireless operator

Leonard George Weller was born on 1 September 1915 in Edmonton, north London, the son of Arthur and Marian Weller. He worked as a toolmaker before the war, and was married with an infant daughter by the time he joined the RAF in 1940.

After training as a wireless operator/air gunner, he was eventually posted to 106 Squadron in early 1943. At 0040 in the early morning of 14 February his predecessor as wireless operator in Lewis Burpee's crew, Flt Sgt Eddie Leavesley DFM, completed his second tour of operations, after a six-hour trip to Lorient. Then, at 1830 the same day, the crew set off again on a ten-hour operation over the Alps to Milan, with a new wireless operator on board, Len Weller.

This was the middle of a very busy period for Lew Burpee, his crew and 106 Squadron in general. A further ten operations would follow in the next four weeks, and Weller flew on them all. By the time the crew were transferred to 617 Squadron, he had been commissioned, so he now outranked his skipper.

Leonard Weller is buried in Bergen-op-Zoom War Cemetery.

Flt Sgt J.L. Arthur
Bomb aimer

James Lamb Arthur was born in Toronto, Canada, on 3 July 1917, the second of the four children of Rev Alfred and Dora Arthur. His father was an Anglican clergyman with a parish in the city.

Arthur was educated at Dennis Avenue School and York Memorial College, where he did well in maths. When he left school he went to work in the Bank of Toronto. He had a great interest in flying, and his youngest sister can still recall the excitement of seeing him, his brother and their father flying overhead in a small aircraft, and using a bedsheet to wave to them. He also had a great love of classical music and took his younger sisters to concerts.

He enlisted in the RCAF in 1941. After first

being selected for pilot training he was then remustered as an observer, and qualified in May 1942. After arriving in the UK he then went on to qualify as a bomb aimer on heavy bombers.

Arthur was posted to 106 Squadron to begin operations in February 1943, but it wasn't until 12 March that he flew on his first operation. Lew Burpee's bomb aimer George Goodings had come to the end of his tour, so the chance of joining an experienced crew with two other Canadians probably looked like a good choice. Their trip took them to Essen, which they bombed successfully from 19,000ft. They reported very heavy flak and 'scores of searchlights'.

Arthur's first operation turned out to be the last that Burpee and his crew would fly in 106 Squadron, and it was therefore the only time that the complete Dams Raid crew would fly together before the raid itself. Fewer than three weeks later they were at RAF Scampton, training for the secret mission which would prove fatal for them.

With just one operation under his belt, Arthur may have been the least experienced bomb aimer to take part in the Dams Raid. Nevertheless the AJ-S crew came through the training successfully.

James Arthur is buried in Bergen-op-Zoom War Cemetery.

Sgt W.C.A. Long
Front gunner

William Charles Arthur Long was born on 11 September 1923 in Eastleigh, Hampshire, the older of the two sons of William and Ethel Long. His father was a baker. The family would later move to Bournemouth.

Long applied to join the RAF around the time of his 18th birthday, but like many young men of his time had to wait several months before eventually being accepted. He was selected for air gunnery training, and qualified in August 1942. He was posted to 106 Squadron in September 1942. He flew on two operations: on 17 October with Sgt Lace on the Le Creusot raid and 8 December, with Flg Off Healey to Turin, before joining Lewis Burpee on 20 December. He then flew on all the twenty-one further operations flown by Burpee in 106 Squadron, as well as a single trip to Berlin on 16 January with Flt Lt Wellington.

William Long is buried in Bergen-op-Zoom War Cemetery.

BURPEE FAMILY

Wrt Off J.G. Brady
Rear gunner

Joseph Gordon Brady, known to his family as Gordon, was born in the small town of Ponoka, Alberta, Canada on 16 April 1916. Ponoka lies in the middle of the province, between Edmonton and Calgary. His parents, Michael and Anna Brady, were both born in the USA, but had moved to Canada and become naturalised. Brady was one of four children, and attended the local schools before taking up employment working in a drug store in 1934. When the war came, after a period as a field ambulance truck driver, he volunteered for the RCAF, and joined up in March 1941. He was selected for air gunner training, and eventually arrived in Britain a year later. After more training, he was posted to 16 OTU at Upper Heyford and arrived on the same day, 23 June 1942, as Lewis Burpee. The two Canadians were quick to crew up together.

Burpee and Brady were posted to 106 Squadron together, and had been joined by Guy Pegler in the latter stages of training. Their first operational trip together as a crew was on a 'gardening' operation to the Silverthorn area on 16 November 1942.

Thereafter Brady flew on every single trip made by Burpee, and was promoted to Flight Sergeant in December 1942 and Warrant Officer in February 1943. He would have had no hesitation in going along with his skipper on the transfer to 617 Squadron, even though they were both very near the end of their tours.

Brady had also been noticed by Guy Gibson, who recommended him for a commission on 10 May 1943, a week before the Dams Raid, describing him as 'smart and efficient'. By contrast, Scampton station commander Gp Capt Charles Whitworth, whose recommendation was also needed, was not so impressed. Brady had been 'nervous and agitated at interview'. However, he went along with Gibson: 'W/C Gibson however has known him for some time and gives a good account of him. I forward his recommendation on the strength of his CO's report.' A week later, it was all too late, and a note on Brady's file merely says 'Recommendation cancelled'.[175]

Gordon Brady is buried in Bergen-op-Zoom War Cemetery.

---

175 Wrt Off J.G. Brady, RCAF personnel file, National Archives of Canada.

Crew 17: AJ-F

Mobile reserve. Attacked Sorpe Dam and returned to base.
Lancaster serial number: ED918/G

Flt Sgt K.W. Brown

Pilot

Kenneth William Brown was born on 20 August 1920 in Moose Jaw, Saskatch-ewan, Canada. He enlisted in the RCAF in 1941 and was selected for pilot train-ing. He was recommended for fighters but after arriving in England, he was posted to a bomber training unit in Kinloss. There he crewed up with navigator Dudley Heal, bomb aimer Stefan Oancia, wireless operator Herbert Hewstone and gunner Grant McDonald, all of whom would stay with him for much of the rest of his career. Their first active posting was however to Coastal Command, flying Whitleys out of RAF St Eval on Channel patrols.

Brown was then selected for heavy bomber training at 1654 Conversion Unit, where one of his instructors was Mick Martin. The low flying specialist was re-portedly impressed by his pupil's abilities in this challenging activity. Brown also formed a complete crew at this unit when engineer Basil Feneron and gun-ner Don Buntaine joined him. The seven were then posted to 44 Squadron to begin operations on 5 February 1943.

On 11 February, Brown flew as second pilot on a raid to Wilhelmshaven in an aircraft captained by Sqn Ldr R.G. Whitehead DFC. He then had to wait until 9 March to fly his own crew on their first operation, to the tough target of Munich. The trip was a fierce baptism, with their aircraft 'coned' by searchlights which meant Brown had to perform a corkscrew in order to escape.

Brown and his crew had completed just five more operations before being reluctantly transferred to 617 Squadron. Dur-ing training, the pugnacious Brown had some run-ins with his new CO, Guy Gibson, whom he regarded as a staunch disciplinarian. Once, after Brown was accused with being late for a brief-ing, Gibson made him wash all the windows of the briefing room. But the CO recognised his skills as a pilot, especially at low flying, and demonstrated his playful side one day by push-ing him into the water when they met by chance in the public swimming pool in Lincoln.

Some time the day before the raid, his regular

HUTCHISON FAMILY

gunner Don Buntaine had reported sick. Bill Divall's crew had been taken off the flying schedule as Divall himself had a knee injury, so Daniel Allatson was hastily reallocated to the front turret of AJ-F.

On the Dams Raid, AJ-F kept so low that at times they were below treetop level. They were detailed to attack the Sorpe, but found it a very difficult target. After several failed approaches, they were able to drop their mine successfully, but did not cause any breach. They flew back to Scampton, again keeping as low as possible.

Debriefing followed, with Sir Arthur Harris sitting in. Although there was an impromptu party going on in the Officers Mess, the all-NCO crew in AJ-F seem to have had a quieter celebration. But they were up and about early enough in the morning for a series of photographs.

When the decorations were announced, all the officer pilots who dropped their mines successfully were awarded DSOs. Ken Brown and Bill Townsend, both Flight Sergeants at the time, were given the rarely-awarded Conspicuous Gallantry Medal. Brown was commissioned in June 1943 and went on to fly on another nine operations in 617 Squadron before being posted out in May 1944. He spent the rest of the war in instructional roles.

After the war he stayed on in the RCAF, rising to the rank of Squadron Leader. He retired from the service in 1968, but carried on flying in the Canadian Department of Transport. He had married an Englishwoman, Beryl Blackband, in 1944 and she accompanied him to Canada, where they had five children. Brown died in White Rock, British Columbia on 23 December 2002.

Sgt H.B. Feneron
Flight engineer

Harry Basil Feneron was born in London on 14 May 1920, the older of the two sons of Harry and Edith Feneron. His father ran an electrical business, where he and his brother both worked after leaving school. Feneron joined the RAF in 1940 and served in ground crew, before taking the opportunity offered in 1942 to train as a flight engineer. He qualified in October 1942 and was then posted to 1654 Conversion Unit, where he joined up with Ken Brown and his crew. He would go on to fly with Brown for the rest of both their operational careers.

The crew were posted together to 44 Squadron on 5 February 1943 and completed six operations between 9 and 27 March. They were then posted again as a unit to 617 Squadron on 29 March.

The relationship between Brown and Feneron was closer than it was between some of the other pilots and flight engineers on the Dams Raid, with

Feneron having more like an assistant pilot role. In the low flying training before the raid, Feneron did an important job looking out for high-tension wires and other obstacles, calling out to his skipper as soon as he saw them. They split the responsibility for forward vision, with Feneron taking the starboard half of the windscreen and Brown the port side.

This spirit of partnership could well have been the reason why they survived the testing low-level flight to the Dams and back, while others didn't make it. Feneron saw Burpee's crash and afterwards concluded that they had been shot down because they weren't low enough.

When they were safely over England, Brown handed over the controls for a while to his engineer while he went aft to examine the extensive damage which AJ-F had endured. He was back in the pilot's seat in time to land at Scampton and Feneron went through his customary ritual of kissing the ground – on this occasion probably with more fervour than usual. He was then able to see the damage for himself, including a large hole a few inches behind where wireless operator Herbert Hewstone had been sitting.

Feneron went on to fly on nine more operations in 617 Squadron before being commissioned and then in March 1944 being transferred into a training unit. He carried out various instructional roles for the rest of the war before being demobbed in 1946. He returned to work in the family business in London, where he stayed until he retired.

Basil Feneron died on 18 November 1993 at his home in Gerrards Cross, Buckinghamshire, where he had lived with his wife, Jean, for thirty years. He had two children.

Sgt D.P. Heal
Navigator

Dudley Percy Heal was born on 5 August 1916 in Portsmouth, one of the three sons of Edward and Ellen Heal. He went to Weymouth Grammar School. In 1936 he started working for HM Customs and Excise, and at the time of the outbreak of war was working in the Waterguard branch in Southampton Docks.

Customs officers were exempt from conscription, but Heal was determined to serve in the RAF as aircrew and therefore volunteered. He was worried that

as an asthmatic he might not pass the medical, but in the event he got through it and was finally enlisted in May 1940.

He was selected for pilot training, but it wasn't until the following year that this actually began. He was sent first to Canada and then on to Pensacola, Florida. Despite undertaking some solo flying he was eventually 'washed out' and returned to Canada. When he remustered as a navigator he was then sent back to Pensacola. He discovered an aptitude for this, and passed out in the top six of his class. This earned him the privilege of flying back from Canada to the UK in an RAF-bound Lockheed Ventura with a ferry pilot.

More training in an Advanced Flying Unit took place, and Heal did even better this time, coming top of the class. This was noted when he was then posted to 19 OTU in Kinloss, where he crewed up with Ken Brown and his Canadian colleagues. Herbert Hewstone also joined them.

After two months attached to Coastal Command, the crew was completed and finally posted to an operational squadron in February 1943, joining 44 Squadron in Waddington. To gain operational experience, Heal was given a first trip with a seasoned pilot, Sgt Forman, on 18 February to Wilhelmshaven. This passed without incident, and on 9 March the Brown crew set off on their first operation together, to Munich. Somehow, they went off course and arrived at the target forty-five minutes late and were even later by the time they got home safely. A rather frosty interview with the Navigation Leader followed, but he escaped any retribution.

After the Dams Raid he flew on all of the Brown crew's subsequent operations until it was disbanded in February 1944. Brown himself had developed hearing problems, and was being sent for medical tests. Heal opted to go to a training post rather than switch to another pilot and crew.

This lasted for a few months, but then early in 1945, he was offered the chance to join 214 Squadron, flying American Fortresses specially equipped for radio counter measures, mainly the 'jamming' of German radio signals. All went well for seven operations but then on the eighth their aircraft suffered engine problems, dropped to 8,000ft and was hit by flak. The crew baled out. Heal and a few others survived and were captured. They were dealt with correctly but some of their crewmates were captured and taken to the village of Huchenfeld, near the town of Pforzheim, which had been severely bombed shortly before. Local civilians, members of the Hitler Youth, broke into the cellar where they were being held, dragged them to a cemetery and shot them.

Heal was held as a PoW for about two months, and was in a group who the Germans forcibly marched away from the approaching American forces. They were eventually rescued, and made their way to an airbase which was flying PoWs home.

After the war, Heal went back to work for the Customs and Excise service and retired in 1978. He married Thelma Davies and had two daughters. They lived in Southampton, and Heal died there on 7 February 1999.

Sgt H.J. Hewstone
Wireless operator

Herbert John Hewstone was born on 24 July 1909 in Stepney, London. He was one of the seven children of George and Lydia Hewstone. The family owned a general store in the area, and George Hewstone also worked as a printer. Hewstone was generally known as Bert to his family, but in the RAF he went by the nicknames of both 'Harry' and 'Hewie'.

He joined the RAF at the start of the war, but it wasn't until 1942 that he began aircrew training, qualifying as a wireless operator/air gunner in June 1942. He was posted to 19 OTU in Kinloss at the end of August, and quickly crewed up with Ken Brown and his colleagues.

After six operations, Brown's crew were posted to 617 Squadron. Before leaving 44 Squadron, they were told how important their role would be in their new posting, and that they would be the 'backbone' of the new squadron. It was Hewstone who expressed some scepticism about this, saying to his captain: 'Skip, if we're the backbone of this squadron, we must be damn close to the ass end.' (Although as a Londoner, he is more likely to have said 'arse' than 'ass'.)

After the Dams Raid, Hewstone went on to fly on all of the Brown crew's subsequent operations in 617 Squadron until it disbanded in March 1944. He was posted to 26 Operational Training Unit, where he served as an instructor for the remainder of the war. He was promoted to Flight Sergeant before being demobbed.

Herbert Hewstone had married Rose Jones in 1938, and they had two children. He died in Havering on 28 May 1980.

HUMPHRIES FAMILY COLLECTION

Sgt S. Oancia
Bomb aimer

Stefan Oancia was born on 5 March 1923 in Stonehenge, Saskatchewan, Canada, one of the nine children of Demitru and Katie Oancia. The family had emigrated from Romania to take up grain farming. Stonehenge is a small community in the southern part of the province of Saskatchewan, near the American border and Oancia went to the local Twelve Mile Lake school.

Oancia joined the RCAF in 1941 and qualified as an observer. On arriving in England, he undertook further training and was then posted to an Operational Training Unit, where he teamed up with Ken Brown and his crew.

Just over a month of joining 44 Squadron and after only six operations, they were sent to 617 Squadron. 'I do not recall volunteering for this transfer,' he later remarked.

After reaching the Sorpe Dam and a final successful drop of their mine, he recorded seeing a large waterspout silhouetted against the moon and falling slowly back into the lake. The crew noticed further crumbling to the surface of the dam wall, but no apparent breach.

Oancia continued in Ken Brown's crew after the raid until it was disbanded in March 1944, and served the rest of the war training other crews. He was commissioned in 1944.

After the war, he returned to Canada and took a degree in civil engineering at the University of Alberta. One of the projects he worked on in later life was, ironically, a large dam in Quebec. He married Ruth Griffith in 1953, but they had no children. Oancia died on 6 May 1999 in Carleton, Ontario.

Sgt D. Allatson
Front gunner

Daniel Allatson was born on 7 November 1923 in Eastwood, Essex. His birth name was Daniel Louis Alberts, and his parents were Frederick and Maude Alberts. He was adopted almost immediately after birth by Samuel and Dorothy Allatson who lived nearby in Southend. Samuel Eli Allatson transferred from the Royal Navy to serve in the newly formed RFC during the First World War. He held the rank of Serjeant-Mechanic, and was awarded both the DFM and the French *Medaille militaire*. Perhaps inspired by his father's service, Daniel

Allatson joined the RAF shortly after the start of the war. His brother also joined the RAF. Allatson applied for pilot training but ended up as an air gunner. He was eventually posted to 57 Squadron at RAF Scampton as part of the crew piloted by Sgt Bill Divall. This crew flew on a number of operations together in February 1943.

Divall's crew was a late arrival in 617 Squadron, replacing Ray Lovell and his crew who returned to 57 Squadron in April 1943. However, despite completing the training successfully, shortly before the raid Divall was himself called off sick, so his crew were resigned to not participating. But then Ken Brown's front gunner, Don Buntaine, also reported sick, so Allatson was quickly drafted in as his replacement. Allatson's name appears on the Night Flying Programme which was typed on the morning of Sunday 16 May 1943, the day of the raid, so the substitution must have been made by then.

Allatson acquitted himself well in what was undoubtedly the most intense operation he had yet undertaken. He then returned to the Divall crew, and took part in the operations undertaken by 617 Squadron in the summer of 1943. These involved attacks on various Italian targets, flying on to Blida in Algeria for refuelling and rearming.

In September 1943, Divall and his crew were detailed for the attack on the Dortmund Ems canal, using a new 'thincase' 12,000lb bomb. The crew was augmented by an extra gunner brought in from another squadron, Sgt G.S. Miles. Allatson was stationed in the rear turret. The operation became the most catastrophic undertaken by 617 Squadron throughout the war, with five of the eight aircraft involved shot down or crashed. Weather conditions were very poor: heavy mist blanketed the canal, making it impossible to see the culverted area which was the intended target. Divall's aircraft dropped its bomb on another section of the canal, but then crashed almost immediately afterwards, with a further explosion. Allatson's turret was blown clear of the aircraft, and his body was found in a field near a farmhouse, with a bruise on his forehead the only external sign of injury.

Daniel Allatson and his colleagues were buried by the Germans in the churchyard at Bramsche. Their bodies were reinterred after the war in Reichswald Forest War Cemetery.

HUTCHISON FAMILY

Flt Sgt G. McDonald
Rear gunner

Grant McDonald was born in Grand Forks, British Columbia on 20 July 1921, the second youngest of the seven children of William and Florence McDonald. His father worked as a carpenter. He went to school in Grand Forks. By the time he left, the war had already started and he applied to join the RCAF. At that stage it was not accepting new recruits, so he went first into the Canadian army, but was able to transfer to the air force a few months later.

After training in Canada as an air gunner, he crossed the Atlantic in May 1942. After more training at a gunnery school near Stranraer, he was posted to No 19 Operational Training Unit at Kinloss, where he crewed up with Ken Brown and his colleagues. They had only completed a handful of operations in 44 Squadron before being transferred to 617 Squadron at the end of March.

After the Dams Raid, McDonald flew with the Brown crew on all its subsequent operations in 617 Squadron, leaving when the crew was broken up in March 1944. In the summer of 1944, he was posted as an instructor to an OTU and remained on instructional duties until the end of the war.

After demobilisation, he joined the Canadian customs service in Vancouver, the same occupation as his sometime crewmate, Dudley Heal. He married Margery Warrian in 1948, but they had no children. He died on 13 May 2012 in Vancouver.

Crew 18: AJ-O

Mobile Reserve. Attacked Ennepe Dam and returned to base.
Lancaster serial number: ED886/G

Flt Sgt W.C. Townsend DFM

Pilot

William Clifford Townsend was born on 12 January 1921 in Gloucestershire, the son of William and Kathleen Townsend. He went to Monmouth School. Shortly after the war started he joined the army, but then managed to transfer into the RAF in May 1941.

He was selected for pilot training, qualified as a pilot early in 1942 and in June of that year was posted to 49 Squadron. He undertook two 'gardening' operations during September 1942, and his first bombing trip was to Wismar on 1 October.

By the end of March 1943, Townsend had completed twenty-six operations and been recommended for a DFM. His regular crew included five of the men who would fly with him on the Dams Raid: flight engineer Denis Powell, navigator Lance Howard, bomb aimer Charles Franklin, and air gunners Doug Webb and Ray Wilkinson.

Townsend's regular wireless operator Jack Grain declined the opportunity to transfer to 617 Squadron, as he was getting married, so when the crew arrived at Scampton they did not have anyone to fill this position. However, George Chalmers, a Scot who had already done a full tour in 35 Squadron, had arrived at the station without a crew, and was fitted in.

Training went ahead throughout April and early May, but dummy Upkeep weapons were in short supply, so Townsend never actually dropped one before the raid. Instead, he flew as second pilot with Les Munro on one test flight at Reculver. Munro flew so low that when the weapon was dropped the resultant splash damaged the rear turret.

On the Dams Raid, AJ-O was diverted to attack the Ennepe Dam, the only crew to be sent to this target, and flew home safely after dropping its mine.

Like Ken Brown, Townsend was awarded the CGM for his role. Five of his crew were also given medals, making them the second most decorated Dams Raid crew after Gibson's. He flew on

YAHYA EL-DROUBIE

YAHYA EL-DROUBIE

Bill Townsend and his crew, photographed outside Buckingham Palace, in June 1943. (Left to right) Ray Wilkinson, Douglas Webb, Charles Franklin, Bill Townsend, Jack Grain, Lance Howard. Jack Grain had been the crew's wireless operator in 49 Squadron but opted out of the transfer to 617 Squadron.

just two further operations in 617 Squadron, both in July 1943 when the squadron was sent on raids on Italian targets with a stopover in Blida, Algeria. He had by then been commissioned and completed a full tour, and in September he was posted to a training role. He remained in the RAF until 1946.

Bill Townsend married Eileen Wall in 1947 and they had three children. At one point he and his wife owned a pub in Oxford, but he later worked as a civil servant, including a spell in the Department of Employment in Bromsgrove, Worcestershire. He died in Bromsgrove on 9 April 1991.

Sgt D.J.D Powell
Flight engineer

Dennis John Dean Powell was born in Birmingham on 21 January 1922, although his family later moved to London. His father, Easton Powell, was Canadian but his mother Ada (née Dean) was from Birmingham.

Powell joined the RAF as a boy entrant before the outbreak of the war and served in ground crew. In 1942, he took the opportunity to train as a flight engineer. He joined 49 Squadron in October 1942, but wasn't immediately allocated a crew. He teamed up with Bill Townsend at the end of the year and then flew with him on fifteen operations before their transfer to 617 Squadron in March 1943.

Like all the flight engineers on Operation Chastise, Powell had a very busy trip. Low-level flying required both pilot and engineer to have sharp eyes and speedy reactions. The two young men in the cockpit of AJ-O certainly displayed both over the course of the raid. After the raid, however, Powell was the only one of the entire crew of AJ-O not to be decorated – a decision which today looks very unfair, but probably reflects the thinking in the RAF of the time.

Powell flew with Townsend and most of the rest of his Dams Raid crew on the two trips to attack Italian targets in July 1943. However, unlike the rest of his crewmates he was only about halfway through a tour, so he then transferred to the crew of the newly appointed CO of 617 Sqn, George Holden.

Holden's first two operations with 617 Squadron had been the Italian trips in July, which he undertook with all of Guy Gibson's Dams Raid crew: John Pulford, Harlo Taerum, Robert Hutchison, Fred Spafford, George Deering and Richard-Trevor Roper. By September 1943, both Pulford and Trevor-Roper had left the crew, so Dennis Powell moved into the flight engineer's seat. He must have regarded flying with the squadron CO as a significant step upwards.

Unfortunately, Powell's first operation with Holden would be his last. On 16 September, Holden led a detachment of eight aircraft on a low level attack to bomb the Dortmund Ems Canal with a new 12000lb 'thin case' bomb. This was to be a catastrophic night for the squadron, and Holden's was the first of five aircraft to be lost.

Approaching the small town of Nordhorn, Holden rose to about 300ft in order to fly above its church. A more cautious pilot – perhaps someone who had flown on the Dams Raid – would probably have changed course to go around the spire. Holden's Lancaster became a simple target for the town's only flak battery and it was shot down, crashing in flames in a farmyard nearby. The bomb inside exploded a few minutes later, devastating the area and killing a woman on the ground. The crew had all been killed in the crash. Of the eight on board, only George Holden and George Deering were positively identified by the Germans. The aircraft loss was witnessed by Les Knight and his crew, flying in formation with Holden. His navigator, Sydney Hobday, wrote to Dennis Powell's mother in 1961 saying: 'We were flying a matter of yards from the machine which carried Guy Gibson's crew – piloted by Sq Ldr Holden – which must have been the one which your son was in. We were very low and they were shot down by light flak.'[176]

Along with the four other Dams Raid veterans who flew in Holden's aircraft, Dennis Powell was first buried in the nearby cemetery at Lingen, but after the war they were all reinterred in Reichswald Forest War Cemetery.

Plt Off C.L. Howard
Navigator

Cecil Lancelot Howard, known to his friends and family as Lance, was born in Fremantle, Western Australia, on 12 January 1913, the son of Henry and Helen Howard. He worked as a commercial traveller before the war.

He joined the RAAF in 1940 and was initially selected for pilot training. Eventually he was remustered as a navigator. He arrived in the UK in late 1941 and was posted to 14 OTU at RAF Cottesmore. He was posted to 49 Squadron in May 1942, where he spent some time in further training in the Conversion Unit. By late 1942, he was flying as the regular navigator in Bill Townsend's crew and went on to complete twenty-five operations by March 1943. By then he had been recommended for a commission, although it was not confirmed until after he had joined 617 Squadron.

On the night of the Dams Raid, Howard was apprehensive as Townsend coaxed AJ-O into the air. 'I had visions of the bumpy (grass) take-off causing the lights under the fuselage to be shaken off so that instead of being 60ft above the ground we would finish up 60ft below it,' he later remembered.

Howard's last two operations in the whole war were the squadron's attacks on Italian targets in July. In September, three days after he had represented the squadron at David Maltby's funeral in Kent, he was listed as 'tour expired' and was later posted to a conversion unit as an instructor.

Howard was released from active service in March 1945 and returned to Australia to be with his wife Marjorie, who he had married in 1941 shortly

---

176 Sydney Hobday, letter to Ada Powell, 1961. www.bonhams.com/auctions/14267/lot/584. [Accessed August 2015].

before embarking for the war. After the war he worked in the Repatriation Department and then at the *West Australian* newspaper. He remained there until ill-health forced his early retirement in 1972. He was active in the RAAF Association but refused an MBE, stating he believed it was awarded to him on behalf of the RAAFA and he considered it insufficient recognition of the work of the Association. He was also involved in the Karrakatta Cemetery association, where he is now memorialised.

Lance Howard founded the Air Force Memorial Estate in Bull Creek, near Perth. The estate provides comfortable housing for ex-servicemen, next to the largest aviation museum in Australia. He and his wife lived there until his death on 26 December 1989.

Flt Sgt G.A. Chalmers
Wireless operator

George Alexander Chalmers was born on 12 February 1921 in Peterhead, Aberdeenshire. As a Scot, he was often known by the nickname 'Jock'. He was educated at Aberdeen Academy before working briefly at a local Crosse & Blackwell factory. He joined the RAF in 1938 as a boy entrant, qualified as a wireless operator/air gunner before the outbreak of war, and was posted first to 10 Squadron in Dishforth. Early in the war, he took part in leaflet-dropping operations over Germany. In August 1940 he transferred to 7 Squadron and later that year to 35 Squadron, where he completed a first tour of operations during 1941.

After about a year in various training jobs, he asked to go back on operations and was posted to RAF Scampton. He was posted in as a supernumerary, without a crew, and told Mick Martin that he would prefer to be allocated to an all-NCO crew if possible. Martin was a bit taken aback by this (perhaps knowing that there were very few of these in the new squadron) but it turned out that Bill Townsend was without a wireless operator, so Chalmers was fitted in there. Townsend's crew did not remain all-NCO for long – by the time of the Dams Raid, Lance Howard had been commissioned, and Townsend followed shortly afterwards.

On the raid, Chalmers was conscious that he stood 'watching history from the astrodome, although everything happened so quickly (at

CHALMERS FAMILY

100ft) that incidents came and went almost before the mind could appreciate them'. When they reached the Ennepe Dam, Chalmers started the rotation of the mine, which caused the aircraft to shudder violently, so everyone was very relieved when it was released. Chalmers himself was able to watch the subsequent explosion from the astrodome.

He was awarded the DFM for his role on the Dams Raid, where the citation noted that he had by then flown on forty-four operations. He was commissioned himself at the end of June 1943, shortly after attending the investiture in London. There he was flattered when the Queen, who was conducting the investiture, identified him as coming from Peterhead.

Townsend and some of his crew finished their tour in September 1943, but the irrepressible Chalmers carried on. He flew first with the new squadron CO, Leonard Cheshire, but then transferred to the crew of Plt Off Bernard 'Bunny' Clayton, an experienced pilot who had been posted from 51 Squadron to 617 Squadron in July 1943 with a CGM and DFC to his name.

Chalmers finally came off operations in July 1944, at the same time as all of the other Dams Raid personnel still flying in 617 Squadron. He was awarded the DFC later in the year, having flown in 66 operations. The citation concluded: "Throughout his long and arduous operational career, this officer has displayed outstanding courage and devotion to duty."

Chalmers stayed on in the RAF until 1954, on an extended service commission. When he left, he joined the Ministry of Defence in Harrogate, working on the technical specifications for RAF services, and developed a specialist knowledge of aircraft refuelling procedures.

George Chalmers retired in 1984. He married Alma Collier in 1941, and they had nine children. He died on 6 August 2002.

YAHYA EL-DROUBIE

Sgt C.E. Franklin DFM
Bomb aimer

Charles Ernest Franklin was born in West Ham, London on 12 November 1915, one of the seven children of Albert and May Franklin.

He joined the RAF in 1940, and qualified as an observer. In April 1942, he was posted to 49 Squadron. Altogether, he flew on twenty-eight operations in this squadron, some of the time with Bill Townsend but also with other pilots. Unusually, he was recommended for the

DFM before he had finished his first tour, with the citation noting his 'marked singleness of purpose in his determination only to bomb the correct target, involving as it frequently has done several runs to identify it positively before releasing his bombs.' The award of the medal came through two days after the Dams Raid itself.

In March 1943, Franklin was offered the chance to transfer to 617 Squadron with the rest of Townsend's crew. On the Dams Raid his job was made much more difficult as a result of the violent shudder caused by the rotating mine, with the result that it took him three dummy runs before he got the line and distance correct. His fourth attempt was successful, and the Upkeep was dropped at 0337. The dam, however, was not breached.

Despite this, Franklin was commended for his efforts and received a Bar to his just-acquired DFM for his work on the night. Only 60 Bars to the DFM were awarded during the whole war, and Franklin's was the only one given to a 617 Squadron airman. He travelled to Buckingham Palace to receive it, and was photographed outside with Bill Townsend and four of the rest of the crew.

The Dams Raid was Franklin's first and last operation in 617 Squadron. In July he was posted on a bomb aimer's instructors course and then at the end of August 1943, he went to a conversion unit as an instructor. During this time, he was commissioned. He returned to operations in July 1944 with 83 Squadron. He flew on a handful of operations with Flt Lt J. Meggeson, but was then taken sick and did not complete this tour.

After the war, Franklin moved to Birmingham and set up a successful catering business with his parents. There was a flurry of publicity about him in 1955 when his name was omitted from the initial guest list for the Royal Premiere of the film *The Dam Busters*, but this was rectified in time and he was able to attend. He died in Birmingham on 25 January 1975, and his funeral was attended by a number of his ex-crewmates. It was widely covered in the press, and a series of photographs taken for the *Daily Mirror* can be seen in agency archives.

Sgt D.E. Webb
Front gunner

Douglas Edward Webb was born in Leytonstone, London on 12 September 1922, one of the two children of Edward and Daisy Webb. After leaving school, he worked briefly for the photographic supplies company Ilford and then for the London News Agency in Fleet Street as a photographic printer.

He joined the RAF in 1940, as soon as he had turned 18, as he wanted to be an air gunner. After a substantial delay, he began training in 1942 and

YAHYA EL-DROUBIE

qualified as a gunner later that year. He was posted to 49 Squadron where he became one of Bill Townsend's core crew, along with Dennis Powell, Lance Howard and fellow gunner Ray Wilkinson. He flew on some 25 operations before the crew were transferred to the new 617 Squadron in March 1943.

Before the Dams Raid started Webb thought that he was going to be busy in AJ-O's front turret, so he scrounged an extra 1,000 rounds of ammunition for each gun from the squadron armoury. And then, with the Third Wave not scheduled for take off until more than two hours after the second, he filled in some of the time having a bath. He recalled later that he was convinced that he wasn't going to come back, and that he wanted to 'die clean'.

Fortunately, his premonition didn't come true. From his seat in the front turret, he was able to see how dangerous the German defences were (he saw the shooting down of Burpee in 'a bloody great ball of fire'), and also appreciate the airmanship of his skipper as Townsend flew as low as he dared. And his decision to bring extra ammunition proved vital, since without it he would have run out during the trip.

Webb was awarded the DFM for his role on the raid. He didn't believe this at first, suspecting he was being set up as part of some elaborate joke. Having checked, he then found a shop where he could buy the appropriate medal ribbons. Due to an administrative error, his actual medal was engraved 'E Webb', missing out his first name.

In July 1943, he flew with Bill Townsend on two of the raids on Italian targets and was then loaned to George Holden's crew for another. It was another stroke of fortune that he did not remain on the Holden crew, as in September they were all killed on the disastrous attack on the Dortmund Ems canal.

Webb was now tour expired, and he was posted to a conversion unit for a spell as an instructor, along with his rear gunner colleague Ray Wilkinson. The pair moved on to other training roles but in October 1944, they both came back on operations with 617 Squadron. He flew his first operation of this new tour in December, and went on to fly on about another ten before the end of the war. During this last phase of the war, Barnes Wallis's 'Tallboy' bomb came into production, but in order to carry this 12,000lb monstrosity, the Lancasters had to be modified. The mid-upper gunner was often left behind, so Webb's opportunities to fly were reduced. Later, when the 22,000lb 'Grand Slam' became available, the wireless operator was also dropped. Webb did however fly on 617 Squadron's last wartime operation, an attack on Hitler's mountain lair on 25 April 1943. Len Sumpter, another Dams Raid participant, also flew on this sortie, making them the only two men to fly on the squadron's first and last wartime operations. (See p169.)

After demobilisation in 1946, Webb rejoined the London News Agency as a staff photographer. He went on to work in the film industry as a stills photographer and then opened his own studio in Soho, where he specialised in theatrical and film portraits. In 1948, he took some of the first professional nude pictures of the model and actress Pamela Green, thereby beginning an association which would last almost fifty years.

Webb had a prolific life in stills photography, cinema and television. His TV work included the title sequences for ITV's *Special Branch* and *The Sweeney*. In the latter, the famous enlarged fingerprints were those of Pamela Green.

Although they were never married, Webb and Green became life partners, and in 1986 when Webb retired they moved together to the Isle of Wight. Douglas Webb died on 8 December 1996 in Yarmouth, Isle of Wight. Pamela Green stayed in the area, appearing in various TV documentaries and giving talks to the local WI, in which she was an active member. She died on 7 May 2010.

Sgt R. Wilkinson
Rear gunner

Raymond Wilkinson was the only child of Christopher and Margaret Wilkinson and was born on 1 September 1922 in South Shields on Tyneside. His father was a miner. Wilkinson worked briefly as a joiner's apprentice before joining the RAF in 1941. He qualified as an air gunner in the summer of 1942 and was posted to 49 Squadron where he became one of Bill Townsend's core crew, along with Dennis Powell, Lance Howard and fellow gunner Doug Webb. He flew on more than twenty operations before the crew were transferred to the new 617 Squadron in March 1943.

As AJ-O flew low across the Dutch and German countryside on the way to its target, Wilkinson was credited with shooting out some searchlights near Ahlen and he was awarded the DFM for his role on the raid.

In July 1943, he flew with Bill Townsend on

YAHYA EL-DROUBIE

two of the raids on Italian targets ,and then in September he was posted as tour expired. He was sent to a conversion unit for a spell as an instructor, along with his mid-upper gunner colleague Doug Webb. The pair moved on to other training roles but just over a year later, in October 1944, they both came back on operations with 617 Squadron. By then Wilkinson had been commissioned.

He joined the crew of the Australian pilot Flt Lt Arthur Kell, and his first operation of this new tour was an unsuccessful attack on the Tirpitz, moored in a Norwegian fiord, which took place on 28 October. Both 617 and 9 Squadrons were armed with Tallboys and set off from Lossiemouth in Scotland on a trip which took more than twelve hours. In very bad weather, the ship was hit by several bombs but was not sunk. After the war it emerged that it had in fact been badly damaged and was no longer seaworthy, but this was not apparent to the Allies. So a similar force set off from Lossiemouth on 12 November to attack it again and once more Wilkinson was in the Kell crew. They dropped one of the four Tallboys which landed directly on the ship. The combined effect was spectacular, although it was not confirmed until the following day when reconnaissance showed the Tirpitz had capsized, with the bottom of the hull visible above the water.

Wilkinson has the unique honour of being the only person to have taken part in both the Dams Raid and the final successful attack on the Tirpitz. He flew on some other seventeen operations before the end of the war, including the raids on the U Boat pens at Ijmuiden and the Bielefeld viaduct.

Wilkinson married his wife Iris after the war, and they attended the Royal Premiere of *The Dam Busters* in 1955. They moved to Australia some time later, and he died in Noble Park, Victoria on 27 July 1980.

Crew 19: AJ-Y

Mobile reserve. Failed to reach Sorpe Dam due to weather conditions and flak damage. Returned to base with mine intact.
Lancaster serial number: ED924/G

Flt Sgt C.T. Anderson

Pilot

Cyril Thorpe Anderson was born in Wakefield on 9 December 1913, the son of John and Gertrude Anderson. He was one of three children. He went to Lawefield Lane School and then on to a grammar school in the city. After leaving school he was an apprentice engineer at Rhodes and Son and became a qualified fitter at British Jeffrey Diamond.

Anderson joined the RAF in 1934 and served as ground crew. When the war started, he volunteered for aircrew and was selected for pilot training in August 1940. He qualified as a pilot in 1942. In the final stages of training he crewed up with all the six men with whom he would fly on the Dams Raid: Robert Paterson (flight engineer), John Nugent (navigator), William Bickle (wireless operator), and Gilbert 'Jimmy' Green (bomb aimer), and Eric Ewan and Arthur Buck (gunners). They were posted together from 1654 Conversion Unit at Wigsley to 49 Squadron at Fiskerton in February 1943.

Anderson's first two operations were the usual 'second dickey' trips, when he flew with Sgt B.A. Gumbley and his crew on trips to Nuremberg and Cologne on 25 and 26 February. (Gumbley, a New Zealander, would join 617 Squadron later in the war. He took part in a number of raids including the attacks on the Tirpitz but was shot down in March 1944, and died along with his crew.)

The Anderson crew's first operation together was an attack on Essen on 12 March 1943. After a successful bomb drop, they lost power in one engine on the way home. Their second trip was to St Nazaire on 22 March.

At this point, it seems that the request from Group HQ to send a crew to the new squadron being formed at Scampton was received by 49 Squadron. The CO nominated Bill Townsend and his crew, who had mostly nearly finished their tour, and therefore fell precisely into the category of 'experienced crews' which had been demanded. He then chose to add Cyril Anderson to the posting, for reasons that have never

DOMINIC HOWARD

LEE RICHARDS

Six of the Anderson crew, photographed after an operation in the summer of 1943. (Left to right) John Nugent, Gilbert 'Jimmy' Green, Douglas Bickle, Arthur Buck, Cyril Anderson, Robert Paterson.

been explained. Anderson, with just two operations under his belt, did not however demur from the request, but asked to gain some further experience in 49 Squadron before moving. He and his crew were therefore sent on three operations in the next five days, flying to Duisburg on 26 March and Berlin on both 27 and 29 March.

Anderson and his wife Rose Darby had married in 1939, and their only son Graham was born in December 1942. Sadly he did not survive infancy, dying at just four months old earlier in March.

With just seven operations to his name, Anderson was one of the small coterie of inexperienced pilots who took part in the Dams Raid. The others with fewer than ten operations were Vernon Byers, Geoff Rice and Ken Brown. There is no doubt that Guy Gibson was not happy with the fact that he had been given men who did not meet the criteria he had imposed, but he had no option but to go ahead with them. In the event, although they all proved that they could handle the tough training regime, he placed them all towards the end of Operation Chastise's battle order.

Anderson and his crew were the last to take off on the Dams Raid, leaving the ground at Scampton at 0015. AJ-Y encountered heavy flak north of the Ruhr and was forced off track. Then the rear turret began to malfunction. By 0228, the time it received the signal to proceed to the Sorpe, mist was rising in the valleys which made the identification of landmarks almost impossible. At 0310, after consulting his crew, Anderson decided that with dawn approaching and a rear turret not working he should turn for home.

The next morning, Anderson was photographed along with the rest of the pilots who returned outside the Officers' Mess, but the crew did not remain long on the squadron, and packed their bags that afternoon. Gibson was not happy with Anderson's explanation.

Anderson and his crew returned to 49 Squadron. Just over a month later, on 21 June, all seven, still together, resumed their operational career with an attack on Krefeld. By then Anderson had been commissioned.

They flew on fourteen more operations after this, but on 23 September they failed to return from an attack on Mannheim. Subsequent research has shown that their aircraft was shot down by a night fighter near Offenbach, as they headed home. Their aircraft was seen flying over the village church trailing fire and crashed into a field. The spot is now marked by a memorial.

Five of the crew were recovered from the wreckage and were buried by the local Catholic priest Fr Jacob Storck on 26 September. The bodies of the other two members of the crew (one was Gilbert Green, the other was not identified at the time) were possibly thrown from the aircraft during the explosion, and were found later. According to Fr Storck, they may have tried to bale out. They were buried on 28 September in Offenbach cemetery. After the war the bodies of all seven were exhumed and identified. They were then taken to Rheinberg War Cemetery.

Cyril Anderson's gravestone in Rheinberg bears a heartfelt inscription chosen by his wife Rose: 'In my book of memory is marked the happy story of a love deep and true.'

Sgt R.C. Paterson
Flight engineer

Robert Campbell Paterson was born on 20 September 1907 in Edinburgh, the son of Robert and Wilhemina Paterson. He was educated at George Heriot's School in the city. On leaving school, he worked as a clerk and then as a driving instructor, being the first person in Scotland to have a franchise from the British School of Motoring. He was also the part-time chauffeur for the author Sir Compton MacKenzie.

PATERSON FAMILY

Paterson was keen on motoring and mechanics and as the war approached joined the RAF to serve as ground crew. In June 1942, he took the opportunity to fly on heavy bombers and qualified as a flight engineer. He was then posted to 1654 Conversion Unit where he crewed up with Cyril Anderson and the rest of his crew, who had been posted in from an Operational Training Unit.

The crew were posted together to 49 Squadron in February 1943, and did their first operation together as a crew on 12 March. After their second trip, they were posted to 617 Squadron but in fact stayed on 49 Squadron to do three more operations, including two to Berlin.

Paterson was the oldest in a crew which was older than the average and had a 29-year-old skipper. This would have singled them out in both the mess and the crew room. After their trip on the Dams Raid, they returned to 49 Squadron and resumed their operational career with an attack on Krefeld on 21 June. They flew on fourteen more operations after this, but on 23 September they failed to return from a successful attack on Mannheim. As they headed home, their aircraft was shot down by a night fighter near Offenbach.

Robert Paterson died three days after his 36th birthday, leaving a wife and a four-year-old son. His school Roll of Honour indicates his modesty, saying that he 'consistently refused to accept promotion and honours.' He is buried in Rheinberg War Cemetery.

Sgt J.P. Nugent
Navigator

John Percival Nugent was born on 9 August 1914 in Stoney Middleton in the Derbyshire Peak District, one of the nine children of Francis and Ellen Nugent. After leaving school, Nugent qualified as a maths and music teacher at St

Mary's Training College, Strawberry Hill, Middlesex (now St Mary's University College). He taught in London, but moved to Brighton at the start of the war when his school was evacuated there. He joined the RAF in 1940 and was sent to Canada for training as a navigator.

On returning to England, he was posted to 25 Operational Training Unit, where he crewed up with Cyril Anderson. They moved on to 1654 Conversion Unit, where the whole crew was formed up. The crew were posted to 49 Squadron in February 1943, and did their first operation together as a crew on 12 March. After their second trip, they were posted to 617 Squadron but in fact stayed on 49 Squadron to do three more operations, including two to Berlin.

Nugent was back in the Peak District when the crews trained for the Dams Raid at the Ladybower reservoir in the Derwent valley. Whether he was able to beat up his family home is not recorded.

After their trip on the Dams Raid, the Anderson crew returned to 49 Squadron and resumed their operational career with an attack on Krefeld on 21 June. They flew on fourteen more operations, but on 23 September they failed to return from a successful attack on Mannheim.

John Nugent is buried in Rheinberg War Cemetery.

Sgt W.D. Bickle
Wireless operator

William Douglas Bickle, known to his family and friends as Douglas, was born in St Ann's Chapel, a small hamlet near Calstock in Cornwall on 6 March 1922, the only son of Percy and Alma Bickle. His father worked as a farmer.

Bickle joined the RAF in October 1940, soon after his 18th birthday, and he was selected for training as a wireless operator/air gunner. After qualifying he was posted to 25 Operational Training Unit, where he crewed up with Cyril Anderson and others who would later fly on the Dams Raid. They moved on to 1654 Conversion Unit, where the whole crew was formed up. The crew were posted to 49 Squadron in February 1943, and did their first operation together as a crew on 12 March. After their second trip, they were posted to 617 Squadron but in fact stayed on 49 Squadron to do three more operations.

After the Dams Raid, the Anderson crew resumed their operational career in 49 Squadron with an attack on Krefeld on 21 June. Altogether, they flew on fourteen more operations in 49 Squadron, but on 23 September they failed to return from a successful attack on Mannheim.

On 9 August 1943, shortly before his final operation, Bickle had married Violet Bickford, a woman from his home village in Wembury, Devon, where her father was working as a NAAFI canteen manager. Violet Bickle remarried after the war, and moved to Liverpool. William Bickle is buried in Rheinberg War Cemetery.

DOMINIC HOWARD

LEE RICHARDS

Sgt G.J. Green
Bomb aimer

Gilbert John Green was born in Malling in Kent on 13 April 1922, the son of George and Gladys Green. His family moved to Southall in Middlesex, where he went to school and joined the a local Air Cadet squadron. He was known to family and friends by the nickname Jimmy.

Green joined the RAF in 1941 and qualified as a bomb aimer in 1942. He was then posted to 25 Operational Training Unit, where he crewed up with Cyril Anderson and the core of the crew who would later fly on the Dams Raid. They moved on to 1654 Conversion Unit, where the whole crew was formed up.

The crew were posted to 49 Squadron in February 1943, and did their first operation together as a crew on 12 March. After their second trip, they were posted to 617 Squadron but in fact stayed on 49 Squadron to do three more operations, including two to Berlin.

After their trip on the Dams Raid, the Anderson crew returned to 49 Squadron and resumed their operational career with an attack on Krefeld on 21 June. Altogether, they flew on fourteen more operations in 49 Squadron, but on 23 September they failed to return from a successful attack on Mannheim.

The bodies of five of the crew were recovered from the wreckage and were buried by the local Catholic priest Fr Jacob Storck on 26 September. Green and one other unidentified member of the crew were thrown from the wreckage by the explosion. Fr Storck said afterwards that they may have tried to bale out, although this has not been verified. Their bodies were not found until after the others, and the pair were buried in Offenbach Cemetery on 28 September, two days after the other five.

After the war, the bodies of Gilbert Green and all his comrades were re-buried in Rheinberg War Cemetery.

Sgt E. Ewan
Front gunner

Eric Ewan was born in Wolverhampton on 3 January 1922, the youngest of the four children of Thomas and Jane Ewan.

He joined the RAF shortly after his 18th birthday and was eventually selected for air gunnery training. In November 1942, while still undergoing training in Yorkshire, he survived a crash in a Wellington in which another crew member was killed. In January 1943 he was posted to 1654 Conversion Unit, where the whole crew which would eventually fly on the Dams Raid with Cyril Anderson came together.

The crew were posted to 49 Squadron in February 1943, and did their first operation together as a crew on 12 March. After their second trip, they were posted to 617 Squadron but in fact stayed on 49 Squadron to do three more operations, including two to Berlin.

After their trip on the Dams Raid, the Anderson crew returned to 49 Squadron and resumed their operational career with an attack on Krefeld on 21 June. Altogether, they flew on fourteen more operations in 49 Squadron, but on 23 September they failed to return from a successful attack on Mannheim.

Eric Ewan was buried first in Offenbach Cemetery. After the war all seven were reburied in Rheinberg War Cemetery.

Sgt A.W. Buck
Rear gunner

Arthur William Buck was born in Bromley-by-Bow, London on 30 November 1914, the younger of the two children of George and Ann Buck. At the time of his birth, his father was employed as a carman. He later became a bus driver.

Buck worked as a commercial traveller before the war. He joined the RAF in 1940 but did not begin air gunnery training until 1942. In January 1943 he was posted to 1654 Conversion Unit, where the whole crew which would eventually fly on the Dams Raid with Cyril Anderson came together.

The crew were posted to 49 Squadron in February 1943, and did their first operation together as a crew on 12 March. After their second trip, they were posted to 617 Squadron but in fact stayed on 49 Squadron to do three more operations, including two to Berlin.

After their trip on the Dams Raid, the Anderson crew returned to 49 Squadron and resumed their operational career with an attack on Krefeld on 21 June. Altogether, they flew on fourteen more operations in 49 Squadron, but on 23 September they failed to return from a successful attack on Mannheim.

Arthur Buck married his wife Minnie Rosetta England in Beckenham in 1941. Along with his comrades, he was buried first in Offenbach Cemetery and then, after the war, reburied in Rheinberg War Cemetery.

Chapter 8

After the raid

THE TWO AIRCRAFT WHICH RETURNED EARLY from the Dams Raid, those of Munro and Rice, touched down at Scampton before one in the morning. Those who had reached their targets began arriving back some two and a half hours later – David Maltby in AJ-J was the first to land at 0311. By four o'clock Harris, Cochrane and Wallis had all left Grantham for the drive to Scampton, and personally greeted some of the later arrivals. AJ-O was the last aircraft to get back, at 0615. It was piloted by an exhausted Bill Townsend, who didn't recognise Harris in his Air Chief Marshal's uniform and pushed past him rather abruptly.

Harris and Cochrane observed some of the crew debriefings. They are both pictured watching Gibson's crew in conversation with an intelligence officer, in a photograph taken by the same Flg Off Bellamy who had pictured them climbing into AJ-G a few hours earlier. After they had been debriefed many, but not all, of the survivors got involved in the two impromptu parties which took over the Officers' and Sergeants' Messes, where the bars were reopened and much beer was consumed. At one point Gp Capt Whitworth's house was invaded by a group who conga-danced around the rooms and stole his pyjamas as a trophy.

Harry Humphries had stayed up all night, but after a wash and shave and some breakfast went to his office to start work. To his surprise and pleasure, all the administrative staff had also reported for duty. Humphries and Sgt Jim Heveron spent much of the morning sending telegrams to the next of kin of the missing. In the afternoon, they were interrupted in this work by Gibson, bearing the news that all 900 aircrew and groundcrew were to be sent on leave the next day. The process of drafting letters to the next of kin didn't begin until Tuesday 18 May, after the leave had begun.

Sometime in the mid-morning a series of photographs were taken. Many of the men posing had not yet been to bed, so some rather dopey and tired expressions can be seen in the pictures. The first two images captured for posterity were taken outside the Officers Mess. One shows the eleven pilots who took part in the raid, along with Flt Lt Harold Wilson, who had withdrawn late through illness. This is shown on p109 of this book. On the far left of the

The Canadian contingent who returned from the Dams Raid. (Standing left to right) Steve Oancia, Fred Sutherland, Harry O'Brien, Ken Brown, Harvey Weeks, John Thrasher, George Deering, Bill Radcliffe, Don MacLean, Joe McCarthy, Grant McDonald. (Crouching left to right) Percy Pigeon, Harlo Taerum, Danny Walker, Bruce Gowrie, Dave Rodger.

shot stands Cyril Anderson, one hand in his pocket. With the exception of Ken Brown, who is standing on the far right and is still in battledress, they are wearing their formal No. 1 uniforms, which suggests that they had all changed especially for the photograph.

Brown doesn't appear in the other photograph, so it could have been taken first before he arrived. This shows twenty-one men – the other eleven pilots plus ten more aircrew, all of whom are officers. These are Lance Howard, John Fort, Sydney Hobday, Edward Johnson, Harlo Taerum, Fred Spafford, Richard Trevor-Roper, Bob Hutchison, Jack Buckley and Len Chambers. Once more, Anderson is on the far left, in the same hand-in-pocket pose. Posing for these two pictures were almost the last thing he did in 617 Squadron. By the afternoon of that day, he had been interviewed by Gibson and posted back to 49 Squadron, along with his crew.

Three more well-known pictures were taken at about the same time. These were photographs taken for the press in Canada, Australia and New Zealand, and show most of the personnel from those countries who returned from the raid. These were taken on the hard standings next to a parked-up Lancaster. All the men who were in No. 1 uniform in the earlier shots are still wearing them, but the rest are in battledress. Rather bizarrely, many men are holding random pieces of flying equipment – mainly Mae West lifejackets or helmets, but in the case of Bob Hay and Lance Howard a map and a binocular case – presumably in order to look as through they have just returned from the mission. This illu-

HUTCHISON FAMILY

The Australians also posed for a group picture after the Dams Raid.
(Left to right) Bob Hay, Lance Howard, David Shannon, Jack Leggo, Fred Spafford, Mick Martin, Les Knight, Bob Kellow.

sion is slightly spoilt by the fact that they are all wearing ordinary shoes rather than flying boots. All fifteen Canadians who returned from the raid are present, plus the American Joe McCarthy, but Tom Simpson and Toby Foxlee are missing from the Australian picture. The two New Zealanders, Les Munro and Len Chambers, stand together for their picture.

The airfield seemed a lot quieter that morning. A Tannoy announcement told everyone on the base what had occurred, but many were more aware of the scale of the losses. Wallis stayed for the morning, mingling with survivors, and very upset with the losses. Roy Chadwick, the Lancaster designer, told his daughter when he got back to Manchester at breakfast time that he was 'in tears when I left'. Cochrane reported him as 'inconsolable' later in the morning.[177]

By lunchtime, the world had been informed of the scale of the achievement. The Air Ministry communiqué had been released to the press, and was broadcast by the BBC:

> The Air Ministry has just issued the following communiqué. In the early hours of this morning, a force of Lancasters of Bomber Command led by Wing Cdr G.P. Gibson DSO DFC attacked with mines the dams of the Möhne and Sorpe reservoirs. These control over two-thirds of the water storage capacity of the Ruhr basin. Reconnaissance later

---

177 Sweetman, *Dambusters Raid,* p234.

Reference :-   No. 617
DO/2/43.   Squadron, RAF. Station,
                                                Scampton, Lincs.

                                                20th. May, 1943.

My Dear Mr Marriot,

    It is with deep regret that I write to confirm my telegram
advising you that your son, Sergeant J. Marriott, is missing as a
result of operations on the night of 16/17th. May, 1943.

    Sergeant Marriott was Flight Engineer of an aircraft
detailed to carry out an attack against the Eder Dam. The aircraft
was seen to drop its load, and when the captain, Squadron Leader
Maudslay, was called by radio, he seemed to be in extreme difficulty.
It is possible, however, that the crew were able to abandon the aircraft
and land safely in enemy territory, and if this is the case, news
should reach you direct from the International Red Cross Committee
within the next six weeks. Squadron Leader Maudslay would, I am sure,
do everything possible to ensure the safety of his crew.

    Please accept my sincere sympathy during this anxious
period of waiting.

    I have arranged for your son's personal effects to be taken
care of by the Committee of Adjustment Officer at this Station, and
will be forwarded to you through normal channels in due course.

    If there is any way in which I can help you, please
let me know.

        Yours Very Sincerely,
                                    Gibson

                                    Wing Commander,
                                    Commanding, 617 Squadron, RAF.

T.H. Marriott Esq.,
Middleton House,
New Smithy,
Chinley,
   nr. Stockport,
     Cheshire.

MARRIOTT FAMILY

Fifty-six letters like this were sent to addresses across the country, and to Canada and
Australia. As can be seen by the date of 20 May on this example, sent to the family of
Jack Marriott, the process took several days.

established that the Möhne dam had been breached over a length of
one hundred yards, and that the power station below had been swept
away. The Eder dam, which controls the headwaters of the Weser and
Fulde valleys and operates several power stations, was also attacked and
reported as breached. Photographs show the river below the dam in full
flood. The attacks were pressed home from a very low level with great
determination and coolness in the face of fierce resistance. Eight of the
Lancasters are missing.

On the Tuesday, every paper carried the full story as its lead. It was only a day or two after news had reached Britain of the final Allied victory in Tunisia, which meant that plans for the invasion of Sicily and then Italy could go ahead, so this daring raid captured the imagination. Nowadays we would call the press and public relations operation mounted by the Air Ministry and the Ministry of Information 'spin', with all the pejorative overtones that that implies, but there is no doubt that the press was given substantial help in the production of their stories, including the release of the dramatic reconnaissance photographs. Of course in war time, with no opportunity to check material and with the only foreign reports coming from neutral Switzerland, Sweden and Spain, it is completely understandable that the press should carry what the official sources wanted them to say.

This would explain why some of the details were either wrong or based on speculation. The *Daily Telegraph*, for instance, informed its readers that 'three key dams' had been blown up, while the *Daily Mirror* was more sensationalist, with a headline reading 'Huns get a flood blitz: torrent rages along Ruhr'. The *Daily Mail* ran a headline over its photographs: 'The Smash-Up: RAF Picture Testifies to Perfect Bombing'. Its story went on: 'Two mighty walls of water were last night rolling irresistibly down the Ruhr and Eder valleys. Railway bridges, power stations, factories, whole villages and built-up areas were being swept away.'

The coverage lasted for days, fed by further information coming from the Air Ministry, as the floods spread further and further down the valleys. 'Havoc spreads hour by hour' one paper recorded, and there was speculation that the third dam might burst at any moment. At the end of the week the news magazines got in on the act. Their coverage continued for several more editions, with one, the *Illustrated London News* on 29 May, carrying an extraordinary double page spread 'artist's impression' of 'how the raid was carried out'. This was drawn by the 'celebrated aviation artist' Captain Bryan de Grineau 'from information given by the Air Ministry'. In it, a Lancaster is shown flying along the length of the Möhne Dam, not directly towards it, which is what actually happened. The ostensible way in which the operation was carried out was explained thus:

> The bomber crews' tricky task was to drop 1,500lb mines in a confined area inside the torpedo net ... in the centre of the dam, where the current would draw them down towards the sluice gates and explode them there. The attack had to be made with perfect coolness, and the mines dropped from a height of sometimes less than 100ft.[178]

---

178 *Illustrated London News*, 29 May 1943.

Poor Captain de Grineau and his editors were being spun a complete fabrica-
tion. This was a cover story, dreamed up by the Air Ministry for public con-
sumption. Gibson was to describe the same fictional technique on his later
US and Canadian lecture tour. At that point, the intelligence services didn't
know that concealing the details of the mine was futile: even as these articles
were appearing in the press, the Germans had already recovered the Upkeep
mine which had rolled free from Norman Barlow's crashed AJ-E and were busy
working out its secrets.

Even the foreign press got in the act. The unnamed journalist writing for the
American magazine *TIME* spun a wonderfully fanciful account:

> Now the planes were roaring 50 feet above the water; now the target
> was dead ahead. Now the bombardiers pushed their buttons, and now
> the big, dark mines, each weighing 1,500 pounds, tumbled from the
> planes. Some landed with a splash in the water; some hit the dams
> fair & square. When the roar of their explosions had subsided, the
> sustained, deeper roar of pent-up waters, suddenly released, struck
> terror into the hearts of those below.[179]

In the meantime, there were vacancies at the head of the squadron's structure
after the loss of both Flight Commanders on the raid. On Tuesday 18 May, David Maltby was promoted to Squadron Leader, and given command of A Flight.
The B Flight position was not officially filled, but both Mick Martin and Les
Munro signed the relevant logbooks as acting flight commanders at the end of
the month. Meanwhile Harry Humphries quietly abandoned his project to get
the signatures of all the men on the squadron. He had posted two large sheets
of paper for them to sign in the crew room before the raid but so many were
now missing that he simply filed the sheets away instead. They now belong to
the Lincolnshire Archives.

Just ten days after the raid, the King and Queen paid a visit to Scampton
(carefully described as 'an air station in the north of England'). To coincide
with this, the list of decorations awarded for the raid was released, and this
prompted more press interest. The list itself was pretty astonishing. Eleven
crews had returned from the raid; two of these were early returns and Anderson in AJ-Y came back with an unused mine. That leaves fifty-six airmen in the
other eight crews, of whom thirty-four were awarded an honour.

---

179 *TIME* magazine, 31 May 1943.

In all the eight crews who dropped their mines successfully, the pilot, navigator and bomb aimer were decorated. Guy Gibson received the highest possible award for bravery, the Victoria Cross. A strict pecking order was followed for the rest of the pilots: the five who were officers were awarded the Distinguished Service Order (DSO) while Bill Townsend and Ken Brown, the two non-commissioned pilots, got the equivalent CGM – the Conspicuous Gallantry Medal (Flying). In the non-pilot aircrew, officers got Distinguished Flying Crosses (DFC) while the NCOs got Distinguished Flying Medals (DFM). Anyone who already had one of the decorations received a Bar to it – in effect another award of the same value.

The awards are set out in the following table:

Aircraft	Pilot	Flight engineer	Navigator	Wireless operator	Bomb aimer	Front gunner	Rear gunner
AJ-G	Gibson VC	Pulford DFM	Taerum DFC	Hutchison Bar to DFC	Spafford DFC	Deering DFC	Trevor-Roper DFC
AJ-P	Martin DSO		Leggo Bar to DFC	Chambers DFC	Hay Bar to DFC		Simpson DFM
AJ-J	Maltby DSO		Nicholson DFM		Fort DFC		
AJ-L	Shannon DSO		Walker Bar to DFC		Sumpter DFM		Buckley DFC
AJ-N	Knight DSO		Hobday DFC		Johnson. E.C. DFC		
AJ-T	McCarthy DSO		MacLean DFM		Johnson G.L. DFM		
AJ-F	Brown CGM		Heal DFM		Oancia DFM		
AJ-O	Townsend CGM		Howard DFC	Chalmers DFM	Franklin Bar to DFM	Webb DFM	Wilkinson R DFM

There is something of a mystery as to why the medals were allocated in this way. The only crew in which all seven members were decorated was Gibson's. That's understandable enough, but it meant that John Pulford was the only flight engineer to be recognised with a medal.

In the other crews, giving awards to the bomb aimer and navigator makes some sort of sense but there seems very little logic in decorating two more wireless operators (Chambers and Chalmers) and four more gunners (Simpson, Buckley, Webb and Ray Wilkinson). This led to six of Bill Townsend's crew (all except the poor flight engineer) receiving medals. They had a difficult enough flight, arriving back last of all, but didn't breach their target. In fact, when front gunner Douglas Webb got the telegram informing him about his medal, he first thought it to be a practical joke.

When the King and Queen came to Scampton, each crew was lined up behind their captain, who stood smartly to attention, toecaps touching a white line painted on the grass. Gibson introduced the King to each of the pilots. Some sources[180] say that each pilot then introduced the rest of his crew, but this is at odds with what can be seen from the few seconds shown on the contemporary newsreels and the accounts of Len Sumpter and Fred Sutherland, who say that they did not.[181]

An official RAF photographer, Flg Off Henry Hensser, recorded the scene. Most of the pictures are in black and white but a few are in colour. When you are so used to seeing wartime pictures in black and white the rich Kodachrome process is almost shockingly bright. Most of the shots show the King and Queen talking to the pilots, but they also inspected the WAAF contingent, spoke to the squadron's armament, engineering and electrical officers and met representatives of 57 Squadron. They also inspected the models of the Mohne and Sorpe dams, and were invited to look at possible designs for the squadron crest. Having chosen the one showing a broken dam wall, with the motto 'Apres Moi Le Deluge', the King signed the artwork.

While there was no word about what Bomber Command planned to do with the squadron, Gibson and others were encouraged to take on various public relations appearances. In the following days Gibson spoke at Wings for Victory events in Sheffield, Gloucester and Maidstone. At the last venue, on Saturday 19 June, the climax was the arrival of four Lancasters, piloted by David Maltby, David Shannon, Mick Martin and Les Munro, beating up the town.

Two days later, the investiture party set off for London. A special train was organised, leaving Scampton by coach at 1330 to catch the train from Lincoln at 1421. Squadron Adjutant Harry Humphries had his legendary administrative skills tested to the limit getting the boisterous aircrew to the station, onto the train and up to London without a major incident. The news that Avro had organised a dinner for the evening of the investiture added to the determination of many to start the party a day early, so copious amounts of alcohol were brought along to ensure that the trip was well lubricated. Tom Simpson and Toby Foxlee wangled their way onto the footplate for part of the trip, and were even allowed to throw some coal into the firebox.[182]

---

180 Sweetman, *Dambusters Raid*, p244; Morris, *Guy Gibson*, p179.
181 Bishop, *Bomber Boys*, p188; Sweetman, Coward & Johnstone, *The Dambusters*, p160.
182 Simpson, *Lower than Low*, p94.

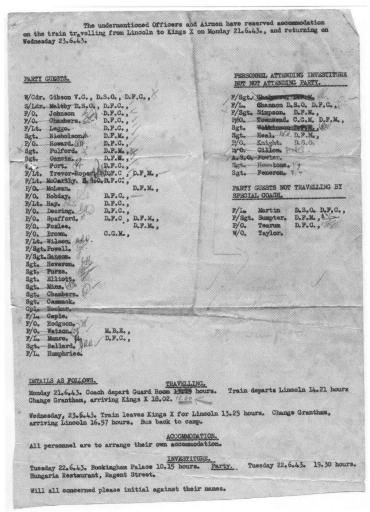

The undermentioned Officers and Airmen have reserved accommodation on the train travelling from Lincoln to Kings X on Monday 21.6.43., and returning on Wednesday 23.6.43.

PARTY GUESTS.

W/Cdr. Gibson V.C., D.S.O., D.F.C.,
S/Ldr. Maltby D.S.O., D.F.C.,
F/O. Johnson   D.F.C.,
F/O. Chambers,   D.F.C.,
F/Lt. Leggo,   D.F.C.,
Sgt. Nicholson,   D.F.M.,
P/O. Howard,   D.F.C.,
Sgt. Pulford,   D.F.M.,
Sgt. Oancia,   D.F.M.,
Lt. Fort,   D.F.C.,
F/Lt. Trevor-Roper, D.F.C., D.F.M.,
F/Lt. McCarthy. D.S.O.,D.F.C.,
P/O. McLean,   D.F.M.,
F/O. Hobday,   D.F.C.,
F/Lt. Hay,   D.F.C.,
P/O. Deering,   D.F.C.,
P/O. Spafford,   D.F.C., D.F.M.,
P/O. Foxlee,   D.F.M.,
P/O. Brown,   C.G.M.,
F/Lt. Wilson,
F/Sgt. Powell,
Sgt. Sanson,
Sgt. Heveron,
Sgt. Purse,
Sgt. Elliott,
Sgt. Minn,
Sgt. Chambers,
Sgt. Cammack,
Cpl. Hocker,
F/L. Caple,
F/O. Hodgson,
P/O. Watson,   M.B.E.,
F/L. Munro,   D.F.C.,
Sgt. Bellard,
F/L. Humphries.

PERSONNEL ATTENDING INVESTITURE
BUT NOT ATTENDING PARTY.

F/Sgt. Chalmers, D.F.M.,
F/L. Channon D.S.O. D.F.C.,
F/Sgt. Simpson. D.F.M.,
P/O. Townsend. C.G.M. D.F.M.,
Sgt. Watkinson. D.F.M.,
Sgt. Heal. D.F.M.,
P/O. Knight. D.S.O.
W/O. Gillon. P.G.
A.S.O. Fowler.
Sgt. Hewstone.
Sgt. Feneron.

PARTY GUESTS NOT TRAVELLING BY
SPECIAL COACH.

F/L. Martin   D.S.O. D.F.C.,
F/Sgt. Sumpter. D.F.M.,
P/O. Tearum   D.F.C.,
W/O. Taylor.

DETAILS AS FOLLOWS.
                    TRAVELLING.
Monday 21.6.43. Coach depart Guard Room 13.15 hours. Train departs Lincoln 14.21 hours
Change Grantham, arriving Kings X 18.02.

Wednesday, 23.6.43. Train leaves Kings X for Lincoln 13.25 hours. Change Grantham,
arriving Lincoln 16.57 hours. Bus back to camp.

                    ACCOMMODATION.
All personnel are to arrange their own accommodation.

                    INVESTITURE.
Tuesday 22.6.43. Buckingham Palace 10.15 hours. Party. Tuesday 22.6.43. 19.30 hours.
Hungaria Restaurant, Regent Street.

Will all concerned please initial against their names.

Harry Humphries's instructions for personnel attending the investiture and party in London on 22 June 1943. Note how the attendees also included squadron 'back room' staff and ground crew.

One of the ringleaders in the antics that followed was David Maltby. According to Humphries, he started at Lincoln railway station by removing the small brass badges saying 'VR' for Volunteer Reserve from the lapels of a young Pilot Officer from the RAF's Railway Transport Office. The Air Ministry had decreed that these were no longer to be worn. 'You won't be needing these, old boy, and may I add you're lucky it's not your trousers,' Humphries quotes him as saying.[183]

---

183 Humphries, *Living with Heroes*, p44.

The loss of trousers became a theme for the journey. The wireless operator in Shannon's crew, Brian Goodale, had his removed by his colleagues in a drinking session in the compartment where Maltby, Richard Trevor-Roper and the rest of the party animals were playing cards. Dressed in his underpants he walked further along the train, to where Humphries was chatting sedately to two WAAF officers. The ensuing exchanges have all the period charm you would expect. 'Ladies were present', so modesty had to be preserved. The gallant Humphries pushed Goodale into one of the train lavatories and set off in search of the missing trousers. He recalled:

> Either I succeeded in getting his trousers back, or I lost mine too. I hoped it wouldn't be the latter. I pushed my way into the carriage where I knew the ceremony had taken place. The wicked gleams were still there. I sighed, hoping for the best. I could see Trevor-Roper there. He would just love to remove my pants! I tried to be offhand.
>
> 'Excuse me chaps, have any of you by any chance seen Goodale's trousers?'
>
> A roar of laughter greeted the question.
>
> 'Why, has he lost them Adj.?' questioned Dave Maltby innocently.
>
> 'You know he has,' I said. 'Now look chaps, I'm not trying to be funny, but he has just walked into a compartment and stood in front of a couple of ladies – like that!'
>
> They roared at this until tears streamed down their faces. Jock Fort gasped,
>
> 'Quite well made, isn't he?'
>
> Another shriek of laughter from all and sundry. I was getting nowhere.
>
> 'I think it's frightfully funny too,' I said, 'but you wouldn't think so if it happened to be your lady friends, now would you?'
>
> The crisis had passed.
>
> 'No, come to think of it I wouldn't,' said Dave Maltby.
>
> He pulled a pair of RAF blue trousers from underneath the seat. They were crumpled and covered in cigarette ash. Dave dusted them in a lazy sort of way and tossed them in my direction.
>
> 'Thanks,' I said, 'I'll make sure he puts them on.'
>
> 'Have a Scotch before you go Adj.' said Trevor-Roper, fumbling in a suitcase.
>
> I didn't really feel like one but thought I had better accept. He handed me the top of a vacuum flask, half full of neat whisky.

A large group gathered outside Buckingham Palace for a photograph. (Left to right) Leonard Sumpter, Harlo Taerum, Jack Buckley, Fred Spafford, Richard Trevor-Roper, David Maltby, Edward Johnson, Mick Martin. Dudley Heal, Guy Gibson, Sydney Hobday, David Shannon, Toby Foxlee, Joe McCarthy, Steve Oancia, John Fort, Danny Walker, Len Chambers, Doug Webb, George Chalmers.

'Go on shorty, let's see you knock that back,' he said.

I gulped, my prestige was at stake. Taking a deep breath I took the contents of the cup at one swallow. I nearly went through the roof of the carriage. My throat burned away at the sudden contact with the raw spirit, my head swam and tears came to my eyes as I gasped for breath.

'I'm proud of you Adj.,' said Trevor-Roper. 'Like another?'[184]

A version of this story also appears in Paul Brickhill's book. Debagging, putting footprints on the ceilings of messes, parading round dining tables with yard brushes on fire – this kind of behaviour was generally tolerated amongst officers on the grounds that they were undertaken by people who regularly put their lives at risk and were simply 'letting off steam'. It's a recurring theme in Brickhill's book, and also in R.C. Sherriff's script for the 1955 film.

When the group got to London, they had been left to sort out their own accommodation, so those without relatives in the city headed to various hotels. Harry Humphries was in a group who went to the Savoy, but others settled for the more downmarket Strand Palace. A lot more drinking followed, and this went on to well into the night.

Somehow, everyone made it next morning to Buckingham Palace where, to

---

184 Humphries, *Living with Heroes*, p46.

Harry Humphries's copy of the menu for the dinner at the Hungaria Restaurant, honouring 'The Damn Busters'.

general surprise, the investiture was conducted by the Queen, as the King was away in North Africa. The delegation from 617 Squadron was first, headed by Wg Cdr G.P. Gibson, VC, DSO & Bar, DFC & Bar, now the most heavily decorated airman in the British empire. The thirty-three other officers and NCOs followed. Afterwards, photographers jostled and shouted as different groups were organised for pictures and newsreel film sequences. Shots were taken of them all: in a group, the Canadians together, the Aussies together, then a bunch of assorted aircrew marching (badly) away.

After another drinking session, some grabbed the chance to catch up on a few hours sleep before the party in the Hungaria Restaurant. The dinner was in honour of 'The Damn Busters', as a famous misprint on the menu card states. In another error, the squadron is congratulated on 'their gallant effort on the Rhur Dams'. Besides the decorated aircrew, there were a number of other distinguished guests. Barnes Wallis was there of course, as well as Roy Chadwick and managing director Sir Roy Dobson from A.V. Roe, and from Vickers Sir Charles Craven and Sir Hew Kilner. The famous aviation pioneer T.O.M. Sopwith was also present, and made a speech before presenting Gibson with a silver model of a Lancaster aircraft. Gibson replied, managing to thank everyone involved, not forgetting the ground crew, the 'back room boys' and the workers at Avro. Then a picture of the breached Möhne Dam, brought by Barnes Wallis to the dinner, was given back to him, signed by most of the people who had taken part in the raid. He had the 'before' and 'after' pictures framed and hung them on his study wall, writing afterwards that they 'formed a historical record of this outstanding accomplishment on the part of the RAF'.[185]

---

185 Quoted in Sweetman, *Dambusters Raid*, p247.

HUMPHRIES FAMILY

R.K. Pierson   J.N.H. Whitworth   J.L. Munro
    C.Craven   H. Kilner   W. Cammack   H.A. Brown

J. Ballard
H.R. Humphries
N.Furze
D.A. MacLean
C.C. Caple   R.D. Trevor-Roper
        J.E. Heveron   T. Hooke
B. Taylor   J. Elliott
        H.S. Wilson
        G.E. Powell   S. Sansom
J.F. Leggo   H.S. Hobday
        T.O.M. Sopwith   E.C. Johnson
C.L. Howard   L.J. Sumpter
        R. Dobson   R. Chadwick
                                                                        R.C. Hay   S. Davies
J. Summers   A. Minns

                                                                        T.D. Simpson

    B.N. Wallis   J. Gammon   V. Nicholson   J. Fort   B.T. Foxlee
        P. Spriggs   H.B.Martin   D.J.H. Maltby   J.C. McCarthy
            F.M. Spafford   G.P. Gibson

This well-known photograph was taken towards the end of the party at the Hungaria
Restaurant. Some of the guests are sitting or kneeling on the floor, others gather behind. For
the first time, everyone in the picture has now been identified in the key above, although
some doubts have been expressed about the correct identification of Sir Charles Craven.

One of the entertainers who turned up at the end of the dinner and provided an impromptu cabaret was 'Monsewer' Eddie Gray, a popular comedian
and an occasional member of the Crazy Gang. Others included Arthur Askey,
Jack Hylton, Chesney Allen and Pat Taylor. Many of the menus were circulated

for people to sign, with several people getting so confused that they signed the same copy twice. Harry Humphries' copy, now in Lincolnshire Archives, has many signatures and the cryptic comment on the front: 'This belongs to H.R. Humphries (I think there is no adjutant just like me) The shit'. It's not clear whether Humphries wrote this himself, or whether it is a contribution from one of his admiring colleagues. As there were copious amounts of free drink on offer – cocktails, a 1929 'Rizling' [sic], a 1930 Burgundy and Commendador port – there is a certain amount of confusion in the accounts of the night. The food must have appeared impossibly exotic to people more accustomed to one sausage a week – crab cocktail, 'caneton farci' (stuffed duck) with 'pommes nouvelles', 'petit pois' and asparagus.

Some time late in the evening, a famous photograph was taken in which a number of people seem pretty worse for wear. Standing rather awkwardly at the back are a number of knighted bigwigs, alongside the newly promoted but always glum-looking Air Cdre Charles Whitworth, whose pyjamas had so famously formed the trophy at the party in the early morning after the raid itself. Most of the uniformed guests form an untidy group, sitting on the floor. In the middle of the front row are Mick Martin, David Maltby and Guy Gibson with several members of their crews around them. Two rows behind his captain, grins Maltby's navigator, Vivian Nicholson, and around his shoulders can be seen an arm, with a hand holding a glass. It is that of Jack Leggo, the squadron's Navigation Leader. In Leggo's other hand there is a large cigar. Further back, with the most raucous grin of all is squadron debagger-in-chief, Richard Trevor-Roper. A few people are obscured, some are looking sideways – but it freezes that moment in time when, in the words of Vivian Nicholson's mother a few months later, they were 'so young, happy and beautiful'.

The train back to Lincoln the next day was pretty quiet. It was probably a good thing that no training took place. However, it started again in earnest on the Thursday and most crews undertook about half a dozen training flights in the next ten days.

The publicity machine was still making demands. During late June and early July, the well-known society and war artist, Cuthbert Orde was commissioned by *The Tatler* magazine to draw portraits of some of the 617 Squadron personnel involved in the Dams Raid. Those whose portraits appeared, in the issue of 1 September, were presumably selected as being the types who would appeal to readers of the magazine. Gibson, of course, has the biggest picture on the double-page spread. There are also sketches of David Maltby, David Shannon, Joe McCarthy, Ken Brown, Bill Townsend, Richard Trevor-Roper and Mick

Martin. The pictures appear to have been drawn on various dates in June and July, which suggests Orde paid more than one visit to Scampton. Orde drew hundreds of RAF portraits during the war, and the 617 Squadron portraits are sensitively drawn and amongst his best work.

Gibson was technically still in charge of the squadron, but high up in the RAF thought was being given as to what to do with him, as well as with the squadron he commanded and the weapon it had deployed. Gibson's name was so widely known that, for the moment, he could not be allowed to fly over enemy territory. If he were to be shot down and killed – or captured – it would present a significant propaganda boost to the Germans. As to the squadron, it was not going to be used on run of the mill bombing operations, even on those in which 'maximum effort' was required to deliver hundreds of aircraft on a mass operation. The squadron would continue to trial different ways of using the Upkeep weapon and also prepare itself to use the new 'thin case' 12,000lb High Capacity bomb which was about to be brought into service.

Sqn Ldr George Holden was lined up to take over command of the squadron. He had been in the RAFVR before the war and so started his training immediately hostilities began. After qualifying as a pilot, he had gone on to fly the Halifax heavy bomber, completing a first tour in 4 Group's 35 Squadron. In October 1942, after a period training, he was posted to take command of 102 Squadron when the previous CO was killed in a freak accident. He had moved on from this posting in April 1943, with a grand total of forty-five operations.

On 2 July Holden was posted in to 617 Squadron as the flight commander of B Flight, on the understanding that he would take charge of the squadron when Gibson left. As he had previously flown Halifaxes, Holden had to become familiarised with flying Lancasters and he took Gibson's crew on two long cross-country training flights on 7 and 8 July.[186]

Around the same time, an official RAF photographer took an extraordinary series of colour transparencies, which are now held in the Imperial War Museum's photographic archive. One is of Holden, who is photographed with Richard Trevor-Roper and David Shannon. Another is of Gibson and five of his Dams Raid crew; John Pulford is the only one missing. (See p113.) There are also pictures of Joe McCarthy, Les Knight, Harold Wilson and their crews. In the background of all of them a dark sky looms, threatening a severe storm. This sequence is completed by a photograph of Gibson and David Maltby, taken in the squadron CO's office. Gibson has a pipe clenched between his

---

186 Flt Lt R.E.G. Hutchison, logbook

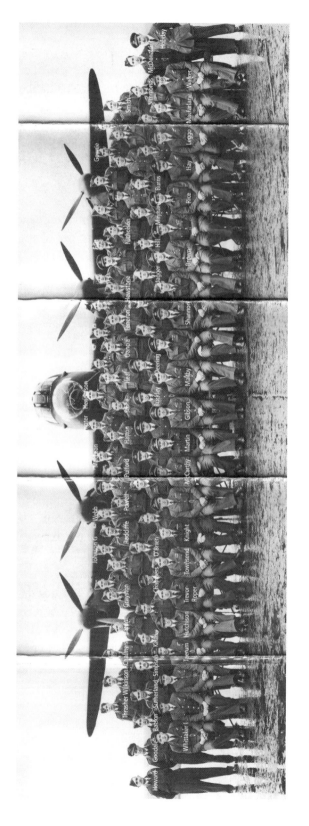

Howard Goodale Batson Thrasher Wilkinson Chalmers Simpson Sutherland Whittaker 1

Johnson G. Webb Grayston Estill Kellow Hutchison Teerum Powell Redcliffe Chambers O'Brien Knight Trevor-Roper Townsend

Hopgood Henderson Pulford McCarthy Hatton Martin Gibson Buckley Malby Deering Nancia Taffenson Cameron Maudslay Heal Shannon Hewstone

Gowrie Nicholson Jagger Hill Maynard Burns Brown Rice Hay Leggo Macfarlane Simmonds McDonald Hobday Smith Walker

617 Squadron Aircrew photographed at RAF Scampton on 9 July 1943. By this time, a number of other aircrew had joined the squadron to replace those who were lost on the Dams Raid. There are eighty-six men in this picture, of whom fifty-seven flew on the Dams Raid. In this annotated picture only those fifty-seven men are named. Of the 133 men who flew on the Dams Raid, eighty survived, so there are twenty-three men missing. Three had become Prisoners of War: Anthony Burcher, John Fraser and Frederick Tees. Of the twenty others, seven had been transferred to 49 Squadron: Cyril Anderson, Douglas Bickle, Arthur Buck, Eric Ewan, Gilbert Green, John Nugent and Robert Paterson. Thirteen more were absent on the day: Frank Appleby, Daniel Allatson, James Clay, Charles Franklin, Bertie Foxlee, William Howarth, Edward Johnson, Les Munro, Percy Pigeon, David Rodger, Grant Rumbles, Frederick Spafford, Harvey Weeks. The picture comes from the Harry Humphries collection and has suffered some storage damage over the years.

teeth, and both men have a finger on the same page of what looks like an air-craft identification manual. (Another photograph often thought to be taken at the same time is of Gibson sitting in a field of poppies, reading a copy of the *Morte D'Arthur*. However, the IWM dope sheet shows that this was actually shot on 26 May by the same Flg Off Bellamy who was on duty of the night of the raid. This photograph was released to the press on the day of the announce-ment of the decorations list.)

These colour photographs appear to have been shot at about the same time as two panorama pictures, one of the aircrew and one of the complete squad-ron, which were taken on 9 July. These were taken by Bassano's, the London portrait photographers, who also specialised in large-format photography. The aircrew picture shows fifty-seven of the seventy-seven men who had landed back at Scampton on 17 May. Of the other twenty, Anderson's crew of seven had been transferred back to 49 Squadron, and the other thirteen were absent for various other reasons. These included Munro's complete crew, who were on leave. The picture also includes three new pilots (Flt Lts Ralph Allsebrook, Wil-liam Kellaway and Bernard Clayton) and their crews, but not George Holden. This photograph annotated with the names of the Dams Raid participants can be seen on the facing page.

617 Squadron finally went back on operations a few days later, on Thursday 15 July. The mission was to bomb two electricity transformer and switching stations, at Aquata Scrivia and San Polo d'Enza. Because these were beyond the 'out and back' flying range of the Lancaster it would be necessary to fly on to another airfield to refuel and reload. Blida, some 30 miles from Algiers, now in Allied hands after the victories in North Africa and used as a launch pad for operations in the Mediterranean, was the obvious choice.

George Holden took charge of one section of five aircraft, while David Malt-by led the other section. Gibson saw them off, watching from the marshal-ling point with Harry Humphries. For many of the crews who flew that day, it would be the last time they saw him.

Everyone was delighted with the chance of getting their knees brown, so they packed sunglasses and tropical kit and stowed their service-issue suitcases and kitbags in the body of their aircraft. It was a long flight but largely without incident, and with very little opposition en route or over the target. All arrived safely although Les Munro's aircraft was damaged by shrapnel from his own bomb as it dropped. Damage was caused to the bomb aimer's panel and a star-board tyre was burst, the latter leading to a dodgy landing.

Blida was fun at first. For many of the aircrew this was the first time they had

Five members of Les Munro's crew in the back of a jeep in Blida. (Left to right) Bill Howarth, Harvey Weeks, Grant Rumbles, Jimmy Clay (with sunglasses and a bandage protecting his injured face), Percy Pigeon.

set foot outside Britain. There was wine to drink, exotic fruit and food to enjoy, sunshine to bask in. Lots of photographs were taken.

Bob Hutchison described the trip in a letter to his family on his return:

> We were some thirty-odd miles from Algiers which town we visited to gain my first impression of life out of England. Naturally I was pleased to get back here again but it was an experience I wouldn't have missed for the world. …
>
> We went swimming in the Med at Sidi Ferruch twice a day and thus got quite a tan. It is the most lovely beach I have yet to see. … I swam for nearly an hour each time after first getting in without stopping and then sat around or dived for shells etc for the rest of the time. Taken all in all an almost perfect holiday.[187]

But then the weather closed in, which meant the 617 Squadron contingent had to stay for a total of nine days. Some people got bored, including George

---

187 Robert Hutchison, letter to parents, dated 'Monday' (probably Monday 26 July 1943), Hutchison family.

Holden, who appalled other members of the squadron by gleefully driving a jeep straight into a flock of goats and goatherds.[188]

Eventually the crews got away and were instructed to bomb the docks at Leghorn (Livorno) on the way back to England. Again, it was a long flight, taking off from Blida at about 2100 on Saturday 24 July and landing after 0500 the next day. The bombing was uneventful, done on a time-and-distance run from Corsica, and everyone got home safely. The crews loaded up the aircraft with souvenirs, crates of fresh fruit and vegetables (Hutchison brought back grapes and lemons for his family) as well as bottles of Benedictine and wine. Martin was wearing a red fez when Harry Humphries met him at the dispersal point.

Round about the same time that the Blida contingent landed some seventeen Lancasters from 57 Squadron also touched down at Scampton. They had been part of the contingent of 779 RAF bombers who had taken part in a massive attack on Hamburg. This was the first of four devastating attacks in the next ten days on the North German city. For the first time, the crews dropped 'Window' – strips of tinfoil designed to confuse the German radar – as they flew over enemy territory. It worked well; so well, indeed, that on the night of the second attack on 27–28 July, a firestorm was created in the densely built-up residential district of Hammerbrook when all the fires joined together and started sucking the oxygen out of the surrounding air. The firestorm lasted three hours and only subsided when all the burnable material in the area was consumed. It is estimated that 40,000 people died.[189] The name given by Bomber Command to the series of raids, Operation Gomorrah – with its connotation of a city being destroyed by the wrath of God, was aptly chosen. Here was Harris's 'area bombing' strategy realising to its full potential.

Doubtless there was discussion in the Scampton messes between the 57 Squadron contingent, who participated in the Hamburg raids, and the 617 Squadron aircrew, who did not. There was certainly resentment that 617 Squadron was not being sent out on routine operations, a feeling that must have been intensified when on Thursday 29 July nine aircraft led by Holden were dispatched on a really soft trip, on the same night as a force of 777 other Bomber Command aircraft were dispatched on the third trip to Hamburg. The 617 Squadron detachment went on a 'nickel run', dropping leaflets on cities in Northern Italy, and going on to Blida again. Seven of the nine flew back two days later, landing at Scampton in the early hours of Sunday 1 August, while Munro and McCarthy had to hang about in Blida waiting for essential repairs.

188 Morris, *Guy Gibson*, p187.
189 Martin Middlebrook and Chris Everitt, *Bomber Command War Diaries*, Midland Publishing 1995, p413.

HUTCHISON FAMILY

Gibson with five members of his Dams Raid crew (Taerum, Deering, Trevor-Roper, Hutchison and Spafford) and new squadron CO George Holden, pose for a picture with ground crew on Monday 2 August 1943. Gibson left Scampton the following day.

By the time the seven aircraft returned, Gibson had been told that he would shortly be going to America under the auspices of the Ministry of Information. On the Saturday, he had been to lunch with Churchill at Chequers and then had a late afternoon meeting with Air Chief Marshal Sir Charles Portal, the Chief of the Air Staff.

He went back to Scampton to say his goodbyes, and complete the handover to George Holden. The pair took five of Gibson's Dams Raid crew (Taerum, Hutchison, Spafford, Deering and Trevor-Roper) on a final flight at 1150 on Monday 2 August. They flew in ED933, a Lancaster converted for Operation Chastise. This had been allocated to Henry Maudslay but had been damaged before the raid, so was not used.

After the flight, the air crew posed for a photograph with some of the ground crew members who had worked on Gibson's aircraft during his time with the squadron. Gibson had prints made immediately and signed each one on the front. He then had the reverse sides signed by all the aircrew, and presented the prints to everyone who was in the shot.

He finally left 617 Squadron and Scampton on the morning of Tuesday 3 August, heading to London. That night he caught a special train to Faslane on the Clyde, and boarded the *Queen Mary* ocean liner for the trip to Canada.

Gibson had been in command of 617 Squadron for just twenty weeks. At the end of August, the squadron would leave its original station at Scampton for RAF Coningsby so that concrete runways could be installed. It had been stationed there for twenty-three weeks, and would never return.

Losses later in the war

Just six weeks after Gibson left 617 Squadron, fourteen more of the 133 men who flew on the Dams Raid would die. Seven were killed on when an operation to attack the Dortmund Ems canal was aborted in the early hours of 15 September. Another seven were amongst the thirty-three men killed the following day when the operation finally took place. In total, of the eighty men who survived the Dams Raid thirty-two more were to die before the end of the war. These were.

15 September 1943 *(617 Squadron: Aborted attack on Dortmund Ems canal)*
AJ-J crew: David Maltby, William Hatton, Vivian Nicholson, Antony Stone, John Fort, Victor Hill, Harold Simmonds.

16 September 1943 *(617 Squadron: Attack on Dortmund Ems canal):*
AJ-G crew: Harlo Taerum, Robert Hutchison, Frederick Spafford, George Deering
AJ-N crew: Leslie Knight
AJ-F crew: Daniel Allatson
AJ-O crew: Dennis Powell

23 September 1943 *(49 Squadron: Attack on Mannheim)*
AJ-Y crew: Cyril Anderson, Robert Paterson, John Nugent, Douglas Bickle, Gilbert Green, Eric Ewan, Arthur Buck

20 December 1943 *(617 Squadron: Attack on Liège)*
AJ-H crew: Edward Smith, Richard Macfarlane, John Thrasher, Bruce Gowrie, Thomas Maynard, Stephen Burns

13 February 1944 *(617 Squadron: Attack on Antheor Viaduct)*
AJ-P crew: Robert Hay

13 February 1944 *(617 Squadron: Shuttle flight back to base after return from attack on Antheor Viaduct)*
AJ-G crew: John Pulford

31 March 1944 *(97 Squadron: Attack on Nuremburg)*
AJ-G crew: Richard Trevor-Roper

30 April 1944 *(460 Squadron: Training accident)*
AJ-L crew: Brian Jagger

19 September 1944 *(627 Squadron: Attack on Rheydt)*
AJ-G crew: Guy Gibson

617 Squadron continued flying throughout the rest of the war, mainly on operations requiring specialised bombing techniques. It was the first squadron to use both the Tallboy and Grand Slam giant bombs, both designed by Barnes Wallis. Just over one thousand aircrew flew with the squadron during the Second World War, and some 210 were killed on active service. Their names are commemorated at the squadron war memorial in Woodhall Spa.

Chapter 9

Afterword

THE DAMS RAID IS ONE OF THE GREAT STORIES of the Second World War, and when a savvy RAF public relations officer gave the men who carried it out the catchy nickname of 'Dambusters' the first step along the path to the status of national icon was taken.

The RAF's Public Relations Directorate had a very sophisticated operation during the war, much envied by the army and navy, and even before the Dams Raid took place RAF top brass were aware what tremendous propaganda the operation could provide if it proved to be successful. This is why an official photographer was present as the aircraft took off and remained on the base until they returned. Massive press coverage followed the raid, helped by careful briefing which lasted for several days afterwards. Then, a month or so later, when the aircrew who had been given decorations travelled to their investiture in London a press officer went with them, ready to provide background copy for the media waiting outside Buckingham Palace.

It helped that Guy Gibson was a natural communicator and readily took to the media operation. He was taken off operational flying immediately after the raid, and then in the autumn he was sent on a tour of Canada and the USA, where he spoke to huge audiences, and mingled with Hollywood stars.

When Gibson came back to England he was given an Air Ministry job writing his memoirs, and provided with an office, a dictaphone and a typist. A few months later, with a draft manuscript finished and given the title *Enemy Coast Ahead*, he persuaded his superiors to be let back on operations, and was killed on only his third flight.

Only a small section of Gibson's text is actually about the Dams Raid, and as discussed above (pp31-4) quite a lot of this part of his book was not actually written by him, but by different journalists acting as his ghostwriter. The book itself wasn't published until after the war, but it was an instant success.

Because Gibson wasn't there to promote the book, the raid might have stayed in the collective consciousness as just one of the war's many daring true stories but for the intervention of Air Marshal Sir Ralph Cochrane. As seen above, he had been instrumental in the formation of 617 Squadron, as the AOC of

Bomber Command's 5 Group, and had been one of those who had briefed the crews before they flew out to the dams. Although he had moved on after the war to head RAF Transport Command he retained a paternal interest in the squadron and was convinced that it needed a special history of its own. He spent four years going through a series of possible authors before lighting on the 'forthright manner' and 'rough personality' of Paul Brickhill, a seasoned Australian journalist who had himself been a fighter pilot during the war.

Brickhill installed himself in a hotel in London and settled down to write the book, which was called *The Dam Busters*. He was, however, a journalist rather than a historian and his research was sometimes less than painstaking. He interviewed a number of the key players who had survived the war, notably Barnes Wallis, Leonard Cheshire, Mick Martin and Dave Shannon. He also used Harry Humphries's material although his rather brusque manner didn't initially go down well with the adjutant and Cheshire had to intervene to persuade Humphries to lend his notes to Brickhill. Some of what Brickhill wanted to write about was still covered by the Official Secrets Act, such as the fact that the 'bomb' designed by Barnes Wallis was designed to bounce across the surface of the water, so this is not mentioned specifically in the first hardback or paperback editions. It wasn't until Brickhill added a further 12,000 words into the 1971 edition that his book told the full story.[190]

Brickhill's gift for story-telling and his terse prose made his book a bestseller when it was published in 1951 and it immediately attracted the attention of Britain's biggest film studio, Associated British Pictures. The rights were purchased, a script was commissioned from the writer of *Journey's End*, R.C. Sherriff, and Michael Anderson was selected as director. ABP had one of the country's famous actors, Richard Todd, under contract and his physical resemblance to Guy Gibson made him an obvious choice for the part. Many other actors were also chosen for their similarity to their real-life counterparts.

Anderson chose to tell the story in a straightforward documentary style, reflecting the script which Sherriff had written with his usual understated economy. As four years had elapsed since Brickhill's book, the government censors gave in and permitted the bouncing bomb to be shown on screen. This led to Barnes Wallis's actual films being used in the scenes where he is trying to convince service and Air Ministry chiefs that his idea will work. A collective 'Wow' must have swept through the nation's cinemas as the general public saw for the first time the big secret behind the successful attacks.

Dramatic licence was also taken with some scenes, such as a wholly fictional

---

190 Stephen Dando-Collins, *The Hero Maker*, Vintage Books Australia 2016, p360.

sequence which shows Gibson getting the idea of using spotlights to measure altitude from their use in a variety theatre. The popular response was, however, overwhelmingly positive, and a piece of British cinema history was made.

Regular repeats of the film on television and its release on video and DVD mean that it is a familiar story to most British people, at least to those above a certain age. This has given the raid itself a singular place in our history, causing it to be part of that catalogue of events and personalities, beloved of journalists and TV documentary list-makers, by which we define ourselves. And it is perhaps the only one of these events which we largely remember through the medium of a dramatised cinema-released film.

As this book goes to press in 2018, we have now reached a stage where you have to be in your 80s to have any direct memory of the Second World War, and well into your 90s to have been on active military service at the time. But this has not stopped public interest in its events.

In a 2017 article in *The Guardian,* historian Daniel Todman suggested that those who reach back to the war remember not the conflict itself but a 'mediated version of it, first produced for the big screen between the 1940s and the 1960s and repeatedly broadcast on television in the decades that followed.'

He goes on:

> 'This is the memory of a repeat of a fiction – and all the more powerful for the simplification it has undergone. The process scrubbed out or ignored much of what characterised the British experience of the war – class division, political conflict, European catastrophe and colonial exploitation. The selective version that remains, badly out of step with a more modern, multicultural and multi-ethnic Britain, excludes many of the country's inhabitants whose forebears were directly affected by the war. For those yearning for a vanished world of wartime unity and late imperial privilege, this is not necessarily a disadvantage.'[191]

The 'memory of a repeat of a fiction' is a phrase which describes well the Dams Raid's position in our national recall of the Second World War. Be that as it may, the Dams Raid was an extraordinary achievement for the time. It was a one-off operation which combined an audacious method of attack, technically brilliant flying and visually spectacular results, and thereby it well deserves its place in history.

---

191 Daniel Todman, www.theguardian.com/commentisfree/2017/jun/03/dunkirk-spirit-brexiters-uk-britain-europe [Accessed June 2017].

Bibliography

A formal bibliography of the works consulted in the preparation and writing of this book follows, but I should begin by acknowledging four particular works which have been an enormous help, and on which I have relied most heavily. These are:

John Sweetman, *The Dambusters Raid*, Cassell Military 2002. This is the authoritative account of the Dams Raid, and has still not been surpassed as a work of record. Much of my account of the build-up and the raid itself derives from this book.

Richard Morris, *Guy Gibson*, Penguin 1995. The most thorough biography of Gibson, which provides much of the background on how the Dambusters myth was first promulgated.

Harry Humphries, *Living with Heroes*, Erskine Press 2003. Very helpful memoirs by the founder adjutant of 617 Squadron.

Helmuth Euler, *The Dams Raid through the Lens*, After the Battle, 2001. Translated from German by Michael Ockendon. Notable for its extensive photographic research.

The two early books on the Dams Raid, Guy Gibson's *Enemy Coast Ahead* (Michael Joseph 1946) and Paul Brickhill's *The Dam Busters* (Evans Brothers 1951) are now both very out of date.Their reliability as source material is discussed in the text. However, they both contain useful information and of course are very important as historical artifacts.

Other books consulted:
Max Arthur, *Dambusters*, Virgin Books 2008.
Kevin Bending, *Achieve Your Aim*, Woodfield 2005.
Dave Birrell, *Big Joe McCarthy*, Wing Leader 2012.
Patrick Bishop, *Bomber Boys*, Harper Press 2007.
Colin Burgess, *Australia's Dambusters*, Australian Military History Publications 2013.
Alan Cooper, *The Men who Breached the Dams*, Airlife 2002.
Stephen Dando-Collins, *The Hero Maker*, Vintage Books Australia 2016.
Jenny Elmes, *M-Mother*, History Press 2015.
Jonathan Falconer, *The Dam Busters*, Sutton 2003.
Jonathan Falconer, *Filming the Dam Busters*, Sutton 2005.
Charles Foster, *Breaking the Dams*, Pen and Sword 2008.

Eric Fry, *An Airman Far Away*, Kangaroo Press 1993.

Barry Goodwin and Raymond Glynne-Owen, *207 Squadron RAF Langar*, Quacks Books 1994.

Stanley Harrison, *A Bomber Command Survivor*, Sage Pages 1992.

Max Hastings, *Bomber Command*, Pan 1999.

James Holland, *Dam Busters*, Corgi 2013.

C.G. Jefford, *Observers and Navigators*, Grub Street, 2014.

George 'Johnny' Johnson, *The Last British Dambuster*, Ebury Press, 2014.

Bob Kellow, *Paths to Freedom*, Kellow Corporation 1992.

Leo McKinstry, *Lancaster*, John Murray 2009.

Martin Middlebrook and Chris Everitt, *The Bomber Command War Diaries*, Midland Publishing 1996.

John Nichol, *After the Flood*, William Collins 2015.

Robert Owen, *Henry Maudslay*, Fighting High 2014.

Robert Owen, Steve Darlow, Sean Feast and Arthur Thorning, *Dambusters: Failed to Return*, Fighting High 2013

Nigel Press, *All My Life*, Lancfile Publishing 2006.

Henry Probert, *Bomber Harris*, Greenhill Books 2003.

Tom Simpson, *Lower than Low*, Libra Books 1995.

Clive Smith, *Lancaster Bale Out*, Tucann 2013.

John Sweetman, *Bomber Crew*, Abacus 2005.

John Sweetman, David Coward and Gary Johnstone, *The Dambusters*, Time Warner 2003.

James Taylor and Martin Davidson, *Bomber Crew*, Hodder & Stoughton 2005.

John Terraine, *The Right of the Line*, Hodder & Stoughton 1985.

Arthur Thorning, *The Dambuster who cracked the Dam*, Pen and Sword 2008.

Daniel Todman, *Britain's War: Into Battle 1937-1941*, Penguin 2017.

Chris Ward, Andy Lee and Andreas Wachtel, *Dambusters*, Red Kite 2003.

F.W. Winterbotham, *Secret and Personal*, William Kimber 1969.

Other books, archive material, journal articles and websites consulted are recorded in the footnotes.

Acknowledgements

Any acknowledgements published at the time of the 75th anniversary of the
Dams Raid should begin by saluting Johnny Johnson and Fred Sutherland. They
and their families do so much to keep alive the memories of their comrades who
also took part in Operation Chastise. I should also acknowledge the late Les
Munro who was a mine of information, and who was still answering emails from
all and sundry until shortly before his death in 2015.

Over the years I have had help from many other members of families of
Dambuster crews. These include: Valerie Ashton, Norma Bagshaw, Dorothy
Bailey, Grace Blackburn, Belinda Brown, Helen Brown, Len Brown, Clare
Burcham, Lewis Burpee Jr, Scott Carruthers, Bill and Lorraine Castle, Viv
Challice, Mike Chambers, Penny Cockerill, Denise Dawson, Roy Eaton, Jenny
Elmes, Richard Farrington, Jean Feneron, Sheila Fenwick, Peter Fort, Simon
Foxlee, Shere Fraser, John and Liz Fuller, Hartley Garshowitz, Mike and
Patricia Gawtrey, Simon Goodale, Vera Goodale, Bill Gracie, Ross Gregory,
David Haworth, Jim Heather, Chris and Debby Henderson, Daniel Hobday,
Rob and Sara Holliday, Robert Holmes, Renee Hopkins, Frances Houlston,
Dom Howard, Colin Hutchison, Gillian Jagger, Nikki King, Dean Leach, Joe
McCarthy Jr, Angela McDonnold, Carole Marner, Paul Morley, June Morris,
Georgina Murray, Katy O'Neill, Gill Owen, Greg Pigeon, Pam Quick, Susan
Richardson, Patti Rodger Kirkpatrick, Liz Shand, Alastair Taylor, Darleen and
Mike Taylor, Mick Tees, Irene Thornton, Michael Townsend, Charles Trevor-
Roper, Adrianne Walters, Veronica Watson, Gary Whitaker, Tony Whittaker,
Daniel Wyatt. Of these, Shere Fraser should be singled out for her magnificent
determination to the cause of truth and justice in the pursuit of her father's
stolen logbook.

Many other people have helped with general points or specific pieces of
information. These include: Heather Allsworth, Malcolm Bellamy, Kevin
Bending, Deborah Bircham, Dave Birrell, Colin Burgess, Steve Darlow, Tim
Dickson, Yahya El-Droubie, Geoff Easton, Nigel Favill, Hugh Halliday, Ray
Hepner, Clare Hopkins, Dave Homewood, Peter Hunter, Graeme Jensen, Joel
Joy, Ken Joyce, Min Larkin, David Layne, Trish Murphy, Volker Schürmann,
Graeme Stevenson, Arthur Thorning, Graham Wallace, Alan Wells.

My sincere apologies to anyone I have accidentally omitted from these lists.

Special thanks are also due to:

The staff at the National Archives in Kew and the RAF Museum in Hendon.

Thea Wrobbel, Matt Wortman and John Nichol for asking me to help on their TV documentary.

Greig Watson and his colleagues at the BBC for asking me to help with research for the 2013 BBC pictureboard.

Peter Humphries and Sally-Ann Maine-Tucker for the use of items in the Harry Humphries collection. This book would have been impossible without this source for so many of the pictures of members of 617 Squadron, and the late Harry Humphries deserves terrific credit for the foresight he displayed in preserving such an important archive.

The Harry Humphries estate and Erskine Press for permission to reproduce material from Harry Humphries's book, *Living with Heroes*.

Colin Hutchison for the use of items from Robert Hutchison's photograph collection.

Clive Smith, for many points of information and especially the proofreading of the final text which saved me from innumerable howlers.

Susan Paxton, whose encyclopaedic knowledge of everything to do with Charlie Williams, the Norman Barlow crew and 61 Squadron spills over into encyclopaedic knowledge of all things Bomber Command.

Dr Robert Owen, the man with a PhD in Dambuster Studies. Every page of this book reflects his input, and it simply would not have been possible without his robust questioning of every detail.

Amy Rigg and Lauren Newby of The History Press, who have produced this book to the highest professional standards at breakneck speed.

And finally, my family. My cousins, John, Charles and Edward Maltby and David Blackburn for their continued interest and support. My brothers and sisters, George, Andrew, Jane and Sarah who have kept on helping and supplying information. (And a special hat-tip to Jane and her husband Peter who have put me up on many trips to London.) My children, Patrick and Aisling, who have astonishingly grown from schoolchildren to maturity without ever knowing a time when their father wasn't obsessed with the subject of the Dams Raid. And Jacqui, my wife, more loyal than I deserve, who has put up with so much, and to whom I owe everything.

Index

Men who took part in the Dams Raid are shown in **Bold**.

Allatson, Sgt D. 15, 17, 74, 85, 86, 106, 262–8, 307.

Allsebrook, Flt Lt R. 303.

Anderson, Flt Sgt C.T. 37, 42, 70–1, 107, 108–10, 279–86, 288, 303, 307.

Appleby, Sgt F.E. 35, 61, 209–16.

Arthur, Flt Sgt J.L. 39, 67, 258–9.

Arthurton, Flg Off M. 82.

Astell, Flt Lt W. 38, 39, 56–7, 63, 83, 89, 91–2, 145, 173, 179–85, 223.

Atkinson, Sgt D. 177.

Baker, Air Cdre J. 27–8.

Ballard, Sgt J. 299.

Barlow, Flt Lt R.N.G. 41, 58–9, 75, 81, 88, 90, 99, 103, 173, 180, 197–207, 292.

Barlow, Gp Capt A. 197–8.

Barrett, Flg Off J.K. 15, 41, 66–7, 244–53.

Bates, Plt Off W. 46–7.

Batson, Sgt R. 35, 64–5, 234–43.

Batson, Sgt D. 242.

Beesley, Sgt J. 38, 49–50, 148, 152.

Bellamy, Flg Off W. 88, 90, 303.

Bergel, Cdr H.C. 86.

Bickle, Sgt W.D. 37, 70–1, 108, 279–86, 307.

Birch, Sqn Ldr P. 55, 174.

Blackett, Professor P.M.S. 23.

Blair, Flt Lt V. 49, 148.

Bolitho, Sgt R. 38, 180–5.

Bower, Sgt G.W. 49–50, 148, 151.

Brady, Wrt Off J.G. 39, 67, 106, 254–60.

Brayford, Flt Sgt W. 64.

Brennan, Sgt C.C. 40, 45–7, 50, 90, 125–33.

Brickhill P. 31, 141, 188, 310.

Brown, Flt Sgt K.W. 17, 40, 42, 68–9, 74, 84, 85–6, 105, 106, 261–6, 288, 293, 300.

Brown, H.A. 299.

Buck, Sgt A.W. 37, 70–1, 279–86, 307.

Buckley, Flg Off J. 54–5, 171, 288, 293, 297.

Bufton, Air Cdre S. 29, 83, 87, 88.

Buntaine, Sgt D. 17, 40, 69, 74, 85, 106, 261–7.

Burcher, Plt Off A.F. 40–46, 89–90, 93–4, 125–33.

Burgess, Flg Off P.S. 41, 58–9, 75, 197–207.

Burns, Sgt S. 38, 63, 103, 223–30, 308.

Burnside, Flt Lt W. 52.

Burpee, Plt Off L.J. 39, 67, 105–6, 107, 254–60.

Burrows, Sgt N.R. 15, 35, 81, 177–8.

Burton, Plt Off 135.

Byers, Plt Off V.W. 34, 42, 61–2, 86, 102, 217–22.

Cammack, Flt Sgt W. 299.

Caple, Plt Off C.C. 78, 299.

Cartwright, Plt Off J.S. 30.

Cassells, Sgt J. 131.

Chadwick, R. 27, 289, 298, 299.

Challenger, Sgt C. 62–3, 224, 230.

Chalmers, Flt Sgt G.A. 70, 108, 269–78, 293, 297.

Chamberlain, Sgt C. 52–5.

Chambers, Flg Off L. 40, 48, 136, 139, 288, 289, 293, 297.

Chaplin, AC 73.

Cherwell, Lord 25.

Cheshire, Gp Capt L 141, 144, 209, 274, 310.

Churchill, W.S. 82, 97.

Clarke, Sgt R. 55.

Clay, Sgt J.H. 35, 60, 101, 102, 209–16, 304.

Clayton, Plt Off B. 274, 303.

Cleveland, Flg Off 75.

Clifford, Flt Sgt 75.

Cochrane, Air Vice Marshal R. 29, 40, 62, 83, 87, 112, 137, 174, 209, 287, 309.

Cockshott, Flt Sgt J. 206–7.

Collins, A.R. 22.

Coton, Sqn Ldr E. 238.

Cottam, Wrt Off A.P. 35, 56, 73, 97, 175–6.

Craven, Sir C. 27, 298, 299.

Cuelenaere, Plt Off M. 60, 213, 215.

Curry, Flt Lt G.W. 165, 168.

Curtin, Plt Off D. 36, 231–2.

Dahl, Flt Lt R. 33.

Dann, Wg Cdr C.L. 160.

Davies, S. 299.

Davis, Dr A.H. 22.

Deering, Flt Sgt G.A. 40, 44–5, 89, 92, 195, 271, 288, 293, 306, 307.

Dierkes, Flt Lt W. 53, 205.

Divall, Plt Off W. 52, 73, 74, 85, 86, 106, 155, 262.

Dobson, Sir R. 298, 299.

Doolan, Sgt 161.

Drewes, Maj M. 123.

Dunn, Wg Cdr W. 86.

Duxbury, Plt Off V. 49, 147, 149, 151, 152, 250.

Earnshaw, Flg Off K. 47, 55, 74, 127–33, 170.

Eaton, Flt Sgt L. 35, 64–5, 104.

Effing, J. 100.

Elder, Flt Lt W. 51, 156–62.

Elliott, Sgt J. 299.

Euler, H. 92, 100, 106.

Everitt, Sqn Ldr H. 120, 140.

Ewan, Sgt E. 37, 70–1, 279–86, 307.

Feneron, Sgt H.B. 40, 68, 107, 261–8.

Fladrich, Hauptman K. 224.

Forman, Sgt 264.

Fort, Plt Off J. 36, 51–2, 94, 154–62, 288, 293, 297, 299, 307.

Foster, Flg Off A.E. 205.

Fowler, Sec Off A. 163, 164.

Foxlee, Plt Off B.T. 40, 47–8, 134–43, 294, 297, 299.

Franklin, Sgt C.E. 37, 69–70, 269–78, 293.

Fraser, Flt Sgt J.W. 46–7, 55, 74, 93–4, 125–33, 170.

Frow, Flg Off B. 201.

Fuller, Plt Off M.J.D. 35, 56, 73, 175–88.

Furze, Sgt N. 299.

Gammon, J. 299.

Garbas, Flt Sgt F.A. 38, 56–7, 180–5.

Garner, Wg Cdr 78.

Garshowitz, Wrt Off A. 38, 54, 56–7, 180–5.

Gibson, Wg Cdr G.P. 29, 30–41, 43–5, 52, 63, 72. 75, 76–7, 81, 87, 88, 89–98, 111–13, 114–23, 125, 135, 140, 154, 173, 217, 261, 292, 293, 294, 297, 298, 299–300, 301, 306–7, 308, 309.

Gillespie, Plt Off A. 41, 58–9, 101, 197–207.

Gillon, Sec Off F. 140

Glanville, Dr W.H. 22.

Glinz, Flg Off H.S. 41, 54, 58–9, 197–207.

Gomme, Wg Cdr C. 61–2.

Goodings, Flt Sgt G. 67, 255, 259.

Goodale, Flg Off B. 54–5, 74, 167–8, 296.

Gowrie, Wrt Off C.B. 38, 62–3, 223–30, 288, 308.

Grain, Sgt J. 70, 269.

Gray, Plt Off C.W. 55.

Grayston, Sgt R.E. 35, 57, 96, 188–96.

Green, Sgt G.J. 37, 70–1, 279–86, 307.

Gregory, Plt Off G.H.F.G. 46, 90, 93–4.

Gumbley, Sgt B.A. 279.

Guterman, Sgt J. 41, 66, 75, 105, 244–53.

Handasyde, R. 79, 82, 86.

Harris, Air Chief Marshal Sir A. 26, 27, 33, 73, 96, 108, 262, 287.

Harrison, Plt Off S. 50.

Haslam, Sgt R. 61.

Hatton, Sgt W. 36, 51–2, 154–62, 307.

Hawks, H. 33.

Hay, Flt Lt R.C. 40, 48, 72, 76–7, 83, 136–43, 288, 289, 293, 299, 308.

Heal, Sgt D.P. 40, 68, 261–8, 293, 297.

Healey, Flg Off 259.

Heavery, Sgt F. 62.

Henderson, Sgt R.J. 53–5, 165–71.

Hensser, Flg Off H. 294.

Herbert, Sgt. W. 52–5.

Heveron, Sgt J. 38, 299.

Hewstone, Sgt H.J. 40, 68, 261–8.

Hill, Sgt V. 30, 42, 52, 74, 154–62, 307.

Hillary, Flt Lt R. 144.

Hobday, Flg Off H.S. 35, 57, 91, 188–96, 272, 288, 293, 297, 299.

Holmes, Plt Off B. 52–5.

Hooke, Sgt T. 299.

Hopgood, Flt Lt J.V. 31, 38, 40, 41, 45–7, 74, 81, 83, 89–90, 92–4, 112, 124–5, 126–33, 140.

Hopkinson, Flg Off D. 38, 180–5.

Holden, Sqn Ldr G.W. 115, 117, 119, 120, 121, 271, 301, 303–5, 306.

Honer, Plt Off 118.

Horsfall, Sgt A. 146–7.

Horsfall, Sgt D.T. 13, 14, 37, 49–50, 97, 146–52.

Howard, Plt Off C.L. 37, 69–70, 105, 107–8, 269–78, 288, 289, 293, 299.

Howarth, Sgt W. 35, 60, 101, 209–16, 304.

Humphries, Flt Lt H.R. 15, 34, 85, 99, 119, 123, 130–1, 158, 236, 287, 292, 294, 295–300, 303–5.

Hurry, Sqn Ldr J. 49.

Hutchison, Flt Lt R.E.G. 35, 43–5, 79, 89, 92, 95, 271, 288, 293, 304–5, 306, 307.

Ibbotson, Sgt W. 38, 49–50, 147–52.

Jackson, Flt Sgt L.J. 244.

Jagger, Sgt B. 54–5, 74, 169–71, 308.

Jarvie, Sgt C.McA. 34, 61, 218–22.

Jaye, Sgt T. 39, 67, 256–60.

Jeffree, H. 86.

Johnson, Flg Off E.C. 35, 57, 96, 188–96, 288, 293, 297, 299.

Johnson, Sgt G.L. 16, 35, 64–5, 104, 193, 232–43, 293.

Johnston, Sgt T.B. 41, 66, 143, 244–53.

Jones, Wg Cdr G.D. 242.

Jones, Flg Off 45.

Keir, Flg Off C.D. 232.

Kell, Flt Lt A. 278.

Kellaway, Flt Lt W. 303.

Kellow, Flt Sgt R.G.T. 35, 57, 91–2, 96, 188–96, 289.

Kilner, H. 27, 298, 299.

Kinnear, Sgt J. 38, 56, 180–85.

Knight, Plt Off L.G. 35, 57, 81, 83, 89, 95, 96, 98, 164, 187–96, 289, 293, 301, 307.

Lace, Sgt 259.

Lancaster, Flt Sgt G.H. 38, 74, 75, 145, 223.

Lancey, Plt Off G.W. 213.

Langdon, Sgt G. 66, 251.

Leavesley, Flt Sgt E. 67, 255, 258.

Leggo, Flt Lt J.F. 40, 47–8, 72, 91, 134–43, 157, 192, 284, 293, 299–300.

Lehmann, Herr 100.

Liddell, Sgt J.R.G. 41, 58–9, 197–207.

Linnell, Air Vice Marshal F.J. 24, 27–8.

Lockspeiser, B. 22, 73.

Long, Sgt W.C.A. 39, 67, 255–60.

Longbottom, Sqn Ldr M.V. 79, 82, 86.

Lovell, Flt Sgt R. 38, 63, 73, 145, 223.

Lyons, Sgt K.M.D. 55.

McCarthy, Flt Lt J.C. 31, 35, 36, 64–5, 75, 83, 99, 103–4, 106, 154, 174, 209, 231–43, 288, 293, 297, 299, 300, 301, 305.

MacCausland, Flg Off V.S. 42, 51, 74, 94, 149–52.

McCulloch, Flg Off D. 52–5.

McDonald, Sgt C. 161.

McDonald, Sgt G.S. 40, 68, 106, 261–8, 288.

McDowell, Flt Sgt J. 34, 61, 102, 218–22.

Macfarlane, Flg Off R. 38, 62–3, 91, 223–30, 308.

McFarlane, Flt Sgt 205.

McKee, Sgt J. 61.

MacLean, Flt Sgt D.A. 34, 64–5, 91, 235–43, 288, 293, 299.

Maltby, Flt Lt D.J.H. 13, 35, 42, 51–2, 56, 82, 92, 94–5, 98, 112, 146, 153–62, 169, 272, 287, 292, 293, 294, 295–6, 297, 299–300, 301, 303, 307.

Marriott, Sgt J. 15, 56, 97, 173–8, 290.

Marsden, Sgt R. 15, 41, 66, 244–53.

Marshall, Flt Lt. L.M. 169.

Martin, Flt Lt H.B. 31, 35, 44, 47–8, 68, 81, 82, 89, 94, 98, 112, 125, 132, 134–43, 165, 188, 224, 273, 289, 292, 293, 294, 297, 299–300, 305, 310.

Mant, Sgt G. 61.

Maudslay, Sqn Ldr H.E. 31, 35, 55–6, 72, 73, 75, 79, 81, 83, 89, 95, 97, 112, 140, 146, 172–8, 180, 256, 306.

Maynard, Sgt T.W. 38, 62–3, 223–30, 308.
Meggeson, Flt Lt J. 275.
Merrals, Wrt Off P. 131.
Miller, Sgt W.A. 55.
Minchin, Sgt J.W. 46–7, 93–4, 128–33.
Minchin, Sgt R.B. 129.
Minns, Sgt A. 299.
Moore, Sqn Ldr P. 55.
Morgan, Sgt I. 49.
Morris, Sqn Ldr G.A. 33.
Munro, Flt Lt J.L. 16, 35, 36, 60, 75, 81–3,
    101–3, 154, 208–16, 269, 287, 289, 292,
    294, 299, 303, 305.
Murray, Sgt J. 85.
Muskett, Sgt R. 64, 242.
Nettleton, Wg Cdr J. 69.
Nichols, Sgt L.W. 37, 49–50.
Nicholson, Sgt V. 36, 51–2, 91, 95,
    154–62, 293, 299–300, 307.
Nind, Sqn Ldr E.F. 114.
Nugent, Sgt J.P. 37, 70–1, 279–86, 307.
Oancia, Sgt S. 40, 68, 84, 106–7, 261–8,
    288, 293, 297.
O'Brien, Sgt H.E. 35, 57, 96, 98, 188–96, 288.
Oliver, Flt Lt W.B. 43.
Osborne, Flg Off G. 45–7.
Oxland, Air Vice Marshal R. 29–30, 40.
Ottley, Plt Off W. 41, 65–6, 73, 98, 105,
    107, 244–53.
Pain, Flt Lt C. 34.
Paterson, Sgt R.C. 37, 70–1, 279–86, 307.
Paton, Sgt 135.
Pegler, Sgt G. 39, 67, 254–60.
Pemberton, Sgt A. 52–5.
Pickford, Sgt L. 49.
Pierson, R.K. 299.
Pigeon, Wrt Off P.E. 35, 60, 101, 209–16,
    288, 304.
Portal, Air Chief Marshal Sir C. 21, 26, 27,
    96–7, 306.
Pound, Admiral Sir D. 26.
Powell, Sgt D.J.D. 37, 69–70, 115, 269–78,
    307.
Powell, Flt Sgt G.E. 38, 299.
Pulford, Sgt J. 41, 44–45, 89, 92, 114–6,
    271, 293, 308.

Pulford, Sgt T. 114–5.
Radcliffe, Sgt W.G. 35, 64–5, 99, 104,
    234–83, 288.
Renouf, Rear Admiral E. de F. 24, 25.
Rice, Plt Off G. 38, 40, 42, 62–3, 86, 101,
    102–3, 145, 155, 165, 223–30, 287.
Roberts, Flt Sgt C.W. 37, 49–50, 147–53.
Rodger, Flg Off D. 35, 64–5, 99, 104,
    235–43, 288.
Rose, Flg Off 78.
Rowe, N. 27–8.
Rowlands, Flt Lt 123.
Rumbles, Flg Off F.G. 35, 60, 91, 209–16,
    304.
Ruskell, Plt Off F. 43.
Sansom, Flt Sgt S. 299.
Satterley, Gp Capt H. 39, 72, 77, 80, 83.
Saundby, Air Vice Marshal R. 26.
Schofield, Sgt N. 170.
Scholl, H. 106.
Schweizer, Hauptman H. 100.
Scrivener, Flt Lt N.H. 52.
Sexton, Flg Off M.K. 51.
Shannon, Flt. Lt D. J. 31, 37, 47, 52–5,
    81, 92, 95, 98, 125, 146, 155, 163–71,
    209, 224, 289, 293, 294, 297, 300, 301,
    310.
Simmonds, Sgt H.T. 36, 51–2, 154–62,
    307.
Simpson, Flt Sgt T.D. 40, 47–8, 89, 98,
    134–43, 293, 294, 299.
Slee, Gp Capt L. 208.
Smith, Sgt E.C. 38, 62–3, 103, 223–30,
    308.
Smith Sgt (RAAF) 135.
Sopwith, T.O.M. 298, 299.
Sorley, Air Vice Marshal R. 27.
Southgate, Flg Off H. 50, 147.
Spafford, Plt Off F.M. 35, 39, 44–5, 89, 92,
    271, 288, 289, 293, 297, 306, 307.
Spriggs, P. 299.
Stephenson, Sgt M. 56–7, 180–5.
Stone, Sgt A.J.B. 36, 51–2, 154–62, 307.
Strange, Sgt H.J. 41, 66, 244–53.
Suggitt, Sqn Ldr W. 116.
Summers, J. 25, 83, 111, 299.

Sumpter, Flt Sgt L.J. 53–5, 81–2, 293, 294, 297, 299.

Sunderland, Sgt E. 57.

Sutherland, Sgt F.E. 35, 57, 86–7, 98, 188–96, 288, 294.

Taerum, Plt Off H.T. 35, 39, 40, 44–5, 89, 92, 113, 195, 271, 288, 293, 297, 306, 307.

Taerum, Sgt L. 117.

Taylor, Sgt A.J. 34, 61, 218–22.

Taylor, Wrt Off B. 299.

Tees, Sgt F. 41, 66, 105, 244–53.

Tew, Flt Lt K.G. 236.

Thiele, Flt Lt K. 61.

Thompson, Flg Off W. 44–45.

Thrasher, Wrt Off J.W. 38, 62–63, 223–30, 288, 308.

Thrasher, Plt Off C. 228.

Tizard, Sir H. 23, 24

Townsend, Flt Sgt W.C. 37, 69–70, 81, 105, 107–8, 115, 269–78, 287, 293, 300.

Trevor-Roper, Flt Lt R.D. 35, 44–5, 89, 92, 174, 271, 288, 293, 296, 297, 299–300, 301, 306, 308.

Tytherleigh, Flg Off W.J. 35, 56, 175–8.

Urquhart, Flg Off R.A. 35, 73, 173–8.

Vine, Sgt H. 61, 221.

Walker, Wing Cdr A. 122.

Walker, Flg Off D.R. 38, 52–5, 119, 165–71, 288, 293, 297.

Walker, Sgt 66.

Wallis, B.N. 21–8, 34, 72, 79, 83, 84, 86–7, 287, 289, 298, 299, 310.

Walters, Flt Sgt A. 247, 248.

Warner, Flg Off J.H. 34, 61, 218–22.

Warwick, Sqn Ldr J. 114.

Watson, Plt Off H. 77–8.

Webb, Sgt D.E. 37, 69–70, 81, 105, 107–8, 269–78, 293–4, 297.

Weeks, Flt Sgt H.A. 35, 60, 101, 209–16, 288.

Weller, Plt Off L.G. 39, 67, 106, 255–60.

Wellington, Flt Lt 259.

Westwell, Sgt A. 64, 236.

Whillis, Plt Off S.L. 41, 58–9, 101, 197–207.

Whitaker, Plt Off A.N. 34, 61, 218–22.

White, Sgt W. 46.

Whitehead, Sqn Ldr R.G. 261.

Whittaker, Plt Off I. 40, 48, 137–43.

Whitworth, Gp Capt J.N.H. 59, 80, 140, 144, 145, 260, 287, 299–300.

Wicken, Flg Off J.F. 43.

Wile, Plt Off F.A. 38, 56, 180–5.

Wilkinson, Sgt J. 34, 61, 218–22.

Wilkinson, Sgt R. 37, 69–70, 269–78, 293.

Williams, Sgt A. 36, 51–2, 74, 154–62.

Williams, Flg Off C.R. 41, 58–9, 197–207.

Wilson, Flt Lt H.S. 37, 73, 74, 85, 86, 287, 299, 301.

Winterbotham, Gp Capt F.W. 23.

Woodward, Flt Sgt I. 199–201.

Woolard, Sgt L.C. 187.

Worswick, Plt Off 118.

Wyness, Flg Off D. 173.

Wynter-Morgan, Gp Capt W. 27–8, 82.

Yeo, Sgt G.A. 38, 49–50, 147–52.

Young, Sqn Ldr H.M. 31, 37, 38, 41, 42, 48–51, 57, 63, 72, 79, 83, 92, 94, 97, 112, 140, 144–52, 173, 181–5, 223.